CORA CRANE

Cora and Stephen Crane
at the benefit party held in Brede Rectory Gardens, August 23, 1899
Gift of Henry W. Walters.

Cora Crane

A Biography
of Mrs. Stephen Crane

by Lillian Gilkes

Indiana University Press • *Bloomington*

1 9 6 0

for Dorothy Brewster and Ted Hodnett

Preface

I THINK it must have been my mother who, in the carefully screened language of a Victorian lady, first mentioned in my hearing the fact of Cora Taylor's association with Stephen Crane. I had been hearing about Cora from the time I could walk—little pitchers have big ears. But from that moment which I cannot date, my interest in the remarkable woman whose strange career had been so deeply enmeshed with the life of my native city of Jacksonville, Florida, took a leap forward. My subsequent years in New York City were taken up with other purposes and cross-purposes, but the idea of writing something about Stephen and Cora remained with me for half a lifetime.

Our old family home was on Forsyth Street, diagonally across from the post office, which then stood on the corner of Forsyth and Hogan. My elder sister, who has always had a passionate love for animals, especially horses, used to stand and watch Cora Taylor drive up in the fabulous victoria—the secret envy of many a first lady of Jacksonville—and enter the post office to collect her mail. Once Cora actually spoke to her, with a smile and a pat on the head, "Hello, little girl!"; and some while afterward my sister obtained permission from the coachman in livery to give the horse, a magnificent black stallion, a lump of sugar. When she rushed home with this thrilling announcement, the roof flew off the old house as our grandmother hit the ceiling, "Don't you dare speak to that woman, or go near her horse!"

By the time I arrived on the scene, my family having meanwhile moved to a newer part of the city, "Cora Taylor," as she was always known to Jacksonville, had already become a legendary figure. Two years after Crane's death on June 5, 1900, Cora had returned to build and operate "The Court"; and when she died in 1910, at the age of forty-five, Cora left all of her property, real and personal, to a local businessman of prominent connections, who had wanted to marry her.

Ernest Christian Budd, a Canadian by birth, was a talented and attractive fellow, trapped in one of those marital calamities which our grandparents, to whom divorce was synonymous with scandal, sanctified in martyrdoms. He was one of my father's close friends, and at that time was making a great effort to drink himself to death. (When I was a small child Mr. Budd gave me a dog. He arrived at our house unexpectedly one evening and pulled out of his pocket a tiny puppy, a beautiful brindled Pitt bull, and presented it to me.) Although my mother, who shared the moral convictions of the well-bred ladies of her day, naturally looked askance at Cora, she had a truly extraordinary understanding of the intricate involvements of the human heart which enabled her in most things to rise above prejudice. Long before Mr. Budd ever saw Cora Taylor he was desperate over his wife's refusal to give him a divorce. He used to confide his troubles to my mother, and Mother's sympathies were entirely with him in the domestic hullaballoo even though she disapproved of many of his habits.

In Jacksonville Crane himself had all but dropped out of memory, and it was Cora who commanded the stage from an unenviable spotlight; elsewhere in literary and academic coteries exactly the opposite was the case. Hardly anyone had heard of Cora Taylor or her connection with Stephen Crane.

In my thinking about this singular fact, over the years, one thing stood out. If the dispersed halves of the Crane story could be brought into focus many new facts not in the recorded biography, yet illuminative of the deeply ambivalent personality of a genius dead at twenty-eight, were certain to be uncovered. But how to bridge this gap? Where were the documents and papers which would unite the scattered puzzle pieces into a factual and intelligible whole?

The answer was given when, one day, in the lobby of the New York Public Library I picked up a copy of Library Columns, the publication of the Columbia University Libraries. It contained an article by Daniel G. Hoffman, "An Unwritten Life of Stephen Crane," describing the new collection of Craneana recently acquired by Columbia. Here then were all of the papers and manuscripts, diaries, notebooks, correspondence, books from the library at Brede Place, which Cora had brought over from England and kept together until her death. Their whereabouts had long been shrouded in secrecy. They came out of sequestration only in 1952, when purchased by Columbia.

In putting together the fragmented Crane story, particularly the Cora half, from these materials, I have been sensible of trying to fill gaps and to correct misconceptions and distortions in the career of this strange and withal remarkable woman. Many gaps still remain unclosed, a task the future Stephen Crane biographer will inherit. Both Cora and Stephen, needless to say, practiced many concealments.

It is understandable that more than half a century had to pass before the full story could be told. In this attempt to tell it I have chosen to keep the focus on the rebel figure of the woman who lived with Stephen Crane during the last three years of his life as his common-law wife: a fascinating, talented, generous-hearted woman who, whatever we may think of some of her actions, suffered greatly for her mistakes.

The writing of this book has placed me under many obligations pleasant to record. My first debt is to Columbia University: to Dr. Richard Logsdon, Director of the Columbia University Libraries, and Professor Lewis Leary, who granted me early access to the Columbia Crane Collection. I wish also especially to thank Mr. Roland Baughman, Head of Columbia University's Special Collections, and his assistant Miss Alice Bonnell, and staff, for responding at all times with the patience of Job to my many demands.

I owe a very large debt to Professor Daniel G. Hoffman, who was working on his study of Crane's poetry while I was doing my research at Columbia, who put no obstacle in my way, and to whose criticism and suggestions when my manuscript came later into his hands this book owes much. I am also indebted to my old friend and former "boss" in Columbia University's Home Study Department, Dr. Edward Hodnett, who read the manuscript in an earlier draft.

Without the generous cooperation of other libraries and the help of many scholars I should not have had access to other new and rare materials of information invaluable to this biography. My first thanks go to Mr. Lester G. Wells, Rare Book Librarian of Syracuse University, and Professor Edwin H. Cady, who opened to me the George Arents Collection of Craneana at Syracuse; also to Mr. Clifton Waller Barrett and the Alderman Library, for unpublished letters of Cora Crane and William H. Crane in the Clifton

Waller Barrett Collection at the University of Virginia; to Dr. John
D. Gordan, Curator of the Berg Collection, and the Trustees of the
New York Public Library for five original drawings by Cora Crane
and other material from the Berg Collection, and for permission to
quote from "The Ghost at Brede Place" and *Bernard Shaw: 1856-
1950: An exhibition from the Berg Collection*, both by John D.
Gordan; to Mr. Edward Connery Lathem and the Baker Library
for letters of Cora Crane to James B. Pinker in the George Matthew
Adams Collection at Dartmouth College; to Professor Gordon N.
Ray and the University of Illinois Library for letters of Cora Crane
to H. G. Wells and Mrs. Wells; to Mr. Robert F. Metzdorf and the
Yale University Library for letters of Cora Crane to Edward Gar-
nett and G. H. Perris; to Dr. Lloyd A. Arvidson and the University
of Southern California Library for two letters of Cora Crane to
Hamlin Garland; to Dr. George P. Hammond and the Bancroft
Library, University of California, for unpublished letters of Cora
Crane to Mr. and Mrs. Moreton Frewen; to Professor William A.
Jackson and the Houghton Library, Harvard University, for per-
mission to quote from an early manuscript page of *The Red Badge
of Courage* (p. 138 f.); and to Mr. Julien C. Yonge, Director-Em-
eritus of the P. K. Yonge Library of Florida History, University of
Florida, for the newspaper article "Stephen Crane Missing."

Special thanks are due the Jacksonville Free Public Library and
its staff for access to newspaper files, and to Miss Audrey Broward,
Reference Librarian, who aided me in innumerable ways far beyond the calls of duty. Another large debt is to Miss Phyllis Pac-
cadolmi and the staff of the Ridgefield Library, who have been
diligent and patient under many extra demands put upon them
through the interlibrary loan service.

The roster of my indebtedness to scholars must begin with R. W.
Stallman, who directed me to many sources and in some instances
shared with me his own material. I am grateful also to Scott C.
Osborn for many kindnesses, including permission to quote from
correspondence about Richard Harding Davis and from two of his
own articles important to an understanding of the curiously involved relations of Davis and Stephen Crane; to Hoyt C. Franchere
for information about Harold Frederic; to Dorothy Brewster for
help with collateral research in New York and London; to Com-

mander Melvin H. Schoberlin for letters of Cora Crane to Mrs. Edward Pease, James B. Pinker and G. H. Perris; to Cyrus L. Day for important information in connection with the *Commodore* disaster; to Alfred J. Hanna for typescript of "An Unfinished Sketch of Cora Crane" by Carl Bohnenberger; to Ames W. Williams, who patiently answered my queries; and to John S. Mayfield, who ascended to a cold attic one freezing winter night to dig out of storage two fat envelopes of material important to the correction of various misrepresentations concerning Cora and her years in Jacksonville.

In the long list of others who have aided me with material, or in various other ways, I wish especially to thank Miss Edith F. Crane for typescript of an unpublished letter from Cora to Stephen's niece, Agnes Crane; for personal recollections of Cora Crane; and for generously and painstakingly furnishing notes which shed much light on the whole background of Crane family relations, especially in connection with the administration of Stephen Crane's will and the episode of the horse, Peanuts.

I am grateful also to Mr. and Mrs. Frederick B. Smillie for typescripts of Stephen Crane's letters to Lily Brandon Munroe Smillie, and for permission to reproduce a letter of Crane's to Dorothy Brandon; Mr. Philip M. Barr for information regarding members of his family and their friendship with the Cranes, for permission to reproduce a portion of a letter from Stephen Crane to his father Mark Barr and to quote from letters of his parents to Stephen and Cora Crane; Mr. Arthur A. Donigian for his interpretation of the will of Stephen Crane, and for his professional advices concerning problems arising out of the law of literary property; Mrs. Hazel P. Brook, genealogist, who looked up property and Howorth family records in Boston; Mr. Paul R. Reynolds for permission to reproduce an unpublished letter of his father to Cora Crane; Mr. Eric S. Pinker for permission to quote from letters of his father to Stephen and Cora Crane; Professor William James for permission to quote from letters of his uncle, Henry James, to Cora Crane; Miss Alice B. Beer for permission to quote from an article by Thomas Beer in the *American Mercury*, "Mrs. Stephen Crane"; Mr. Richmond Barrett for the gift of a newspaper clipping of Crane's article in the New York *Press*, "Stephen Crane's Own Story," for a photograph of the Hotel St. James, and for permission to quote from his letter to the *American Mercury* and to reproduce the Stephen Crane autograph cited therein; the Trustees of the Estate of Joseph Conrad and Messrs. J. M. Dent, agents, for permission to quote from letters of Joseph and Jessie Conrad to Stephen and Cora Crane; Mr. Spencer Curtis Brown for permission to quote from letters of his father to Cora Crane; and Messrs. A. P. Watt, agents, for assistance in obtaining necessary permissions to quote from a letter of A.E.W. Mason to Vincent Starrett now in the possession of R. W. Stallman, and from other letters of Mason to Cora Crane now in the possession of Trinity College, Oxford.

As all efforts to trace descendants or literary executors of Robert Barr have proved fruitless, permissions on the Barr letters could not be obtained. The letter of Harold Frederic which appeared in *Stephen Crane: Letters* (ed. R. W. Stallman and Lillian Gilkes, New York University Press, February, 1960) is here used again by permission of New York University Press. For permission to quote from letters of Kate Frederic to Cora Crane, I am grateful to the heirs of Kate Frederic.

Many old friends in Jacksonville, and some newer ones, have contributed generously toward making this book possible. For assistance in obtaining access to records, and for much other information relating to the period of Cora's residence I am heavily indebted to Mr. Richard P. Daniel and Mr. Philip S. May; to Mr. Alton B. Wetherington, president of the Title & Trust Company of Florida, for records pertaining to the Hotel de Dream, the Court, and Cora's other real estate holdings, and to Mr. George E. Drady who located and kindly interpreted them for me; to the late Abbie Barrs, who copied for me records of the Circuit Court of Duval County; to the Director of Evergreen Cemetery and Mr. S. A. Kyle for burial records, and other information from Mr. Kyle regarding the circumstances of Cora Crane's death; to Mrs. Byron West (Helen Hunt) for the newspaper story which she wrote of the election eve parade; to the late Henry W. Walters for personal recollections of Cora Crane, and for photographic negatives; to Mr. Frank Elmore for the newspaper account of Carry Nation's trip "down the line"; to the late John W. Alsop, a former mayor of Jacksonville, for several colorful anecdotes; to Mrs. Dorcas Broward Drake for a photograph of the *Three Friends;* and to innumerable others who contributed information but have chosen to remain anonymous.

Materials and kind assistance have also come from England. My heaviest obligation there is to Mr. Roger M. Frewen of Brede Place for the gift of many photographs of the house and its occupants, for typescripts of unpublished letters of Stephen and Cora Crane to Mr. and Mrs. Moreton Frewen, the Christmas dinner menu, press clippings of *The Ghost* performance, the garden party, etc. I am deeply indebted also to Mr. and Mrs. Nicolas Pease of the Oast Cottage, Limpsfield, for background information concerning Ravensbrook Villa and the Oxted-Limpsfield locale, for the story of the puppy Velestino's misbehavior in Paris; and for the gift of original photographs of Adoni standing beside the dogcart with the two little Pease boys inside it, and of the luncheon meeting of the Society of American Women in London inscribed in Cora's hand to Mrs. Edward Pease. I also thank Mr. W. N. Rees, editor, and the *Nottinghamshire Guardian* for microfilm of Cora's story "Cowardice" which was published in the *Guardian*.

Thanks are due for permission to quote from the writings of Stephen Crane to Alfred A. Knopf, Inc., publishers of *The Work of Stephen Crane* and of *Stephen Crane: An Omnibus*, and holders of the literary rights to Crane's manuscripts and uncollected writings both published and unpublished; and for quotations from Beer's biography *Stephen Crane*, without reference to which nothing more on Crane can be written. I am grateful to Mr. William A. Koshland, Knopf's attorney, for assistance rendered in obtaining these permissions. I am also obliged to the Syracuse University Press for quotations from *Stephen Crane's Love Letters to Nellie Crouse*, ed. Edwin H. Cady and Lester G. Wells; and to *American Literature* for quotations from two articles by Scott C. Osborn, "Stephen Crane and Cora Taylor: Some Corrections," and "The 'Rivalry-Chivalry' of Richard Harding Davis and Stephen Crane." To New York University Press, publishers of *Stephen Crane: Letters*, I am grateful for permission to reproduce or quote from many of the letters appearing in that collection.

I thank Miss Irene Koby for typing the manuscript, and Miss Louise D. Peck for additional help with typing; and Mr. Clarence

Korker for his painstaking work in salvaging irreplaceable originals of photographic negatives, which had become curled and cracked almost beyond rescue.

I am grateful to Pauline Gelert and Marjorie Hogg for help with indexing.

I also wish to thank my sister, who has lived in enforced intimacy with Cora and Stephen for several years and borne it well.

LILLIAN GILKES

Ridgefield, Connecticut

Table of Contents

Mrs S. Crane.

List of Illustrations

17

PART ONE

(November, 1896 — January, 1899)

An early photograph of Cora, perhaps taken during the time of her first marriage. Stephen Crane Collection, Syracuse University Library.

... the Tall Swift Shadow of a Ship at Night

chapter 1

ON A bright spring afternoon in 1897, at the entrance to the Jacksonville post office, a small plump blonde woman stepped from a victoria driven by a dignified Negro in pongee livery. Her general appearance was striking, but she was not overdressed according to the fashions of the day, which emphasized ruffles. Her mass of red-gold hair showed beneath a mountainous hat billowing with ostrich plumes. Her shapely arms were sheathed in black lace gloves which came to the elbow, and she carried a tiny lace parasol. At each step she took across the sidewalk the tips of her small slender feet peeped from under the hem of her gown. Her features were a shade too heavy for beauty, but there was about her an extraordinary vitality, particularly in her eyes, of a remarkable blue depth, and her high coloring, unaided by rouge. The color of her hair also was natural—though some thought otherwise. Men's eyes followed her down the street, but housewives and matrons put up their parasols to protect their vision from contamination.

The woman was Cora Taylor and she came every day to get her mail. She was expecting a letter from the young man who forgot to write, the genius already famous at twenty-five as the author of *The Red Badge of Courage*, that marvelous boy who Mr. Howells had said could do things Mark Twain could not.

Cora was thirty-one, but it was something to look younger than you were. "Virtue," she thought, "never yet atoned for wrinkles, men ask us women to be forever young and pretty.

Though a woman must be rather more than pretty—and may be rather less—to attract a fin de siècle man." But Cora never appeared in public, even to drive out in her rig to take the air, without the woman companion who now, under a small lace parasol much like her own, waited in the victoria in front of the post office. On these outings the handsome carriage, with its liveried coachman and fine black horse, the dusters spread upon its seat cushions a different color each day to match Cora's costume, burst like a sunset on the community—as no doubt she intended it should. She was "very much in the grand manner, a sort of Tannhäuser Venus."

Love comes like the tall swift shadow of a ship at night. Stephen Crane had written her that, and now where was he? A war against the rule of the Turk was going on in the Mediterranean island of Crete, and he was crazy to get into it, to go among the fighting and the dying, to see with his living eyes how men behaved when they touched the great death, inflamed by dreams and commands, or simply knowing nothing of what it was all about. The *Red Badge* had been written before Stephen had seen war. Many nights, as the hours fled into dawn, they had talked about these things in the privacy of her rooms in her own hotel in this seaport town, where feeling on the side of Cuban freedom boiled in the breasts of local sympathizers and the atmosphere of conspiratorial adventure hung thick as cigar smoke in waterfront back rooms. Why did she not hear from him?

Cora, too, had experienced something of the *Zeitgeist* that sends men forth to wars and discovery. Hers was a florid and exuberant era. Men had invented torpedo boats to dive down and annihilate the enemy under the sea and balloons to ascend into the clouds. Captain Peary was slogging across the Arctic ice cap nearer and nearer the Pole. Some twenty years earlier Stanley the reporter had fought his way through the jungles of "darkest Africa" to rescue David Livingstone. Here in America, the Claflin sisters—Victoria and Tennessee—had demonstrated to a scandalized public that a woman possessed of wit and charm, and sex appeal, could be successful in Wall Street, publish a newspaper, or even run for the Presidency. From her Fifth Avenue chateau Alva Vanderbilt stormed the citadel of Mrs. William Astor with a ball that set all of New York's Four Hundred jimberjawed, and capped it by marrying off her daughter to the young Duke of Marlborough. Nellie Bly, Joseph Pulitzer's girl reporter, had completed her record-breaking dash around the globe in seventy-two days, six hours, ten minutes, and eleven seconds, to cabled plaudits from Jules Verne: "Hurrah for her and for the manager of the World! Hurrah! Hurrah!" If Cora had had an envious nature, she would have liked to change places with Nellie Bly.

But whatever eccentricity of Fate had set her down in these Florida sticks two years earlier, Cora viewed it as a lark and remained to go into a business that mocked the parental restraints she had known as a child in her great-grandfather's house in Boston. For it was one thing to have been born into a romantic age, quite another to reconcile oneself to the fact that the spirit of boldness in men got them decorated as heroes, but in women just the reverse. The woman who cast aside her "modesty" because she found life dull with such an encumbrance risked social excommunication! So Cora Taylor, née Howorth, resolved *never* to be afraid of anything, least of all the artificial pressures of convention. And she was not.

> I am a strange woman to whom fear of many kinds is unknown. I could dare, or do, some strange things without flinching if I were driven.

Now she had consulted her lawyer about disposing of the lease on the Hotel de Dream, and was making plans to join Stephen. But it was the third week in March—almost a week since he had left for New York—and still "a bitter silence— the silence of the sea at night."

2

ON THE southwest corner of Ashley and Hawk streets in 1897— Hawk later becoming Jefferson—in the LaVilla district, stood a frame building of dilapidated elegance, over the door "a semicircular sign . . . bearing in great letters of gold the inviting legend 'Hotel de Dream'." This building burned to the ground in the fire which destroyed a large part of Jacksonville, then a town of

25,000, in 1901. No photographs of this structure have come down to us: that gleaming, gold-lettered advertisement is what is remembered of its exterior.

LaVilla, once a separate municipality, was then the back yard of the busy port and railway terminal that was Jacksonville. Its once fine houses were blackened by smoke and cinders from the railroad yards, as aristocracy gave way to commerce and slums. Lot 6, Block 124, according to city records saved from the fire, was in 1877 conveyed to one Marcella Pons for the sum of $250. Next recorded is a bill of sale dated March 21, 1895, from Carrie B. Mudge to Cora E. Taylor for $1,000, covering chattels consisting of furniture, etc., for a dwelling described as a "furnished boarding-house"—furnished according to the tastes of gentlemen—the term a euphemism for places of questionable character. Mrs. Mudge, the wife of a not-too-respectable attorney specializing in divorces, had already subleased the place to Ethel Dreme (who is listed in the City Directory for 1895 as the proprietress of a "furnished boarding-house" located at the same number on Ashley and Hawk streets). Ethel Dreme had debts amounting to $1,480, which were assumed by Cora Taylor in the purchase, bringing the actual price paid to $2,480. A marginal notation standing opposite the bill of sale reads "Hotel de Dreme"; a further notation states that the instrument covers also "lease, good will, and right of possession."

That good will clause was meant to be specific, but it did not satisfy Cora. She intended to stay in business, and her business included meals served to transients who desired room and board. A boardinghouse in fact, with some stretching of the term—but no telltale red light outside the door. Actually, no girls were boarded on the premises. Gentlemen brought their own, or met them by prearrangement. Cora's hotel was not far from the old Sub-Tropical Gardens, now Water Works Park, at a safe remove from Ward Street, street of the brothels, familiarly known to the initiate as "the line."

So not content with the bill of sale that made her responsible for Ethel Dreme's debts, Cora presently obtained an assignment of lease from Marcella Pons. This was for the unexpired lease of Carrie Mudge, which still had two years to run, the rental $50 a month "except for the months of May, June, July, and August when the rent shall be $40 per month, payable in advance, the lessee to pay all repairs except leaks in the roof." The following year, the lease was redrawn under a five-year renewal starting from date, the rent $50 a month with no off-season reduction. Under its new management, the place was making money.

Oddly enough, both leases were recorded in the name of Cora E. Stewart—as the bill of sale was not. Cora was still legally married to her English husband, Captain Donald William Stewart, younger son of a baronet.

Why was she known as Cora Taylor? The dense smog of scandal, folklore, suppressions, and hearsay that envelops the figure of Cora Taylor sixty years later yields no clue. It might have been an assumed name, possibly a random choice adopted as a business designation from motives similar to Stephen Crane's selection of "Johnston Smith"—"the stupidest name in the world"—as a pseudonym for his authorship of *Maggie*.* A local explanation makes Cora the common-law wife of a man named Allen Taylor. There is an Allen Taylor listed in the City Directory for 1895, but this fact alone seems to prove little. By 1895 Cora Taylor was prospering independently of lovers or liaisons as the successful new mistress of Ethel Dreme's old establishment.

From a dingy relic the new Hotel de Dream was suddenly transformed into something approximating a modern night club. On a smaller scale, it was probably as much like Lulu White's or any of the luxurious sporting houses of the New Orleans Vieux Carré as its new mistress could make it. When and under what circumstances she had seen the delta city is conjectural, but her familiarity with its tenderloin can hardly be in doubt.

Resorts like the Hotel de Dream and the pleasure palaces of the Vieux Carré belonged to an era when men led a life apart from their womenfolk. To comprehend the place that such resorts filled in the separate masculine world, one must journey back to a time long antedating the Kinsey reports and the dissemination of Freudian ideas. Outside the domestic circle, men had their clubs

---

* Crane's first novel, *Maggie: A Girl of the Streets*, was published at his own expense in a cheap yellowback edition in March or April, 1893. Crane told a young admirer, Willis Clarke, who visited him at Brede Place, that in the hunt for a pseudonym he asked his friend Post Wheeler, editor on the New York *Press*, what he thought was the stupidest name in the world. Wheeler suggested Johnson or Smith, and Johnston Smith went on the cover by mistake. See Beer, p. 90.

and barrooms which excluded women, their political hustings and business offices where in the America of our grandparents' youth the presence of a woman was still a rarity. Night spots thrived on the social and religious prohibitions on drinking, gambling, or card playing in the home, as well as on the banishment of sex from the bedroom except for reproductive purposes; and the new mistress of the Hotel de Dream was in these things a student of human nature. She was also a devotee of the night hours:

> Whatever is too precious, too tender, too good, too evil, too bashful for the day happens in the night. Night is the bath of life, the anodyne of heartaches, the silencer of passions, the breeder of them too, the teacher of those who would learn, the cloak that sets a man in with his soul. The seeds of great deeds and of great crimes are alike sown in the night. The lover and the lustful person, the thief and the thinker, the preacher and the poacher are abroad in the night.

The Hotel de Dream was not by any means the only popular night spot in Jacksonville, or the only one known to Crane. There was also "Lyda's," right on "the line" in Ward Street. And Lyda owned an autographed copy of Crane's first work, *Maggie: A Girl of the Streets*—his landlady once used the yellowback edition to light the fire. Its inscription read: *"To Lyda from her friend Stephen Crane. Jacksonville, Fla. February 18, 1897."* Lyda de Camp was a well-known madam, and it is evident that Stephen Crane had some sort of dealings with her at the very time he was falling in love with Cora—who, technically at any rate, was not a madam. Cora may or may not have been aware of this; but an amusing postscript is provided in Cora's diary when years later, back in Jacksonville, she notes that two or three of her girls who had been causing trouble deserted to Lyda: "Good riddance!"

But the Hotel de Dream, smartest of nighttime spots the city afforded, was given a class-A rating by the clerk at the St. James, who kept "a list of the better houses of ill fame for the intelligent guidance of guests of the hotel." So writes Richmond Barrett, a gentleman from Newport, Rhode Island, whose parents wintered every year at the famous old inn. The traditional sporting-house "Professor"—the piano player, Negro or white, but always impecunious—was in round-the-clock demand for his song and dance accompaniments, and Cora remained in the parlor rooms during the first part of the evening to greet the guests and start things off. For she knew they came to see her. Her personality and wit drew them back and kept their dollars rolling in. With her luminous smile and a bright word for each, she passed among the tables, joining in conversation when some youth or balding cavalier pleaded to buy her a drink—beer or champagne: no spirits or hard liquor was served to the public. Cora disliked drunkenness. Beer was one dollar a bottle, the standard price "down the line."

Later, as couples began to leave or drift upstairs, Cora said good night and, with her companion, Mrs. Ruedy, withdrew to her own apartments, to which none but the inner circle gained entrée. To these favored few she was "Miss Cora," or sometimes "Ma."

3

"ALOOF" was the newspaperman Ernest W. McCready's word for her—"a touch of the marble awaiting a Crane to impart the glow of his particular something." McCready wondered in one of his letters "if anyone ventured really into Crane's one big romance? . . . One carries gold in wartime, or on campaign, and there was drink a-plenty, of course. Yet even before we knew that Crane had not only staked the claim but that there was instantaneous mutual attraction (I'm no bio-chemist, you'll guess) we never proposed to her that a little love interlude would be profitable to her and quite irresistible to us. Why? It was, after all, the Hotel de Dream." Of Cora he retained after thirty-seven years a still vivid impression. There is, he declared, such a thing as "class," and Cora had it. "Fact is, she was a cut above us in several ways, notably poise and surety of command of herself and others. If she had any false notes I was then all too unskilled in recognizing authentic 'class' or lack of it, to detect any."

Stephen Crane probably arrived in Jacksonville sometime between November 10 and 14, 1896, and headed right for the Hotel de Dream. Correspondents drifting in and out of the city on their way to Cuba put up at the St. James and hung around the known purlieus of the Junta, in the hope of coming upon some filibustering scoop for their papers. After they had turned in their wires for the day, their favorite evening diversion was going "down the line."

Cora's place was known to them all. Crane spent a good deal of time there, waiting for a blockade-running ship to take him across to the island. A chancy business, but gambling was in Crane's blood. He was incidentally observing the life he wrote about in those strange stories that horrified editors like Mr. Gilder of the *Century* but found instant favor with a less squeamish minority who were addicted to the new realism championed by William Dean Howells and Hamlin Garland.

One eyewitness, whose later testimony is open to question, provides an account of the first meeting between Stephen Crane and Cora Taylor, at which he claims to have been present: Cora and Crane supping on quail and champagne in her rooms at midnight, she happily patting her poet and filling glasses while he conversed in his acrid drawl with the informant, a local "doctor" invited in to help entertain him. True, quail and champagne were sporting-house fare in those plushy days; but the rest of the "doctor's" story is fabrication.*

McCready describes a dinner at the Hotel de Dream at which he, Captain Ed Murphy, the big genial young Irishman who skippered the filibustering *Commodore*, and one other young journalist— Stephen's old friend from Asbury Park days, Ralph Paine, a son of Jacksonville—"sat in at the 'family board.'" "Paine carving the noble bird," the table was "lavish as to victual and drink, but not vulgar; and the Hostess' authority and *standard* ran through the whole stable, imposing a decorum that yet escaped any constriction of natural spirits and wasted no inspiration due to licker." Then, dinner eaten down to the plum pudding, and the mood growing mellower, a remarkable thing happened. "Murphy and Crane were thinly incog. Presently, as the Skipper hoisted a few more and a few more he revealed his friend's identity. The news pierced the lady's very liver."

Cora, an avid reader whose tastes in literature were catholic, had in her rooms a copy of one of Stephen Crane's novels—probably *George's Mother* (on the flyleaf of which appears Stephen's tender

---

* In a letter to R. P. Daniel, George M. Powell lays claim to having been an invited guest at the Hotel de Dream on the occasion of Crane's first meeting with Cora, and to various other things. See Appendix Three, "Controversy: Sources of Misinformation." Both men were attorneys of Jacksonville.

inscription with the Jacksonville dateline, November 4, 1896: "To an unnamed sweetheart"). McCready suggests that he and Ralph Paine eavesdropped "between sessions at the roulette wheel and learned then and thereafter . . . that our Mr. Crane had discovered the lady reading his book." At any rate, both were witnesses to the effect on Cora of the electrifying discovery that the anonymous and now glowing young man who had just eaten a "Christmas" dinner was none other than her favorite author, whose mud-bespattered name signified to Cora the brightest star of genius.

McCready's memory was faulty. What he described as happening at a Christmas dinner must have been an earlier encounter between Cora and Crane, which may have occurred at a Thanksgiving party at the Hotel de Dream; and he had no knowledge of the tender inscription. (It has been suggested that November 4 may have been intended for November 14 as Crane, whose time sense was notoriously off calendar, was in Cambridge on the seventh reporting a Harvard football game.) Since Crane did not sail with Captain Murphy in the *Commodore* until December 31, he and Murphy could not have been, on this occasion, "newly come from death and the sea," as McCready says; and Ralph Paine spent Christmas marooned on one of the Florida Keys. But McCready was probably wholly right in dating the inception of the romance from Stephen's discovery of her possession of his book.

4

CORA HOWORTH, who called herself Cora Taylor, belongs in the tradition of those European women—authors and courtesans—who, with their intellectual curiosity, wit, and immense personal charm, achieved renown in the salons over which they more or less unconventionally presided: the Aphra Behns, Ouidas, George Sands, de Staëls, and Récamiers. But the United States, too, in the fast-growing years after the Civil War, had produced its own crop of glittering hostesses. In the front ranks was Mrs. Frank Leslie, who had won sensational triumphs on the stage as "Minnie Montez," a scorching beauty who was at one time married to the brother of Oscar Wilde, later to E. G. Squier, an archaeologist, and later still to Frank Leslie, under whose name she managed his vast publishing empire after his death in 1880. And there was Mrs. Jack Gardner, the arts queen of "Fenway Court," whose liaison with the painter, John Singer Sargent, was for a decade the scandal of Beacon Hill. Among these, Boston-born Cora might have held her own with distinction. But fortune did not smile on Cora. For one thing, she evinced the old-fashioned predilection for falling headlong in love and marrying her lovers; and she did not live long enough to witness the revolutionary changes in morals and mores which swept the nation in the aftermath of World War I.

On both sides of her family, Cora Howorth had come from highly literate people. The Massachusetts Vital Statistics on file in the State House in Boston record the birth of a daughter, Cora Ethel Eaton, to John and Elizabeth Howorth, July 12, 1865. John Howorth, "artist," was born on "Long Island" (actually in Brooklyn), and Elizabeth Holder Howorth in New York City. Cora, an only child, was born at 26 Kneeland Street in the downtown part of old Boston, in the home of her great-grandfather, George Howorth, an art dealer who had a small gallery at the same address. George Howorth was an authority on the restoration of oil paintings. A special process he discovered netted him a modest fortune, which he quickly turned into a sizable one by shrewd investments in Boston real estate. He was also the author of a monograph on the subject, issued in 1859 from the Boston press of George C. Rand and Avery. A note in M. M. Swan's *The Athenaeum Gallery* (Boston, 1940, pp. 120-121) states that the fashionable portrait painter, Chester Harding (1792-1866), "agreed to get Mr. Howarth* to line the picture"—his own portrait of Daniel Webster—for hanging, and that "the bill was fifty dollars." The Fine Arts Committee report for 1865 says, "Trumbull's 'Sortie of Gibraltar' . . . has gained much by Howarth's skillful treatment, and it will be an attractive feature in the Spring Exhibition." George Howorth, as a young man, had arrived in this country from England with his wife Mary about the time of the War of 1812, and seems to have lived for some years in Philadelphia, where his son John was born.

* The nineteenth century had no standardized spelling, especially of proper names, until very late. In wills, property deeds, and other public records, the Howorth family name therefore appears under a variety of spellings. "Howarth" and "Howorth" both perhaps are corruptions from the Yorkshire "Haworth," associated with the moorland home of the Brontës.

This John was a resident of Brooklyn, New York, at the time of the birth of his eldest son John, Cora's father, in 1836. In 1833 we find George Howorth living in Connecticut, and four years later —in 1837—he moved his family from there to Boston.

Boston in 1837 was the arts capital of America, and to the canny vision of old George it must have seemed a more attractive center than either Connecticut or the city of Brotherly Love for the pursuit of those professional ambitions which were to lead to the amassing of a solid fortune in mortgages and leases. In 1853 George Howorth purchased the roomy red-brick mansion on Kneeland Street with "land and buildings." In one of the separate brick buildings which stood on the property the art gallery must have been housed.

When George Howorth died in August of 1864—eleven months before Cora's birth—several other members of his numerous family, in addition to Cora's parents, were living in the Kneeland Street home. Besides the old man's widow, Mary, there was an Eleanor Howorth, Cora's grandmother, also widowed (her father's mother), and her father's two brothers, George, Jr., and William L. Howorth. George, Jr., apparently served with the union forces in the Civil War, attaining the rank of Captain.

William L., the youngest of the three brothers, had a distinguished record in the Navy. In 1863, at the age of twenty-two, he was appointed Mate and subsequently Acting Master, in which capacity he received a citation for gallant service in "assisting to destroy and ram the Confederate vessel *Albemarle*" on October 27, 1864. Receiving an honorable discharge when the war ended, he re-enlisted the following year and was again appointed Acting Master; two years later he was commissioned an Ensign. On April 4, 1869, he resigned from the service, subsequently becoming an engraver. Little else is known of William beyond the fact that he never married. His only importance in the story lies in a strong attachment to his little blonde-haired neice, which must have endured to the end of his life. For when he died, about 1895 (the exact date is unknown), Cora was named sole heir and executrix of the small estate he left.

Her mother's people, the Holders, were descended from a mixture of English and German stock—musicians, craftsmen, makers of musical instruments, and men of letters. Elizabeth Holder's mother, Sophia Bunn, was born in Lispenard Street, Manhattan, in the neighborhood of the old City Hall, the daughter of Reuben Bunn, who had a shoe business. Cora's maternal grandfather, Charles Holder, is credited with having been the first piano maker in New York City and sending to the gold-rush parvenus of San Francisco their first piano, one of his own make. To the marriage of Charles Holder and Sophia Bunn seven children were born. One of Cora's uncles, Elbridge Gerry B. Holder, was a successful young composer of popular music—according to his wife, her Aunt Mary —but he earned his living as a piano salesman. Cora seems to have had a special affection for this aunt by marriage and one other— her mother's own sister, Mrs. Abbie Holder Cates of Everett, Massachusetts. They were the only relatives with whom she remained in communication more or less continuously over the years.*

The Holders came early to prominence as one of the leading Quaker families in America, and to Christopher, the first to leave England, sailing in the little ship *Speedwell*, belongs the honor accorded in the Beatitudes to all who suffer persecution for Righteousness' sake. The *Speedwell*, thirty-six years earlier, had been one of the original Pilgrim ships to sail from Delfthaven with the *Mayflower*, but owing to the sabotage of her captain, Governor Bradford notes in the *History of Plymouth Colony*, she was forced to put back to Plymouth harbor. The ship seems to have been bad luck to Christopher, for when he and eight other Quaker nonconformists sailed on it in 1656, they were barred from setting foot ashore in the Massachusetts Bay Colony, imprisoned on shipboard and sent back to England. But in August of 1657 Christopher Holder and some others of his faith came again to America in the *Woodhouse*, a boat built by a gentleman named Robert Fowler, and this time were allowed to land. The story of Christopher Holder's

* A scion of another branch, Charles F. Holder, is the author of a genealogical history of the family in America (*The Holders of Holderness*, Pasadena, 1902), whose talented members included Joseph Bassett Holder (1824-88), the naturalist, and his son Charles F. Holder (1851-1915), the biographer of Darwin and Agassiz. It has been suggested as a possible explanation of the fact that this work makes no mention of Cora's grandfather, Charles Holder, or her uncle, Elbridge Gerry B. Holder, that their descendants were not reached by, or they failed to answer, the questionnaires. John Greenleaf Whittier, the Quaker poet, also was a relative of the Holder family. (Daniel G. Hoffman, *The Poetry of Stephen Crane*, p. 112n.)

deportation and second voyage to America is in the ship's log kept by Fowler.

From Elizabeth Howorth's brother, Thomas Holder, to whom she had given a photograph of herself, comes an affectionate tribute to one seemingly possessed of the graces canonized in "womanhood":

> Sweet Sister Lizzie
> Whose features portrayed
> From affection's memory
> Never shall fade

But poor Elizabeth, perhaps in all innocence, seems to have done her share to make Cora a rebel even as a toddler. From Cora's story, "The Lavender Trousers" (an unpublished autobiographical contribution to Stephen Crane's series of boy stories, the Whilomville tales) and from "The Angel Child," Crane's own story of the small imp who was Cora, we gather that mother and daughter must often have clashed—the child headstrong, charming, and emotionally perhaps just enough like her strong-willed mother to loathe being like her, all the passion of her nature and intelligence pitted against the curbs of Elizabeth Howorth's pettitcoat conventionality.

The Kneeland Street household fell apart when the old grandfather died. His wife survived him only one year. Then as quarrels over the inheritance and the property broke out among the heirs, which Elizabeth probably did nothing to allay, George, Jr., left to board with a family in nearby Washington Street, and William took a room in Dix Place. Their mother stayed on with John and Elizabeth in the big house until 1869, when she too died.

But old George's spirit lived on, for a while at least. Little Cora's impressionable years were spent in an atmosphere in which art and its appreciation formed an important part of daily life. (Cora proved not to be without talent herself, though she probably never received any formal training.) Then when she was only six years old, her young father died, at the age of thirty-five, of tuberculosis of the lungs.

Whatever the measure of John Howorth's gifts as a painter, his grandfather's hopes of continuing the family connection with art centered on him. In George Howorth's last years he may even have turned over the management of the art gallery to his favorite grandson, meanwhile devoting his own great energies to the equally congenial task of creating a fortune in real estate. Howorth real estate transactions, in Kneeland Street and adjacent areas, fill innumerable pages of old ledgers. In his will, the old man left all of his property real and personal to "my beloved wife Mary," and named her "sole executrix." "In case she does not survive me, then my grandson John is to be my sole executor," and John was directed to pay to each of his brothers the sum of $600, smaller cash sums to two granddaughters and a niece. John was to inherit all the rest.

Growing up amidst wealth which he had done nothing to create, John Howorth probably had little of his grandfather's business acumen. His grandmother, at any rate, did not make him her executor, but named instead an unknown gentleman the nature of whose connection with the family is not divulged. To George, Jr., who seems to have been her favorite, she willed $1,200 and "2 large portraits painted by Otis" (Bass Otis, 1784-1861); and to William, the granddaughters, and the niece, smaller cash sums each. Then, scrupulously carrying out her husband's intention of making John his heir after her death, she left to him all the rest "real or mixed." This included the art gallery.

We have a glimpse of John Howorth in Cora's "The Lavender Trousers," and Crane's "The Angel Child." In both these stories, the father of "little Cora" is represented as the artist-dreamer under the rule of an overpowering, conventional wife, and either by design or coincidence he bears a marked resemblance to another gentle dreamer, Stephen's father, the Reverend Jonathan Townley Crane: the Dr. Trescott of Whilomville.

John seems to have taken into partnership one E. A. Pierce, with whom he continued to operate the art gallery until about 1868. What happened next is not clear. The business failed, or John disposed of it in some other manner—perhaps to his partner. Signs of increasing ill health must already have appeared; and now the character of "Sweet Sister Lizzie" reveals itself in a somewhat different light. In the same year, 1868, a curious transaction took place: John sold the Kneeland Street property to his brother-in-law Reuben Holder, a resident of Bangor, Maine, and Elizabeth promptly bought it back a few days later. By this maneuver the homestead was brought under his wife's name without appearing to have come to her from her husband, thus depriving the other brothers

Cora at the age of eleven months.

Cora's mother in 1864. The iden-
tifying inscription is in Cora's
hand. The verse is in the handwriting of Cora's uncle, Thomas
Holder. Both photographs courtesy Columbia University Crane
Collection.

of any possible grounds for suit under the homestead law to obtain their share. The scheme must have originated with a clever lawyer; but, if it was at gentle John's own wish, Elizabeth probably had a hand in it; for when John died, on November 17, 1871, all the rest of the real estate left by George Howorth was likewise in Elizabeth's name. Aside from sundry small articles, clothing, and some accounts due—mostly worthless—the only other items in John's estate were a schooner yacht and "trifle boat"—i.e., a sailboat and dinghy. The estate was appraised at the low figure of $1,000. But as John died without a will and the Court heeded Elizabeth's petition to be named administratrix, this—or the equivalent in cash—also came to her.

So Elizabeth had her way in everything pertaining to the property. But even before her husband's death, she had begun to mortgage the real estate—in Chelsea, Dorchester, South Boston. In 1872 Kneeland Street was widened and the City of Boston paid her $10,700 for the land they took, a slice off the frontage of the brick mansion's lot.

With business pressing hard on residential doorsteps, other signs of change had begun to appear in Kneeland Street. The great fire of 1872, which laid waste a vast segment of the business and financial district but spared the Howorth house, acted as a spur to the postwar rise in property values. Exactly two years later—in November, 1874—Elizabeth and her new husband, Charles O. Manny of New York City, put a mortgage on the house for $18,000.

Charles Manny seems to have taken his wife and young stepdaughter back to New York; and at this point we lose track of them. Years later, Cora told Edith Richie, a friend in England, that both her parents had died when she was a small child, and that she had been brought up by her grandfather, who died when she was fifteen, leaving her his money but no guardian. This, of course, was her version—with omissions unexplained. However, if Elizabeth Howorth Manny died any time soon after she remarried, there is nothing to indicate that she ever named Charles Manny, or anyone else, to be her child's guardian.*

* A search of vital statistics in Boston and Manhattan yields no information as to the death of Elizabeth Howorth Manny, from which it must be concluded that she did not die in either of those places. I have also been unable to come on any trace of Charles O. Manny, his occupation, place of residence, or year of death.

We have no indication as to who Charles O. Manny was, or where or when Elizabeth met him. But his entrance into the family must have created sharp complications for Elizabeth if the small Cora resented and disliked her stepfather. Had the second marriage been unhappy? Did the restless and rebellious teen-ager run away from her stepfather's home to live with her Aunt Mary Holder, then widowed? Or had Aunt Mary simply taken Cora to live with her, for whatever reasons? How did Cora come into her substantial inheritance from the fortune of Great-grandfather Howorth? These questions remain unanswered. But the property-minded Elizabeth must have devised some means of preventing the unspent portion of her first husband's wealth from falling into the hands of her second.

It seems fairly certain, at any rate, that Cora went to live with her Aunt Mary, whose home, at 156 West 128th Street, was in the neighborhood of Oscar Hammerstein's dazzling new Harlem Opera House. But even this was too far from the center of things where she longed to be; and the bright lights were calling. About the time she became twenty-one, she moved downtown to a boardinghouse at 365 Fifth Avenue. However much Aunt Mary may have disapproved of this move, she seems to have had some sort of comprehension of her niece's waywardness and not to have taken her to task. Cora was free to return. For many years afterward, very likely to the end of the old lady's life—or her own—Cora continued to use Aunt Mary's home as a permanent address. Aunt Mary did not slam the door.

But what did she intend to do now, alone in her new freedom? "Nice" girls did not stay, unchaperoned, in hotels; and the better class boardinghouses, whose conservative elegance many preferred to the gaudy luxury of the great commercial hostels, "let in" no one without an introduction. "Incredible New York" of the eighties, where a woman could be arrested for the crime of appearing in public "red in the face!"

That was the eighties; the nineties offered pious protection to the droves of female waifs loose upon the city in search of employment and independence. Wrote one young woman from Brattleboro, Vermont, to the editor of the New York *Press,* "The only position I have in view is one not paying over five dollars a week. I shall be absolutely alone there and know nothing about the city."

The writer asked to be directed to "some respectable place where I can board within my limited means."

The editor responded to the letter, August 27, 1897, with a long informative article, captioned in large type: "DOORS ARE OPEN FOR GOOD GIRLS—Working Women Can Choose from Three Homes. . . ." Heading the list was the Margaret Louisa on East Sixteenth Street, "oldest and most aristocratic of these much needed abiding places. . . . The process of disillusionment and disappointment awaiting the young woman from other towns who has come to New York as her Mecca is not the less painful, but certainly is more safe, amid the comfortable surroundings and wholesome Christian atmosphere of the Margaret Louisa." After this warning homily, the article stated that a single room might be had for the sum of fifty cents a day, or a room with two beds for eighty cents. But no one might remain longer than five weeks; applicants were being turned away at the rate of a hundred a day. Meals in the restaurant were priced at "ridiculously low rates." "While this handsome house does much for the woman earning fair pay," there was also a home at 48 West Fourteenth Street for girls earning under six dollars a week. Here there was no time limit, and no restrictions as to faith or creed, but when a resident got her pay raised above the six-dollar ceiling she was "asked to leave her room for a less prosperous sister." This house in the writer's opinion was "not as prettily furnished" as the Margaret Louisa, but everything was pronounced "comfortable, if it doesn't exactly harmonize." Girls making as much as four to six dollars a week were expected to pay two-fifty to three dollars, "which includes breakfast, dinner, and a packed lunch the matron prepares for each to take with her to work." At that time (1897), some thirty young women had found accommodations here. In a more expensive category was the Grannis Home at 5 East Twelfth Street.

But safety, if it meant going to live in one of the places where girls were "protected" and young men callers driven away at ten o'clock—just when the evening was mounting to its best—was hardly Cora's idea of living. How lucky, she thought, that she wasn't obliged to seek employment at any of the drab occupations then open to "womanhood"; that she did not have to join the hordes of factory girls earning a miserable two or three dollars a week, for whom the ultimate choice lay between an overcrowded slum tenement or the street. She had no silvery voice like the fabulous Lillian Russell, but she had other talents, and Great-grandfather Howorth's money. And of one thing she was sure: the place to grasp the rainbow was the Gay White Way!

The sentiments expressed by Mrs. Pell, a firm champion of woman's independence, in the *American Woman's Home Journal* a decade later, were also Cora's—and might even have found favor with Elizabeth. In a series of articles, pro and con, on the theme of whether or not American womanhood was being corrupted by bargain counters, Mrs. Pell wrote:

Women growing more avaricious? It is the best thing they can do, but I do not think the bargain counters are to blame. Every day's change in our modern civilization brings women more and more in contact with the world. It is the instinct of self-preservation that is teaching women to be avaricious. . . .

They are learning the value of money for the first time, and as a result they are learning the need of getting money and the power it brings. The bargain counter may help them along, but it is only one factor among many. There is no sex distinction in dishonesty. Men have always been avaricious. . . . Until a woman began to handle money she had no need to become greedy, but the ability to become greedy, which is nothing more nor less than the ability to become a good business woman, is speedily developed by circumstances. . . .

There was little of avarice in Cora's composition. But since it was a man's world, hence necessary for a woman to attach herself to one of the creatures if she was to have any fun at all and avoid making herself conspicuous, perhaps the first thing to do was to get herself a husband.

In 1886, 365 Fifth Avenue was but a stone's throw from the opulent splendor of the Hoffman House bar with its celebrated painting of nudes by Bouguereau, the Brunswick Hotel whence the rival leaders of the great new "coaching" sport set out on their gay sprints into Westchester, and the Fifth Avenue Hotel at Twenty-Third Street. From Union Square to Forty-Second Street the area lying between Broadway and Sixth Avenue was also the neighborhood of the great restaurants: Luchow's, Delmonico's, Mouquin's, and Louis Martin's, where "the foyer was hospitable to well-groomed ladies who seldom disdained invitations to an evening of diversion." But more and more, too, it was becoming a region of boardinghouses rubbing elbows with the millionaire mansions which lined the Avenue from Washington Square to Forty-Second Street. The fact that Cora and young Mr. Murphy both resided at 365 Fifth Avenue, as shown on the marriage license, is strong indication that they met and grew better acquainted in one of these boardinghouses.

Nothing is known of Thomas Vinton Murphy except that he was born in New York City, the son of another Thomas Murphy and one Mary Gibbs, that he was twenty-five years of age and in the dry goods business. He and Cora Howorth were married by a minister, the Reverend Edward M. Deems, on September 21, 1886.* The bride was twenty-one. The romance was short-lived, a minor episode in the career of one whose dream of life hardly fitted her to be the wife of an obscure dry goods vendor. In all probability, a good slice of what remained of the Howorth fortune played a prominent part in the divorce settlement, if it was not the initial attraction.†

But how did Cora get to England, presently, to meet and marry Captain Stewart, who belonged to the smart racing set of Ascot

* The first clue to this hitherto unknown marriage came to light on the English marriage license issued to Cora and Donald William Stewart, where she appears as "Cora Ethel Eaton Murphy, formerly Howarth," and under head of "Condition," "the divorced wife of Vinton Murphy."

A Thomas Murphy, appointee of President Grant, was involved in customhouse scandals in the Port of New York. The New York *Nation*, March 9, 1871, reporting a Congressional investigation of the affairs of the customhouse, refers to charges that Collector Murphy undertook the management of the customhouse not mainly with a view to efficient and economical collection of public revenue, but made appointments and dismissals with reference to political activity. Murphys are legion, and there is no direct evidence linking Cora's ex-husband with the son of this Thomas, who seems to have been a member of the Tweed Ring. But Cora's later statement to a correspondent that she had "seen the dark insides of politics in three cities" leaves the question open, at least as an interesting speculation.

† It may be worth recalling here that when the fair Miriam Follin, who later became Mrs. Frank Leslie, stepped off the path with a young New York jeweler's clerk, a shrewd and determined mother took the matter to court. The court action was dropped when the young man agreed to marriage, but on the wedding night he left his seventeen-year-old bride, who then "found herself in the anomalous position of having lived with her husband before marriage and having separated from him immediately afterward." The Victorians, it seems, were often far more resourceful in disposing of such embarrassments as an unwanted bridegroom than they are given credit for.

and Goodwood, and exhibited a fondness for American showgirls? With her curious adherence to the forms of her genteel upbringing, those "limits of decorum" which might not be overstepped while discarding the restraints, it seems unlikely that Cora would have traveled alone to London. Was Thomas Vinton Murphy then a dry goods exporter, and did his business perhaps require a trip abroad accompanied by his wife? Or did Captain Stewart, who had been severely wounded eight years before in the Afghan war, meet her on a trip to America undertaken for his health? And did they elope? They were married, at any rate, in the Register Office in Somerset House, London, on January 26, 1889—just two years and four months after the date of Cora's marriage to the dry goods merchant in New York. But this time there was no minister to pronounce the benediction: it was a civil ceremony.

The date and place of Cora's divorce from Thomas Vinton Murphy are blotted out. Because she remained an American citizen and her first marriage took place in New York City, it seems likely that the divorce was obtained in the United States, probably in New York City. A search of records in London, at any rate, yields no information. There is in the United States no central agency such as exists in Great Britain, where all marriage and divorce records are required by law to be placed on permanent file, and the number of New York City courts alone is formidable. However, British thoroughness in checking on the status of divorced persons who remarry would certainly have required "Cora Ethel Eaton Howorth, divorced wife of Thomas Vinton Murphy," to submit proof of her divorce before she could be so described on an English marriage license. In view of Captain Stewart's rank, moreover, and the social prominence of the Stewart family, it seems altogether improbable that he would have brought a woman to whom he was not legally married to live under his family roof at 73 Harrington Gardens.

The Stewarts were of Scottish lineage. Cora's father-in-law, Sir Donald Martin Stewart, field marshal and commander-in-chief of Her Majesty's forces in India, now retired, after several times receiving the thanks of Parliament was created a baronet in recognition of distinguished services to the Empire. Those were the days when the Empire offered a career to young men from the upper ranks of the middle class, as well as to younger sons of the aristocracy. In his youth, during the Indian Mutiny, Sir Donald had made a famous ride from Agra to Delhi carrying dispatches which, says the *Dictionary of National Biography*, "forms one of the romantic episodes of that heroic year" (1857). On his retirement from active service Sir Donald, who had previously held important posts in the Indian government, was made a member of the Royal Commission on Indian Civil and Military Expenditures and later appointed governor of Chelsea Hospital, a home for retired servicemen in London.

His youngest son too was a hero at twenty, mentioned in dispatches, decorated with the star and medal with clasp. But many more stars and medals, from as many campaigns, were collected on the person of Donald William Stewart by the time he was married to Cora Howorth, at twenty-eight.*

In the England of Queen Victoria, gentlemen did not "earn" money. If they inherited no estates, they served the government or entered the army. Younger sons were endowed or they left the country. For a son of the lower peerage, a war hero who had been his father's aide-de-camp, to unite himself outside the Anglican Church with an American divorcee suggested a bohemian bent that may well have brought censure upon the hero's head. He apparently quickly returned to an orthodoxy requiring Cora's submersion in a domestic circle presided over by a Victorian autocrat in the person of a retired field marshal, a price she may have been unwilling to pay for acceptance in the family. Her husband at any rate had resigned his commission the year before the marriage took place, and some while afterwards he entered the colonial service.

* Cora's husband was made a C.M.G. in 1897, and knighted (K.C.M.G.) in 1902. The Colonial Office List (London), 1905, p. 579, has on record that he joined the 92nd Gordon Highlanders in 1879; served in the Afghan War, 1879-80; was present at Lord Roberts' march from Kabul to Kandahar, was severely wounded, and received medal and clasp, star for the march; served with 92nd in the Transvaal War, 1881; was A.D.C. to commander-in-chief in India, 1882-1884; served with the mounted infantry, Sudan campaign of 1884-1885, receiving medal and clasp, Khedive's star; served as political officer with the Ashanti expedition of 1896, receiving star; Res. of Ashanti, 1896; served in northern territories of Gold Coast, 1897, and at the occupation of Gambaga and connected operations; was commissioner and commander-in-chief, British East Africa Protectorate, 1904.

He died on October 1, 1905, while serving as Commissioner and commander-in-chief in the Protectorate (now Kenya Colony).

Cora at the time of her marriage to Donald William Stewart. The inset photograph of Stewart is from a page headed "THE KING'S BIRTHDAY HONOURS: PROMINENT RECIPIENTS," in *The Illustrated London News*, November 15, 1902, captioned "Mr. Donald W. Stewart, C. M. G. / Chief Commissioner of Ashanti (New K. C. M. G.)."

Cora's photograph courtesy Stephen Crane Collection, Syracuse University Library.

Whatever the degree of her culpability, she certainly had neither talent nor taste for the role of "Empire widow," with a husband stationed somewhere in India, Afghanistan, the Sudan, or the Transvaal, coming home on occasional short leave to beget a child; and Donald Stewart evidenced no inclination to sacrifice his career for the little woman, who, if she objected to his going through her inheritance, was every bit as keen on a good time as he.

The immediate cause of the break between them disappears in the mists. A Jacksonville attorney alleges that Cora once confided to him that Donald Stewart spent her money "with such facility that she told him to get out of her life, and he obligingly went." He did no such thing. If this was Cora's version, later circulated for her own reasons, it was not the whole truth. For the one thing confirmed is that *she* left *him;* that Donald Stewart held his wife wholly to blame for their matrimonial debacle; and that her subsequent desertion so wrought upon his injured self-conceit that, embittered and wishing to blot the whole thing from memory, he recorded himself in *Who's Who* (1902) as "unmarried."*

When next we hear of Cora it is in Florida. How did she get there? And what was she doing in those "lost" years between Harrington Gardens and the Hotel de Dream?

Had she drifted in with one of the "remittance men"? English younger sons, these, who came to Florida to build fortunes in orange culture—of which they knew nothing—got rooked by land sharks, and were frozen out: a sad sight, balancing a tea cup and shivering in white ducks on the piazzas of the old wooden hotels along the river, having lost all but the clothes they stood in.

The common gossip is that with a friend, an unknown Lady Grace Hamilton, she arrived on a bewildering assortment of millionaire yachts, a flotilla with a list of hosts from which the reader may take his choice: William B. Astor, who had extensive real

---

* During one of her recurrent cycles of going "broke," Stewart allegedly offered to set Belle Livingstone up in "a large tea-room" in London—where presumably, entertainment and refreshment would not be confined to tea drinking—and shortly before his return to Nairobi, in 1904, where he was then Governor of the Protectorate, he presented her with £1,000. "Sir Donald on occasion could be every inch the severe official, but whenever he called on me in gubernatorial mood I would always ply him with whisky and soda until he thawed into his usual genial self. I saw a great deal of Sir Donald while he was in London that time." (Belle Livingstone, *Belle Out of Order*, New York: Henry Holt, 1959.)

estate holdings in Jacksonville and presented the city with a site for a clubhouse and yacht basin; Pierre Lorrillard, tobacco king and sportsman; Hamilton Disston, Philadelphia financier who is credited with laying the foundations of future Florida prosperity by sacrificing a large part of his fortune to refunding the State debt. The yachting party went slumming "down the line"—so runs the fable—but after a disagreement with their host the two ladies were "dumped," and the yachtsman sailed away leaving a substantial check pinned to the pillow of each. One hears no more of Lady Grace Hamilton. But a variant of the story asserts that the yachtsman extricated himself from an embarrassing situation by setting Cora up in proprietorship of the Hotel de Dream.

Legend matches the peacock and barnyard plumage of the era, and legend again puts Cora and the ghostly Lady Grace in Shanghai for a rendezvous with the yachtsman—where they are supposed to have been living in a blaze of Mongolian splendor that would make the pleasure dome of Kubla Khan look like the meanest Bedouin tent. Again the story trails off into the mists: Cora had come to Shanghai from Japan, or from India, where she had been living with her husband. But records of the Colonial Office in London give no hint that Captain Stewart, after quitting the Army in 1888, was engaged in Her Majesty's Service anywhere outside the British Isles until the year 1896, when he went to the African Gold Coast (now the Republic of Ghana) as political officer with the expedition against the Ashanti tribes. Were Cora and Captain Stewart, then, "blowing" the last of her inheritance on a holiday junket around the world? There is nothing, however, in Cora's notebooks, into which went a conglomeration of travel notes, observations on life, and quotations from her diverse reading, to indicate that she ever penetrated farther into the Orient than Constantinople—where she afterwards was with Stephen Crane.

One other story, given currency by Richard Harding Davis, who "was never intimate with Crane"—and certainly never fancied Cora!—is that "she was the mistress of a Jacksonville politician when Crane met her." There is no concrete evidence that she was ever anybody's mistress before she knew Stephen Crane. As Davis himself was not in Jacksonville at the time of which he writes, we may conclude that he was repeating local gossip. And whatever we may think of her looseness of conduct—her "laxity of worlds"—it must be conceded that were promiscuity truly a component of

Cora's personality, she would hardly have gone to the trouble of marrying the lovers with whom she was at different times in her life involved. Besides, Cora had seen far too much of politicians ever to choose them for her intimates. When she was later obliged to avail herself of their good offices—the sharp edge of the knife blade pressed against her own neck—her opinion of ward politicians stood at zero.

We return to the question persistently in the foreground of her baffling story from which so many of the key facts are missing: how did it happen that she, Boston born, the child of wealth, descended on one side from Quakers, musicians, and makers of musical instruments, and on the other from artists whose religious roots had sprung from Church of England soil, became the mistress of a pleasure resort in Florida? Such questions are susceptible to no final answers, but certain contributing factors—cultural, environmental, psychological—have already been noted.

One motive for her break with convention (which was not limited to sexual conduct) was certainly her intense curiosity, her craving, however perverse at times, to escape from the commonplace. "Unenthusiastic natures, how much they miss! . . . I have lived five years in one all my life," she wrote in her diary. "I have never economized in sensation, emotion. I am a spendthrift in every way." In this pursuit of heightened stimulation she is, as one writer sees her, at one with those Decadents who, like the English poet Dowson, "cried for madder music and for stronger wine"; and also at one with Stephen Crane.

But while Crane's compulsive urge to make his body "a testing ground for all sensations of living" led him to seek heightened experience in the adventure of war, Cora as a woman not unnaturally looked for it in love, which despite her worldliness she, like her older contemporary Ouida, continually viewed through the golden mists of a romanticist's dream:

> There was a woman—young, world-worn, selfish, floating on the
>   swift dream of desire, never able to reach the smooth sea
>   of satisfaction—
> until one day—
>   *He* came, and with him came once again melody in the
>   notes of birds . . .
>   (from "What Hell Might Be")

Cora, for one thing, felt none of Crane's obsessive guilt, the poisoned fruit of his early indoctrination with the idea of a direct relationship between sin, damnation, and carnal love. On the contrary, like Ann Veronica, the heroine of H. G. Wells' once controversial novel, when she "wanted a particular man who excited her . . . she pursued him and got him. With gusto . . ." To have followed up this unwomanly behavior by walking out on a husband, one who was an English aristocrat—what more was needed to convince the righteous that here, indeed, was a dangerous hussy? Cora perhaps gloried in the epithet. She herself, with supreme self-confidence and enjoyment, took the first steps toward the Hotel de Dream, in jubilant defiance of the Victorian climate.

When the Women's Rights movement in the United States became entangled with the free love ideas of Victoria Woodhull, its priestess and militant standard-bearer Susan B. Anthony lost no time in disavowing the Woodhull faction. H. G. Wells, who remained to the end of his life a rather muddled advocate of free love despite occasional reservations and recantations, regarded the furor over Women's Rights as of secondary importance, the movement itself he termed "vindictive." "If women wanted to be free," Wells writes in his autobiography, "the first thing was surely for them to have complete control of their persons, and how could that happen unless Free Love and Neo-Malthusianism replaced directed and obligatory love and involuntary child-bearing, in the forefront of their programme."

Cora, with little use for programs, likewise considered Women's Rights as a political movement of secondary interest, and she would no doubt have agreed wholeheartedly with Wells' formulation of the case for sexual freedom for women. We cannot know to what extent she may have been influenced by current free-love ideas, but her notebooks yield this illuminating statement:

> The maintenance of the physical welfare of man, in spite of his superiority over woman, being quite impossible . . . without a violation of the laws of chastity, he allows himself the wildest liberty in this respect, and denies equal or indeed any freedom of conduct to woman, his, in his opinion, physical and mental inferior.

Ibsen evaded the question of what happened to Nora Helmer after the slamming of that door which echoed around the world,

marking her exit from "the doll's house." But it may not be altogether fanciful to imagine that Ibsen's Nora and Cora Howorth
Stewart might have met at the Hotel de Dream.

Although her establishment was primarily a place for the enjoyment of superior food and entertainment, Cora, like Crane, pursued her own unconventional theories of "rescue," and from diary
entries it is at least inferable that she felt she was performing a
worthwhile philanthropy in also furnishing to the clients of the
Hotel de Dream, if they wished to avail themselves of it, a trysting
place amid civilized surroundings. It is important to keep in mind
that, in her view, such associations had nothing in common with
debauchery—though she later extended this rationale to include
prostitution.

> What is a kiss? . . . It warms your blood and sets your heart
> beating. . . . And makes your eyes twinkle like stars on a frosty
> night. It isn't a thing ever to be forgotten. No language can express
> it, no letters give the sound. Then what in nature is equal to the
> flavor of it? What an aroma it has! How spiritual it is! It is not
> gross, you cannot feed on it! It does not cloy, for the palate is not
> required to test the taste. It is neither visible nor tangible, nor port-
> able, nor transferable. It is not a substance, nor a liquid, nor a
> vapor. It has neither color nor form. Imagination cannot conceive
> it. It cannot be imitated or reproduced and so is immortal. It is as
> old as creation, and yet is as young and fresh as ever. It pre-existed,
> still exists, and always will exist. Millions and millions of souls have
> been made happy, while millions and millions have been plunged
> into misery and despair by a kiss. And what is it? Simply a pointing
> and parting of the lips.

We shall see in a later chapter by what stages of rationalization
Cora arrived at agreement with Mrs. Warren, the madame of
Shaw's play—which was having a stormy history of suppressions
in England—that girls were better off in a well-run house of prostitution than in factories where they were employed as sweated
labor.

Nothing at the Hotel de Dream was "vulgar." The newspaperman McCready's remark is significant, for Cora undoubtedly derived a powerful feeling of protection from her ancestral roots
and cultural background. As long as certain standards of propriety
and taste were maintained, it seems never to have occurred to her

that she could not defy with impunity the governing mores in sexual matters. This egotistical blindness or indifference to the consequences of some of her actions produced tensions and cross-purposes which were ultimately to plunge her, like Isadora Duncan, into extremes of recklessness and emotional chaos in which the fibres of personality break.

Richard Harding Davis, writing in 1913 to Mrs. Charles Sidmore, an English friend of Cora's who had warmly defended her, cautioned: "But if you are thinking of writing anything about Crane for God's sake say nothing about her until you have talked to Ralph D. Paine. He knows all the facts of the matter." And he added, straining to be fair, "Mr. Paine has a very high opinion of Mrs. Crane. Any decent man will tell you she was a loyal wife to Crane as long as he lived. . . ."

But Ralph D. Paine, who knew "all the facts," died without revealing them. In 1924 he wrote to Thomas Beer: "I promised myself long ago never to write about Cora. I do not want to put anything on paper, even now, for fear of being misunderstood. What I am afraid of is that some smart Aleck will get the yarn from the wrong person and dish the dirt for the 'sophisticated' to have a good time with. She was a fine person in so many ways. . . ."

5

ALTHOUGH the most famous literary men in America had done Stephen Crane the honor of noticing him (even if principally to attack him), of "society" he had no knowledge beyond Delmonico's and Asbury Park summer hotels. He was curious about it. Meanwhile "society" persisted in the uncharitable notion that he was a morphine eater, drunkard, lecher—and a despoiler of "womanhood." In the tourist city on the edge of the wilderness the moody and shy young man who got along badly with women unless they were a few years older, or nonconformists like himself, must have found in Cora's company welcome relief from "the same old women"—who reminded him of certain "feminine mules" encountered in Port Jervis and Asbury Park—"sitting on the hotel porches saying how well the climate suits them and hurling the same lances with their eyes to begin bloodshed." Cora had moved in charmed circles of London society in the brief period of her marriage to Captain Donald William Stewart—later K.C.M.G. Her trunks and dressing-table silver were marked with a coronet. Her husband's family home, 73 Harrington Gardens, was in South Kensington, a fashionable new part of the London West End. Helen Trent and Lily Brandon Monroe, two other women to whom Stephen had been briefly but intensely attached, had also lived abroad; and the first Stephen Crane, who arrived in Massachusetts in 1635, was from a family that had owned land in Surrey which Stephen someday would like to visit. Except for a couple of months in Mexico, he had not been outside the United States.

This tousled young man with the intense eyes and "strange melancholy beauty"—Howells' words—could astonish and overwhelm Cora with the realism of his depictions of the area around New York's Chatham Square and the human derelicts encountered at nighttime under the El. He could entertain her with tales about the artist's studio in East Twenty-third Street where he had lived for eight months with three friends, all of them sleeping on the floor and dining off buns, sardines, and potato salad from the free lunch counters. The idea of potato salad for breakfast made Cora shudder!

If they laughed together over the childhood episode in which his older brother Ed figured as the rescuer of his manhood, carrying Stephen off to be shorn of his "little Lord Fauntleroy" locks, she could counter with the pranks and misdeeds of "little Cora, the angel child." Both were rebels, and the glow of shared iconoclasms probably exceeded that of the champagne—which Stephen disliked anyhow.

"One of the greatest pleasures of having been what is called bad," Cora said—and he must have grinned at this, remembering thundered warnings in his maternal great-uncle Bishop Peck's published treatise, *What Must I Do To Be Saved?**—"is that one has so much to say to the good. Good people love hearing about

---

* Jesse Truesdell Peck, Bishop of Syracuse, great-uncle of Stephen Crane. A copy of Bishop Peck's tract, *What Must I Do To Be Saved?* (New York, 1858), is among the books from the library at Brede Place now in the Columbia University Crane Collection. The possible influence of this work on the mind and imagination of Crane, in boyhood, is convincingly argued by Daniel G. Hoffman in *The Poetry of Stephen Crane*.

sin. . . . Good, oh, but I'm glad to be far from that goal!" Her dislike of "good" people extended to those "good for one," who produced within her "a kind of rabbia. I want to bite them." The only reason, she thought, for associating with anyone was in the pleasure derived from the association. But of course a line must be drawn somewhere. One could not go about with a murderer, however amusing: "His moral deficiencies might produce unpleasant consequences for oneself!"

But no woman, she was sure, "who is absolutely and entirely good in the ordinary sense of the word gets a man's most fervent, passionate love, the love beside which all other feeling pales. How deadly dull to herself must the good woman be, how limited her imagination. . . . I wonder if husbands are so often unfaithful because their wives are good? I think so. They cannot stand the dreary monotonies and certainties. They give them reverence and affection, and go to the women who are less good and love them." She had, she now confessed, "an incessant longing for love and sympathy," but desired not reverence: "it goes to passion's funeral! . . . The world, my world, is generously and munificently lax. . . . But there are limits of decorum, certain proprietorial domains upon which we may not openly poach. Zeus has unquestioned right to Io; but woe betide Io when she suns her heart in the smiles that belong to Hera!"

A man's mental rank she felt was usually determined by his estimate of woman. "If he stands low he considers her—heaven help her—such a one as himself. If he climbs high he takes his ideal of her along with him, and to keep it safe, places it above himself."

Stephen's love-making resembled none of the varieties she knew much about. "Brevity," he had said, wooing her with poetry, "is an element that enters importantly into all pleasures of life, and this is what makes pleasure sad; and so there is no pleasure but only sadness."

Taking sharp issue with such a lugubrious philosophy, Cora told Stephen of her marriage to Captain Stewart, of her flight from the house in Harrington Gardens when her husband, bedecked with stars, ribbons, and crosses, refused her a divorce. And the earlier marriage fiasco in New York. Her marriage to Captain Stewart could still bring sadness when she thought of it, sadness for what cannot be restored: youth, innocence, the rapture of "first" love, and belief in the existence somewhere of a good and glorious future just around the corner.

> I wonder how many of us wish ourselves transported permanently to that time when we didn't know champagne from *alter feiner* madeira, or dry hock from sweet sauterne? When an attractive face made us feel ready to abjure all the sinful lusts of the flesh and become inheritors of the Kingdom of Heaven? I should like to feel it again. But how can we, when we have been intoxicated with many things . . . success and experience . . . and know the world backwards and ourselves mercilessly?

Musing on these lost things, Trilby's lover came into her mind, Little Billie, in whose sensibility, chivalry, and genius she saw Stephen reflected:

> What do I not feel for you? I cannot tell yet. It is too vast to be measured, and alas, weighted with such a burden of sorrow and regret.

A few men, Stephen had said to Nellie Crouse, "can treat a woman tenderly not only when they feel amiable but when she most needs tender-treatment." But did he tell Cora about Nellie Crouse? Helen Trent? Lily Brandon Munroe? The others he had worshipped with a boy's abandon? Or the ex-actress Amy Leslie, drama critic for the Chicago *Daily News*, who had once loaned him money and about whom he worried now because he had found out that she was in love with him? Amy, old enough to be his mother, was down on her luck. But "not one man in three thousand," he told his friend Willis Hawkins, could "be a real counsellor and guide for a girl so pretty as Amy." He was leaving that now for Hawkins to unsnarl.

Crane responded all his life to beautiful women, but he had come a long way since his infatuation during a summer at Asbury Park, when he was twenty-one, with the bewitchingly lovely Mrs. Munroe, to whom he sent the manuscript of *Maggie*. Her husband, in a fit of jealousy, destroyed the manuscript along with photographs and all of Stephen's letters except four that her younger sister Dorothy saved. Two-and-a-half years later—in January, 1895— while Lily was living in Washington with her husband, Stephen arranged a meeting with her there and tried to induce her to go with him to Mexico. He was going on a trip west for his health, he said, then south across the border to write stories and articles for Irving Bacheller's syndicate. Their meeting—its hopelessness a prelude to parting—took place amid the shattering noise of hammers, in the chilly corridors of the Library of Congress, then under construction. Lily was moved by the desperation in the boy's passion, but she thought him too much of a visionary.

Back in New York, arranging for his western trip, Stephen was introduced at a tea party in Thirty-fourth Street to beautiful Nellie Crouse, who at once became "a curiously potential attraction." Her image stayed with him through a six months' absence. When in the town of Puebla, Mexico, he saw an American girl in a new spring gown who reminded him poignantly of Miss Crouse, he suddenly turned and headed back to New York. Nellie helped him to forget Lily.

"I am often marvellously a blockhead and incomparably an idiot," he wrote her on his return from Mexico, "I reach depths of stupidity of which most people cannot dream. This is usually in the case of a social crisis. . . . A social crisis to me is despair." And to her he also confided his unsentimental and strangely joyless vision: "The final wall of the wise man's thought . . . is Human Kindness. . . . If the road of disappointment, grief, pessimism, is followed far enough, it will arrive there. . . . Therefore do I strive to be as kind and as just as may be to those about me and in my meagre success at it, I find the solitary pleasure of life." He intended to die in his thirty-fifth year: "that is all I care to stand." (To a later confidant, Karl Edwin Harriman, he made it thirty-one.) "But I expect to make a sincere, desperate, lonely battle to remain true to my conception of my life and the way it should be lived. . . . It is not a fine prospect. I only speak of it to people in whose opinions I have faith. No woman has heard it until now."

Hardly the spirit in which to conduct a successful courtship! Nellie Crouse wanted a "man of fashion," and Stephen was not a gentleman in her sense of the word. "As for the man with the high aims and things," he protested, ". . . I shouldn't care to live in the same house with him if he was at all in the habit of talking about them."

On the subject of marriage, Stephen and Cora understood each other perfectly: Cora had found domestic and sexual incompatibility worse than any fear of scandal; Stephen had called marriage "a base trick on women, who were hunted animals anyhow. But

something had gone out of him with those unfledged episodes of
boy love. Worship would henceforth have no part in his love for a
woman—the "reverence" that slew passion, Cora thought.

Cora's taste in dress was of the *beau monde*. But Stephen's frequently slovenly appearance, the boyish, soft lock falling over one
eye, the rest of his hair "sailing in the general direction of the last
wind," only made her want to fill him up on good food. And she
knew about food! She could see that he went around half starved,
never taking any care of himself. And when he peered at her from
behind the blond lock, a look half quizzical, half humorous in those
gray-blue eyes that seemed to bore right through all the shams to
the very soul of Truth—the rush of talk released in him because of
her—she wanted to laugh. And comb his hair.*

And what of Crane's feelings, "his one big romance"? The two
love notes written to "C. E. S.," and the book inscription, must
speak for themselves. In the judgment of Daniel G. Hoffman, the
interpreter of Crane's poetry, Stephen Crane had found in Cora
Taylor a woman who "combined with the peculiar qualifications
required for his psychological needs deep sympathy for his literary aims and his ideals of conduct"; while to Cora, "he must have
seemed the fulfillment of all she had dreamed and sought in her
curious career of libertinism. . . ."

He had always declined to join in the usual hue and cry against
the "fallen woman," based on the concept which denied her a mind
and will of her own. "This girl in Zola is a real streetwalker," he
wrote of Nana. "I mean, she does not fool around making excuses
for her career. You must pardon me if I cannot agree that every
painted woman on the streets of New York was brought there by
some evil man." Again, "most streetwalkers would be demimondi-
anes [sic] if they had money. Lots of women are just naturally
unchaste and all you jays know it."

Crane could sympathize with the cry of Hebba Gabler, yoked to
a good man who bored her: "I sometimes think there's only one
thing in this world I'm really fitted for . . . boring myself to death!"
He had no use for the popular notion that the woman who com-
mits a sexual offense is somehow more culpable than the man in a
world which tolerated prostitution so long as it was kept suffi-

* Stephen had written Nellie Crouse: "Of course I am admittedly a
savage. I have been known as docile from time to time but only under great
social pressure. I am by inclination a wild shaggy barbarian."

ciently out of sight, within variously prescribed legal boundaries. This is not to suggest that Crane condoned vice or promiscuity. He simply detested the whole atmosphere of moral hypocrisy glorified under the double standard. And if brothels were a part of his rebellion, as one biographer remarks, there was certainly much more than that single common denominator in the attraction between Cora and himself.

In the precarious balance between Crane's romantic idealism and his pessimistic view of reality, personal honesty was "the supreme responsibility of the individual." Cora's peculiar combination of unconventional honesty and hedonism must have made a deep impression on him; her energetic courage, intelligence, and humor, too: masculine qualities, which in an earlier rebel, George Sand, had seemed to the vacillating Chopin a source of strength.

Somewhere in all their midnight discussions of poetry, love, marriage, chastity, and the social position of woman, that other night side of herself must also have raised its voice: the voice of a female Decadent who had stepped over the line to gather the *fleurs du mal*.

> Sometimes I like to sit at home and read good books, at others I must drink absinthe and hang the night hours with scarlet embroideries. I must have music and the sins that march to music. There are moments when I desire squalor. . . . The great unwashed mood is upon me. Then I go out from luxury. The mind has its Westend and its White Chapel [sic]. The thoughts sit in Park Lane sometimes but sometimes they go slumming. They enter narrow courts and rookeries, they rest in unimaginable dens— seeking contrast—and they like ruffians whom they meet there and hate the nation of Policemen keeping order. . . . I never know how I shall spend the evening until the evening has come—I wait for my mood.

Quite possibly in this Baudelairean version of the emancipated woman, Crane perceived something like a guarantee of certain cherished male freedoms, assurance that Cora would not try to saddle him with the usual feminine paraphernalia of domestic encumbrances.

He could hardly have gotten farther away from the image of both his parents: his devout mother with her "vacuous, psalm-singing religion," or the gentle and kindly dreamer who was his father, the Reverend Jonathan Townley Crane. On both sides of his family Stephen Crane had come of a line of Methodist theologians. The harshness of his mother's creed of sin and damnation contrasts with his father's milder belief in brotherhood and redemption through love. The psychological conflicts resulting from these warring family religions were to bedevil him to the end of his life, especially in his relations with Cora.

Another minister's son, Robert H. Davis, writing of his only meeting with Crane, describes a youthful Don Quixote bent on rescue of the Magdalen; and Thomas Beer details involvements resulting in blackmail, scrimmages with the metropolitan police, fisticuffs provoked by anonymous outraged defenders of the public weal. A girl in a blue coat, with "sunny hair"—Davis writes—had come out of the shadows, "stopped, and looked at Stephen Crane":

Straightway he detached himself from my side, tossed his cigarette into Greeley Square, placed his left hand upon his heart, removed his hat, and made a most gallant bow. I have never seen a more exquisite gesture of chivalry than this youth sweeping the pavement with his black felt.

Under the flickering shadows of the arc lights . . . I got for the first time a blinding flash of the romantic Crane. A lock of soft hair lay upon his high, white, and shapely forehead. . . . Around the mouth hovered an elusive smile, while the whole posture of the body suggested the dancing master about to begin a minuet.

I was not a hero-worshipper. . . . Nevertheless at that moment I discerned an almost indescribable luminous beauty in the eyes of this modern Villon. They were large, the iris seemingly out of proportion to the pupil, blue . . . , brilliant, flashing. . . .

"A stranger here?" inquired Crane with the utmost delicacy in his speech as though addressing one lost in a great city. . . .

"Well, suppose I am a stranger. Can you show me anything?"

"Yes," replied the author of *Maggie*, "I can show you the way out, but if you prefer to remain—" Crane made another gesture with his felt and bowed with an air of magnificent finality. . . .

"You shouldn't hang out here, kid," said Maggie in a throaty voice. "You look cold. You can't stand it. This fat guy [Davis] can."

The girl sauntered off utterly indifferent. . . .

"This is a long cañon," said Crane. "I wonder if there *is* a way out."

But did Cora Taylor really wish to be rescued from the life she was pursuing, with marked success, at the time of her meeting with Stephen Crane? Undoubtedly—by him; we have the answer in her own words. To Crane she wrote in the interval between his departure from Jacksonville and their subsequent reunion in London, both bound for the Greek war:

You are my guiding star. You have just broken out of the clouds which have enveloped me for years in darkness. I never realized true happiness or joy until I met you. [And again:] Even when love is so base as to be only a thirst for pleasure it rarely dies with the first embrace, and who can say he possessed the entire woman in one night of love? . . . Cold sagacity misjudges us. But love illumined by truth, truth warmed through and through by love—these perform for us the most blessed thing that one human being can do for another. They show us to ourselves; they show us what we really are, what we have been, can be, shall be.

Was she referring in the pronouns to all women? All women "fallen" like herself? Or to all lovers?

She does not particularize. But in another journal entry, in her Memorandum Book, she confides, "There are moments when a woman feels ready to exchange all she possesses for the one thing she misses most." And now she herself was about to do just that.

6

ON THE afternoon of New Year's Eve, 1896, the old tugboat *Commodore* lay at her dock in Jacksonville while a steady procession of Negro stevedores carried boxes of rifles and ammunition up her gangplank, destined for the island of Cuba, where a revolution against a corrupt and despotic colonial administration had been simmering for upwards of two years. Everything was described as "perfectly open"; the revenue cutter *Boutwell*, "the old isosceles triangle that protects United States interests in the St. John's," lay at anchor a few miles downstream. The tug took aboard sixteen Cuban patriots going to fight for freedom; farewells were exchanged in two languages and ballads sung to the strumming of guitars. Somebody was overheard to say in Castilian, "It is all fixed. She will sink"; but this scare rumor was later officially discounted.

Stephen Crane, correspondent for the New York *Press*, had signed on as able seaman. He wore a money belt filled with gold supplied by the Bacheller-Johnson syndicate, for which he was also to write articles.

The ship's officers and the leader of the Cubans were detained at the customhouse, as a "mournful twilight" settled down over river and shore before the hawsers were finally cast loose. Two miles downstream the *Commodore* grounded on a mud flat in dense fog. The *Boutwell* came up at dawn and dragged her off; they changed pilots opposite the little fishing village of Mayport and were delayed again waiting for the tide to take the ship across the shallow bar at the river's mouth.

When word reached Jacksonville of the series of mishaps delaying the *Commodore's* sailing, Cora Taylor sent a note to the ticket agent of the Florida East Coast Railway, who was also manager of the Jacksonville Terminal and liaison man with the Cuban Junta, asking a favor. This gentleman replied by messenger, with regrets: "Believe me, my dear friend, if it were possible to arrange it I would go in a minute for I would very much like to see Stephen before he sails." Next morning, before breakfast, came another communication from the agent:

Henry has gone down to the bar as I understand the boat will not go out until the weather permits. . . . But I think if you get a launch you can reach him okay. I would love to go down with you . . . but being alone and it the first of the month . . .

Then suddenly the weather cleared to a brisk, blowy, cold-bright winter day "and the fine golden southern sunshine fell full upon the river. It flashed over the ancient *Boutwell*," Crane reported, "until her white sides gleamed like pearl, and her rigging was spun into little threads of gold." The spirits of all aboard ship were raised to a pitch of mirth and enthusiasm, but Cora's heart was near bursting with a mixture of emotions. Only the cook Montgomery had a queer feeling come over him, "one of those damnable feelings," he said later.

Some twenty hours after Cora's return to Jacksonville in the chartered launch, the news began coming over the wires: THE COMMODORE SINKS AT SEA   Twenty Men Are Now Safe in Jacksonville With Friends BUT EIGHT OTHERS MAY BE AT THE BOTTOM   Three Men Were Drowned as the Steamer Sunk—One Died on the Beach and Five Are at Sea on a Raft—The Newark and Three Friends Are Still Looking for Them, but There Is Little or No Hope That Any More Will Be Saved.

Then for twelve more interminable hours tragedy screamed out of the headlines and Cora, frantic with anxiety, could learn nothing definite. Her good friend at the Jacksonville Terminal called on her, fearing the worst. The newspaper editor left his desk to bring her more of the story from incomplete reports coming in. At nine o'clock in the evening of January 2 (Saturday) the room clerk at the St. James dispatched a gloomy note to the Hotel de Dream:

My dear Miss Cora:

I am very sorry that I have no encouraging word to send you. The eleven men who were saved have arrived in town. One of them saw Mr. Crane get out of his berth and dress himself with the same non-plussed [sic] manner characteristic of him. He entered the boat containing the 16, which is reported to have swamped. There is conflicting rumors as to the empty boat being washed ashore. Some say it has been washed ashore at Port Orange—others say not. The Operator at New Smyrna tells me that he has it pretty straight that it came in bottom up. God save Crane if he is still alive. You are welcome.

Morton

But Morton was misinformed. Stephen Crane did *not* enter the boat which capsized—the number of its occupants seven, not sixteen—but remained on the tug until ordered by the captain to go forward and lower the dinghy. Then he, with Captain Murphy, the cook Montgomery, and an oiler, Billy Higgins, took the ten-foot dinghy, in which they drifted about for thirty hours until they were washed ashore at Daytona. Higgins, struck by an oar or caught under the boat as it capsized in the breakers, was drowned, dying on the beach as the others were being hauled in. Rescuers from the town turned out with food, brandy, and dry clothing.

Early Sunday morning came a hasty but more encouraging bulletin from the faithful ticket agent: "I don't know the truth. But I think everybody is safe. But I will let you know if I hear anything else. I may drop up to see you later." Then a wire from Stephen, and Cora wired back: "TELEGRAM RECEIVED. THANK GOD YOU ARE SAFE. HAVE BEEN ALMOST CRAZY. C.T."

Morton telegraphed the castaway:

THE WAKE HELD AT THE ST. JAMES LAST NIGHT TURNED INTO A JUBILEE TODAY. JUST CARRIED THE NEWS DOWN HOME. ALL WELL THERE. CONGRATULATIONS FROM THE GANG. I AM RIGHT HERE WITHIN CALL. ANYTHING I CAN DO COMMAND ME.

Morton, to whom the Hotel de Dream was "home," presently sent off a second wire to Crane in Daytona relaying congratulations and the assurance of money to follow from Stephen's old friend, Edward Marshall, then Sunday editor of the New York *Journal*.

All day Sunday the wires between Jacksonville and Washington were kept hot. The warship *Newark*, then in port, was still without orders to lift anchor. Telegrams had reached Junta headquarters the day before from two of the Cuban survivors urging that the filibuster tug *Three Friends* be dispatched to the rescue of the seven Americans who, if alive, were clinging to a hastily improvised raft. Until the arrival of Crane's telegram, Cora had believed him one of the seven.

Filibustering was a lucrative trade carried on under the noses of the authorities, who for the most part looked the other way. A local historian testifies, "In 1896, when the Cuban revolution was at the height of its military success the romantic and hazardous business of filibustering men and arms from the Florida coast to Cuba reached considerable proportions." The *Three Friends*, the already famous flagship of the so-called "Cuban fleet," had made her first getaway on March 11, 1896, and piled up a record of some seven successful runs. On her last trip, however, the fast little tug had run afoul of a Spanish warship after unloading her contraband cargo on the Key of No Name. Armed to fight the Spaniards with a Hotchkiss gun mounted on her bow, the tug had opened fire on the pursuing vessel, and was seized on arrival in Jacksonville and interned by the Collector of Customs under pressure from United States Government agents. Her officers and crew were arrested on a charge of piracy. Ralph D. Paine, and Ernest W. McCready of the New York *Herald*, passengers on the *Three Friends* at the time of this incident, judged it the better part of wisdom to hole up in a twenty-five cent lodging house until the affair blew over.*

This little flurry over the *Three Friends*, which took place dur-

---

* The *Three Friends* was not "a government tug" as stated in Berryman (p. 165), but was owned by three Jacksonville citizens who were partners in the filibustering trade, hence her name. Her owners were N. B. Broward, then Sheriff of Duval County, later Governor and U. S. Senator; A. W. Fritot; and George R. Foster. As Foster's connection with the romantic enterprise was a carefully guarded secret, the third member of the triumvirate has been confusingly identified in local sources under various names. (My authority is Mr. Foster's daughter, who authorizes the secret to be made known.) When the *Three Friends* was chartered by the New York *World* as a press boat, immediately after the American declaration of war against Spain, many of the correspondents lived aboard her, among them Stephen Crane. The *Dauntless* entered the service of the Associated Press.

ing Christmas week, was intensely upsetting to everybody. Paine and McCready faced being tried with the others for violation of the neutrality laws. The ship's owners were "sick and tired of giving bonds for Johnny O'Brien [captain] and the rest of the bunch." The *Three Friends* seemed headed for confiscation, and the United States Court was "acting mighty mean and stubborn about it."

In these circumstances, the Collector of Customs, Cyrus R. Bisbee, was understandably reluctant to allow the *Three Friends* to sail without authorization from Washington, especially as the *Dauntless*, equally notorious sister ship of the *Three Friends*, was owned by his son. But the Sheriff of Duval County, Napoleon Bonaparte Broward, former tugboat captain, a colorful figure in politics, and later an able governor, was part owner of the *Three Friends* and no more afraid of the wrath of Washington than of the gunboats patrolling Florida waters or of the Spaniards themselves. When the elder Bisbee, ex-Senator Wilkinson Call, and J. M. Barrs, attorney for the *Three Friends*, in a series of telegrams to the Secretary of the Treasury put her on record as a mercy ship, the mayor of Jacksonville and Sheriff Broward on their own authority sent her to look for the people on the raft. But too late.

Cora had meanwhile been putting the heat on representatives of the Florida East Coast Railway. Whether because the official conscience belatedly awoke from its sabbath doze or because (as was rumored) she paid for it, a special train was at last got off to Daytona—eighty-five miles away—to bring back the other survivors of the shipwreck, Crane among them.

On Monday Cora wired Stephen: "COME BY SPECIAL TODAY. NEVER MIND OVER CHARGES. ANSWER AND COME SURELY. C.T." But the harassed gentleman at the Jacksonville Terminal had more on his mind than the health of Stephen Crane. "Rushed to death trying to get down to rescue the other people," he did not know "if SC would be able to come up on the train."

Not able? Then, oh . . . he must be ill! The thought so panicked Cora that she hastily packed a bag and left word with the assistant manager at the St. James, Mr. James Harrison, to send one more wire, which he did:

CORA WILL BE THERE NOON TRAIN

M ST JAMES

[acting manager]

When Stephen, haggard and dirty, was brought into the St. James lobby still in his seaman's shirt and dungarees, now shrunk to half their size, he caught sight of the precocious nine-year-old daughter of the Barrett family and called out: "Where's that album?" The little girl, an avid collector of autographs, had conceived a romantic attachment to Stephen Crane as "the divinely appointed Savior" of Cuba and was in the lobby to greet him; Stephen, who told wonderful stories to his own nieces and their playmates, was always a special charmer to little girls. The present hero-worshiper grabbed her autograph album, which she kept at the hotel desk, and Stephen, who before his departure had been too rushed to sign it, now wrote his name alongside those of William Jennings Bryan and the owner of the *Police Gazette:*

Stephen Crane, able seaman S.S. Commodore

"That newspaper feller was a nervy man," the cook Montgomery said in an interview for the New York *Press.* "He didn't seem to know what fear was." Stephen was the last man in, before Captain Murphy, when the boats were launched. The cook said he rowed in the heavy seas "as well as the others, although he was so worn out he could hardly hold his oar straight." And in the January 7 edition, Stephen Crane, hero, was all over the front page —a bright yellow halo around him! The cook had mentioned Crane's rescue of a sailor from drowning, a detail which must have caused the hero to curse immoderately as Cora sat by his bed with the papers. It was all right for a man to act like a hero as long as you didn't call him one—the sort of thing Dick Davis made an ass of himself for. Crane's own dispatch to the *Press,* a long, brilliantly-worded account of the sinking, carried no heroics spotlighting the unprepossessing little figure of Stephen Crane. The ironic contrast to other times, when his name had adorned the metropolitan papers with a less sanctified notoriety, must have laughed out at him from the headlines. The year before, in the Dora Clarke affair, against the advice of his friend Theodore Roosevelt, then Police Commissioner, Crane had insisted on testifying in court on behalf of a woman unjustly arrested for soliciting and had even let himself be put down in the police book as her "husband." "If it were necessary to avow a marriage to save a girl who is not a prostitute from being arrested as a prostitute," he

The St. James Hotel, Jacksonville, Florida. Gift of Richmond Barrett.

The "Three Friends." From a painting in the possession of Mrs. Dorcas Broward Drake.

wrote in a *Journal* article, "it must be done, although the man suffer eternally." The newspapers had blown up the story in headlines: STEPHEN CRANE AS BRAVE AS HIS HERO; and there were repercussions yet to be felt.

But a filibustering expedition in waters patrolled by the ships of two navies is scarcely a holiday excursion. Ill at the outset, nerves overstrung, Stephen had had no sleep in the thirty hours out of Jacksonville before the *Commodore* foundered. Now Cora fussed over him, fed him, nursed him—probably at the Hotel de Dream—until he was able to get out of bed, and time passed quickly. The two of them and a gentleman whose first name was Camille—an out-of-town guest of the hotel—played cards, Stephen keeping score on the back of a discarded page of *The Red Badge*. What the game was does not appear from the scoring, but Stephen was, as usual, an inveterate loser.

In the shelter of Cora's arms was rest, recovery. His mother had died when he was twenty, worn out from a life overburdened with childbearing, widowhood, church preaching, and work for the Temperance Union; and Stephen, the fourteenth child, had known little of that refuge of mother love.

> Should the wide world roll away,
> Leaving black terror,
> Limitless night,
> Nor God, nor man, nor place to stand
> Would be to me essential,
> If thou and thy white arms were there,
> And the fall to doom a long way.
>   (*The Black Riders*)

These lines were written to one of his early loves, Helen Trent. But knowing these things now, security, woman's love, to be only illusions to cheat Death with and Love the greatest illusion of all, where was Happiness? For the old thunderer Bishop Peck's descendant, for whom compatability with an unfallen woman probably had become a psychological impossibility after the last humiliating failure with Nellie Crouse, there was to be no escape from the doom envisioned in carnal love. His older brother Will had told him not to believe in Hell when his uncle had scared him "with the lake of fire and the rest of the sideshows." Under the mounting strain of this ambivalence, rooted in childhood, it was to be Cora's mission in their life together to harmonize and ease the warring elements of personality.

And to Cora's romantic heart the miracle of love was everything. "Men and women are not meant to kill their strongest feelings and impulses but only to understand them, to know when to govern or to let themselves be governed," she told Stephen—who had once shocked an Englishman in New York with the statement that there is no such thing as sin except in Sunday schools. "In passion there is fire, and does not fire purify as well as burn?" Her conscience had never been "a stalwart combatant" of her wishes. "If an action doesn't seem to you wrong, nothing in the world will prevent your doing it, provided your desire is sufficiently strong." But no one, she granted, is entirely consistent.

> We do many things in the excitement of companionship which our consciences fail to ratify in the secrecy of self-communion. We thus tacitly admit that we are irresistibly moved by the vibration of a common chord of humanity. If we are piped unto it seems reasonable to dance; and yet no one dances to his own solitary piping. If more allowance were made for the innocent impulses common to men, as gregarious animals, there might be less of the dangerous sense of the pleasure of forbidden fruit in their enjoyment.

Although she chided Stephen with his concern that she had so far been unable to secure a divorce, Cora, too, was anxious about this barrier to their legitimacy in which she now perceived "a more binding yoke than the law imposes." To Stephen she said,

> I've no claim upon you. But I know now—though I did not always think so—that the obligations we have incurred in the past are chains forged whether we will or no, to bind the future. We cannot escape from them; they hang upon us and make life a burden and a misery. When one forsakes the standard of duty there seems nothing left. Wrong doing brings its punishment, and remorse kills the sweetness of life.

So she renewed appeals to her brother-in-law in India to use his influence as the elder brother to persuade her husband to grant her a divorce. She made no mention, of course, of her desire to marry Stephen. Colonel Norman Robert Stewart, heir to the baronetcy, was the officer in command of the Merwara Battalion in Deccan. Although they had never met, he had always stood by her in domestic quarrels and had himself been divorced and re-married the year before—a fact Cora must have counted on in the present situation.

Stephen, also mindful of inconvenient obligations, wrote again to Willis Hawkins, to whom in November he had expressed gratitude "for allowing me to plant certain responsibilities upon your noble shoulders." These "responsibilities" had to do with weekly payments to Amy Leslie, which were to be withdrawn from a sum deposited with Hawkins for the purpose. Hawkins had agreed to act as one of Crane's literary executors in case his journey in the *Commodore* "was protracted by causes which you can readily imagine." (The will made at this time was lost, and Crane later made a new one at Brede Place.) But now Stephen was "troubled over Amy," whose neurotic symptoms were becoming alarming, and begged his friend, "Telegraph frankly Amy's mental condition."

Stephen, in the midst of his worries about the past and his precariously forming plans for the future, was writing "The Open Boat," begun and finished in Jacksonville. Ralph Paine and Ernest McCready, having dinner in one of the private dining rooms of the Hotel de Dream, were an invisible but enthusiastic audience when "The Open Boat" was read aloud for the approval of Captain Murphy—and perhaps of Cora, too.*

Stephen, thinking long thoughts of Cora and the implications of their plans, was also writing to his brother Wilbur in Binghamton, New York, to tell him of the shipwreck and how it felt to be a castaway. Wilbur Crane, once a rower on the Columbia crew, had taught Stephen how to swim.

---

* McCready says that he and Ralph Paine were dining together in another room of the Hotel de Dream when Crane read aloud to Captain Murphy the story of "The Open Boat." "Paine and I were in one section of the house and did not that night encounter Crane—whom P already knew—but only heard distantly the Murphy party. But we returned some nights later—Christmas eve. . . ." McCready confuses dates here, having evidently forgotten that the *Commodore* sailed on December 31, and has the Christmas party follow the shipwreck; it was, of course, the other way around. McCready's timing is contradicted by Paine, who says that he (Paine) sailed in the *Three Friends* on December 14 and spent Christmas Day marooned on the Key of No Name. (*Roads of Adventure*, p. 121.)

There were unpleasant social incidents, which might foreshadow the future. The Barrett children, out bicycling with their mother one morning in the neighborhood of the Sub-Tropical Gardens, passed on the road a well-known victoria driven by a coachman in pongee livery. Stephen, alone in the rear seat, gaily waved his hat. The children hailed him with glee, but their mother acknowledged his greeting with only a chilly little bow.

A Jacksonville attorney told his wife at supper one evening that Stephen Crane had come into his office that day with Cora Taylor and a crazy request: "I want you to give me a paper to protect this lady." At the little strangled sound coming from his wife, the lawyer said, "I simply told him I was too busy."

When the United States Government seriously cracked down on filibustering in the early part of 1897, the looming war in Greece began to attract the attention of some of the correspondents. Stephen wrote: "I am going to Greece for the *Journal* and if the Red Badge is not all right I shall sell out my claim on literature and take up orange growing." On March 11 he wrote his brother Edmund that he had been "for over a month among the swamps further South, wading miserably to and fro in an attempt to avoid our derned U. S. Navy. It can't be done. I am through trying. I have changed all my plans and am going to Crete."

To Crane, the actual location on the map of those "swamps further South" probably meant little, for like Poe's "ghoul-haunted woodland of Weir" their true locus was in the miasmas of his own troubled psyche. "In the imagery of his writing," as in life, Hoffman says, "Crane sought to transfer sexual initiative and guilt to the woman." In one of the poems in "Intrigue," Crane writes:

> Thou art my love,
> And thou art a priestess,
> And in thy hand is a bloody dagger,
> And my doom comes to me surely—
> Woe is me.
>
> *(The Black Riders)*

Was he hiding out from Uncle Sam's patrol boats and at the same time honeymooning with Cora? With a genius for putting himself in the wrong, hardly out of hot water with one woman before compromising himself with another, he was perhaps being careful in the only way he knew—flight. Taking Cora with him, he fled to the swamps of the Indian River below Daytona, where the gossips and the officials investigating the *Commodore* disaster could not get at him for questioning. How long they remained among the big oaks and cabbage palms, where the egrets waded, is anybody's guess. It was probably not as long as Stephen represented to his family. For Cora it was the golden time of their romance. She recorded it in sentimental verse, later in a prose sketch afterwards published in *Smart Set.*

Stephen had once told his family that if he ever met a woman with golden hair he would marry her. (Lily Brandon Munroe and Nellie Crouse were both blondes.) If marriage must wait upon Captain Stewart's humor, they could go meanwhile to some distant place where Cora's "past" and Stephen's troubles with New York police courts would be locked away behind an ocean. Why not England, whence his Surrey forebears had come? In the European countries, she must have urged, if you had a name and position, the legal formalities of domestic cohabitation were not too closely scrutinized.

What, then, was the meaning of that demand upon the lawyer for a "paper to protect this lady"? No record of any transaction exists. If there were one, lost perhaps in the Jacksonville fire, it probably had to do with the sale, or some form of transfer, of Cora's five-year lease on the Hotel de Dream. Business was excellent at the Hotel de Dream, and if Cora was lucky in finding a purchaser on short notice it is hardly surprising. Up to the year 1910 Florida leases did not have to be recorded, and seldom were. The earlier records pertaining to the property at Ashley and Hawk Streets were a notable exception in this respect. Florida law now permits, and did then, action against a defaulting tenant within a twenty-year limit. Long before this statutory limitation had expired, Cora Taylor was back in Jacksonville, her credit unimpaired. There is no record of a default action, in this particular case, ever brought against her in the local courts.

"You are now *au courant des evenements,*" Cora presently wrote Stephen, "and there is nothing to do but await developments." With her shrewd knowledge of human beings, she must have realized that he was as irresistibly pulled toward battlefronts as she was by her own unorthodox ideas of necessity and fulfillment. She was wise enough not to try to stop him. But why not go with him? Men have persuaded themselves that there is a glory in gunpowder and killing, theirs peculiarly and by right. How much longer, she wondered, can they expect women to swallow this fairy tale? Had not Florence Nightingale and Clara Barton discovered on the field of glory need of women's hands? To look upon the scenes of war, where women were still forbidden by custom to trespass except as agents of mercy, and to write about them, would be a grand adventure—an experience to unshackle one forever from the thrall of "womanhood."

Characteristically, with her flexible acceptance of what she could not prevent—turning it into a lark—she brushed up on her French and German, acquired somewhere in her early education and travels (on the continent perhaps with Captain Stewart), bought grammars and dictionaries, and began to put down in her notebooks all sorts of foreign idiomatic phrases for possible use in conversation. Even Moslem prayers and proverbs, unearthed with phonetic spelling! Stephen, always self-conscious and inhibited outside the English language, said he had "tried to learn French because my mother thought it was important but no foreign language will ever be my friend." But foreign tongues held no terrors for Cora, who sailed along fluent and untrammeled.

Stephen saw his brothers in New York and said nothing to them of marrying. Neither the lawyer's cold shouldering nor the gossip would wash out of his memory. A man of honor, and things spoken in love's ardor withal, now he wavered. Then over dinner with an artist friend, Corwin Knapp Linson, who in the hungry days had let him bunk in a corner of the studio in West Thirtieth Street, he confided his dilemma. "With a reserve characteristic of him when speaking of a woman," Linson wrote in two hundred pages of shyly worshipful memoirs, "he told me of her he was to marry, touching so lightly on their meeting in Jacksonville that no memory of it remains." But, from this somewhat expurgated version of the romance in Florida, Linson gathered that the girl had "suffered from unfortunate circumstances." "She could sail on the same steamer and be married in England. But there were tongues. 'The weasels would draw blood anyhow.' He hated to leave her alone but his job was to go on to Greece and come back when the stew was over. 'What would you do, CK?'"

"Just that," Linson replied, never doubting that Steve would "always do the right thing." The war "could not last long; Prussian-officered Turks would do the business of Europe's rotten politics, and all he would have to do would be to see the Parthenon and come home and get his wife! It did turn out that way, only instead of New York it was England."

After this advice from Linson, a gentle and uncomplicated youth, the terrible silence ended for Cora with the arrival of the letter she had been waiting for. And she poured out her heart in reply:

> I feel as if you had been restored to me after five years of separation! I wish I could write you every hour in the day. It is hard for me to express my love for you on paper. . . . I am delighted with your letter, it seemed more like the dear one I knew and loved so well . . . the bitterness that filled my heart has entirely passed away and I look forward with much pleasure to the coming of your letters. . . . We are both older now . . . and I believe much wiser. Had you given yourself time in the past . . . to consider the probability of my sincerity when I so often repeated that you were dear to me, you would better feel what that separation cost me and better understand the pleasure your letters give me now. . . . Jerome, I think it was who said, in writing of love, even when it brings misery it is a wild romantic misery all unlike the dull worldly pain of other sorrows. . . . Perhaps you recall the words, I think them beautiful as truth is beautiful.

Her love would endure "till the angels doubt, and the stars burn out," therefore, "looking back through the dark avenues of time into the fading past let your fondest memories be those of your loving Cora."

And when a last brief note came, scrawled perhaps in the hurry of boarding the ship that was to take him to England, she replied with:

> Only a line that you may know I am thinking of you and to say that I should indeed be happy if you were with me, or even if I had sufficient time to sit down and write you a long letter, for whilst writing it I might delude myself with the happy thought that you were by my side and I was talking to you. But fate wills otherwise and I can only add goodnight—be good and I *love you*.

Grecian Lark: War and Romance

And you love me.

I love you.

You are, then, cold coward.

Ay; but, beloved,
When I strive to come to you
Man's opinions, a thousand thickets,
My interwoven existence,
My life,
Caught in the stubble of the world
Like a tender veil—
This stays me.
No strange move can I make
Without noise of tearing.
I dare not.

(The Black Riders)

chapter 2

THESE autobiographical lines from one of the poems in *The Black Riders*, written fully three years before Crane set eyes on Cora Taylor—probably in the autumn of 1893, about the time of his first wounded renunciation of Lily Brandon Munroe —are a key to his dilemma with respect to Cora. The women he had loved previously had in common social eminence, backed by solid means, such as he, the artist wastrel, could never hope to reach. The pain he suffered on losing Lily is certainly echoed here. Nellie Crouse did not come on the scene before publication of *The Black Riders*. It was at Lily he flung the hurt denigration of "coward." Now, however, the shoe had shifted to the other foot: Cora, unlike

Lily, did not return to the husband she no longer loved and who apparently had not much feeling for her; and Stephen found himself "cold coward" before the social punishments envisioned in the love she offered him.

They did not sail together, Crane apparently hugging the illusion that this gesture to appearances might somehow avert the hateful tongue-wagging that was certain to come. In London while the laggard ship was bringing Cora to him, Stephen was being introduced to celebrities: Anthony Hope; Sir James M. Barrie; Justin McCarthy, a member of Parliament who had been to Greece and written a novel about it.* In the heady glow of acceptance on equal footing by such notables, his old antipathy to top hats and titles was beginning to loosen; he liked London.

He was introduced at the clubs by Harold Frederic, the big, blond *Times* man from the Mohawk Valley. Frederic's novel, *The Damnation of Theron Ware*, had the year before sounded a new note in English fiction, foreshadowing *Elmer Gantry*. It was a realistic study of a Fundamentalist minister whose faith succumbed to the combination of Darwinian ideas, a red-haired siren, and a hedonistic priest who introduced him to his own view of Roman Catholicism. The book, which failed to scandalize all the nice people, promptly went through six editions.

Frederic had been unhappily married in Utica, New York, to a cheerless woman who stubbornly refused him a divorce. He had forsaken her and their four children for a sweet, sparkling, high-spirited girl from Oswego who was a Christian Scientist. By her he had three other children. With her he enjoyed an easy, happy freedom at Homefield in the pleasant little village of Kenley, Surrey—an hour's train journey from London. Mrs. Frederic and her

---

* Anthony Hope, pseudonym of Anthony Hope Hawkins (1863-1933), English author of romantic novels, best known for *The Prisoner of Zenda* (1894), which started a fad for the swashbuckling school of Balkan intrigue which continued up to World War I. Sir James M. Barrie's novel *The Little Minister* was published in 1891 and later adapted for the stage. His famous play *Peter Pan* was to become permanently linked on Broadway with the name of Maude Adams, who achieved her greatest success in the title role. Justin McCarthy (1830-1912), British historian, novelist, and journalist, who was the leader of the Irish Home Rule Party in the House of Commons. Not to be confused with Justin Huntly McCarthy, his son, likewise a member of Commons, historian, novelist, and poet.

four also were living in England at this time; and the astonishing fact is that Frederic lived back and forth in both households, sometimes quitting Homefield to spend as much as a fortnight with his legitimate family. With his twenty-year-old daughter Ruth, who seems to have accepted Homefield uncritically, he had a warmly affectionate companionship; he used to drive with her about the country in search of rare plants, and once had taken her with him on a trip to Germany.

Frederic was an able editor and his popularity in England won him a host of friends as well as enemies; he kept his job as London chief of the New York *Times* in spite of these domestic irregularities. After Frederic's death, a visiting American of rather strait-laced views wrote Cora Crane his impressions of a visit three years earlier to the home he found "a marvel, a miracle—the happiest home, it seems to me, I ever saw"; and he had come to like its master "as well as any man I ever knew. . . . Harold told me that for the first time in years he was now free of evil. He said his mind was calm, his conscience clear. His marital relations were pure, his children growing up in an atmosphere of love. I myself saw the side of the picture he turned toward me and had to admit its beauty. Except for the *other* side, I felt it was absolutely perfect. But there *WAS* the other side."

Frederic it was, the year before, who first introduced Stephen Crane to the English novel-reading public with an exuberant review of *The Red Badge of Courage*. He followed this with a dispatch to the New York *Times*, January 26, 1896: "Stephen Crane's Triumph—London Curious About the Identity of America's New Writer."

Crane now called on his publisher, Heinemann, whose chief editor Sidney Pawling had written him in December: "We think so highly of your work—of its virility, actuality and literary distinction that we have been pleased to place it prominently before the British public." He arranged through Heinemann to cover the war in Greece for the *Westminster Gazette*. Richard Harding Davis, also bound for the Greek war, staged a luncheon for him at the Savoy to which came all three of the lions—Barrie, Hope, and McCarthy—to sit down with the most unlamblike Frederic in honor of the youthful genius from the United States.

There was no love lost between the host and his young guest.

While Stephen considered Davis an egotistical fool, the dandified idol of college youth deemed the author of *Maggie* and the Bowery tales a gifted but unwashed lunatic, a boor with suicidal proclivities and unfortunate leanings toward low associations. Each however recognized in the other a core of professional integrity, and when Crane in New York later became the butt of mud-slinging abuse, Davis, with his own brand of *noblesse oblige*, came to his defense. Crane reciprocated at San Juan by helping Davis, then stricken with sciatica, over the rough trail to his own bivouac at El Poso, all the while under fire from the Spaniards on the hill. This was to come; but meanwhile, since reading *The Red Badge* sometime in 1896, Davis was eager to meet the young author who "seems to me to have written the last word as far as battles or fighting is concerned. . . ."

There is considerable uncertainty as to whether they had met before. Davis told Thomas Beer that at the Lantern Club* in New York he had heard Crane express opinions against drug-taking. This would have been in 1895 or 1896, but Davis' statement to Beer was long after the fact and his recollection of things unconnected with his professional reporting has often proved unreliable.† Crane's unflattering opinion of Davis, set forth in a letter to Nellie Crouse—January, 1896—may or may not have been arrived at first hand. Crane was sometimes given to snap judgments of individuals whom he never personally knew, as in the case of his violent antipathy to R. L. Stevenson. Davis, at any rate, was in Key West that winter of 1896-97 while Crane was in Jacksonville and

---

* The Lantern (original spelling was the older form Lanthorne) Club, which had its headquarters in a loft over a rickety old building on William Street in Manhattan, almost under the Brooklyn Bridge, had come into existence as a meeting place where young writers and newspapermen could hold forth over a hot noon meal in lively debate on anything from politics to one another's work. They chipped in to hire a Negro cook. Irving Bacheller was the Club's founder and president; other charter members were Willis Brooks Hawkins, Edward Marshall, Edward Townsend, and Post Wheeler. Crane joined in the summer of 1895, after his return from Mexico. Guest speakers were often invited to attend the luncheons, among them Davis, Theodore Roosevelt, Mark Twain, and Ethel Barrymore; but it is not on record that Davis was ever a member of the Lantern Club.

† See Beer, p. 133. Scott C. Osborn finds it "odd" that Davis and Crane should not have met before March, 1897, but concludes: "In reading Davis' letters, published and unpublished, I formed the tacit policy of taking at face value what he said if he wrote it during or immediately after the event; but

the swamps below Daytona with Cora. The only regular rail route to and from Key West was through Jacksonville and Tampa. In Jacksonville, Davis must certainly have paused to visit Junta headquarters for his newspaper, and would in all probability have spent an evening at the Hotel de Dream, formed his own impressions of its dazzling mistress, and heard repercussions of gossip.

In London, where he was the intimate of literary moguls and the popular hero to whom foreign secretaries salaamed, Davis was in his element. Even Crane must now have been impressed. At the Savoy luncheon Davis got a different impression of the youth who was by turns loquacious and taciturn: "He is very modest sturdy and shy. Quiet [sic] unlike I had imagined." After all he had heard in New York bars and, more recently, in Florida, this was giving "Stevie" the benefit of the doubt.

Stephen had probably been two or three days in London when Cora joined him, chaperoned by the ever devoted and enigmatic Mrs. Ruedy. The fourth day after his arrival, they left for Paris. On the train to Dover, Stephen prudently occupied a separate compartment from the two women. He and Harold Frederic, who had come along to see him off, were presently joined by Davis, on his way to Greece by way of Italy; and at Dover, on the dock, Frederic introduced Crane to a tall, reserved Canadian: Arnold Henry Sanford Bennett.

In the next few minutes, a collision occurred which was to have a permanent effect upon Stephen Crane: Davis recognized Cora Taylor. The moment that the *chevalier sans peur et sans reproche*, whose values were almost everything Crane's were not, caught sight of Cora in the crowd milling about the customs booth, Crane the untidy bohemian became transformed into an "irresponsible." Animus flared. Here is Davis' version of the incident:

"Stephen Crane came with me *also a bi-roxide blonde who*

---

if he were depending on his memory for meetings, dates, and places I frequently found him in error. . . . That's why I doubted his sweeping statement that he had often at dinners and at the Lanthorne Club heard Crane express prejudice against drug taking. He might have heard Crane say this almost anywhere—Greece, Cuba, etc.—and assigned the statements to other places and times. Another reason why I decided to take his statement at face value is that in his letters home during 1895-6-7 he never mentioned the Lanthorne Club or Crane—with the exception of the letter in September 1896, in which he praised the Red Badge." (Scott C. Osborn to Lillian Gilkes, April 30, 1956.)

*seemed to be attending to his luggage for him and whom I did not meet."** [Italics mine. L.G.]

Later, from Athens, Davis repeated his abusive characterization of Cora, with embellishments, referring to her as, "a Lady Stuart [sic] who has run away from her husband to follow Crane." Whether or not this questionable use of the title "Lady Stewart," which was picked up by the other correspondents, originated with Davis cannot be known; but it is an interesting speculation. There is no evidence that Cora ever made formal use of it; but she may possibly have teased Davis with it, while he, whose vanity sometimes rendered him humorless, would not have realized he was being "took." When she observed the Davis back solidly turned upon her, it would have been exactly in character for Cora, in whom consciousness of ancestry and position was whimsically conjoined with humor, to ask Harold Frederic to introduce her—and throw the title at him while Crane looked on in agonized silence.

But in Paris, Cora and her traveling companion apparently kept their distance from Stephen. The fiction that they were in separate parties must have been strictly observed during their stay. Meanwhile Stephen went sightseeing with Sanford Bennett, but was strangely unimpressed. Funerals disgusted him, Notre Dame bored him; only the children sailing their boats in the fountain of the Luxembourg Gardens, and a cavalry trooper on horseback who might have been at Gravelotte, revived his fugitive interest.

Bennett remained in Paris when Crane, with Cora and Mrs. Ruedy, entrained for Brussels about April 3 or 4. A strong bond had sprung up between Crane and Bennett in those few days together.

All that is known of Mrs. Ruedy is that she was of a retiring disposition, a native of Akron, Ohio (a city romantically associated in Stephen's memory with Nellie Crouse and an "intolerable duf-

---

* Of special interest is the fact that the second part of this sentence was deleted from *Adventures and Letters of Richard Harding Davis,* edited by his brother, Charles Belmont Davis, as were also other later unflattering references to the Cranes in Greece, including his remark, "a Lady Stuart. . . ." But with due allowance for Davis' moral disapproval, one can but wonder why Davis went out of his way to speak of Cora at all, in conjunction with Crane, when writing to his family. Was he afraid some whisper might get back that he had shaken hands with the mistress of the Hotel de Dream? For "whom I did not meet," read "on whom I turned my back"—and the answer is clear.

fer" who bored him), somewhat older than Cora, and that Joseph Conrad familiarly referred to her as "the good Auntie Ruedy." The cruel portrait of the elderly companion of Nora Black in *Active Service*—Crane's novel of the Greek war—has perhaps been too easily accepted as a facsimile of Mrs. Ruedy; the autobiographical elements in this novel have been widely misrepresented as well as overstressed.

In Brussels it was still Cora who enjoyed the sights. When they visited the art galleries, the realism of Rembrandt's wonderful "Anatomy Lesson" made a deeper impression on her than the master's name, which she promptly forgot: ". . . the corpse upon the operating table is so truthfully depicted that it is said to be possible for a professional eye to diagnose the nature of the disease which caused death.Yet all this skillful painting does not make the picture an agreeable one." Scarcely a production, she thought, to hang in one's dining room.

They spent a day in Bruges, city of "the marvellous Middle Ages," where Cora was struck by a general absence of ambition among the women of Flanders. Ideal mothers they were, and very religious, but undisturbed by "even a whisper of rebellion." "The new woman," she concluded, "has no place in Flanders."

On the train to Frankfort their Yankee dander was roused by the story of a resident of that city who was actually sued in the courts because he complained to officials of the Royal Prussian Railway that the sleeping-car porter had failed to waken him when his station was reached in the night. The man had no redress. Stephen was sure such a thing could never happen in America, where fewer "granite heads" were to be found amongst officialdom and public servants were gifted with a sense of humor. The incident so impressed him, he wrote it up in one of the series of syndicated newsletters on which he and Cora presently were to collaborate. Then, on the way to Munich, the western terminal of the Orient Express, Stephen began to worry about his lack of languages in a war that would be fought in foreign tongues. From Basel he wrote:

I now know that I am an imbecile of rank. If nobody shoots me and I get back alive through those Indians in London I will stay home until there is a nice war in Mexico where it does not matter what you talk so long as you can curse immoderately. Willie Hearst has made a bad bargain.

But Cora's spirits were not dampened. She no doubt had arranged the itinerary, and as the train rolled on across borders skirting the southern tip of the Black Forest and cutting across the northern edge of Switzerland past Lake Constance, the wheels clicked a tune of happiness. This was their second honeymoon, the real one, and all the more delicious after doubts and separation! The presence of a third party, the older woman napping in a corner of the compartment or gazing out of the window, affected her not at all; she refused to let herself be bothered by anything.

From Munich they made short excursions; and if Stephen's interest in sightseeing remained lukewarm, Cora's did not. She was enchanted with the lovely old Bavarian town of Landshut, viewed "standing where the road begins to rise towards the Castle . . . to the right the mellowed red brick of St. Martin's ancient Gothic church, with its tower of many quaint irregular stages, and the stone porch with gay fifteenth century traceries." She rejoiced that it had not yet been spoiled by tourists. "Not a glaring object, hardly a modern house to mar the charm of its slightly curving main street, genuine Mediaeval . . . with quaintly gabled roofs"—a contrast to Oberammergau where the traces of tourists were everywhere visible, and where—from the eagerness of all whom she met to finger silver—she judged money to be a conspicuous factor in productions of the Passion Play in modern times. "What must it have been like, or rather, the people, when to them the . . . Play was a purely religious and sacred thing?"

After a day in Oberammergau, "the village known all over the world," they moved on to visit Linderhof, the favorite palace of the mad King Ludwig "whose suicide ended the madness." Cora describes it, "a small chateau with a beautiful garden, a masterpiece of the landscape art"; but the statues were "a blot on the picture, all poor samples." She mentions the Kiosque with its Turkish fittings, but was more taken with the Blue Grotto, which she recognized as a copy of the celebrated cavern at Capri. Although the Grotto was excavated out of the mountainside, "half the rocks are only wood," but so perfect in her opinion the imitation of Nature, "it forms an artistic whole." Lights behind blue glass "shed the requisite color over the small lake and waterfall"; there is a boat in which the King used to lie dressed as Lohengrin, and on one side facing the waterfall a rocky projection known as *Die Lorelei* after the famous promontory on the Rhine.

The party setting out from Munich seems to have included two other people: a young Englishman named Ferris—a theological student—and an American journalist referred to in Cora's sketchy notes only by the initials "S.S." This may have been Sylvester Scovel, Stephen's old friend whom they later saw much of in Athens, although there is no other identification or evidence to connect "S.S." with Scovel. Cora and Stephen had chosen a more "unusual" route than Davis to get to the war in Greece, one filled with discomforts and perils which if known to the tourist in advance "would certainly banish all pleasure!" But the casual bohemianism of their Bavarian ramble calls to mind one other, half a century earlier, when George Sand, Liszt, and the Countess d' Agoult set forth from Switzerland for Chamonix—not to report a war, but merely to express themselves. This was not yet the era when wars had become global and nuclear weapons a shadow of evil encompassing the earth; laughter and the carnival spirit were still possible within sight and sound of the more serious business of life and death upon an uneasy planet.

Cora kept a record of all stages of the journey to Constantinople, a rough diary on loose sheets of lined legal cap paper—the kind Stephen preferred and obtained in quantity from his brother William, the lawyer in Port Jervis. But ten pages at the beginning unfortunately are lost, and the account breaks off in the middle and again at the end where other pages have vanished. Cora was as careless as he in the matter of dates; she usually omitted them, and what she meant by her reference to "time for a Presidential election in the U. S.," it is impossible to say. Was she confusing the election with McKinley's inauguration? The sentence continues, "and we take advantage of it to go and see the Consul and get passports, F. [,] S. and myself being without them. S. S. with his usual foresight had procured his long ago in America. They are not needed in Europe until one goes to Turkey, Iran or Russia."*

A note on Ferris, who is "improving physically in the life he now leads, he drinks but little and reads much"; then they are "again in Wien"—Vienna—for one day only, "and will take the Oriental [sic] Express to Varna. I have ordered a fur-lined overcoat for our young parson, who insists on travelling in a top hat and who had not warm enough clothes to travel in Bulgaria in win-

* This held true until World War I.

ter." Sixty years ago when trains were unheated April in that part
of the world was still winter; and it was typical of Cora's open-
handedness that she could not sit complacently in the compartment
while opposite her the young man in a top hat shivered without
a proper overcoat. They stopped over in Budapest, a charming
city and one she wished to visit again; then back to Vienna to
board the Orient Express for Varna, a dingy little Bulgarian port
on the Black Sea.

"Until the Danube River is reached—and I am sure the man who
wrote the 'Beautiful Blue Danube' never saw it at this point—the
train service is as good as on Club Train from Paris to Londres. All
the rest of the journey . . . was perfect misery." Though wrapped
in furs, with rugs and hot water cans, everyone suffered from the
intense, bitter cold. It was everywhere in Europe an unusually
severe winter. On the shores of the Danube they met crowds of
picturesque Moslem pilgrims on their way to Mecca, "mostly
dressed in the long coats and hoods one sees in Russian pictures,
each with a long staff and loaves of bread hugged tightly to their
dirty breasts. We crossed the river on small boat to the Bulgarian
side, where for the first time passports were necessary." [Bulgaria
being then under Turkish rule.] But the passports sought in Vienna
must not have been obtained, for she notes with a swell of patriotic
pride: "The American citizen is evidently very much respected in
that half-civilized land—for the outside of one passport [Sco-
vel's?] with USA printed on it was enough and the official took his
hat off with a 'good day' in excellent English."

The dirt and conditions of filth in which the lower classes existed sickened her. The name of a shed in the wilderness where
they stopped for a meal none of them could eat escaped her, but
the toilet accommodations were unforgettable! She enjoyed "a
good laugh when I think of the undignified position of a member
of the French Embassy surrounded by peasants and one or two
passengers, who by the way, were limited to one woman and a
child trying to reach Constantinople in the shortest time, and five
or six men, all members of different legations."

These were the only tourists, as few persons bent on pleasure
were foolish enough to go by way of Varna in wintertime. So it
was a very tired and disgusted party "that reached that wretched
hole . . . miles over frozen, snow-covered desert, with nothing to
eat and empty flasks, and nothing to see but an occasional shepherd

working like one of his own half-starved sheep, as they are all dressed in sheepskins. . . ." And there what a prospect awaited them! A raging tempest and an old hulk of a ship anchored some distance out. While it looked as if the small boats with their few miserable passengers would never live through such seas, the travelers were obliged to take their chances

on a watery grave even before reaching the boats, as one by one, as the little craft rose on a huge breaker we jumped to be caught in the arms of the dirtiest sailors I ever saw. Twenty minutes of hard pulling landed us on the Austrian Lloyd *Danae*, soaked to the skin. . . . They were considerate enough to give us our supper before sailing. The old ship was rocking and tossing in such a manner that few sat the meal out. The anxious, strained look that usually precedes *mal de mer* was on every countenance. I must have been born for the sea as I never experience it. The journey is supposed to be seven hours—it took the *Danae* on that memorable trip from Sunday at 6 P.M. till Wednesday night to reach Constantinople. . . . When ships are unfit for Indian and such service and reach the respectable old age of 30 or 40 summers, and their owners no longer care to pay the high rates of insurance, they are put on the Black Sea. The *Danae* belonged to this class. She was a terrible old tub with only the Captain, first and second Mate, and five sailors to manage her. The accomodations were too funny—little hen coops for cabins. Ferris and I took what is called the "ladies" cabin, a good size room with six berths—S, SS and Mathilde [Mrs. Ruedy] had three little hen coops, the berths so short that it was impossible for anything but a child to stretch its legs. There were about twenty second-class passengers, mostly Turkish ladies and some few Albanians; and 200 steerage—a villainous looking lot, all Turkish men. The cargo was 5,000 live chickens when we started, dead ones before we reached the Bosporus. The wind was howling and rain falling when the anchor was pulled up in Varna harbor. It soon blossomed into a gale. At midnight the gale became a hurricane—waves mountains high, the poor old ship with no freight to steady her groaning and tossing about like an egg. As one by one the heavy seas struck her she trembled and it seemed as if she would fall in pieces. The darkness was intense, no one could stand or even sit up, so all who had berths had taken to them. The poor wretches on the lower deck huddled together for warmth and protection from the heavy seas that almost drowned them, as they had little shelter. It was bitter cold. I crawled out into the cabin to see if anyone was still alive belonging to our party; they were, but wished they were dead, all deathly sick. The horrors of that night, in fact all the journey, were added to by the sounds of breaking crockery and glass. There was not a bit of whole china left after that trip. Mr. Kauffman, whom I found on the floor of the main cabin, moaning and praying in different languages—wildly clutching the stair rail—said the Second Mate had just told him the Captain was drunk, had to get drunk or freeze (nice discipline) and had not the slightest idea what part of the Black Sea we were in, they had lost all control of the ship and we were floating about at the mercies of Pa Neptune. Just then a monster wave struck the *Danae*, she keeled over on one side and the engines stopped. I crawled to the different cabins trying to rouse S, F, S and poor Mathilde but no use—they longed for death in preference to the agonies of *mal de mer*. Kauffman the talkative was speechless and green with fright, but the end had not come. The machinery was broken and it took ten or

We know that the battered old tramp finally reached her destination, but the narrative breaks off here, pages charred at the edges and watersoaked as if from a bath in the Black Sea. The rest is lost, except a fragment of page 23: "Many are the stories told by the guides—we have one who is a character. Steve named him 'Alabasta Sebastopoli'."

They lingered in the city of Constantine long enough to visit Saint Sofia, and to see the inside of a Turkish harem, where Stephen came upon a fragment of manuscript in Latin dating back probably to the Crusades.* They gathered notes on that headline enigma, "the Turk," for use in a series of articles dealing with the Eastern Question, which eventually appeared in the *Westminster Gazette* under the caption, "With Greek and Turk." Then on April 26 Cora, who was actually the first woman war correspondent, the Marguerite Higgins of a little "bath-tub war" in the Balkans, was sending under the by-line of "Imogene Carter" her first dispatch from Athens: "War Seen Through a Woman's Eyes."†

* This manuscript fragment turned up in a scrapbook left behind at Brede Place and recently unearthed there by Mr. Roger M. Frewen, grandson of Moreton Frewen and present owner of Brede Place. The Cranes may have obtained it as a souvenir from their host, the sheik of the harem.

† The unpaged clipping of this article (in the Columbia Crane Collection) does not show the name of the newspaper in which it was published.

2

Turkey did not declare war on Greece until April 17, although fighting had been going on much earlier in border raids of Greek armed bands into Asia Minor and northern Epirus, and Greek landings on the Turkish-held island of Crete had occurred more than a year before. Severe cold weather continued beyond the usual season, the New York *Press* reporting April 14, "Snows, rain and bitterly cold winds have made campaigning in the mountainous districts hard, and all dispatches are being delayed."

A forgotten little war lasting only one month! But for many years, since the Ottoman Empire (the advance symptoms of its dissolution quickened by a Greek nationalism that was grandiosely termed pan-Hellenism) entered the stakes in the old imperialist poker game of the Western powers, the Eastern powder keg had been intermittently sputtering. Great Britain and France in alliance with Russia—then intent on her own pan-Slavism aimed at annexation of Constantinople and control of the Dardanelles—were jockeying with Germany and her weakened ally Austria-Hungary in the contemplated division of the estate of "the sick man of Europe," the Turkish Sultanate. A prominent Greek stated in an interview with the Associated Press correspondent: "Whether or not Europe insists on the integrity of Turkey, Greece is not animated by selfish views or with any desire for annexing territory to the kingdom. She demands not only complete independence for heroic Crete, but the same independence for Epirus, Macedonia and Thrace"—meaning, of course, the direct opposite of what he said, that is, "independence" for these provinces from Turkish rule under a Greek confederation, which would eventually emerge as a united nation. The pattern, outlined in the New York *Journal*, is familiar:

May 18, 1896	revolution broke out in Crete.
August 1	proposal for intervention by the Powers failed.
September	Powers protested Greek intervention.
October 4	Greece proclaimed sympathy for Crete.
January 4, 1897	Powers hurried warships to Crete.
February 15	Greece sent small army to Crete to "restore order."
February 24	Greece defied Europe in behalf of Crete.

March 13	Russia called for troops of each Power to act in concert in Crete.
March 25	Allied fleet bombarded Cretans.
March 28	Powers decided to blockade Cretan ports.
April 6	Greek irregulars crossed frontier into Turkey.
April 17	War declared on Greece by Turkey.

But this was not war as "Imogene Carter" was there to see and report it. She cared little for "history in the past tense," war as waged by the diplomats and viewed by the historians. In "War Seen Through a Woman's Eyes," she says:

> To a woman, war is a thing that hits at the hearts and at the places around the table. It does not always exist to her mind as a stirring panorama, or at least when it does she is not thinking of battles save in our past tense historic way, which eliminates the sufferings. One cannot, however, be in any part of Greece at this time without coming close to the meaning of war, war in the present tense, war in complete definition. I have seen the volunteers start amid flowers and tears and seen afterwards the tears when the flowers were forgotten. I have seen crowds rave before the palace of the King, appealing to him for permission to sacrifice. . . . I have seen the wounded come in hastily and clumsily bandaged, unwashed and wan, with rolling eyes that expressed that vague desire of the human mind in pain for an impossible meadow wherein rest and sleep and peace come suddenly when one lies in the grass. . . .

The unknown soldier's sacrifice "in the present tense" had for her little of the romantic appeal that it exerted upon the imagination of Stephen Crane, but if that image of "an impossible meadow" was cribbed from Stephen it was also apt. "In Athens one can get an idea of war which satisfies, it is true, the correspondents of many London newspapers. . . ." A gratuitous jab, this, at the army of café experts loudly conversant in every war, and whose participation in this one from a safe distance filled "Imogene Carter" and Stephen Crane with deep disgust. "War here is tears and flowers and blood and oratory," she summed up. "Surely there must be other things. I am going to try to find out at the front. . . ."

The last straw in the patience of a weary old Sultanate had been reached on April 6, when the Greek irregulars poured over the border into Turkey proper: an action timed to coincide with the crossing of the northern frontier by other bands of insurgents. The Associated Press correspondent went to Larissa and learned that "the invaders numbered upwards of 3,000. Among them Signor Cipriano and his Italian volunteers."

On the eve of these developments, a monk from Mount Athos assisted his abbot and two deacons in a solemn religious ceremony at Koniskos—rendezvous of the northern insurgents—at which all members of the invading body partook of the sacrament and registered the oath of allegiance, "Liberty or Death." The men, all fully armed, wore the national costume, fur caps bearing the badge and initials of the Ethnike Hetairia—Greek patriotic society—embroidered in blue and white, with the words "En Jonto Nike" crossing the initials in black. General Makris, knowing more than he cared to impart of these movements, left with his staff for the Greek outpost near Elassona. Headquarters disclaimed all knowledge of the raid, or the raiders; but a prominent Greek in close touch with the League (the Greek National Society) and its plans was more talkative. "For years," said this gentleman, "thousands of Greeks, even little children, on receiving a shilling have been in the habit of putting half into a national box for the cause of pan-Hellenism. . . . Now that a great moment has come in Greek history, we have seized upon it."

In Athens, while the news was hailed with delight by crowds of cheering Athenians, the Crown Prince Constantine was uttering to Frederick Palmer face-saving disclaimers which nobody believed. It was an open secret that by the end of the week at least 10,000 Greek "irregulars" would be in Macedonia, Albania, and Epirus. Like flies in August the Greeks were suddenly everywhere at once, while the Turks, asleep, appeared helpless before the superior organization of the rebel leaders.

The city presented a scene of wildly patriotic bustle when Stephen and Cora, Mrs. Ruedy—and possibly Sylvester Scovel—arrived from Constantinople about the time war was declared. What had become of the gay young theologian Ferris, in his top hat and the fur-lined overcoat presented him by Cora? Soldiers jammed the streets and cafés, cheering for war. Enthusiasm and confidence were high among Greeks of all classes, shopkeepers locking their doors and going off to join the army, leaving in charge teen-age boys who threw away the keys and followed their employers.

All over the world, this little "bath-tub" war was attracting attention. The amount of sympathy it generated among diverse segments of the population finds a parallel only in the South American independence struggles of the nineteenth century, under the leadership of Simón Bolívar, and the more recent example of republican Spain. From Italy some 2,000 "Garibaldians," led by the son and grandson of the great Italian, arrived to fight for the Greek cause, while others were leaving Italy in such numbers that the Italian government finally stopped all visas and sent a protest to King George. But Edward Abbott reported May 1: "Garibaldians continue to arrive, and today a French officer and a Russian officer obtained permission to lead their own men to the front." A London report, April 12, told of the arrival of thirty volunteers at Arta, among them young Clement Harris, soon afterwards killed at Pente Pegadia. The twenty-three-year-old youth —symbol of the many who left home and family to die, like Byron, in the "holy cause" of Greek liberty—was, ironically, the son of the British admiral who had directed the bombardment of Crete.

Another of the English volunteers was the journalist H. N. Brailsford, who was later editor of the London *New Statesman and Nation* and a contributing editor of the American weekly *The New Republic*.

The New York *Press* reported that the clergymen of New York City, Brooklyn, and Philadelphia "have joined a movement to aid the Greek cause. An appeal for funds will be read from many pulpits tomorrow." At the same time, hundreds of Greeks living in the United States were returning to Greece to fight for their homeland.

Greece also had her own Joan of Arc. Nineteen-year-old Helen Constantinides, whose parents had been killed by the Turks, declared that she had no fear of death and would fight in the front ranks. An excellent shot, she dressed in an army uniform and, cheered by thousands of enthusiastic Athenians, left for the front under the escort of her brother.

But Miss Constantinides and "Imogene Carter" were by no means the only women taking an active part in the little war. Inspired perhaps by the women's suffrage movement then gathering momentum, women all over the world seemed to have come to the conclusion simultaneously that war was their business, too—in one way or another. Mrs. Ormiston Chant, the English social reformer, under the auspices of the Red Cross, reached Athens early in April and set out with the Greek royal princesses the next day for Larissa—center of hostilities in the north—to join the hospital corps there. An appeal, "Send what you can to the Union of Greek Women," from Olga, "Queen of the Hellenes," to the women of America found immediate response in the heart of Clara Barton, who issued a special plea for contributions to the American National Fund in Aid of the Greek Red Cross. The National Fund, headed by Solon J. Vlastos of New York, was supported by Mrs. Clarence A. Postley, treasurer of the DAR, and Mrs. T. Henry Gelston of the Hoffman Arms, who formed a committee and placed coin boxes in prominent hotels all over New York.

Other women in the United States helped as best they could. A Barnard College senior, Miss Anne Sumner, skipped graduation and offered her services as a nurse through the Greek Consulate in New York. A sister of General Grant donated a letter written by the General and a leaf from his casket to be sold for the Greek war fund. Mrs. Robert Hoe, wife of the American millionaire printing-press manufacturer, noticed three men buying revolvers in a Twenty-third Street store and spoke to the clerk. "Those are Greeks, madam," said he. Said Mrs. Hoe, "I'll pay for their purchases."

"Imogene Carter" of the New York *Journal* meanwhile was running into unexpected competition from one Harriet A. Boyd, whom the *Journal* described as "a bright American girl" and Smith College graduate, who went to Athens to study modern Greek and volunteered as a nurse when the war broke out. Miss Boyd, the *Journal* announced, was "trying to get attached to the hospital corps" and would send back "special letters to the *American Women's Home Journal* [a Sunday Supplement published by the New York *Journal*] on the active work done by women in the field and in the reserve." Her first article describing her experiences in probationary training had appeared in the Sunday edition of April 25. But Miss Boyd seems to have been no less keen on being first to the goal as a war correspondent; her next article date-lined from Volo, May 5, was featured in a big spread with headlines:

ONLY WOMAN WAR CORRESPONDENT AT FRONT

I left the Piraeus on the transport Thrace eight days ago, bound for the front in accordance with the Journal's instructions. I am the first woman war correspondent in the field. . . .

But "Imogene Carter" had already scooped her by six days! Her dispatch, April 29:

WOMAN WAR CORRESPONDENT AT THE FRONT
Goes for the Journal
Imogene Carter Braves Perils of the Field of War
Only Woman on the Scene

I start today for the front of the Greek army to see how the men fight. I learn that even the English nurses have returned from the hospitals of the army because the Turks fire on the Red Cross flag with the same enthusiasm with which they fire on the lines of battle.

From this and from other rumors I am quite sure that the Journal will have the only woman correspondent within even the sound of guns.

Acquaintances among the foreign residents here all strongly advise me not to go. At first I was flatly refused letters of introduction to people at the front in an effort to make my going impossible, but, as a matter of fact, I do not believe altogether in the point of view of the women of Athens, and, at any rate, I am going.

She was not going to be beaten out at the innings by any "bright" sister who hid behind the Red Cross emblem! And she had already scored earlier with her story of "War Seen Through A Woman's Eyes"—April 26 date line—which now placed her one-up on her rival. This piece did not appear in the *Journal* but in some other paper not identified in the heading.

But as to the *Journal* puzzle of two women contenders for first place: Harriet Boyd had as she herself feared—in the dispatch of April 25—washed out on her final examination for admission to the hospital unit, the lectures being "all in Greek." She must then have cabled the *Journal* in New York and through its managing editor Sam Chamberlain got the assignment of woman representative for the paper at the front. "Imogene Carter's" job probably was arranged by Stephen in Athens through John Bass, the *Journal* man in charge of its field correspondents. All records from that time were lost in a fire which destroyed the old *Journal* building on Nassau Street, but the most probable explanation of this confused situation is the mix-up of arrangements separately concluded in Athens and New York. There can be no doubt about the *Journal's* eagerness to have a woman correspondent at the front.

"Mrs. Stephen Crane as war correspondent during the Graeco-Turkish Scrap"—the inscription in Cora's handwriting. The photograph is a duplicate of the one Cora presented to Stephen, inscribed: "To me old pal Stevie/Imogene Carter." Courtesy Roger M. Frewen.

Seeking letters of introduction, Cora and Stephen hastened to call upon the United States Minister, Mr. Eben Alexander, a modest, kindly North Carolinian, a scholarly gentleman of the old school, of whom Crane has drawn a warm portrait in *Active Service* and who seems at once to have taken a strong fancy to the young American couple. When Stephen sent him copies of his books, Alexander thanked him, saying he should have valued the books in any case, but "they are all the more to me because of the friendly feeling that told you to give them to me." A family man with a wife, grown daughters, and a sixteen-year-old son—all but the married daughter with him in Athens—he exhibited a fatherly interest in the difficulties of these attractive young people, lovers who could not marry, who undoubtedly confided in him. Taking them both to his heart with the same warmth of affection given to his own, he wrote Stephen the following July, in reply to their invitation to visit him in England, that "it would be altogether lovely to drop in on you and Mrs. Stewart." He had missed them both so much as almost to wish "you hadn't come at all."

His regard for them took concrete form. While Stephen was away from Athens on a short expedition, Cora sought out women prominently identified with the war effort. Conspicuous among these was Mme. Ralli, wife of a cabinet minister who had recently resigned to become leader of the opposition. Mr. Alexander, trying to arrange an immediate meeting, enclosed in a note to Cora a card of introduction "which you will not need. Her house is just behind this hotel, No. 3 Muses' Street." Also enclosed was a note in Greek "which may possibly help you along somewhere."*

Crane's return to Athens on April 28 from northern Epirus where guerrilla fighting was going on around Janina coincided with the arrival from Florence, via the sea route from Brindisi, of Richard Harding Davis. Davis wrote his family on April 30, 1897, that Crane had been searching for him "all over Albania," and "told me he had been in Crete all this time that I have been in Florence."

But at this point in the odyssey of Stephen Crane in Greece the trails crisscross and knowledge breaks down.

A recently discovered Crane dispatch date-lined April 26, "On

---

* Mr. Alexander's note, addressed to "Mrs. Stewart," unfortunately omits the date and gives only the week day, "Wednesday."

Board French Steamer Guardiana," presents a birds-eye picture of
the Allied Fleet—the "Concert of Powers"—anchored in the Bay
of Suda to "keep order" after the bombardment and blockade of
the Cretan ports. The large, mountainous island of Crete lies 150
miles southeast of the Greek mainland. If Crane was ever there he
must have hopped a boat from the Piraeus, possibly the *Guardiana*
then in port, almost immediately on arrival in Athens. But it is also
quite possible that he may have faked the Cretan dispatch. In one
other instance, an account of a nonexistent Greenwich Village
fire, so successful was he in fooling the readers of the New York
Press and W. D. Howells, who called it "a notable piece of realistic
reporting," that the story was only recently discovered to have
been a journalistic hoax. For was he not, after all, the genius of
The Red Badge of Courage who had never been within sound of a
shell "hootling overhead" until he came to this little Balkan war
to find out—among other things—if *The Red Badge* was "all
right"?

The "Powers" had been in the Bay of Suda since early January
and the bombardment took place on March 25. No fighting of any
importance was going on at this time in Crete. Crane's dispatch,
published in the Louisville *Courier-Journal*—a paper he had not
signed up with—was by this time old news. Moreover, it appears
from the wording of the dispatch that, if he was on it at all, he remained aboard ship for the *Guardiana*'s return trip to Athens—
without even going ashore!

But Stephen may well have had another motive for wanting to
go to Crete unconnected with newsgathering—viz., to throw the
correspondents in Athens off the scent regarding his relations with
Cora. The Dover incident must have hit him like a blockbuster!
Always thin-skinned and now recoiling before the inevitable gossip, it must not become known to his colleagues that he, Stephen
Crane, had traveled across Europe with a woman Davis had publicly cut dead in the presence of Sanford Bennett, Frederic, and
himself. And if he could make it appear that he had boarded the
ship bound for Crete at Marseilles, instead of the Piraeus, that
would take care of everything. He had obviously not been near
Marseilles. But he had probably spent five or six hours sitting out
in the harbor of the Cretan capital; he may also have ridden a
horse over the border from Epirus into Albania. His statement to

Davis, in any case, was certainly stretching the truth and he might as well have saved himself the trouble. The ruse fell flat. For within twenty-four hours Davis had learned through grapevine channels all the scandalous details of Stephen Crane's affair with the clever and energetic Mrs. Stewart, who had charmed her way into Athenian social and diplomatic circles and was said to be seeking an audience with the Queen.

Davis gossiped to his family: "I left Athens on the 29th of April. . . . Crane and Bass and I went off together, Crane accompanied by a Lady Stuart. . . . She is a commonplace dull woman old enough to have been his mother and with dyed yellow hair." The fact that Cora was working on assignment under Bass as were the other *Journal* correspondents left Davis unimpressed. Once more he figuratively turned his back and, incurably disgusted, repeated the slander: "He [Crane] seems a genius with no responsibilities of any sort to anyone, and I and Bass got shut of them at Velestinos after having had to travel with them for four days. They went to Volo. . . ." The last statement, as to Volo, does not correspond with the account in Cora's diary of the journey to the battlefield of Velestinos; nor does this:

Crane came up for fifteen minutes and wrote a 1,300 word story on that [the battle of Velestinos]. He was never near the front but don't say I said so. He would have come but he had a toothache which kept him in bed. It was hard luck but on the other hand if he had not had that woman with him he would have been with us and not at Volo and could have seen the show toothache or no toothache.

As late as the 1920's, there were those who reacted *en pleine colère* to a woman's invasion of the war correspondents' field.* But "Imogene Carter" remained unruffled by gossip or professional jealousy. Armed with Mr. Alexander's letters, which included an introduction to the Crown Prince, whose headquarters

---

* Cecil I. Dorian, drama critic of the New York *Tribune*, was in England at the outbreak of World War I and covered the war on the continent for the Newark *Evening News*. Then the only newspaper woman at the front and the only woman allowed to visit the trenches, her dispatches, signed "C.I.D.," attracted much attention, subjecting her to a murderous fire of gossip and professional antagonism. Clare Sheridan, the sculptress, daughter of Clara and Moreton Frewen, underwent a like experience of character assassination while serving as a correspondent in Turkey and Mexico, 1921-1922.

were then at Pharsala, at nine o'clock in the evening of April 29 she set out with Crane, John Bass, Davis—and probably also the other *Journal* correspondents, Julian Ralph, Franklin Bouillon, Edward Abbott, and Langdon Perry—by steamer for Stylis. Mrs. Ruedy remained in Athens, but Cora, enough of a Victorian still to defer to propriety in these highly unconventional circumstances, took along a young Greek peasant girl as her maid.

Her rough diary continues:

> Left 9 P.M.—stopped noon, next day Chalkis. Got left—dispatch boat, with new minister war on board. Took us on board, caught up our steamer and were transferred. Arrived Stylis 6 P.M.—went ashore sail boat. Got carriage—drove to Lamia which was reached midnight. Bunked on floor, weird hotel. Cafe—soldiers. . . .

Next day, May 2, at seven o'clock in the morning they left by carriage for Domokos, arriving at five in the afternoon. All along the route they met shepherds and goatherds driving their flocks before them, and whole village populations fleeing down from the frontier away from the advancing Turks. The household goods of these people were transported on camels and in carts, some modern Greek carts, some ancient Turkish vehicles with huge wooden discs for wheels. The children were piled on top. Volunteers went by continually, guns on shoulder and cartridge belts slung around their waists, but they had no uniforms.

Domokos, situated on top of a mountain, was "a grim old tumbledown place of narrow cobbled streets, very Turkish in appearance, with human beings and guns saved from Larissa mounted on top of the houses, and crowds of curious people everywhere." At seven o'clock the same evening the party left Domokos and drove to Pharsala, meeting more fleeing villagers, more flocks in great numbers, some camped along the roadside. They passed a dead soldier. Then on the outskirts of Pharsala, where they were halted by outpost sentries from the Crown Prince's forces, they separated. Davis and Bass took the route to Velestinos nearby; Stephen and the other correspondents went on to Volo; and Cora, who seems to have thought Bass intended to wait with her in Pharsala for an interview the next day with the Crown Prince, drove on into town with the now worn-out and very cross little Greek maid to look for a place to sleep. She speaks of "Bass desertion," and notes that "Davis gave deserted house article."*

Not a soul remained in Velestinos. Davis and Bass, having made themselves comfortable in the empty house of the mayor, were regaling themselves on provender left behind when a distant boom of guns announced the beginning of the battle.

Cora continues with the adventures of "Imogene Carter": "At one o'clock in the morning the diligence stopped in front of a dismal coffee house called 'The New World.'" Her dragoman suggested going at once to Headquarters for permission to sleep in some abandoned house, but deciding it was too late, she persuaded the coffeehouse proprietor to let them sleep there.

"I found myself in a barnlike room whose walls bore faint traces of vanishing whitewash," with a bare and very dirty floor, and in one corner a tiny counter at which coffee, native cognac and mastika were dispensed to patrons. It was dimly lighted by two oil lamps. To one side was an ancient pool table; a few old benches stood against the walls; and distributed over the remaining area were many little tables and chairs. "The proprietor shooed out a few straggling soldiers, and I went to bed on the pool table." She had first thought of rolling up in her rugs and sleeping on the floor, but the filth made it impossible; the condition of the benches was little better. "My maid who had grumbled constantly at everything and cried over our dinner of black bread"—which Cora herself found "very sweet and good"—"now flatly rebelled, so I paid her and sent her to the diligence by which she returned to Lamia. And so I was alone, the only woman in Pharsala or within many miles of it." . . . A frightening thought, even to one unused to fear!

But the old coffeehouse proprietor, with true gallantry, arranged her rugs for her on the pool table, then got his rifle and "patrolled"

---

* In her rough notes of the trip to the front, hastily scrawled on cheap, lined tablet paper, Cora dates the departure from Athens "9 P.M. April 30"— contra Davis' April 29. Her usual carelessness in regard to dates makes me inclined to rely on Davis in this instance. But if Davis is correct, the various stages of the journey recorded in Cora's notes leave an extra day unaccounted for. The party must then have been in Domokos and Pharsala on May 1, instead of May 2, Davis and Bass proceeding to Velestinos on the night of May 1. But the battle of Velestinos did not begin until May 4. See Davis' "deserted house article" in *A Year From a Reporter's Notebook* (New York: Harpers, 1898).

around it while she slept. Every few minutes came a knock at the door, some late soldier wanting a drink; the old man had "locked" the door by piling a table and chairs against it. Several times these were pushed away and soldiers broke in, to be told that an American woman was sleeping on the pool table and they would have to get out. Having finally made fast the door in some way, as the knocks continued the old man would mutter something in Greek and shake his fist at the door, "then look toward me, and if he caught me peeking out from a corner of my blanket"—and peek she did, to be sure—"he would lay his head on his hand, then pat the rifle. . . ." Toward daylight she fell asleep, to be awakened after what seemed but an instant by loud knocking and a voice demanding admittance. The old man roused up, to resume his muttering and fist-shaking as the voice repeated, "The Gendarmes command you to open!" and with a glance directed at the lady on the pool table, and a shrug of the shoulders, he presently opened the door. The place was instantly filled with officers loudly calling for coffee. Cora lay quiet a quarter of an hour; then she sat up, put on her hat, and climbed down on a chair—inconvenienced by the voluminous, long tweed skirt she had not removed.

"It was embarrassing, but I tried to look as if it was my usual manner of sleeping and waking!" She was moved to admiration by the polite manners of these Greek officers. "They also tried to appear unconscious—and when one did look at me, it was in a respectful manner."

At Headquarters no one was up. "The Crown Prince sleeps late, so I had to wait until 9 or 10 o'clock"—with no place to go in the meantime. Then an empty house, one of the best in the village, was put at her disposal:

> High on the hills, and the view from the balcony superb. The entire plain of Pharsala—where Caesar defeated Pompey in 48 B.C. —lay before me covered with waving grain. On each side of the road crossing it toward Velestinos troops were encamped. They were far out and looked like the tin soldiers children play with. I could see them moving about in long lines and in squads of about fifty—and some on tiny horses. Occasionally a cavalryman, with orders perhaps, would gallop up the road towards Pharsala growing larger and larger as he approached. Infantry soldiers were also constantly coming and going along this road, increasing or dimin-

ishing in size. . . . On the mountain opposite, a flash attracted my
attention, messages being sent by the mirror system of field tele-
phoning. Just below me to the left was the jail, queerly con-
structed, the roof covered with storks' nests. The storks were
flying about making queer noises and flapping their wings: the
only inhabitants of Pharsala not afraid of the coming Turk and
who did not desert the home nest. . . .

But perhaps she lingered too long admiring the view and com-
muning with the ghosts of history. On her return to Headquarters,
at any rate, there was no interview. It was the day before the big
battle then forming around Velestinos and the jittery Crown
Prince, who had left his army at Larissa after ordering a retreat
in the moment of victory, and filling the railway carriages with his
baggage over the protests of officials and a disgusted populace, was
again packing up for another hasty departure.

3

CORA rejoined Stephen in Volo, "a small seaport on the Aegean
surrounded by mountains, a mosque in the foreground. Warships,
one French, one English, the rest belonging to the Greek fleet, lay
at anchor in the harbor." Cora describes "lumpy looking mountains with patches, brown, red, different greens, black rocks, and
shadows." Houses and shops were closed. On the morning of May
4 they breakfasted in a deserted railway carriage, and were joined
by a French officer they had met at a wayside station on the journey coming from Constantinople. "Mouse ill. . . ."

"Mouse" was probably a nickname for Stephen, who must then
have been suffering from the dysentery which presently felled
him. Already he may have been too ill to be out of bed; this would
account for his going on to Volo on May 2 at midnight to look
for a hotel, leaving "Imogene Carter" to cover the royal interview
which never took place. And how typical of Crane's wryness, to
hide his illness and humiliation behind that most unheroic façade—
a faked toothache!

The battle of Velestinos, which decided the war, lasted two
days. Davis, jubilant at having beaten Crane, with his usual luck
witnessed the entire fight from the infantry trenches. He says

[May 4?], "Crane came up for fifteen minutes. . . ." Cora says, "3 P.M. word has just come the Greeks have killed 2,000 Turk Cavalrymen"—news which sent hope high again in beleaguered Volo. "Got horses—rode to Velestino—warned to turn back, but kept on. Went on mountain. Battery No. 2. Under actual fire, shells overhead." Whether this was the first or second day of the fighting is far from clear. At some point Cora, probably with Stephen, was going among the reserves waiting behind the trenches to gather information on "What troops eat—how cooked." With John Bass, they seem to have spent most of the afternoon of May 5 with Mountain Battery No. 2, witnessing from the heights at sundown the Greek retreat—the sullen retreat of an army which had again had victory within its grasp. A shell flew over her head barely missing her, but making headlines for Imogene Carter's dispatch from Volo. Among the last of the correspondents to leave, they had a run for it to catch the train for Volo. Then the Turks shelled the train.

Cora had picked up on the battlefield a fat, waddling puppy Stephen immediately christened "Velestino, the Journal dog," which later figures in a story by John Bass, "How Novelist Crane Behaves on the Battlefield."* The piece was written over sour objections from Davis, who told his family and Bass, ". . . there was nothing to be said about what Crane did except that he ought to be ashamed of himself. . . ."† The puppy starred again in "The

---

* Bass attributes the puppy's rescue to Stephen. But according to a note in Cora's hand on recto of a photograph of the dog, taken from the scrapbook found at Brede Place, it was she who picked up the puppy on the battlefield.

† There seems to me little room for disagreement with Scott C. Osborn's suggestion that Davis had Cora in mind for his characterization of the actress in his comedy, *The Galloper* (1906), based on the Greco-Turkish War: "an attractive, dashing-looking woman of the adventuress type" who is pursuing her divorced war correspondent husband in an attempt to collect alimony. As to Davis' alleged "attack" on Crane in his portrayal of Channing, the degraded correspondent in the short story "A Derelict," opinion remains divided. Beer issued a vigorous denial "on behalf of a dead and generous man" (Beer, p. 246). Mr. George Matthew Adams unreservedly states: "The late Robert Emmet MacAlarney is authority that Richard Harding Davis's story 'A Derelict' is about none other than Stephen Crane. He was Channing. My memory is that Bob Davis [Robert H. Davis] confirmed this fact. So the book is placed in my Stephen Crane Collection." (Quoted from Herbert Faulkner West, *A Stephen Crane Collection.)*

Dogs of War," a charming vignette of a correspondent and his dog, dashed off by Stephen in the swirling confusion of the journey back to Athens.

Volo was panic and bedlam, the dog lost, later recovered at Chalkis. Food and furnishings had all been moved out of the only hotel in Chalkis, but they managed to get tea. The town was emptying before the arrival of the Turks, expected that night. Every boat gone, they got permission from the Greek flagship to be taken aboard a man-of-war which brought them as far as Ossa.

Back in Athens, angry crowds surrounding the royal palace, which had been placed under heavy guard, called for the Crown Prince's resignation as commander-in-chief. At the hospitals, the Queen and the royal princesses were insulted. A bulletin was given out from the palace that King George was suffering from cardiac spasms, his physicians pronounced "a change of air" to the island of Milo or Scyra "absolutely necessary."

Stephen wrote from Athens, "this is not a king's war, not a parliament's war, but a people's war." And Mr. Ralli, leader of the opposition, said the Greeks wanted a republic: matters which went unperceived by the diplomats in the capitals who fiddled with the idea of mediation. The headlines read:

AUTONOMY FOR CRETE INSISTED UPON BY GERMANY; GREECE MUST OBEY POWERS; POWERS WILL INSIST GREECE CONFIDE HER INTERESTS UNRESERVEDLY TO THEIR HANDS.

The Prince and Princess of Wales called at Buckingham Palace to present a special appeal to Queen Victoria for intervention on the side of the Greeks. But the German Kaiser, William II, complained bitterly that had he been permitted by the Allied Powers to "modernize" the Turkish army, having already sold them guns and begun building with German capital the Berlin-Bagdad Railway (Orient Express), there would have been no war!*

There was still Domokos ahead, and the Greeks, waiting at Thermopylae where 2,500 years before they had held the pass

---

* The last link of the German-built Orient Express was not completed until a few years after the little Greco-Turkish War ended. In 1897, travelers going by the overland route through the Balkans to Constantinople had to do as Cora and Stephen did: finish the journey by tramp steamer across the Black Sea. The alternative was the long sea route via the Mediterranean and Aegean ports, through the Dardanelles.

against the hosts of Xerxes until defeated by treachery, were "eager for another chance at the Turks." But with treachery in the air, the former high enthusiasm was already giving place to sullen frustration and panic; the outcome was a foregone conclusion. In an article in the *Journal* May 24, 1897, Crane expressed the mood of the correspondents, whose sympathies were overwhelmingly on the side of the Greeks: "I'd like to write a dispatch telling of a full-blown Greek victory for a change."

As the American Legation was quartered in the old Hotel Grande Bretagne, where most of the correspondents put up, he and Cora were seeing a good deal now of Mr. Eben Alexander and his family, and of Sylvester Scovel. Stephen's friend, who seems to have liked Cora immediately, had earlier viewed with misgivings their connection (of which they made no secret to him), fearing it would be Crane's ruin. Now he was changing his mind, seeing Cora's influence as beneficial, only sorry for them in the anomalous situation. "She urges him along"—Scovel was writing to his wife —"but even if he wished to, he can't marry her, as her husband . . . will not divorce her."

Stephen was writing articles on the Eastern Question for the *Westminster Gazette*, strolling with Julian Ralph over the Acropolis ruins, and climbing Lykabetos, the sharp rocky finger upthrust behind the hotel with a view of the Gulf of Aegina—Salamis a blue dream in the distance—where the Greek allied fleet overcame the ships of Xerxes in 460 B.C. He was also reading Tolstoy and coming to conclusions about art and Henry James; and unaccustomedly flush, he was enjoying the pleasant sensation of lending money instead of being always a borrower. He sent $100 to Willis Hawkins for Amy Leslie, and presently another $125.

Cora's finances probably were in a less robust condition, the money from the sale of the Hotel de Dream business already spent. They would need an anchor to windward until they could establish themselves in England. She suddenly thought of Uncle William's bounty, which all at once shone with the lustre of a fortune heaven sent. Ensign William L. Howorth, USN, was at the time of his death unmarried and a resident of Monmouth County, New Jersey. Cora had written once about taking out administration papers, but since then, occupied with the Hotel de Dream, she had not found time to do anything more about it. The reply to her present inquiry reached her after her return to England. Dated

June 12, 1897, coming from Messrs. Tallmadge & Tallmadge, a Chicago firm of "Solicitors for U.S. Claims," it was not encouraging:

... we do not see how you can take out letters of Adm [Administration] on the estate of the late William Howorth USN in England—as this officer was a citizen of the United States and had no property in England. The courts of England would not take cognizance of such an application. . . . If you are to return to the United States you can take such action when you get home.*

Meanwhile, between visits to the home of Mme. Ralli, which was a sort of diplomatic listening post for the upper enclaves of Athenian society, Cora was writing an article on Greek lithographs, to form one in the series of syndicated newsletters issued from London—though never published:

> There are no illustrated papers in Greece, but the war has developed a great and breathless movement in lithographs. They hang in every shop window and upon the day of some new issue there is always more or less popular excitement over the particular feat in art of the moment. As can be seen from the appended illustrations, these pictures are strictly immense. Perhaps the greatest of all in breadth of treatment is the one called "The Bombardment of Prevesa." It has breadth of treatment in a large degree— the scene of the festivities really extends over a goodly portion of the Turkish province of Epirus. Judging from an ordinary estimate of distance and the stature of men, the soldiers in this picture are about a mile high. Prevesa is denominated No. 1 and is that extraordinary collection of pink and white candy houses on the left. Arta is thirty-five miles from Prevesa under ordinary circumstances, but it is plain that the Greek soldiers who are crossing the pontoon can sprint down there in about two minutes.

> * * *

> The anguish in red and blue and white which represents the fight at Velestino is not so notable for breadth of treatment, but at any rate it is a very bluggy creation. The figures in green uniforms represent the regular cavalry of the Greek army. The equestrian

---

* Carl Bohnenberger, Assistant Librarian of the Jacksonville Free Public Library, had access to the papers which are now the Columbia University Crane Collection, while they were still in Jacksonville (see Appendix Three), and made a hasty examination of them for cataloguing. On coming on this letter from the Chicago firm, he seems to have jumped to the conclusion that "Lieutenant William Howorth" was Cora's brother. Beer also thought Cora had a brother.

heroic just below where the Greek battery is shooting out of the sky is a noble portrait of Smolenski. If there is anything nobler in the picture it is probably the bugler, who is situated just above Smolenski's outstretched sword. It is plain to even a casual observer that the Turks are having rather a hard time of it. The Greek artists have a way of killing Turks in these pictures which is almost monstrous. The Turks don't get a show. . . .

Its humor saves the piece from malice; and because her real subject is the war, seen through the popular art of the shop windows, she cannot conclude without sketching Smolenski, "the hero of the people, the man who has reaped the popular glory of the war. . . ."

. . . The Crown Prince deemed it necessary to retreat from Pharsala and he also ordered Smolenski to retreat from Velestino. This I suppose had something to do with the strategy of war . . . but everyone hears now that the order to retreat nearly broke Smolenski's heart. People say he shed tears.

. . . And it is distinctly the opinion of the Grecian people that Smolenski has done almost all that has been well done, as far as leaders go, in this war. In appearance he is a man of medium height and rather stout, but his clothes fit him so well that he remains a military figure [with his small black mustache reminding her of the popular idea of a French duellist]. . . . His manner is quick, sharp, and at times imperious—although like all bold, stern and very brave men, he has a smile that . . . lights and softens his face.

At the end of the war Stephen, already ill before Velestinos, succumbed to dysentery, the malady known to every soldier in wartime. Heedless of Cora's pleadings, he at first refused to keep to his bed, then was prostrated.

And now too, in the depletion of illness and in his profound disillusionment over the war's outcome, the black riders of his own guilt feelings bore down upon him. All sorts of jealous doubts and misgivings came to perch upon his sickbed:

> Thou art my love,
> And thou art the ashes of other men's love,
> And I bury my face in these ashes,
> And I love them—
> Woe is me.
>
> *("Intrigue")*

Stephen Crane and John Bass in Greece. Columbia University Crane Collection.

Cora, nursing him, tried to divert him from his dejection, in which guilt and the many problems presented by his association with her were uppermost. How could he ever take her back to America, both to be flayed alive by the gossips and professional guardians of other people's morals, whose only career in life is baiting their fellow creatures? How present her to his family in whom he had not confided, fearing what their reaction would be—her "past" and the unsettled divorce hanging over them a perpetual threat? It must have seemed to Crane that this passion had involved him, like the minister in *The Scarlet Letter*, in a jungle of lies and deceptions from which there was no egress, and like Dimmesdale he suffered the remorse of those eternally damned by their own moral cowardice.

"Well, as Sancho Panza says—this youth considering his weak state hath left in him an amazing amount of speech!" And he looked then, Cora thought, "like some angel in a church window designed by Burne-Jones, some angel a little blasé from injudicious conduct of its life."

Hanging and wiving go by destiny, she reminded him. "But there are a few, always brief moments in life, when we find out what happiness means; and it would be a thousand pities to shorten them . . . by reflections which are quite sure to present themselves with all necessary rapidity." For, like Trilby, she believed we ourselves to be the makers of our own hell on earth, surely punishment enough.

> I don't think you or I have so many friends in this world that we can afford to lose one. . . . But we can be different. We can say here and now that we will love each other, so that our love will never die as long as we live, can't we?

The words were a plea, but to Stephen Crane it all seemed far less simple than that. And perhaps for the first time shaken by his negativism, she turned away to hide the grief ready to burst from the wound he had given her.

> I am not one of those fools who think that the souls created for each other must needs come together—that destiny draws them from the uttermost ends of the earth, and trifle as we may with our best hopes, fate is stronger than they are, and true to the pole-star of ultimate happiness. I know the world too well to believe in nonsense like that. I know that every day, every hour, men and women are constantly casting themselves away, men on the wrong women, women on the wrong men, and that all this is a tangle that will never, never be undone!

Yet something within her, she didn't know what name to call it by, "makes me hate to have things die out, fade out, the way they seem to do. I would like to get something that would last. . . ."

And then because he wished it, and because some wisdom of her heart told her that the struggle between them for the fulfillment of their love begun in Florida, the promise of a life together, would never be resolved without adjustments painful and difficult on both sides, she consented to his stipulation that they should go apart for a period of one month, a testing period in which both might come to some dispassionate conclusions as to what course the future held.

> A month will pass by without our touching hands. . . . Ah, but how little, in some respects, do you understand the heart of a woman such as I am! The trouble is, you have met so many and formed your opinion from their standard, and measure me accordingly. . . .

4

EVERY human being has known moments of wavering, but there were prolonged stretches in the life of Stephen Crane when he seemed not to know his own mind. But no creature so ridden by conflicting drives, toward respectability and away from it, toward the love of one woman and away from the ties and responsibilities love engenders, eschewing domesticity and in love with the roving career of war correspondent, to the sacrifice ultimately of both health and talent, can ever be seen all of a piece. Hence the dilemma of so many discouraged and frustrated biographers, for the penetration of Crane's dualism must certainly begin any satisfying exegesis.

What was he trying to prove to himself when he sent Cora away? That he did not love her? Or was it the old nihilism of a precocious adolescence that still had him by the throat?—the nihilism of the figure in *The Black Riders* who ate of his own heart, holding it in his hand, chewing, and saying:

> But I like it
> Because it is bitter
> And because it is my heart.

Stephen and Cora, in varying degree, were both stamped with the emotional and mental attributes somewhat loosely identified as *fin de siècle:* an ultraromanticism which collapsed into disillusionment and over-refinement of the senses. But the tonal character of Cora's response to life was never that of nihilism. Like

Ouida,* whose books she must have read, Cora embraced life as a yea-sayer, abandoning herself to its potentialities of good and evil, happiness and suffering; and not until the first shock of encountering the negative side of Crane's personality was she even partially disillusioned. Any account of these two lives, baffling as they appear to the biographer, must take note of this difference and start from there: a difference which was certainly basic and all-pervading in their relationship, at times no doubt productive of friction, at other times uniting them in the attraction of opposites.

In an age when the average woman's lot was "an ideal subjection, their managing arts"—as R. L. Stevenson put it—"the arts of a civilized slave among good-natured barbarians," Cora lived chiefly in and for her emotions. Sometimes, she could write with a gift for philosophical observation put into terse and witty prose which reminds one of the older memoir writers, or of Ouida's *Views and Opinions*, the product of her analytical mind—a faculty Stephen lacked. But her attempts at verse were generally awful! The torrential character of her emotionalism, the violent energy with which she worked at it in her writing, must indeed have irked and frightened Stephen with his inherent distrust of emotionalism in any form. At times, no doubt, he fled from it.

It is interesting to compare *Active Service*—Crane's novel of the Greek war, begun in England the following winter—with a

---

* The popularity and fame of Ouida (Marie Louise de la Ramée, 1839-1908) was even greater on the continent than in England and America, for she was among the earliest of the Tauchnitz authors and her books were translated into many languages. Temperamentally, Cora and the older woman had much in common: the same constitutional energy, the belief in life and the transforming power of love, and in all things the same headstrong inclination. Intellectually, they were poles apart. Ouida's atheism was alien to Cora's strong Roman Catholic leanings, while Cora lacked the training in political thinking Ouida had from her French libertarian father. (See Monica Stirling, *The Fine and the Wicked: The Life and Times of Ouida* [New York: Coward-McCann, 1958].) But with due allowance for these dissimilarities, it seems hardly possible that Cora could have remained unimpressed by Ouida's literary achievement, let alone her stupendous commercial success. It is surprising that, while Cora sprinkled her notebooks with quotations from George DuMaurier's *Trilby*, we find no line of Ouida anywhere recorded. In "Ouida's Masterpiece," one of his few sorties in literary criticism, Stephen Crane had written on Ouida's best-known novel, *Under Two Flags*, praising the book's emphasis on nobility of character.

short story of Cora's, probably written about the same time, called "The Red Chimneys." Both are mediocre examples of fiction. But for Cora let it be said that the clichés and mannerisms of this particular story, the wooden dialogue, the melodrama reminiscent of very stale Byron and rancid Poe are no worse than the same faults in Stephen's novel, common as they were to the general level of potboiler fiction of that time.

Both tales have a certain basis in actuality. Written off the surface of the mind, each comes straight out of its author's subconscious. In the story development the autobiographical elements in both thus appear in reverse, transformed by the writer's guilt feelings into the exact opposite of the situation as it worked out in real life. In Crane's story the war correspondent-hero Coleman is in love with the beautiful, virtuous, and perfectly conventional daughter of a college professor who takes a party of students to Greece to study archaeology. Marjory—Nellie Crouse, Lily Brandon Munroe?—her parents, and the students, all are trapped in Turkey when the war breaks out, and Coleman, whose suit is banned under pressure from a disapproving mother (Lily's father had disapproved of Crane), nobly sets forth to rescue them. Coleman is being pursued by the beautiful, unconventional, and not entirely virtuous Nora Black—an actress! In a hang-over from too much champagne Coleman succumbs momentarily to the wiles of Nora Black, and thinks, "To go to the devil, to go to the devil with this girl would not be a bad fate!" But he casts her off, marries the insipid Marjory, and virtue triumphs.

The theme of Cora's story is illicit love; the situation, a young and attractive woman tied to an elderly dying husband—who takes much too long about it and is, moreover, a supreme egotist. The lover refers to the husband as "that self-satisfied duffer who slumbers contentedly, not because he thinks you are too good, but because he thinks he is too unparallelled and astounding a person ever to lose the love of a woman." "Ah, the sin!" the heroine repines. "You would never be happy with a bad woman"; but she quickly amends this Freudian slip: "No, I didn't mean that . . . I meant that I, I could never be happy if I were a bad woman, I would be afraid—of you." On the next page she succumbs to temptation: one long kiss; and in this moment of bliss she promises to go away with him. The lover gloats in his chamber the next day, for nothing could prevent her going *now*, "nothing but death," she had said. At that moment, a messenger arrives with a note begging her beloved's forgiveness: the distracted girl has "chosen death."

The falseness of this tale is so completely at odds with Cora's own behavior in actuality, her vigorous pursuit of her heart's desire and the fearlessness with which she defied convention, that one cannot but marvel. Did the old ghosts still have to be laid? Was she, too, still ridden by the nineteenth-century fetish of sin and remorse? Here, it would seem, are two crows downed with one stone: Donald Stewart the spoiled young man with his ribbons and crosses, his self-conceit and his vices—if such they were— who crushed her early love; and Donald Stewart the aging invalid husband, embittered, who stood between the legalization of her happiness now with Stephen, abolished both at a single stroke. So does love triumph—in death only—for Ophelia deserted by Hamlet, Cleopatra betrayed by Antony. So too for Cora's distraught heroine, in death, self-inflicted, is virtue re-established on the throne of maidenhood unsoiled. One wonders how much her ambition to rejoin society, after she met and fell in love with Crane, was responsible for this piece of sentimental trash.

> Farewell; even the bitter asphodel outlives love's rose;
> The fruit and blossom of the dead for us. . . .

It must have been a dark and dreadful time, indeed, for Cora: another one of the agonizing separations. She sought comfort in the knowledge that she still looked younger than she was, and that she knew how to dress and to charm. "Chic, *savoir faire*, tact, manners, and dress not clothes, these fetch the men of today." But to look younger than one is, she thought "as pleasing to Antony as it would be to Cleopatra, for, look at it boldly as we will, face it as courageously as we may, age is tragic. It means 'get out of the way!' *Faites place aux jeunes*. It means the retired list, respectability and inanition." But she knew it was not only years that age women, rather, the events they are reckoned by. She had lived five years in one all her life, a spendthrift in every way. "*Dum vivimus*."

But she could not, even in despair, remain for long unresponsive to the spectacle of life around her—more especially in its humorous aspects. Traveling west to Venice from a point unnamed, a four-teen-hour train ride, she decided to break the journey and rest overnight in the Austrian town of Gratz. After a little dinner, refreshed, she inquired what the amusements were; the *kellner*—waiter—informed her that there was "a most amusing play" done by an English company. It had been months since she had seen a play in English; she went.

> It was *Carmen Up to Date* I believe, and really very funny dialogue. And given by an excellent company. So I highly enjoyed all the jokes. After a bit I noticed everyone in the house looking at me, and laughing when I laughed—finally an old Austrian officer who sat beside me leaned over and asked if it were "really so amusing?" After that each time I laughed he would say, "Do tell me what they said then." It was too ridiculous trying to translate English slang and jokes into my bad German, and at each effort of course I laughed more.

There were not, she supposed, half a dozen people in Gratz who spoke English. But it was a *great* place for retired Austrian officers.

And then Crane himself put an end to the separation, much before the stipulated month was up.

> Of all the sweet letters you have ever written me, and there have been many, none were so sweet . . . and that is why I am light-hearted tonight. My heart swells with gratitude and love, and peace and charity for the world, and is as clean and pure of all doubt, hate, envy . . . as the heart of the penitent when he leaves the confessional. I have read your letter no less than twenty times already. . . . Not that it is difficult to understand, for it is plain and sincere, therefore beautiful and it fills my soul with perfect delight.

No longer would she doubt that he cared for her, she felt calmly assured that in forming that letter the mind dictated as the fingers traced what the heart prompted.

> It contents me to think that for the present you love me, and for me the morning of hope is born. . . . If the good Genii of our childhood states should ask me to name a wish and promise it would come true, mine would be to spurn distance long enough to give you one good strong hug.

chapter 3

WITH the signing of the armistice on May 20, there was gloom and demoralization in the streets and cafés of the Greek capital where a month earlier had been flowers and cheers. Crete was not to be annexed and any thought of a Greek republic had gone out the window. In superficial harmony, the Powers dictated the terms of the peace treaty, acting together to give the moribund Ottoman Empire a new lease on life for another fifteen or twenty years at the expense of little Greece. (The wife of the Crown Prince Constantine was a sister of the German Kaiser.) One by one, and in bunches, the disillusioned correspondents were leaving the city.

Stephen, going by the sea route, was arrested in Marseilles.* With him were two Greek boys he had picked up, war refugees, the brothers Ptolemy, twins to whom the prospect of quitting their

* On rough yellow paper in Stephen's handwriting is this note:

> New York 290
> 201
> Took up collection 43 dollars
> Captain's own money pd to Paris
> In Paris, 100 police, commissioner of minister of interior
> Arrested in Marseilles   No tickets
> Salife   Shalife   [cancelled]
> Sharefe millionaire

The first part of this memorandum, a puzzle, seems to refer to Crane's Atlantic crossing from New York. The collection taken up aboardship may have been for the crew, or some undesignated charity. But the next line vanquished country under the protection of a "rich" American journalist who would find them employment somewhere within the golden orbit of his influence was an opportunity not to be passed up. But the French authorities seem to have insisted on visas for the expatriates, and were even more volubly unpleasant concerning the matter of railroad tickets. In Paris, where the party was to meet Cora, Stephen was ambushed by "100 police" and haled before an official from the Ministry of the Interior. The cause of these latest commotions was the puppy Velestino, by now a figure of importance in literature, who further distinguished himself when the hotel proprietor presented his master with a bill for damages—for 100 pounds! Leaving the dog shut up in the hotel bedroom, Stephen had gone sight-seeing with the Greeks, while Velestino amused himself chewing holes in the carpet and draperies. Cora and Mrs. Ruedy had not yet arrived from Venice. The rest of the story is not on record, but in view of the well-known proclivities of Parisian hotel proprietors when dealing with troublesome Americans, it may be supposed that a settlement was reached for a somewhat lesser amount.

Sometime in early June Stephen and Cora, with their retinue consisting of Mrs. Ruedy, the Greeks, and Velestino, arrived in England to set up housekeeping at Oxted, Surrey, in a plain brick villa Harold Frederic had found for them. The villages of Oxted and Limpsfield adjoin, and Ravensbrook Villa, just over the line in Oxted, was the corner house next door to the Oxted Laundry.† House and garden lay in a hollow at the foot of a long steep slope down which Robert Barr often came striding through mists or rain

---

strongly suggests that Crane, headed for Paris, borrowed money from the captain of a *westward* bound ship on which he was a passenger. The memorandum would seem to be proof that at some time he passed through Marseilles. But the evidence in Cora's diaries seems conclusive in putting him there on the *return trip from Athens to Paris*—and not at the outset, as some have thought. The theory that he went by sea from Marseilles to Greece is certainly invalidated by Cora's account of the crazy Black Sea voyage on which he was with her.

† Ravensbrook in recent years has been cut up and turned into flats, with several other small villas dotting the garden area. One of these villas, which is still named "Cranes," was occupied for a while by the poet W. H. Davies.

for a roisterous evening of poker and talk with Crane and Frederic. From his own house, Hillhead, at Woldingham, the lights of Ravensbrook were visible shining out of the valley; Frederic's Homefield, at Kenley, was within easy walking distance, too. Older than Crane, both were oathful men whose racy humor and gusto put "Stevie" at ease. They were "the three musketeers." Barr, a Scot born in Glasgow, whose boyhood was spent in Canada, had been a dozen years a newspaperman in Detroit, part of the time as editor of the Detroit *Free Press*. He had then gone to England to write novels, which had earned a spotty livelihood for the wife and young daughters who lived with him at Hillhead. Ten years earlier in London, with Jerome K. Jerome, he had founded *The Idler* magazine.

Furnishings at Ravensbrook were sketchy, but with one of the Greeks, Adoni Ptolemy, installed as butler, Cora and Stephen made ready to welcome Sylvester Scovel, who came in July, just missing the Queen's Diamond Jubilee. With Cora's divorce still in deadlock and no word from India, they determined to put on a bold front and announced themselves as "Mr. and Mrs. Stephen Crane." Stephen told Constance Garnett they had met in Athens. The story traveled conveniently, leaving to surmise when and in what place they had married. Mr. Eben Alexander wrote from Athens: "I fancy that you have settled down in England . . . a decent country to live in, though lacking the clear sky of Greece." Missing them both "sorely," and anxious to go home, Alexander hoped to leave by the first of August, reaching London the sixth or seventh. "If so I will surely shake hands with you. . . . My kindest remembrances to Mrs. Stewart. I am not likely to forget either of you." But the Minister after all did not visit England, probably returning home by another route. This was a disappointment; then came grief with the loss of Velestino.

He had been smuggled in somehow past the customs men; in Great Britain the quarantine law against bringing dogs in from abroad was strictly enforced. Then, in spite of his hardy mountain shepherd breed, the puppy, unused to the English climate, contracted a sickness neither their nursing nor vets could cure, and on August 1 in Cora's bedroom he died "with all the pillows under him which our poverty could supply." An hour later Stephen wrote Scovel, "tonight Cora and I want to speak to you because you are the only one [who] will understand. . . ." Indeed, the only one besides Alexander who already understood so much! For eleven days they had thought of nothing else but saving the puppy's life. "He made a fine manly fight, with only little grateful laps of his tongue on Cora's hands . . . we are burying him tomorrow in the rhododendron bed in the garden. He will wear your collar in his grave."

Kind neighbors left the transplanted Cranes no time to feel loneliness. A mile away in Limpsfield, at the Pendicle, was the Pease family: Edward Pease, the Quaker secretary of "that miscellany of enquiring and experimenting people which constituted the Fabian Society"—as H. G. Wells describes it in *An Experiment in Autobiography*. Pease's wife Margery was a tall, ruddy-complexioned Scotswoman with a pronounced burr in her speech, a fountain of energy and kindliness, who later went into politics and until her death at eighty-seven was the Labour Party's standard-bearer in an unconquerable Conservative stronghold. Others who swiftly befriended the Cranes were Miss Margaret Gill and her father at Arden Cottage, the elderly Mr. Gill a widower in poor health whose last days were brightened by many readings of Crane's novel *The Third Violet;* the lively and eccentric Garnett household at the Cearne; and Ford Madox Hueffer,* of whom Stephen later wrote Sanford Bennett after a typical exhibition of Hueffer rudeness to Bennett's wife:

You must not be offended by Mr. Hueffer's manner. He patronizes Mr. James. He patronizes Mr. Conrad. Of course he patronizes me and he will patronize Almighty God when they meet, but God will get used to it, for Hueffer is all right.

At this time Hueffer occasionally lent his presence to the open-house Thursdays at Ravensbrook. Edward Garnett took Stephen to call on Hueffer, who was then in an energetic gardening phase of his oddly quirked personality; and Crane, in a burst of enthusiasm for the history-drenched English landscape, planted a rose

* The Hueffer family of Münster, Westphalia, were prominent as bankers, printers, and newspaper proprietors; Hueffer himself was a grandson of the English painter Ford Madox Brown, and a nephew of D. G. Rossetti. In 1919 Hueffer dropped his Teutonic surname, probably because of anti-German feeling after World War I, and began calling himself "Captain Ford."

tree in Hueffer's garden at Gracie's Cottage. David Garnett asserts
in his memoirs that Crane settled at Oxted in order to be near his
distinguished father; but although Stephen's respect for Garnett
as the foremost English critic was awe-filled, and the two households were on comfortable visiting terms, other evidence to support the statement is lacking. The man most responsible for Crane's
coming to live at Oxted was certainly Harold Frederic.

Although they were delighted with these new friendships, Cora
and Stephen were more attracted by history than by Fabian experi-
mentalism in social reforms or the occasional excursions into free
love of some individuals of their order—which, writes David Garnett, were frowned upon by "the majority who feared to have the
Free Love label permanently fastened upon their body." Anxious
about their own legitimacy, the Cranes left radicalism and politics
to others and looked to genealogy to bolster their precarious domestic status. This may have been Cora's idea. For she now was writing to her Aunt Mary in New York for particulars of the Holder
family origins, and of individual claimants to distinction; and gave
encouragement to Stephen in tracing back the pre-Revolutionary
roots of the ancestral Stephen Crane of Essex County (New Jersey) to a remote Surrey baronetcy. Writing to an elderly genealogist, Charles Woodruff Woolley, Sr., a distant family connection who lived in Buffalo, Stephen displayed an interest in titles
and heraldry which quite upset the old gentleman's Yankee blood.
"We did not know," he acidly commented, "that our Stephen
Crane was a descendant of Sir George Carteret. . . . We have read
of the Townleys having been allied with Royalty, but paid no
attention to it as we were not particularly interested in 'Royal
blood,' 'Coats of Arms,' 'Crests' and 'Quarterings.' " But Stephen
Crane, who had got his artistic education on the Bowery, his old
"university"—as he told someone at Mrs. Garnett's who thought
he was referring to a school of fine arts—was now obsessed with
the desire for respectability and in process of exchanging his early
bohemianism for the new look of an English squire.

To Cora, whose rebellions had never encompassed bohemianism,
the social climate of England was the habitat and congenial ocean
in which she comfortably swam, though it was some while before
she got around to hunting up her Howorth kinfolk, the collateral
descendants of old George. Of these, an elderly cousin, Miss Kate

Howarth of Yew Tree Cottage, the Moor, Hawkhurst, seems to have been marked with the family endowments of artistic talent. Miss Kate later came to Brede Place and made a drawing of the oak-paneled living room with the great hearth, as it looked to a romantic eye probably at about the time the house and lands passed from the Oxenbridges to the Frewen family.

"Life in an English country house is perhaps the most delightful manner of living in the world," Cora was writing now—in one of the syndicated London newsletters—"and society should be forgiven if it grows silly over it. . . ."

So she thought; but Stephen was restive. The strains and stringencies of "settling down" brought a return of old wanderlust, albeit with diminishing force. The South African fight was off, but he wrote his brother Edmund in July, "Expect to hear from me in the Soudan." Later he confided to William Howe Crane that he was eager to go to "a frontier row in India"; then again the Sudan; and the Klondike for Bacheller, where he "hoped to be able to do a service for Ted"—Edmund Crane, who seems to have been briefly struck with the prevalent gold fever. Post Wheeler, one of Stephen's old editors on the New York *Press* and also a brother in the Lantern Club, had quit his job and gone to the Klondike; but if Crane ever thought of joining Wheeler out there he should have been swiftly disillusioned by the series of articles then running in the *Press* depicting the cannibalistic horrors inflicted on the carcasses of deluded gold hunters by Alaskan mosquitoes with teeth like dinosaurs. It was "no place for consumptives," in the opinion of the writer.

And the Cranes were householders now, with a position to maintain. Their immediate worry was finances. The weekly newsletter going out under the pseudonym of "Imogene Carter" to ten different papers in the United States brought them in some ready cash. Whose idea this was, originally, there is no knowing. But a woman's column featuring chitchat of the social world, fashion news, travel notes, sports, the doings of the aristocracy and of visiting royalty was, at the turn of the century, still a novelty to American readers, to whom the daily newspaper was as much a necessity as the morning cup of coffee. The series, which ran intermittently for ten weeks as a Sunday feature, appears to have been sold directly to a list of papers with which Stephen retained contacts from his days as roving reporter for the Bacheller syndicate. According to Cora's listing, the New York *Press*, San Francisco *Chronicle*, and Philadelphia *Press* were the only papers that bought all ten articles; the seven other papers each bought only the first five, being replaced in the series by another group of seven which bought the last five. A form letter addressed to the editor and signed by "Imogene Carter" accompanied each of the weekly offerings, with a list of papers to which the articles had been syndicated for that week:*

> Ravensbrook
> Oxted, Surrey
> England

Dear Sir:

I enclose No._____ of my series. I hope if they do not suit your columns you will let me know at once, or if you do not care to receive them I would be glad to receive your advice any time as to what kind of stuff your readers prefer.

> Yours very truly,
> Imogene Carter

Date-lined London, the articles appeared in print ten days or two weeks later; and for some reason not immediately clear they were unsigned, having no other identification than the general head, "From a Special Press Correspondent." Though it bought all the series, the New York *Press* did not use them all, and the pieces used do not correspond altogether with Cora's numbering; the make-up men evidently shuffled them around, rearranging them to suit the ideas of the Sunday editor, Curtis Brown, who had replaced Edward Marshall. The *Press* also had at this time one other

---

* The wording of three different form letters used by Cora is similar except that in one instance she reminds the newspaper editor, "The price of the letter remains four dollars." Her list of papers to which the articles were syndicated: San Francisco *Chronicle*, New York *Press*, Philadelphia *Press*, St. Paul *Pioneer Press*, Boston *Globe*, St. Louis *Globe-Democrat*, Pittsburgh *Dispatch*, New Orleans *Times-Picayune*, Omaha *Bee*, and Galveston *News*. The pieces were numbered seriatim by Cora, but some numbers and sheets are missing and manuscript pages—some seventy in all—are jumbled, thanks to her incurable habit of leaving off page numbers. But by comparing paragraph first sentences with files of the New York *Press*, I was able to identify all five of the letters published in that paper under dates August 15, 22, 29, September 26, and October 10. The remaining five which had been bought by the *Press* presumably never appeared in its columns.

woman special correspondent who occasionally sent back fashion notes from Paris, and a man who sent travel items from various resort spots on the Continent. That the team of "Imogene Carter" and Stephen Crane had to face competition from these two may account for the omission of some whole articles and other subsections, while still others bearing on the Greco-Turkish war and the Eastern Question probably were dropped when their topical news value disappeared.

A portion of letter Number Three (Cora's numbering) dealing with conversion of the Parisian millinery establishment, the Maison Virot, into a stock company owned by international shareholders was among the pieces that did not appear. Others not printed were on "gruesome traffic in murder" of Russian children; cycling as a fad; the dress reform movement; Queen Wilhelmina of Holland; dress of the women of Flanders; the visit of the Duke and Duchess of York to Ireland; etiquette at the Court of Denmark. Still others omitted were Cora's article on Greek lithographs, Number Four in her listing; her account of their visit to a Turkish harem; and Stephen's political articles on the Eastern Question then running in the *Westminster Gazette*.

A letter written by Stephen in November to his American agent Paul R. Reynolds has sown confusion and sprouted a theory that "Imogene Carter" did not write the Greek dispatches signed with her name, a misconception now clearly traceable to Stephen's allusion to the London articles:

You might go to Curtis Brown . . . and say how-how for me. Then tell him this *in the strictest confidence*, that a lady named Imogene Carter whose work he has been using from time to time is also named Stephen Crane and that I did 'em in about twenty minutes on each Sunday, just dictating to a friend.

The second part of this statement—an exaggeration and a whopper—undoubtedly refers not to the dispatches, which Curtis Brown never saw, but to the London Letters. And as for "the strictest confidence," the reason, of course, was Cora!

In respect to the newsletters, the problem of determining who wrote what is made more difficult by the fact that Cora sometimes worked from rough notes dictated by Stephen, who afterwards revised her copy or allowed it to stand with only minor corrections; he then added his signature in the form of a few typical Crane-isms, of idea or phraseology. Again, sometimes a skeleton draft was provided by him and filled in by her, or certain articles begun by one and finished by the other, or whole pieces separately completed by each.

Only a psychiatrist would be able to say why Cora's handwriting varied so much in this period of her life, often showing marked differences—attested to by the diaries—that superficially seem to point to several different writers on a page. Stephen Crane wrote a clear, even, and somewhat immature script tending toward a backhand, with a trick of circling his periods—an old newspaperman's habit, the circled dot scribbled on copy margins for the printer. But as though mocking the later claims of learned investigators, Cora picked up the backhand and the circled periods, probably in unconscious imitation of Stephen. Oddly enough, while both are common to the holograph manuscripts and correspondence of this period, they vanish when she left England permanently after Crane's death, seldom if ever to reappear in later samples of her penmanship.

But without getting involved in the intricacies of handwriting, it is possible in most instances approximately to determine authorship on the basis of content and phraseology. Letter Number Two date-lined August 12, New York *Press* issue of August 22, under the caption "European Gossip of Dress and Sport" provides a fairly typical example of how they worked. The lead article, "Goodwood, the Duke of Richmond's Great Race Track," probably was drafted by Cora with minor revisions by Stephen. A subsection describing feminine costumes worn at the races by members of the Royal Family and the upper aristocracy is certainly hers. "London Society Women's Bracers," dealing with the increase in consumption of alcohol, notably champagne, on the distaff side as a result of the increasing strain from the social pace, bears the unmistakable stamp of Crane's sardonic thrusts; likewise other sections on the Empress of Germany, Cowes, and Mr. Ogden Goelet's yacht. Numbers One and Three appear about evenly divided; Four and Five, totaling sixteen items, are with but two exceptions probably wholly by Cora.

Stephen at this time was writing "The Monster" and "The Bride Comes to Yellow Sky," two of his most famous stories, so Cora was left to finish the London articles after an interruption caused by a carriage accident, and a trip to Ireland with Harold and Kate Frederic. Driving over for a luncheon party on August 19, Frederic's birthday—the date is important—a horse badly harnessed ran away, overturning their carriage and nearly killing them. "They, dear people, took us in and cured us," Cora wrote Scovel in October, "and then carted us off to Ireland where we had a delightful three weeks in the wilds. . . ." A week at Homefield, "laid up" and nursed by the devoted Frederics, became a month in Stephen's recollections to brother Will; ill luck in pressing damages for their injuries rankled in Cora's memory, along with a prejudice against lawyers. She was "disgusted with the English justice shown Americans," she later told Moreton Frewen. "It seems the job masters here [livery stable keepers] can take mild Americans out in their traps which they can, without fear of punishment, turn upside down and dump the passengers out on the road, ruin their clothes and scar them for life. So I never want to see another lawyer if I can avoid it."

But the Irish holiday, shared with such gay gypsy companions as Kate and Harold Frederic, raised their spirits momentarily. Stephen was full of "the joys of the pig-market, the delirium of a little taproom filled with brogue . . ." and wit able to cut an Englishman's "skin into strips . . . the ancestral dagger of fast sharp speaking from fast sharp seeing."

The London Letters had brought them in $400 at the rate of four dollars an article from each of their subscribers—and the Cranes lived on this money as long as it lasted. "Rotten bad"—Stephen told Reynolds—as the pieces were, he proposed to his agent another series "signed and much better in style," of which nothing more was heard. He had been "in dreadfully hard luck" since coming to England, he wrote Will Crane at the end of October, a month laid up from the carriage accident, and though in the three working months he had earned close to $2,000, the actual sum paid in was only about $120.

I am just thinking how easy it would be in my present financial extremity to cable you for a hundred dollars but then by the time this reaches you I will probably be all right again. I believe the sum usually borrowed was fifteen dollars, wasn't it? Fifteen dollars—fifteen dollars —fifteen dollars. . . .

He could remember "an interminable row of fifteen dollar requests," including one to Hamlin Garland to get back half the manuscript of *The Red Badge* then in hock to a typing agency. There was one other to a fellow journalist who "borrowed" a check from his boss to help Crane retrieve his manuscript, and got fired when found out.

Painting the picture larger than life, he told his brother he was working now on a big novel that would be much longer than *The Red Badge (Active Service*, though he had not yet begun it). All of his friends here considered "The Bride Comes to Yellow Sky" his very best thing.

I am so delighted when I am told by competent people that I have made an advance. . . . There seem so many of them in America who want to kill, bury and forget me purely out of unkindness and envy. . . . All the hard things they say of me affect me principally because I think of mine own people—you and Teddie and the families. . . . Now Dick Davis for instance has come to like the abuse. He accepts it as a tribute to his excellence. But he is a fool. Now I want you to promise me to never pay any attention to it, even in your thought. It is too immaterial and foolish. Your little brother is neither braggart or a silent egotist but he knows that he is going on steadily to make his simple little place and he cant be stopped, he cant even be retarded. He is coming.

For a man who had so often raised the flag of rebellion and shouted his personal nonconformity into the ears of Mrs. Grundy, he was displaying all at once a singular tenderness toward social opinion. "Sometimes," he wrote, " I think you and old Ted worry about me and you may well worry!" He had managed his success like a fool and a child, but it was difficult to succeed gracefully at twenty-three. ". . . you ought to see the effect of such things upon my family," he had told Willis Hawkins at the time of the dinner given him, two years earlier, by the Society of the Philistines in Buffalo. "Aint they swelled up, though! Gee! . . . It's great. I'm no longer a black sheep but a star."

To Will now: "However I am learning every day. I am slowly becoming a man." For now he had a home and a woman in it, a woman who worshipped and believed in him. That made easier the belief in himself which, in the past, had come and gone—mostly the latter—like a bird on the wing. He could not mention Cora yet to his family, so he gave his address in care of his London publishers, William Heinemann. "My idea is to come finally to live at Port Jervis or Hartwood. I am a wanderer and I must see enough—but afterwards—I think of P. J. & Hartwood. . . ."

Sanford Bennett lived in England, and friendship, hospitality, decorum would presently require an invitation to Bennett to bring his young French bride to visit Ravensbrook House. But Bennett had been with them—Cora and himself—on that fateful Channel crossing, and although they had maintained the strictest propriety until they left him in Paris, he had witnessed the Dover encounter that soured Dick Davis. So appearances must be mended. Dating his communication from Paris, September 2, Stephen wrote: *

Frederic and Mr. Heinemann have been urging me to stay in England for a time. So my wife—after practicing nine days I can write that without a jump—and I will be hunting a house or an attic in London pretty soon.

This letter, first published by Thomas Beer, is mainly responsible for the widespread belief that Stephen Crane and Cora Taylor were formally married—either in Paris or in Athens with Mr. Eben Alexander performing the civil ceremony. But Alexander, as we know, sent regards to "Mrs. Stewart"—in the letter of July 7. Had Crane entrusted this short and puzzling note announcing the marriage which never took place to Scovel, or some other friend, to be mailed from Paris—and no questions asked? The possibility seems weighted by Cora's letter to Scovel of October 17, and other circumstantial evidence that places Stephen and Cora in Ireland with the Frederics on September 2. The alternative possibility that they were again in Paris at some time after the mid-June arrival in England seems definitely ruled out by the counter-evidence, however incomplete.

* Thomas Beer, who first published this letter to Bennett (p. 158), had his own reasons for bypassing the then unpublishable story of Cora Taylor and her relationship with Stephen Crane. In justice to Beer, it should be remembered that he did not have access to much other data now available in the papers Cora brought over from England and kept together until her death—now the Columbia University Crane Collection.

2

"So HELEN has a sweetheart?" Stephen remarked in the letter to his brother William. Odd to think of his favorite niece, Will's oldest, no longer the little girl in pigtails he told stories to in Port Jervis, but "sweet sixteen." Stephen sent his love to his sister-in-law Cornelia, and praised her cookery.

Cora, too, was a talented cook. Her Southern hot biscuits—"little flat rolls" to their English guests—served with jam at teatime when visitors dropped in, were already famous, and her doughnuts later adored by a no less finicky gourmet than Henry James. She was also an accomplished hostess, never thrown into panic by "a social crisis." At a luncheon party where he met the Cranes on their return from Greece, Mr. Edmund Gosse had found her "very vivid and agreeable. . . ." He described her as "a small, plump woman. . . . She was most entertaining." An American, he wrote "had become very long-winded on the subject of a reported quarrel between an Exalted Personage and his mistress. The possible consequences of this rupture were discussed more than exhaustively, and we were all close on madness when Mrs. Crane said, 'Well, if the Prince *has* left her, I suppose we must all just grin and bear it.' This ended the matter." When Sanford Bennett brought his French wife to Ravensbrook, Cora's absence from the room momentarily left Stephen swamped with seven or eight callers, and Ford Hueffer holding forth on the subject of modern French painting. Addressing her in a lingual atrocity which presumed to be French, Hueffer unfortunately undertook to instruct Mrs. Bennett on the subject of Seurat. The lady who had long been a friend of the Seurat family attempted to correct some of Mr. Hueffer's ideas of the man and his work. Tensions developed; Stephen was nervous, everybody uncomfortable till Cora, returning, said in what Bennett called a "dangerous" voice: "Mr. Hueffer, Mrs. Bennett speaks English very well. Let's change the language—*and the subject.*"

Others, including Bennett, who liked her, were rasped by Mrs. Crane's lack of regard for crinoline and lace. Neighbors who called on the Cranes to express appreciation for a cold remedy Cora had sent a young relative of theirs (named Vere after one of Ouida's heroines) were scandalized when in reply to polite interrogations concerning Mr. Crane's illness in Athens Mrs. Crane bluntly came out with it: "Dysentery." She discussed diseases at meals, someone else reported; and some of her remarks at other times revealed, distressingly, that "she knew too much about life." An Englishman recalled her once having related a gruesome murder story at Lamb House. Robert Barr, who had a warm liking for Mrs. Crane and considered her "a capital wife for Stevie," said Henry James could not abide her. An American school friend of Stephen's noted that he also "had to hear a great deal from some English friends about Mr. Henry James and his intense sufferings when he had to 'endure' Mrs. Crane. Maybe! I do know that he came bowling over from Rye one day with a carriage load of people, all stuffed shirts, and announced that he had brought them to lunch. Mrs. Crane was mad as a hornet, but did not show it. She vanished into the kitchen and concocted a lot of extra lunch in a chafing dish."

"Cora was a dear. Her heart was as big as all outdoors," an American woman testified. And Vere—the objections of her family melting before Cora's warmth—was allowed to become a frequent visitor at Ravensbrook, where she found both Cranes "so nice and gay"—until she was suddenly warned that she "must not go to see Mrs. Crane again. . . . One of my uncles had picked up the gossip about her from Clement Shorter [editor of the London *Illustrated News*]." But Vere adored Mr. Crane, who had found out the secret sorrows of her young life, and formed an attachment to Cora which survived later assassinations of gossip and the years. When Vere dropped in one day while Cora was dressing for a luncheon, Cora invited the girl into her bedroom—a thing no Englishwoman would have done. Delighted with the naturalness and easy informality of the Ravensbrook household, Vere later expressed surprise at the daggered criticism of Mrs. Crane's unconventional style of dress. "She was plucky and gay and kind-hearted. . . . She seemed the apogee of smartness to me, especially her American shoes."

Smartly dressed for formal occasions Cora Crane undoubtedly was, though there were periods when her wardrobe was reduced to one garment for street and one for evening wear. She knew the difference between "dress" and "clothes." At Goodwood she had observed the Princess of Wales "elegant in a mauve and white frock trimmed with lace, and a mauve toque with red flowers"; but

Lady Randolph Churchill "in the same frock she wore at the royal garden party—gray with a green waistband—did not look her best." Cora was satisfied that Englishwomen had come round to face the fact that the same costumes worn during the London season "will not do for the Continent," if they were not to be outshone by the Parisiennes and Viennese. Delighted with the flowing lines and sapphire splendors of Mrs. Patrick Campbell's costume as "Ophelia," she singled out for particular mention the use of pearls which "soften all that glitter"—an effect of too many jewels. Always in these fashion notes she wrote with sure knowledge of materials and a professional eye for details:

> Society women are about to adopt much lighter colors for their winter street dresses, or at least the leading modistes are planning the adoption. The new styles are of white, pale gray, or fawn colored satin-finished cloth skirts, with trimmings of braid or appliques of velvet or fur, and fasten on the side.
>
> A fawn colored skirt, with a coat of golden brown velvet, trimmed at the neck and wrists with sable . . . was shown me. A skirt of white cloth, appliqued with black velvet, a blouse coat of ermine fur, a toque of white velvet, with ermine tails fastened by a small diamond buckle, and a tiny muff, also of white velvet and ermine tails, were being made for a beautiful blonde. The muff had a small pocket for the stems of a huge bunch of violets.
>
> In Paris, at Felix establishment, I saw a very handsome short seal coat. It was made with a vest festooned with sable tails and lace. This was destined for the Princess Soltykoff, who, by the way, is an American and a widow.
>
> For a slim figure, the coats that fasten on the side are much better than those fastened primly in front. Now that we have the small sleeve this is also true of the dress bodice. For those who cannot afford a variety of costumes dark green and the new shade of purple are suggested.

At home, Cora discarded her American shoes for the Greek sandals she had had copied by the Oxted shoemaker, anticipating Isadora Duncan. Her regular costume was a species of blouse and skirt—"a weird kind of wrapper," as Sanford Bennett described it— which she made herself and which was probably an adaptation to long-skirt requirements of the classical Greek chiton, with long sleeves added to lend a touch of the medieval. The effect was strange, to say the least, and economy no doubt the chief virtue, the blouses and skirts costing "next to nothing" to make. In the

New York of 1912 such a habit might speedily have found its way out of Greenwich Village into the Fifth Avenue shops.

But even more than this unconventional getup, what gave sharpest offense to Victorian notions of propriety was Cora's habit of sometimes appearing before company with her hair down her back. "If you are prepared to shudder," Bennett commented, "because a woman lets down her hair in front of seven or eight friends during a poker game, I suppose she was *farouche*." "Her complexion was very fresh," writes one of Stephen's nieces who saw her later on a visit to Port Jervis, "her hair golden, very soft and fine and very abundant." With her remarkable blue eyes and rosy skin coloring, the mass of golden hair worn usually in a simple coil was probably her most striking feature. Bennett vouches for its state of nature, adding that certain colors made it seem artificial; but unbound and in conjunction with the "weird wrapper," the first impression was to his conservative mind somehow "awful, . . . like a dance hall girl in the morning." But Cora believed it good for the hair to hang loose several hours a day, exposed to air and sun. Citing the example of Sarah Bernhardt who "at 55 looks younger than 35," she wrote in a newsletter, "Women are beginning to recognize . . . that they made a mistake in curling and waving their hair."

In a letter to a friend the widow of R. L. Stevenson gossiped, "She is nine or ten years older than Mr. Crane and 'all the tongues are wagging.'" Never noted for her tact, Fanny Stevenson herself was eleven years her husband's senior; and Crane's abomination of the Stevenson cult had traveled. "I believe in ghosts," he had scoffed. "Mr. Stevenson has not passed away far enough. He is all around town."

Clearly, both Cranes were outspoken on the wrong subjects usually at the wrong times. Stephen, who had felt that you could have an idea in England without going to jail for it, now complained to the critic James Huneker:

They will believe anything wild or impossible you tell them [Bothered with questions, he had told somebody his father was a Presbyterian cardinal!] and then if you say your brother has a bathtub in his house they—ever so politely—call you a perjured falsifier of facts. . . . It has not been the habit of people I meet at Mr. Howells or Mr. Phillips or Mrs. Sonntag's to let fall my hand and begin to quickly ask me how much money I make and from what French realist I shall steal my next

Velestino. Inscription in Cora's hand. Courtesy Roger M. Frewen.

Below, Adoni Ptolemy with Nicolas and Michael Pease in front of the Pendicle, the Pease home at Limpsfield. Gift of Mrs. Nicolas Pease.

"Velestino".
Picked up by Mrs Stephen Crane in the midst of the battle of Velestino Greece.

book. For it has been proven to me fully and carefully by authority that all my books are stolen from the French. . . . Now I am going to wave the starry flag of freedom a little even if you contemn the practice in one who knows not Balzac and Dostoywhat'shisname. . . .

Irritated by the matrimonial dilemma that made him for the time being an exile, Crane's Anglophobia exploded intermittently in the London Letters: ". . . taken with all the silly and fabulous ideas which the British public has in regard to American million-aires, this new boat [Mr. Ogden Goelet's yacht] causes a dull won-der which a British peer could not manufacture by the expenditure of twice the cost. . . . They look upon the owner as they look upon some popular chimpanzee in the Zoological Gardens." But it was perhaps symptomatic of the state of Anglo-American relations at the turn of the century that these ill-natured jibes should have found their way into print. Even Cora, rubbed the wrong way by an article praising London beauties "which reads like a florist's catalogue," came back at the author with a blast of her aroused Americanism. This wight had simply gone through the social register conferring on females therein all the "poetical" stock terms—swanlike throats, ruby lips, beautiful complexions—all of which to Cora seemed "ridiculous, if it were not like to be taken seriously by the Englishman who has never been nearer to London society than the sidewalk in front of some well-known house" and who will "immediately . . . and solemnly swear that the Parisiennes and the Americans are nowhere. This kind of a fact goes into an English head like a pin into a cushion, but unlike the pin, it never comes out."

In the *New Review* that fall there was running *The Nigger of the Narcissus*—a work by a new and little known author. Joseph Conrad was a discovery of Edward Garnett's. "It is a crackerjack," Stephen wrote Garland in America, who confessed he had never heard of Conrad, although English critics were already noting a supposed influence upon *The Nigger* of *The Red Badge of Cour-age*. So when Crane's editor, Sidney Pawling, asked him again whom he would like to meet, he promptly named the other Heine-mann author. A luncheon was arranged by Pawling, and when he left them at four o'clock, Crane and Conrad, still talking, started on a tramp through the London streets which wound up with din-ner at ten in a Piccadilly restaurant.

Conrad, a Pole of aristocratic birth whose family had suffered under the Russian czars, had gone to sea at the age of seventeen, later married an English wife and embraced English citizenship. He was much older than Crane, though a beginner in the art in which the younger man was already near the peak of his fame. Theirs was a singularly undemonstrative friendship of two artists, founded on their common vision of the creature man as a lonely pigmy in a universe indifferent, when not actively hostile, to his humanity. They were joined in the silent bond of temperamental stresses and complexities which they never discussed. To this friendship Crane brought none of the artistic reservations which, in spite of the warm personal affection on both sides, occasionally ground on his relations with Barr and Frederic; and it was free of the "impassable" barriers of youth and age of which Howells was always conscious. Here was a man whose genius Stephen could admire wholeheartedly; a spiritual elder brother who did not look down from a pinnacle of seniority, pardoning his callow youth, but who rather looked *up* to Stephen as man and artist, with full comprehension of his mature powers. Whereas to Garland "he was always a boy," albeit a marvelous boy, Conrad envied Stephen— and told him so. "I am envious of you—horribly." And later: "You are the greatest of the boys—and you are as good as I want you so you needn't trouble to apologize."

So, when directly after their meeting which climaxed in the London ramble, Conrad sent him the manuscript of *The Nigger*, Stephen wrote at once:

It caught me very hard. I felt ill over that red thread lining from the corner of the man's mouth to his chin. It was frightful with the weight of a real and present death. By such small means does the real writer suddenly flash out in the sky above those who are always doing rather well.

He said he had written Bacheller and "told him to be valiant in the matter of 'The Nigger,' " and had dispatched "some other little notes to America," which brought Conrad's grateful acknowledgment by the next post:

I must write to you before I write a single word for a living today. . . . If I've hit *you* with the death of Jimmy I don't care if I don't hit another man. . . . The world looks different to me now since our long powwow . . . therefore I write to you as though we had been born together before the beginning of things.

Looking back across the years and the void opened by death, Conrad with his deep perception of the shadow-lines noted that his young friend "had not the face of a lucky man." He had kept, he said, "an abiding affection for that energetic, slight, fragile, intensely living and transient figure" with the quiet smile that "charmed and frightened one," not like a ray but like a shadow.

But now Stephen must go to Ivy Walls, in Essex, for dinner and the night; Mrs. Conrad, expecting a child soon, could not leave home. Stephen and Conrad talked and smoked the night through. Two months later, when the baby Borys was born, a great box of flowers arrived from Cora. Then on February 19 (1898), when Borys was five weeks old, the Conrads came to spend a week at Ravensbrook. Since they came without a nurse, a large armchair for the baby to lie in was drawn up beside Mrs. Conrad's place in the dining room. The Greek servant Adoni grew so attached to the child he could hardly bear to have him out of sight, and if the door were left unlocked would creep into the bedroom, ecstatically beaming, to watch him bathed by his mother. The latter found this somehow frightening; and Stephen was made nervous and shy by Jessie Conrad's air of self-assurance, which contained a trace of smugness. The visit, nevertheless, was enjoyed by all of them. Conrad, who in advance had recommended "a strong iron cage" and a "reliable keeper" for the infant, was deeply touched by Mrs. Crane's "kind forethought" in providing a cradle—borrowed, of course, probably from their Limpsfield neighbor, Mrs. Pease.

3

HUEFFER, whose love of tall tales quite often interfered with veracity, was probably not far wrong in his estimate of the literary flotsam descending upon Ravensbrook that autumn of 1897 as "the most discreditable bums any city can ever have seen." But for the rest of Stephen Crane's English reception, when one has separated the grain of truth from Hueffer's customary exaggerations—not untinged with malice—one is inclined to agree that Crane "was done about as well as highbrow England could do him."

Stephen had been introduced at most of the clubs and the Embassy circle presided over by Mr. John Hay. In London he and Cora were invited to dinners and theatre parties, while among their Limpsfield-Oxted intimates no eyebrows were lifted and no doors slammed on account of the vagueness which hung over the domestic arrangements at Ravensbrook.

But the highest-paid writer in England, with the possible exception of Kipling, was not unnaturally an object of unfriendly curiosity to fourflushers who envied him and lied about him; and rumors of his wife's past already were crossing the ocean. The too hospitable Cranes soon found themselves beset by a hooligan mob. From Fleet Street and Park Row they came to get a look at the fabulous boy, to visit an old friend, "to check up on the rumors." They came with notes of introduction, and with manuscripts; they invited themselves and the Cranes invited them. They came and they encamped. By November Ravensbrook was overrun, and Stephen trying to work. Edward Garnett knew of a place "less accessible" to London, a fourteenth-century manor house belonging to a friend of his—Moreton Frewen—half in ruins but unoccupied. Cora made a mental note of it, and flung herself into the immediate duties of bodyguard and social secretary.

> As Stephen is asleep [she wrote Sanford Bennett on November 29] I have taken the liberty of opening your telegram. Will you do a distracted wife a favour? I know that Stephen wants to see you as soon as possible. But we have been overwhelmed with callers all week. He is desperately trying to finish a story. Just this morning a literary boy who lives in the neighbourhood imposed himself on us from 9 to 4! So I am *not* going to tell Stephen that Mrs. Bennett and you have arrived in London. Please telegraph or write again, day after tomorrow. I know this is rude. . . .

Next day came an American lawyer with a note from their good friend John Scott-Stokes, a cousin of the Duke of Norfolk. Stephen was pleasant to him "in a quiet, boyish way"; Cora invited him to lunch, and in the middle of lunch Harold Frederic arrived with five other men. The lawyer, Frederic, and the five remained through the afternoon. Frederic was not satisfied until Stephen had given a demonstration of his excellent marksmanship with his Mexican revolver—the weapon later described by Irving Bacheller to Cora as "the longest revolver I ever saw." "Some children came over from the next house to watch," the lawyer recorded, "and Mrs. Crane made biscuit for tea."

And then Crane fled. "I have been staying at this hotel [Brown's in Dover Street]," he wrote on December 3, "two days so as to finish some work. Cora just now wires me that she has got rid of some people who have been boarding with us for three days, so I can go home."

Had Cora Crane been a wife who scrimped and saved for her husband, like Jessie Conrad, much might have been different. As it was, she was improvident, luxury-loving—as she herself said, "a spendthrift in every way." So the locusts consumed more game pies, the empty claret and brandy bottles piled up in the cellar, and the bills went unpaid. "In one way Steve and I are the same person," she told a friend of Stephen's. "We have no sense about money at all." Cora's young friend Vere met her coming home one day in the London train "with a positive bower of orchids, and some costly white flower. No English family in the same circumstances would have spent three or four pounds on flowers for a small dinner. . . ."

In January Stephen signed a contract with his London agent, James B. Pinker. Reaching home very late, lugging a huge hamper laden with caviar, foie gras, and oysters, he found Hueffer there and probably also Frederic—Robert Barr was in Algeria. The occasion called for a celebration. Nervously fagged from the day in town, but in high spirits, he sat on into the small hours talking, laying plans, dispensing things from the hamper, and moistening it all with champagne, which the others drank. The checks coming in now from Pinker averaged twenty pounds per thousand words, seldom falling below ten, and sometimes hitting as high as thirty (then about $150).* "As you see, I am buckling down and turning

* Reports of the prices Crane received for his work, large even in figures of today, have been greatly exaggerated. Beer states (p. 183) that Pinker was paying him forty pounds for every thousand words. It was probably nearer ten pounds—which at that time would have been upwards of forty *dollars*—averaging out perhaps at twenty, Hueffer's figure (in *Portraits from Life*, p. 25). Mason's figure of one hundred pounds each for twenty "Battle" stories must be halved both ways! (A. E. W. Mason to Vincent Starrett, October 4, 1945, letter now in the possession of R. W. Stallman.) The number of stories in *Great Battles of the World* actually totaled nine, and Crane received fifty pounds from *Lippincott's Magazine* for each. See Pinker and Perris correspondence, Chapters V, VI, and VII.

out stuff like a man," he wrote Paul Reynolds in New York. "If you hold your fine gait it will only be a short time before we are throwing out our chests."

Fine it was while the chesty feeling lasted—and the champagne —to contemplate all those thousands of words yet to come, each thousand worth twenty or thirty pounds with Stephen Crane's name on it. But to one who had long declared, and probably now sensed in the organs of his body, that Death had picked him for a loser, especially fine to call the hand and take the winnings—and play host for a change! Perhaps it helped him to forget the hot iron on his flesh back in the lean garret days, of those fifteen-dollar requests and appeals like this one to Acton Davies: "Please send me $5 by this bearer. . . . Am going to Ed's at Lakeview and need some grub. Other wise I shall eat the front door, his baby and the cat." His family had not known of his privations then. But he told Karl Harriman later: "I was foolishly proud. . . . I hated to borrow money from my brothers. . . . I borrowed too much which I have never paid back. . . . They have never asked me for a cent and that hurts like hellfire."

Irksome as her hostess duties sometimes became when the arriving rabble had to be wined and fed at all hours of the night, Cora probably thought Stephen's literary reputation would benefit from keeping open house; and he liked company as much as she. But both were given to counting chickens before they were hatched, and their helpless good nature was bankrupting them. By December Crane was begging Reynolds to sell "The Monster": "For heaven's sake raise me all the money you can and *cable* it, *cable* it sure between Xmas and New Year's"; and, appealing to Acton Davies to collect from two men who had borrowed money from him in Greece, he wrote, "I took X——'s note for $300 and Y—— owes me about $250. . . ." He hated to press nice fellows, "but it costs me more to live over here than I was led to believe and some of these Comanche braves seem to think I am running a free lunch counter. Seven men have been staying over Sunday."

While to Cora's eyes and to others, the future looked rosy, Crane himself only half believed in it. His English expenses, he told Reynolds, "have chased me to the wall'; he was ill, too, with winter colds. Then ill-luck struck hard, the cursed luck that seemed ever dogging him around the globe. In January (1898) Amy Leslie sued him in the New York Supreme Court to recover $550 of the

$800 she professed to have loaned him the year before. So once more, the name of Stephen Crane was spread upon the front pages of the metropolitan journals—in mud.

STEPHEN CRANE SUED

Charged With Making A Serious Mistake In A Bank Deposit

. . . On November 1, 1896, the plaintiff alleges that she gave the defendant $800 to deposit in the bank. Instead of depositing it in her name, she says, he placed it to his own credit. . . .

In the absence of final evidence, one can only guess at what lay behind a charge so astounding. Crane as a borrower had piled up a mighty record, and now since the winds of prosperity had blown upon him money slipped through his fingers like butter; but circumstantial evidence in this instance is mostly in his favor. At the time of the Philistine dinner engineered in his honor by Elbert Hubbard in Buffalo, Amy Leslie had written to him from Chicago and from this correspondence—which she herself probably at some time destroyed—seems to have developed a friendship which on her side quickly blossomed into a hopeless passion. Amy followed him to New York, where she lived with a sister whom Crane described to Willis Hawkins as "weak, very weak." With his quixotic penchant for rescuing female unfortunates lost in the jungles of Manhattan, it seems altogether probable that *he* was trying to help *her;* and that the $800 "loan" may have been, at his urging, set aside to forestall indulgence of an unfortunate weakness, hers or her sister's, such as alcoholism or drugs. That Crane meanwhile may have used the money, intending to replace it, also is entirely probable. At any rate, before going filibustering in the *Commodore* he deposited with his friend Hawkins $500 to be used for weekly payments to Amy Leslie, and other disbursements for his own needs, this sum to be followed by more; and from Athens, as we have seen, he sent another $225 earmarked for Amy. Hawkins kept careful account of these disbursements, and from his notations it appears that about half of the original $800 was paid out to Miss Leslie in weekly installments. Then doubtless sensing trouble ahead—from the tone of her communications to him—Hawkins wearied of the neurotic appeals of a mentally sick woman and called a halt. Hawkins' refusal to accept other money, i.e., the two checks from Greece for $100 and $125, apparently was seized upon by Miss Leslie's attorney as a pretext for the suit.*

Robert Barr had given an affidavit for Stephen, submitted for reading before posting to Crane's lawyer; he was sailing for America on March 20 and offered "to go anywhere and testify to what I know for use at the trial."

Cora took refuge in philosophy. "Never fret over either of two things, what you can help and what you cannot!" Pessimism she saw as "the religion of the unsuccessful." One must cultivate the habit of seeking the best in every person and in every event, so look for good, not evil, in all things. "The bane of our life is that cynical contempt which finds in all things only weakness . . . something to be criticized and despised."

She was doing her best to protect Stephen from the invading "Indians." But delay in selling "The Monster" compounded the gloom intensified by debts and the lawsuit. Conrad's visit had provided a bright interval; so about the middle of March Cora wrote urging another visit to Ravensbrook. But Conrad declined, fearing "the company of a wretched creature like me *wont* do any good to Stephen." He was in an "unhealthy mood himself, and suffering from an attack of gout. "Dear Stephen," he presently wrote, "I am

* On December 28, 1897, Hawkins wrote a final, emphatic letter to Miss Leslie's attorney, George Mabon:

Dear Sir:

Your letter addressed on the outside to me and on the inside to "Willis B. Hawkins, Esq., Agent," is before me. I do not know of any such person as "Willis B. Hawkins, Agent."

For your personal information, I will say that I did, at one time, more than a year ago, receive a certain sum of money from a friend who wished me to pay it out in certain prescribed manners. I paid it all out in those manners, and I hold receipts for all the items. When that sum was paid out my connection with the matter ceased.

For your further information, I will say that a long time afterward, I did receive another sum of money from the same friend, but I returned it to him and declined to make any further disbursements for him. I hold a receipt for this sum.

I presume you will agree with me that I do not have to receive and disburse money for my friends if I do not wish to.

I make this explanation to you merely to enable you to decide whether you desire to proceed further in the direction indicated.

Yours very truly,
Willis B. Hawkins

like a damned paralyzed mud turtle—I can't move—I can't write—
I can't do anything. But I can be wretched, and, by God! I am!"

After the visit to Ivy Walls Conrad had written Garnett, "I had
Crane here last Sunday. . . . He is strangely hopeless about himself"; and on February 5 to Stephen, ". . . I am wondering how you
have passed through your crisis . . . it hurts me to think you are
worried." He and Garnett had concluded that Stephen must be
kept quiet, "but who is going to work that miracle? We trust in
Mrs. Crane and in the sagacity of publishers. That last is not much
to trust to—I admit."

Whatever its merits and shortcomings as art, in the conception
of "The Monster" was spilled a large measure of its creator's own
heart's blood. The story joins two key Crane themes: rescue and
the deflation of heroism. The hero, a Negro servant whose face has
been horribly burned in performing the act of heroism, ends up as
an object of both pity and derision while his benefactor, who protects him, in turn suffers ostracism in the community. A typical
Crane reversal. But would not he, Crane, have suffered ostracism
at home in Port Jervis for his rescue of Cora? And was not he too
a sorry figure, stripped of heroics: a monster to some? Reynolds
had written him that Richard Watson Gilder protested when the
story came in to the Century: "Good heavens, we couldn't publish
that thing with half the expectant mothers in America on our
subscription list!"

When Harold Frederic strolled over one morning from Homefield and Stephen read the story aloud to him and Sanford Bennett,
Frederic abruptly told him to throw the thing away. Then the
mounting tensions Cora and Conrad had both observed burst forth
with violence. "What was wrong with people anyhow. Here was
a lot of ink on white paper and 'a story with some sense in it.' Why
be frightened? His hopeless failure to catch the emotional view-
point of average readers," says Beer, "or, for that matter, of average writers came flashing up. 'Men of sense' would not care if
Henry Johnson had a face or no." Stephen thrashed up and down
the room arguing passionately, beating his revolver butt on the
furniture—the Mexican revolver. The battle lasted through luncheon; and when Frederic presently turned his fire on Conrad's novel,
the revolver crashed down fatally on a dessert plate, Stephen shouting, "You and I and Kipling couldn't have written The Nigger!"

Frederic, whose enemies have accused him of every crime in the book, from ignorance and untruthfulness to ill manners and plagiarism, was the last man to hold rancor. He had been offered a house in Ireland, "a mansion" overlooking the sea with seven bedrooms, a bath, and two boats—one a sailboat—and had thought of it, he told Crane, "solely with reference to your sharing it with us." Expenses would be light; he was going there to finish his book; he and Stephen could "work as well as loaf."

But the quarrel over "The Monster" had blown a fuse and Stephen reacted with peculiar psychological violence. Irrationally, the Irish house became a blazing issue, a symbol of bohemian laxity, as certain all too obvious parallels between the Frederics' illegitimacy and his own rose up before him nakedly revealed. Accordingly, when a few days later Harold and Kate walked over from Homefield one evening in February to discuss with Stephen and Cora plans for their joint occupancy of the house in Ireland, their reception fell woefully short of expectations. The subject brought on another explosion, worse than the one before. Cora made peace, and two days after her letter in which she endeavored to calm the roiled waters, came a grief-stricken reply from Frederic, taking all the blame on himself:

February 8, 1898

My dear Cora:

Forgive the informality of my taking the matter away from Kate, and myself answering your characteristically kind and straightforward letter of Sunday.

I left Ravensbrook on Saturday dismayed at the proportions of the mistake I had made in opening up the Irish business at all. My error arose from my taking as my guide the very delightful memories we both have and cherish of the Irish trip last Autumn. I had not at all realized—up to the time of our discussions last week—that so much had changed since then. You see you and Stephen then were still in the chrysalis stage, so to speak, of housekeeping and you were both relatively fresh from the haphazard, bohemian life of the campaign in Thessaly. It was comparatively easy for you both, therefore, to fall in with the general views of the organizer of the picnic. How charmingly you both did so we shall never forget. And you were both ill, too, and that contributed its very sweetening effect, in our minds, to what we look back upon as one of the happiest times in our life. It has been borne in upon me, however, by practically every word that has been exchanged about the new project, that the conditions are all altered—and I am greatly distressed and angry at my own simplicity not having seen in time to avert the unhappy blunder of making the proposition.

I am more vexed at my own stupidity than you can think—but it never occurred to me that since last autumn Ravensbrook has defined for itself a system and routine of its own—quite distinct, as is natural, from the system of Homefield—and that an effort to put these two side by side under one roof would necessarily come to grief. There would be the common bond of great and deep personal attachment between the two households, of course—but when it came to a test of strength between that and the divergent impetus of two wholly different sets of habits, I have seen too much of the world to doubt that the bond would be injured much more easily than the habits would be harmonized. And God forbid that that should happen.

I don't want to go any further into the matter. It is all very heart breaking to me—to us—and I wish with sharp emphasis that Mrs. Rice had never offered me the house at all. As I have said, I take all the blame upon myself for not having realized that, under the changed conditions, the things that we had so pleasantly in a community of comradeship would recede into the background, and that our points of difference would rise up and rush forward. . . . I think . . . if we were all off on a holiday, with no necessity of work for either Stephen or me, we could probably take a sufficient number of these differences by the scruff of the neck, and thrust them back where they belong. But with the necessity of work weighing upon us both, I am frankly afraid of the experiment.

Yet I have built so fondly on the project of having some long, good fishing days alone with Stephen—and there are such a multitude of like attractions for us all . . . I want earnestly to set before you a kind of alternative. Do you and Stephen and Mrs. Ruedy carve out of your spring a three weeks of entire leisure (and I will make that period free for myself, or nearly free) and come over and visit us at Ahakista. Everything then will be perfectly simple, and I surely need not waste words in saying how warmly you would be welcome. Bring Adoni with you.

Kate is going to write you tomorrow. Meanwhile I beg you both to read into my letter all the regret and affection which your hearts will tell you I wanted it to contain.

Yours always,
Harold

At Frederic's urging Crane had begun the novel *Active Service*. As he worked on it, his interest only lukewarm, another idea occurred to him for a book dealing with celebrated battles in history, to be called *Great Battles of the World*. He probably thought of this book as a potboiler to pull him out of the financial hole, seeing in it lucrative possibilities for advance serialization. So he employed, or persuaded, Kate Frederic, who had had professional experience in research, to undertake the gathering of his material. It was to be another collaboration, like the London Letters, in which most of the labor would be done by the other person. Harold supplied a book of "naval names"; and Kate began her investigations with the Battle of New Orleans. According to Stephen's friend C. Lewis Hind—editor of the London *Academy*—one Colonel Hinds of the Mississippi Dragoons, an ancestor, had the dubious honor of setting off this battle prematurely with an attack unauthorized by the commander General Andrew Jackson. Kate found records of the New Orleans engagement "confusing," and there was no mention of this incident. But it might be "true as truth; historians lie so."

But now the house by the sea receded further into the Irish mists. War clouds were gathering over the capitol dome in Washington. After the *Maine* disaster all London was tense, Stephen tight-lipped and waiting; and Harold Frederic lay incurably ill of a cardiac embolism. Stephen sat at the bedside of his friend. Then one day in April, white-faced and eager, he was racing wildly over London with Conrad, desperately trying to raise sixty pounds to get himself to Cuba and the imminent war—which was then only two weeks off. They had no luck till Conrad led him into the office of *Blackwood's Magazine* and pledged his own work as security for the advance. Stephen gave a receipt for the loan to *Blackwood's*, had Cora make a copy, and borrowed another ten pounds from Sanford Bennett.

Conrad had the feeling, later, that he had led his young friend that afternoon by the hand to his doom. "But, indeed, I was only the blind agent of the fate that had him in her grip! Nothing could have held him back. He was ready to swim the ocean."

Stephen left a note at Sanford Bennett's rooms: "Sorry not to have seen you. I have raised the wind and sail tomorrow. Nothing I can do for Harold. Barr will look after him. Write me at Hartwood, N. Y., care of Edmund Crane. . . ." And then he went home to break the news to a despairing woman, who wrote in her journal:

> Oh, happy is the human being who has never yet had occasion to cry: "I cannot bear it!" But we bear things. Somehow we bear them, though that endurance leaves us forever after with a mark upon us.

Ravensbrook: Heartache, Waiting, the Prodigal's Return

chapter 4

CRANE'S self-pity was not a pose, as Davis believed, but the expression of that negative side of his personality which came more often into ascendancy after his twenty-fourth year. With two unsuccessful courtships behind him, he was all too aware that his early iconoclasms had earned him the uncomfortable reputation of "failure" and "black sheep." Perhaps when the final story of his short, troubled life is told, his biographer will conclude that he cared too much for his own good about what certain people thought of Stephen Crane, and about public opinion in general. Oversensitiveness to the judgments of others was undoubtedly one of the things that did most to destroy him, as was his hopeless inability to organize his life on a footing he could pay for in dollars and cents.

If we assume a connection, however remote, between an artist's inner drives and the projections of his imagination, Berryman's observation—that the typical Crane character "normally is *pretentious* and *scared*"—has point. In 1893, in an early draft of *The Red Badge of Courage*, Crane had said of the young soldier Henry Fleming:

He was of the unfit, then. He did not come into the scheme of further life.

. . . It was a barbarous process with affection for the man and the oak, and no sympathy for the rabbit and the weed. He thought of his own capacity for pity and there was an infinite irony in it.

Much cruelty lay in the fact that he was a babe.

Admitting that he was powerless and at the will of the law, he yet planned to escape; menaced by fatality he schemed to avoid it. . . . He now created in thought a secure spot where an all-powerful eye would fail to perceive him, where an all-powerful stick would fail to bruise his life.

There was in him a creed of freedom which no contemplation of inexorable law could destroy. . . .

To Nellie Crouse he had spoken of "the majestic forces . . . arrayed against man's true success—not the world . . . —but man's own colossal impulses more strong than chains." He had fought with the world, but the real fight henceforth would be carried on against those "colossal impulses": the compensatory forces of his own nature whose potency for his undoing he never really understood, ". . . but this other battle—it is to last on up through the years to my grave and only on that day am I to know if the word Victory will look well upon lips of mine."

So now bruised by the inexorable, the all-powerful stick wielded by Amy Leslie; hard-pressed to support the Ravensbrook establishment; and menaced by the continuous threat of exposure of his ambiguous marital relations, which in any court would be branded bigamy or adultery, he was running off to another war. And like the raw recruit who also ran, Henry Fleming, he would make his lonely stand not by his own hearthside, in his study guarded by a devoted woman, but in the violent crucible of the battlefield.

For Cora, it had been love at first sight—whatever the phrase may mean to a later day—"the old chords were struck, and withered emotions bloomed again." But now she felt that she had been abandoned. She had borne two separations already in their seventeen-month romance; how was she to endure yet another, this one of unknown duration? And with Stephen far away, how know that he still cared? "A man is content to know that he is loved, but woman doubts unless she daily hears the sweet refrain." Was it true, then, that one could not find true love; or simply, that men love best their own pursuits? She was stabbed anew by this paradox of the sexes: that "to men even the most exquisite joy palls when it ceases to be a novelty. Not true of women." Hence, in woman's love the sharpest pain comes "not from deception, but from being undeceived."

Circumstances [she reflected] are the lashes laid onto us by life: some have to receive them with bared backs, others are permitted to keep on a coat. That is the only difference. But when we come to think about it, it is rather absurd to expect to have uninterrupted stretches of happiness; happiness falls to our share in detached bits, and those of us who are wise content ourselves with these broken fragments.

For she recognized that "2,000 years of human experience, modified by Christianity, has taught us to make the best of what chance may take from us, as well as of what chance may bring."

She was endeavoring to make the best of it, though finding "the art of knuckling under a hard one to learn." Harder still, to practice with good grace! But she would not remain at home in the ugly little red-brick villa to weep and repine, penned in by four walls with a thousand reminders of the absent one, or to suffer the platitudes of well-meaning friends. Harold Frederic had made a partial recovery from the cardiac disorder; so accompanied by Mrs. Ruedy, taking various dogs and the peerless Adoni, Cora set out to join the Frederics at Ahakista—the Irish house Harold and Kate were then occupying.

Conrad, who disliked Frederic and disapproved of Stephen's association with him, wrote to Cora on April 19: "We imagine how lonely you must have felt after Stephen's departure. The dear fellow wired me from Queenstown. . . . Jess is very concerned about you and wishes me to ask you to drop her a line on your arrival in Ireland." Her going there, however, he thought a good thing,

as solitude after separation is sometimes very hard to bear. We thought of asking you to come here at once but on receiving Stephen's wire I imagined you were all in Ireland already. However, you will be more entertained and more comfortable at the Frederics for a time, and on your return to England I hope you will have the will and the courage to undertake the risky experiment of coming to us with Mrs. Rudie. [Conrad was continually stumped by the spelling of this name.]

Cora did not go then to Ivy Walls, and on June 27 Conrad wrote again apologizing for not having replied to her letter with news of Stephen. Stephen in Cuba " in the thick of everything" and going to write for Blackwood—that was good! He himself was deep in gloom: oppressed by household troubles calamitous to a writer's routine, worried too that Jess had to slave at housework, cooking, washing baby clothes, because he couldn't afford a servant yet. "Oh! for a success, a beastly popular success! . . . Garnett told me you had secured a house after your own heart. My congratulations on that. . . ."

In March, both Cranes near lunacy from the incursions of the "Indians," Cora had written to Edward Garnett inquiring about the "less accessible" house in Sussex. Garnett replied on March 13, enclosing an agency's description and "a bad map," with his blessing and the warning, "Go without expectations." For no telling how the place had run down with only a farm bailiff encamped in its ancient walls. It was near Battle, scene of "the affair between William the Conqueror and all England in 1066," post office Northiam; but the best way to go was by train to Hastings and be driven over in a fly, a distance of eight miles.

So on her return from Ireland Cora first saw Brede Place—and fell fast in love with it! Garnett was again helpful with practical advice. He had gone over the house himself with an architect (his wife's brother-in-law W. H. Cowlishaw) and advised Cora to submit the architect's report to the owner, Mr. Frewen, with the suggestion that they halve costs for necessary repairs as landlord and tenant each would benefit.

Gentleman, sportsman, adventurer, promoter, currency expert and bimetallist, as well as diplomat ex officio, Moreton Frewen was a colorful figure out of that romantic mid-century when the Empire builders were extending the outposts of Her Majesty's realm on the Dark Continent and in Asia, penetrating jungle and desert, probing to the farthermost island reef. Endowed with the imaginative vision of a tycoon, he always had a fortune by the tail and somehow it always got away from him. "Winning new capital with his smile, Moreton launched one splendid crash after another." A cattle ranch in Wyoming had brought bankruptcy; a gold-crushing machine, invented by him for use in Australia, produced no gold but crushed the inventor instead. Asked whether Frewen were rogue or fool, one of his backers, Lord Desborough, replied: "Worse than either, he's a genius!" In India, where he was engaged in straightening out the finances of a maharajah, he had encountered a spectacled, shy young man who pressed on him a manuscript, entreating him to seek its publication on his return to England. His efforts miscarried; but when Rudyard Kipling's *Plain Tales From the Hills* later brought fame to the unknown author, Moreton Frewen took a wicked delight in having the last word, writing to chide the editor of a London daily who had returned the manuscript as "not up to standard."

Frewen had married Clara Jerome, eldest of the three lovely daughters of "the remarkable Mr. Jerome" of Wall Street and racing fame. Her sister Jennie was already Lady Randolph Churchill, and mother of a future great statesman. The original demesne of the Frewens was Brickwall, at Northiam, but Brede Place had come into the family in 1708 when Sir Edward Frewen purchased it from the Oxenbridges. For long intervals the house had been left without occupants, its farm acreage the chief interest of its owners; but when Moreton and Clara returned from Wyoming in 1885, after the cattle-ranch disaster, they took it over as a residence until the wealthy Mr. Jerome made them a gift of a small town house in London. Mrs. Frewen afterwards bought the house and game park—one hundred acres—from her husband's brother, Sir Richard Frewen; but only the bailiff's family had lived in it since.

In a short story, "Cowardice," Cora has recorded her impressions of that first visit to Brede Place. The country round about was given over to hop culture and sheep farming; the hill on which she stood was belted by a wide marshland through which threaded a still, dark ribbon of river—the Brede—its bankless sides confined within dikes. Opposite, another hill rising sharply from the far edge of this flatland was "clothed with trees in matronly foliage and draped as for a harvest festival" with long ropes of the pungent hops; the marsh itself, "a smooth carpet of purple, blues, and violet-green," with patches of yellow, orange, and white lilies. The lilies and tall grasses fringed with copperish bracken cast small shadows on the miniature plain. Her eye was caught by "hundreds of shorn sheep glued to the earth. A heron, his head pleated into his neck, rested on one leg beside the river. Overhead, small floating white clouds moved like ducks upon a blue lake. To the right the marsh faded into a gray line, the sea; and to the left, another gray line, the far horizon." The straight white road on which she stood stretched downhill across the marsh and up the slope opposite to

Brede village, the square tower of an ancient church just visible above the treetops, red tiles and thatch roofs showing spottily through the leaves. In a slight dip to the right of the village, encompassed by a ragged mat of century-old hedge, rose the five tall chimneys of the house, their red Tudor brick silhouetted toothlike on the cobalt sky.

As she drew near, her eyes took in the leaded windows with casings of Caen stonework, choked with ivy, through which protruded the noses of gargoyles flattened by centuries of rain. Begun in 1370, in Edward III's time, the house had been added to in the early 1500's by Sir Goddard Oxenbridge, at which time the original plaster and timber was replaced by brick and stonework—very narrow Tudor bricks only six or seven inches long.

Weeds grew high against the walls, but Cora had eyes only for the thrills within, beginning with the white owl's nest lodged in an oak beam of the entrance hall. On the first floor, above the chapel, was the priest's room with a small closet concealed behind oaken panels covered over with linen cloth, and a stairway leading down from high in the chimney to a labyrinth of subterranean passages where "in the cassock-hunting days of Cromwell the household priest could hide"—though several of the Oxenbridges were Roundheads. The caretaker—a woman whose looks she liked—explained that these passages connected with the river a mile away, and for almost a century, while the house was unoccupied, had been used by smugglers. The chapel, built by Sir Goddard, who had been one of the courtiers in attendance on Henry VIII at the Field of the Cloth of Gold, had a single long oriel window carved in cinquefoil. Cora was shown the Gallows Room over the dungeon, "with the spot of blood on the floor that neither soap and water nor the footprints of time could wear away," and the oak beam overhead from which the legendary lord of the manor hanged his wives in true Bluebeard style; the rust-eaten hook in the beam and the mark at the side where the pulley had rubbed. Here, too, in this room when the wind was high, and the night wild, were heard the cries of children! For the house had its ghost, Sir Goddard, the ogre who according to legend ate a small child for his dinner each night. In actuality Sir Goddard appears to have been a mild and benevolently inclined old gentleman, who left a will giving to each of his servants of both sexes four months wages and a suit of black cloth; to friends his silver cups, his horses and kine; and to his good wife Dame Anne his house and lands at Brede. Nevertheless, as late as 1929—according to Viscountess Wolseley in the *Sussex County Magazine*—"few cared to pass at night the Groaning Bridge" where the maligned old knight was supposed to have met his end. Legend has it that the children of the locality were his executioners. After filling him full of beer—presumably of his own manufacture—they laid a saw across him, and "the children of East Sussex rode upon one end and the children of West Sussex upon the other."*

Cora knew at once that she must have this house. Stephen would find wry entertainment in the *mise en scène* of "Groaning Bridge" and "Gallows Room"; and perhaps the ghost who scared off thieves and gypsies after dark would keep away the "Indians"! So now with a return of her old bouyancy she began to construct new hopes.

Garnett, in the letter of March 13, had facetiously remarked that "Stephen's eloquence" would quickly unlock the entrance-ways to Brede Place in case the caretaker showed reluctance to admit them. From this letter it appears that Crane had been contemplating an inspection tour of the house with Cora when his departure for Cuba abruptly put an end to these plans. She must have written him at once after her visit, which was sometime in May. While awaiting his reply, she had obtained the architect's estimate for necessary repairs, and forwarded a copy to the Fre-

---

* While the ghost legend probably did not originate with smugglers, it is thought to have been encouraged and widely circulated as a smokescreen for their nighttime activities. For almost a century smuggling had been a trade generally followed by the populations of Surrey and Sussex counties. To farm tenants, it was a means of augmenting their meager substance; to land-owners, it sometimes brought in more annual increment that rents or crops. It was everywhere an accepted rule that horses and vehicles might be borrowed for transportation in an "emergency" and later returned to the owners with no questions asked. A story is told of a squire who ordered his groom to harness the mare to the wagon for a journey to town. "Beg pardon, sir," replied the man, "but the mare is not in the stable." "Oh well, then," said his master, "get me a horse from somewhere." "Beg pardon again, sir, but the wagon is not in the stable either." This standing together of upper and lower classes made it next to impossible for the revenue officers to make arrests, and even Parliament was helpless in putting down the traffic—largely in French cognac and gin from Holland.

Brede Place, circa 1929. From the *Sussex County Magazine*, October, 1929. Courtesy R. W. Stallman.

wens. "I understand . . . that . . . in about two years time," she wrote Mrs. Frewen on June 4, "you are thinking of making extensive additions to the old house." In that case, the Cranes "would not like to spend too much" on renovations. It had been rented as a farm house for fourteen pounds a year. "We think that £40 per year as the house *is* will be a fair rental. And we will make the repairs named in the architect's report"—which was raising the ante over Garnett's proposal of halving costs. These expenses to make the house "habitable," exclusive of repairs to the stable and "building a small conservatory"—for which she asked the privilege—would, Cora pointed out, treble the sum already going for rent.

The impatiently awaited cable from Jamaica did not come until June 8, and when it did there was no mention of Brede Place—only Stephen's complaint that he had received no letters from Cora. Two days later Cora wrote to Moreton Frewen that she was expecting to hear from Crane "any day now that he is satisfied with my arrangements for Brede. I can, however, safely say that we will take it on the terms named in my letter and as soon as I hear from Mr. Crane I will write you a formal letter to that effect." She was glad Frewen did not think lawyers necessary, having had "such an awful dose of them the past few days"— referring to the carriage accident the previous August. "By next week I hope to forward you the formal letter and will then have the architect start repairs. And try to be already in camp at your wonderful old house when Mr. Crane returns." She would be very much obliged to Mrs. Frewen for the literature on the early history of the house. Would Mr. Frewen object to its being used in an article? And might she ask for the photos he had told her he had of Brede? She would try to arrange to keep the caretaker, would go to Brede one day next week and see her, and then write him.

The news that her letters were not getting through to Stephen was deeply upsetting to Cora, in more ways than one. She probably replied by cable, and then wrote again giving full particulars as to Brede Place; and on June 16 she dispatched an anxious note to an unknown recipient, possibly the manager of the Key West Hotel, or Crane's chief at the New York *World*:

Dear Sir: Mr. Crane cables me that he has recieved [sic] no letters from me. Will you kindly let me know if you forward them as received? As it is of great importants [sic] my letters reach him.

Yours truly

Cora Crane (Mrs. Stephen Crane)

And on the same day, she wrote again to Moreton Frewen. His letters of June 13 and 14 were both awaiting her on her return to Ravensbrook "from a four days driving trip . . . with friends to Tunbridge Wells and then on to Brede. From there to Rye and Battle." Cora was "quite in love with that part of England. . . . Mr. Crane will be delighted with the idea of camping in your old house. I am so glad that there is a chance of our keeping it longer as I want to take some roses from this place and of course we would have so little good of them in one year." She was planning to go to Queenstown to meet Stephen, "with an American lady [Mrs. Ruedy] who is stopping with me. It will give us great pleasure to come to you for one day." But she feared it would be September or even October "before this war business is settled so that Mr. Crane will return." She had had another cable that morning from Port Antonio (Jamaica) saying "he had been *fighting*. To see what it is really like I suppose. But it's very distressing to me. A good book should be written while we are at Brede Place which may please you as adding a wee bit more history to the place. When the workmen are through I will write you."

This, then, was not yet the "formal letter." But thus occupied with plans for the "wonderful old house" and the future that would bring Stephen's return, Cora managed to get through the long summer months. Then disquieting news of Stephen's health reached her, whether from Stephen himself—which seems most unlikely—or through the malice or misdirected kindness of an unknown informant. The answer to this question is one more of the puzzle pieces still missing from the story. And difficult to fit into the known chronology of Crane's feverish zigzag course during his nine months of absence from England is the letter Cora received in September, from Dr. Edward Livingston Trudeau— the great lung specialist and founder of the cottage sanitarium at Saranac Lake in the Adirondacks—presumably in reply to an inquiry from her earlier in the month:

September 16

Paul Smith's
In the Adirondacks
Paul Smith's, N. Y.

Dear Madam
Your husband had a slight evidence of activity in the trouble in his
lungs when he came back here this summer, but it was not serious and
he has improved steadily I understand since he came. I have only examined him once but he looked very well and told me he was much
better last time I saw him.

Very truly yours
E. L. Trudeau

Was Stephen at Saranac twice then, that summer of 1898? Or
does Dr. Trudeau's allusion to "when he came back here this
summer" point to an earlier visit in another year? And did Cora
know of it? Certainly, his brothers did not. But Richard Harding
Davis told Thomas Beer that Crane was coughing badly and
spitting blood on his return to New York from Cuba. Was this
trip to Saranac sandwiched in between his July 13 arrival in Old
Point Comfort on a transport bringing back the wounded, and
his departure in August to cover the Puerto Rican action for the
New York *Journal?* Cora's letter to Dr. Trudeau has not been
preserved and the Sanitarium's records show nothing to indicate
that one Stephen Crane, novelist and war correspondent, was ever
a patient there. But Dr. Francis B. Trudeau, son of the founder,
suggests that his father, who carried on a large practice outside
the Sanitarium, at Paul Smith's and in the town of Saranac itself,
may well have treated Crane as a private patient in either of those
places.*

The real significance of this Trudeau letter is in the startling
revelation that Crane had actually had treatment from the foremost authority on lung tuberculosis in the United States, and
now must get himself patched up to go back into the war. It
would seem that he either misjudged the optimistic tone of Dr.
Trudeau's report, or in the clutch of those egocentric "colossal

* Dr. Francis B. Trudeau to Lillian Gilkes, September 28, 1954. Since the
death of the younger Dr. Trudeau in 1956, the Cottage Sanitarium has been
disbanded as a hospital, but its laboratory facilities continue in operation as
a research center.

The living room at Brede Place, with the furnishings used by the Cranes during their stay there. Courtesy Roger M. Frewen.

A corner of the dining room at Brede showing Sir Goddard Oxenbridge's Tudor Bricks. The bench and mugs are also of his period. Courtesy Roger M. Frewen.

impulses," which appeared to the youth Henry Fleming as salvation and self-discovery, he did not particularly care.

2

ALL sorts of gossip began to drift like floating seaweed across the Atlantic. Cora's alarm over Stephen's health touched frenzy with a report that he had been seen aboard a hospital ship, quarantined with the then mysterious and deadly killer of the tropics: yellow fever! Still another report said typhoid. Whether he actually had yellow fever is debatable, although Cora in a letter to Moreton Frewen later refers to it as a fact. He did have a delirious craving for orange ice-cream soda and pickles! And he was quarantined during the voyage to Old Point Comfort on a subsistence diet of canned tomatoes. When he was released from quarantine, where he had lain in the scuppers as the transport crawled and beat her way up the Atlantic coast, he was a chattering, half-delirious wreck so wasted that Mrs. Bolton Chaffee, who had visited the Cranes at Oxted three months earlier, did not recognize the wraith who bowed to her from the verandah of the Hotel Chamberlain. When she realized who he was, she immediately took measures for his physical care. They were seen together. Then sprouted another weed: Crane disappeared, to elope to San Francisco with the wife of Brigadier General Adna R. Chaffee—the hero of El Caney— where the twain were reported living together "in adulterous splendor." "You must be careful about feeding runaway dogs," Stephen wrote the alleged corespondent. "Mr. Bemis [Floyd Bemis, a Southerner] informs me that you and I are sinners and that we have flown to San Francisco. They have promoted you to the rank of Mrs. Brigadier General Chaffee.* Perhaps it is not known to you . . . that my name in New York is synonymous with mud. Give my regards to your husband and tell him the cigars made many correspondents happier. My friends will pile a mountain of lies on me but they will smoke my cigars as freely as I smoke theirs. That is cynicism."

In August Cora went with Mrs. Ruedy to visit the Conrads at

* Beer (p. 196) says, "General Chaffee had no wife possible for this purpose," but the *Columbia Encyclopedia* reports him married.

Ivy Walls. Knowing nothing of the complications presented by the Stewart marriage and the rest of Cora's "past," Jessie Conrad reports this visit "marred by her very real anxiety as to his [Stephen's] whereabouts, and a fierce jealousy as to his possible fancy for someone he might meet. In vain I assured her of my complete conviction that Stephen was deeply attached to her, and that his first thought as soon as he was able to get a letter through would be of her."

How long Cora was without word from Stephen is far from clear. William Howe Crane says twenty days, but it was certainly longer. Crane's letters at best were infrequent. To Paul Reynolds Cora wrote on September 25, "The last news I had direct from him was dated from Key West August 16th."

On September 22 a copy of the September 10 *Florida Times-Union and Citizen* had reached her, with an item in a gossip column that Crane was "missing!"

CUBAN GOSSIP
(Havana, Sept. 7, via Key West and Miami, Sept. 9)

. . .

STEPHEN CRANE MISSING

Stephen Crane, the novelist, also a member of the Journal staff, who entered Havana as a tobacco buyer about ten days ago, and was stopping quietly at the Hotel Pasaje, is missing, and fears for his safety are entertained by his friends. The police had been shadowing him several days before he disappeared.

Several other correspondents who recently arrived here, and who were immediately spotted, have been warned against attempting to send a line out about the situation previous to the arrival of the American Commission. Ruz, the Mexican newspaper man, has been released.

By this time the war was over, but the peace treaty had not yet been signed; Havana was still a no-man's land to Americans. The demoralized city, with sanitary facilities disrupted, was a pesthole of epidemics, and no one was allowed in or out. Another story going the rounds of the bars was that Stephen Crane had been taken prisoner and was languishing somewhere in a Spanish dungeon. A correspondent who did not know Crane picked up this yarn from two Hearst men and immediately put a report over the wires that he was "lost," perhaps done away with. He was later "found" when the same correspondent recognized a slight man in a white suit, whom he had encountered prowling the streets at midnight, as the gaunt individual who sat down beside him in the American Bar one evening and gave his name as Stephen Crane. Still another version of Crane's "disappearance" turned up in the Hearst Press: he was "hiding" in a Havana rooming house.

Cora, "in great distress of mind," could get no information out of the *Journal* office in London. By now, too, she was in financial straits, and she continued in her September 25 letter to Reynolds:

> I am in *great* need of money. And I fear that we will lose our home here if I cannot get money to pay some pressing debts. The Journal is behaving very shabily [sic]. I have been served with two summonds [sic] so you can see how bad matters really are. If you can collect any money due to Mr. Crane please cable it to me without delay. This being so helpless in a foreign country together with my fears for Mr. Crane are almost driving me mad.

She begged Reynolds to use his influence with Mr. Hearst, and now, all her battle flags waving:

> He has no right to allow a man like Stephen Crane to be missing for over three weeks without using means to find him. And if he allows Stephen Cranes [sic] wife to be turned out of her home, while Stephen is risking his life in his service, I have told Mr. Creelman I would let every correspondent in London know about it. Both Harold Frederic and Robert Barr would let the world know over their own signatures. I beg you to let me hear any news by cable.

On the same day—September 25—overwhelmed by the avalanche of rumors now crashing into Crane's silence, Cora cabled the Secretary of War, Russell A. Alger. The message was referred to the Adjutant General's office for transmission to the United States authorities in Havana:

MRS. STEPHEN CRANE DESIRES INFORMATION CONCERNING THE WHEREABOUTS OF HER HUSBAND, STEPHEN CRANE, WHO ENTERED HAVANA SEPTEMBER 1ST AS A TOBACCO BUYER. MISSING SINCE SEPT. 6TH OR 8TH.

She followed this up with a letter repeating the cable message, with other letters to the British Consul at Havana, and a cablegram to

William Crane at Port Jervis. She did not cable Reynolds—William Crane to the contrary, who afterwards saw her cabling everybody all over the map.

The consternation produced in the Crane family circle by this bombshell, a cable message from England from an unknown woman announcing herself as Stephen's wife, may well be imagined. One wonders which caused the greater shock—Steve missing, or the fact that he had a wife! "Some of his wife's letters and cables were not judicious," William Crane later remarked to Thomas Beer. "She cabled to a very talkative newspaperman she had known at Jacksonville and he put a yarn around that Steve had abandoned her . . . . there was a great deal of nasty talk about it."

But William Crane is again in error in supposing the Florida story, or the Hearst version with which he seems to have confused it, inspired by Cora. Putting reports together, Robert Barr, to whom she now turned in this trouble—Harold Frederic was again near death from a cerebral hemorrhage, and Conrad occupied with moving his family to Pent Farm, their new home in Kent—judged the prodigal more harshly:

If what Hurst [sic] cables is true, then I should hate to put down in black and white what I think of S. Crane. If he has not disappeared, and if he has been drawing money for himself, while leaving you without cash, then that article about his disappearance in the Florida paper is a put up job, and he does not intend to return.

Frederic had been saying Steve was not coming back; on what grounds, Barr wondered? James Creelman, London chief of the New York *Journal*, had told Barr he was certain at least some of Cora's communications had reached Crane. "If in these circumstances you think it worth while to go after such a man, then there is nothing to do but consider the ways and means."

Cora meanwhile was changing her mind about love and noting in her journal:

There is no spirit of Evil, we are betrayed by our own passions and the chief of these passions is love. It is the nemesis that stalks through the world, haunting all men and goading some to great wrong. . . . I passed one of those days that outweigh an eternity, a day full of useless feeling; a day of self-forgetfulness and waking dreams, when what one has longed for in visions in the night actually stands before one. . . . But I may come to feel as if all this had been a dream, as if it had happened to some other girl I once knew, not to myself.

As to ways and means—Barr, with no illusions about their chances of success, but leaving no stone unturned, wrote a letter on September 27 to the Director of the North German Lloyd introducing "Mrs. Stephen Crane who wishes to make some arrangement with you regarding deferred payment for passage to New York." Her husband, the celebrated novelist, had been with the American troops during the war in Cuba and recently in Havana was captured by the Spaniards. "He is certain to be released as soon as the Americans get in there. Mrs. Crane is naturally very anxious about him and wishes to get to Havana. As soon as Mr. Crane reaches New York he will pay the amount due you, should you see your way to let Mrs. Crane cross on one of your boats."

A similar letter was drafted for presentation to the head of the American Line in London, Mr. Parton. Letters from Creelman or Frederic, Barr thought, would have more influence—but the latter was not now in a position to do anything. Should Cora use these letters, he advised her, "take with you the Florida paper to show . . . the item regarding Stephen's disappearance." Barr hadn't mentioned the fact that Stephen was a correspondent, "as the first question they would ask would naturally be, Why does not his paper furnish the money?" Still, it seemed the only way to get passage without paying money down. Then Barr had a better idea: perhaps Heinemann would come to their aid with fifty pounds. "Stephen's publishers have, in a way, security for any money they advance, and if you think Stephen would carry out any bargain you made on his behalf you might promise them some forthcoming books. . . . If you cannot raise money from Heinemann, then we must all of us put together what we can . . . and get you over to New York." Creelman had said he would go two pounds, and once Cora was there Barr was optimistic that "Hurst [sic] would forward you on to Havana."

And what of the prodigal meanwhile? He had not been out of the city! Only moved from the Hotel Pasaje to a rooming house to save money, where he was holed up, quietly doing his writing.

While Will and Edmund Crane were pulling all the wires they could in the furor back home, it was Cora's cable to the Secretary of War that finally blasted Stephen out—just as during that other dreadful time of the *Commodore* disaster, hers was the pressure which launched the *Three Friends* and dispatched a special train to bring up the shipwreck survivors. But the cablegram was stuck in the Adjutant General's office till October 9, reached Havana on the eleventh, and it was not until the twenty-seventh that a report came back from Major General J. F. Wade, in charge of evacuation of Americans from the island. General Wade had inquired among some of the correspondents and reported: "After these inquiries, Mr. Crane called and expressed regret at having caused so much trouble. I do not know his business or why he has not corresponded with his family."

The rooming house was run by a hard-bitten Amazon named Mary Horan who mothered, bullied, and fed bountiful meals to the newspaper boys under her roof. At night, she drove Crane into the streets to walk off cumulative tensions from his hours of strenuous writing. The letters he had written Cora, some five or six, and given to one of the servants to mail, never reached her. He was writing steadily, furiously now "story after story, article after article, and sending them on [to his American agent] with brief penciled scrawls on cheap ruled pad paper; sometimes his vehement notes were written in a shaky hand on old telegraph blanks. Always they glowed with enthusiasm over his work and appealed for instant payment." He was sending dispatches still to the New York *Journal* and working on the Greek novel *Active Service*. Enthralled by the exotic color of the Cuban capital he began a long romance, a tale of love between a daughter of an old aristocratic Spanish family and a stranded American sailor, but presently destroyed it. In October he sent off to Reynolds a strange new batch of poems called *Intrigue* on which critics are agreed in finding little merit—harsh, jealous, bitter love poems, some of which seem to have had Cora in mind, others inspired by some lost love, probably Lily Brandon Munroe. Lily received at least one, possibly more letters from Crane written from Havana, which were among those afterwards destroyed by her husband; and a letter to her younger sister Dorothy Brandon, dated May 19 "Off Havana" and postmarked "New York June 19," reveals the fact that he had stopped in Washington on his way to Cuba expressly to call on the Brandons:

My dear Dot: I do not know if you will forgive me but at least let me explain that I was the victim of a strange set of circumstances. When I was in Washington I suddenly recieved [sic] notice that there was to be a big fight off Havana and I was to go there instantly. I flew; I did not telegraph because I could not explain well enough by wire and returning now from Porto Rico I find my first real opportunity to write you a note. Will you forgive me? I have not changed in the least and you may be sure that the S. Crane you knew so well long ago would not seem thoughtless if he could help it.

I am going to England as soon as the war is over and I wish you would send me the address of your sister there.* My address will be Key West Hotel, Key West. Adios.

S. C.

3

ONE would like to think Stephen's apologies to General Wade and Miss Brandon had been followed by an expression of regret to Cora. It is problematical. She, at any rate, noted in her journal: "Promises made in the time of affection require a better memory than people commonly possess." And again, "The smallest worm will turn when trodden on."

In two short fictional pieces written about this time, Cora's pent-up emotions were released. Both are allegories using a stylized phrasing, and both of more interest autobiographically than as literature. The one called *What Hell Might Be*, published in *Smart Set* in November, 1901, recites her meeting with Stephen: linked with an image of "ancient oaks," the line, "Out of the glare they went into a quiet spot," describes the Daytona idyl. The love relationship is then pictured in the flowery style of late romanticism, and the piece concludes:

> Then the man was taken from the woman to do his appointed work in the unknown life beyond, saying to her: "Be patient; work and wait as I shall wait until we meet again, dear heart."
> And the man passed and the woman did as he bade her. She was patient, she worked, she waited. At times she sank into that fathom-

* Not his old flame but another sister, Stella, then living in Switzerland, who later became Mrs. Schmidt of Baden-Baden. The original of Crane's letter is in the possession of Mr. Frederick B. Smillie.

less depth of woe known only to the lonely of heart; then she would remember that *he was waiting for her*, and she was patient and worked again.

Years passed and the woman's golden hair silvered; the dark eyes that *he* had loved faded and closed in dreamless sleep. Greedily grasping the ferryman's hand, she, too, passed into the shadowland.

But he was not waiting for her! Ages, cycles she wandered far . . . through the unknown land, peering into each passing face . . . weeping, weeping, always weeping; never resting; ever seeking the love of her life.

At last she saw him. "Yes, it is my beloved!" she cried, holding out her arms to him.

He did not know her.

The other piece, unpublished, with the title *The Poor Soul*, is on the same theme of love denied and the troubled soul wandering loose in Hell, with echoes of Paolo and Francesca:

There was once a young girl who, having gone astray and died early, got into Hell, and there the Holy Peter kept hearing her cry out of the flames, "Paul! Paul!" and that so touchingly that the worst devil could not have ridiculed it. So one day the Holy Peter went to the gate of Hell and asked: "Child, why are you always crying Paul! Paul! and that so miserably?" So the maiden replied, "Ah! dear Holy Peter, what are all the torments of Hell? Nothing at all. My Paul suffers much more, how will he endure without me? I pray you only for one thing; let me go once more on earth and let me see for one moment how it fares with him. I will then gladly remain in Hell for one hundred years longer!" "A hundred years," said Holy Peter, "consider, child, that is a long time."

"Not to me. Oh, I pray you let me once more look on my Paul on earth, and then I will certainly be quiet and take things as they come, patiently." The Holy Peter resisted long, but the poor soul gave him no rest, so at length he said: "Well, for aught I care, go; but you will repent it." And so the poor soul went on earth to Paul and when she got there she found her Paul and he was with others! and so the poor soul went quietly back to eternity and only . . . said, "I will now go back to Hell and will expiate." And the Holy Peter said to her: "The one hundred years which thou hast promised are forgiven thee; in one minute thou has gone through more than one hundred years of Hell." This is the story of the poor soul.

4

IN ONE of his frantic appeals Stephen had written Reynolds: "I have got to have at least fifteen hundred dollars this month [October]. . . . For Christ's sake get me some money quick here by cable." Reynolds, presumably, was advancing money for living expenses against manuscripts sent from Cuba. Stephen was also drawing money from the New York *Journal*; his last dispatch was filed on November 9. None of this money reached Cora.

On October 18 word had come from the British Consul at Havana, Cora told Reynolds, that Crane was no longer with the *Journal*. The Consul thought she had no further cause for worry about Crane's health or the police, "but he does give the impression that something is wrong." Stephen was "in some sort of difficulty." He had left the Hotel Pasaje; the Consul did not know his address, but had advertised in a local paper saying he had cables and letters for him. Magazines were asking for stories; and Crane's affairs in England, in a chaotic state, needed his attention—as evidenced in the plagiarism by *Illustrated Bits of* "The Bride Comes to Yellow Sky." Cora had transferred the copyright to Heinemann, who was suing the tabloid. "Very much worried," she urged Reynolds to "use every effort to induce Mr. Crane to leave Cuba and return to his work."

Cora feared "money trouble"; or worse, she saw Crane victimized and captive in the clutch of some designing female. She no doubt envisioned Mary Horan's place as a bordello from which Stephen must at all costs be rescued. For was he not a noble-hearted babe, who slew no dragons but involved himself in rescue of soiled virgins and she-vipers who turned and stung—like Amy Leslie? It was necessary for her to believe this.

Not knowing which way to turn, she addressed a desperate appeal to Conrad, who wrote in haste from Pent Farm to say he would do what he could but not to build any hopes on it, "a *most* remote chance," though the only thing he could think of. A poor businessman himself, Conrad could give her no "hints as to raising money on life insurance." Couldn't John Scott-Stokes advise her?

What kind of trouble is Stephen in? [Conrad queried.] You make me very uneasy. Are you *sure* you can bring him back? I do not doubt your influence mind! but not knowing the circumstances I do not know how far it would be feasible. In Stephen's coming back to England is *salvation* there is no doubt about that. Will he come? *Can* he come? I am utterly in the dark. . . .

Davis S. Meldrum was literary consultant in the London office of William Blackwood & Sons, Conrad's publishers. Conrad's plan was to ask Meldrum for another advance of fifty pounds for which he proposed "three securities": (1) Stephen's work; (2) Cora's property, the furniture at Ravensbrook on which she was to give a bill of sale; and (3) "my own undertaking to furnish them copy to the amount advanced should unforeseen circumstances [the not unlikely circumstance of Crane's death] prevent you and Stephen paying him back as soon as he may expect." The approach to "old man Blackwood" Conrad thought should be made through Meldrum, an admirer of Stephen and "*most* friendly"; for, though a man of good will, Blackwood "must be handled cautiously." So too thought Robert Barr, who was kept informed of the new plan; and Conrad, to whom Cora must have shown the Consul's letter, added: "I am sure you are doing and planning for the best. That is the way to rescue poor Stephen. I only wish I had something to pawn or sell; you would not have to wait long for means. As it is I've only my work and that I've offered . . . for what it is worth."

Still without a line from Crane, Cora sighed to Conrad: "How few of us realize that we are not important items in the machinery of life, and that real joy is found only in anticipation." Her letters were "one long inky howl." And into her journal went the embittered observation: "When a man does exactly what he likes and with a perfectly natural air, his friends allow him latitude so long as his domestic circle remains outwardly untroubled."

She was apprehensive that details of the Meldrum transaction might leak out to the gossip hunters, but Conrad reassured her: "I must mention here that the originals of your letters are destroyed and that the whole matter is treated on a perfectly confidential footing." He had had to let Meldrum in on the exact state of affairs "as far as we all on this side are aware of them. Would Stephen come back by himself if written to? Would he tell us *how much* is wanted to enable him to leave Havana? Would he recognize the engagements we would enter into . . . ? His future is here—I firmly believe—but will he see it? Whatever happens the matter must be kept quiet, and his reputation shielded." Conrad noted that Blackwood was already miffed. "A short letter from Stephen saying that he could not send anything would have made all the difference. It is too late now.* What do you think of writing him a strong letter urging his return and saying that we keep £50 ready for that purpose. . . . Please write."

On November 9 Cora sent Reynolds another of the communications William Crane deemed "injudicious":

> I *know*, that a friend [Conrad] has written him, and that the letter should reach him not later than the 11th of this month, offering to cable him enough money to get home if he needs it. It is the opinion of all the men who know, that Stephen's future is in England. . . . He has a great vogue here and now he must return if he is ever going to do more great work. A man must have pure wholesome air if he wishes to succeed in art. I beg you will advise Mr. Crane to return to England. He has a great future and a wonderful home awaiting him [Brede Place].

She would write, herself, to the people who had written about stories "and tell them you have stories of Mr. Crane's."

And now Reynolds was the recipient of the following from William Crane, dated November 10:

> Stephen Crane, my brother, telegraphs me from Havana to loan him some money and asks me to notify you.
> Can you tell me what the urgency is or whatever you may have to do with it? . . . I have written him at Havana, but my letters were returned as uncalled for. Do you know his city address there.

Stephen's admirer, John Scott-Stokes, the Duke of Norfolk's cousin, had come forward meanwhile to make himself responsible for three cables to Crane in Havana, and for others later sent to New York. Stokes, with a high position in the London post office, wrote Cora on November 14: "Cable dispatched to 75 Aguacale . . . this morning. Same text as Friday with addition. . . . Money shortly through General Wade." Stokes would accept no money

---

* It is significant that no story of Crane's ever appeared in *Blackwood's Edinburgh Magazine* after "The Price of the Harness," in the December issue (1898). "Old Man Blackwood" was "through" with Stephen Crane.

for the messages he sent. "What I have done is off my own bat. . . .
So that is quite clear, is it not?" Again in January, over Cora's protests, he wrote: "I don't think the cables I sent for you came to
more than £15 if so much"; anyhow, he had not the slightest intention "of ever asking you or Stephie for it and the receipts went
into the waste basket. If you two prosper you may someday send
me a cheque for some amount not greater than £15 and I will
spend it on a motor car and the babies [the Frederic children] and
paying Dr. Hugo's long bill!"

Stokes had recently been ill himself. Harold Frederic was dead.

At the time of Frederic's stroke in August Cora, who adored
children, had immediately taken in at Ravensbrook Helen, Héloïse,
and Barry, so that Kate might be relieved of their care to devote
herself to nursing Harold. He had willfully gone back to cigars
and whiskey, and he persisted in overwork. Then, one week before his death, Frederic—fed up with doctors who could not cure
him and wishing to please a devoted woman—consented to dismissal of the "medicine men" and to the substitution of a Science
practitioner at his bedside. On October 19 he died. Kate and the
practitioner, Mrs. Mills, were held for manslaughter.

Kate and her children were penniless; Frederic had made no
provision for his dependents. Homefield did not belong to him.
To cap it all, this was the critical moment seized upon by the grocer and the butcher to cut off the Crane's credit and to serve Cora
with court summonses.

She ran up to London to see Creelman, counting on help from
him. But the *Journal's* representative was out of the city; the trip
was for nothing. Robert Barr suggested also trying to see the grocer, who might be induced to withdraw the summons. "The bill is
so small that I was amazed at his action"; Barr thought it was
prompted by "spite and servants' talk." This summons, he assured
Cora, need not worry her; he would keep it to show Creelman.
There were eight days yet before anything could be done. Were
not his own bank account "in a state of relaxation, needing a
tonic," he would send her a check at once,

but if there is no cash before the eight days I will go to this grocer,
and make myself personally responsible . . . and he will accept my
surety. The trouble is that the butcher may do likewise and his bill
is more serious. [The butcher did] . . . Of course the grocer is per-

fectly within his right . . . It has been noised about . . . that you are going to leave . . . so doubtless, having been bilked before, he fears he is going to be cheated again. The only person at fault is Stephen Crane, and as he is not within cursing distance there is no use in swearing.

Barr was sure the cash would be in from the *Journal* before many days. Though housebound with rheumatism he hobbled up to town and, while waiting to see Creelman, consulted a lawyer who assured him, he told Cora, that "unless you gave the grocer your personal guarantee to pay, he cannot collect. All you have to do is to give notice that you are a married woman, that it is your husband's debt and that he is in America and will pay when he returns. It would be better to have a lawyer do this. I will see you tomorrow."

But "Old Man Blackwood," then negotiating with Reynolds for "The Price of the Harness," seems to have soured on further outlays to erratic genius. Meldrum—his man Friday—who judged a bill of sale pretty flimsy security and "Mrs. Crane's promise on behalf of her husband . . . legally, absolutely worthless," was nevertheless moved by his high opinion of Crane as a writer to promise Conrad he would do what he could among his own personal acquaintances. Perhaps "young Maqueen" (John Maqueen, a London publisher) would advance Mrs. Crane the money to fetch Stephen home. But Maqueen, as it happened, was already halfway across the Atlantic bound for New York. On November 30 Blackwood heard again from Meldrum:

Let me say again that I should have been very sorry had you advanced money further to the Cranes. I fancy he is far more foolish than you know. I can find no justification for the man, though I can [find] many excuses for one with such a strange and all-on-edge temperament as his. But as I gather from your letter that you object to my personally moving in the matter, I have told Conrad and the Mrs than I can do no more.

So now falling back on Barr's suggestion of a publisher's advance against future works—"worthless" or not as a guarantee—Cora proposed to James Pinker that a group of Crane's early stories be put into book form: probably the only unsold manuscripts she could lay hands on. Pinker advised against it. "I do not think it would be possible to dispose of the stories on the understanding that it should be announced that they were written when Mr. Crane was a lad, and it seems to me that if Mr. Crane does not think them good enough to stand on their merits, it would be better not to let them go out." She sent three of the tales to Pinker anyhow, who evidently had no trouble selling them; a loan for the means to live, obtained from Heinemann through Sidney Pawling, was quickly repaid out of advances against the magazine rights. But while publishers in Pinker's judgment were more willing to advance money on a long book, he as author's representative must be in a position to offer a definite book for delivery on a definite date. "I will gladly do all that is possible if you will tell me exactly how matters stand with regard to Mr. Crane's future work."

If she only knew!

Sometime before he left for Cuba, Crane seems to have been contemplating an historical novel dealing with the American Revolution, and the part taken by his New Jersey ancestors, "who were pretty hot people" in that war. So now that the book of short stories would not do, these plans for the Revolutionary novel, vague as they were, must have been exhumed. Cora communicated them to Pinker, who communicated in turn with the house of Methuen and its editor Grant Richards. Pinker also let it be known to Richards that Crane would be bringing back with him material for a second book of war experiences. Then, as the publishers quite naturally wanted confirmation of their tentative agreement concerning the novel, another of Jack Stokes' cables was dispatched in all haste to Crane in Havana. Pinker also cabled. When the reply was received, there was a misunderstanding over the size of the advance. "I am glad to know the terms," Pinker wrote Cora on December 1, "though they do not quite agree with your instructions, as I understood Mr. Crane wished for only £75 now." Pinker thought he could persuade Methuen to increase the payment, but before negotiating further he would like an assurance from Mr. Crane that he would be able to deliver the manuscript by the date specified (July). On December 9 Pinker wrote again: "I presume that you have a formal power of attorney from Mr. Crane [which she had not], as you will need it, if the publisher should ask for its production"; and on December 12, with reference to Crane's continued absence: "The circumstances weaken one's hands very much, so that we cannot do as well as we ought."

While these negotiations were in progress, word came from Havana which brought joy to Cora and Conrad. On receiving the money sent by Stokes through General Wade—an advance presumably from Methuen, or Heinemann, or both—Stephen announced by cable through Thomas Cook & Son that he had sailed for New York.

True, the lights of Broadway were a long way still from Oxted, but their darling boy was homeward bound at last! Cora lost no time in relaying the news to Conrad. And they were like two fond parents rejoicing together at the bedside of a beloved, wayward, wholly unpredictable child who by one of God's miracles had just been spared to them. "You made us quite happy with your letter," wrote Conrad on December 4. He had had a couple of pretty bad days himself after hearing from Meldrum "about that wretched McQueen. . . . It was an immense relief to hear that you had been lucky in some other quarter. Do you think Stephen will be in England before Christmas?" The story in *Blackwood's* ("The Price of the Harness" had just appeared in *Blackwood's Edinburgh Magazine*) was "magnificent." It was Stephen all himself, and a little more; and the very truth of art. "There is an added ampleness in his method which makes me augur a magnificent future for his coming work. Let him only come—and work! . . . Ah! but I do feel relieved. . . ."

5

ONE woman's rigid determination to hold on to the husband who wished a divorce in order to marry another woman had not seemed to the friends of Harold and Kate Frederic sufficient warrant for their excommunication from the society of decent people. It was, after all, a situation not uncommon, in the United States or in England, at the turn of the century. But when, in connection with the trumped-up murder charge against Kate, the details of Frederic's private life were dragged through the courts after his death and brutally converted into a public scandal (which delighted his enemies), Cora, recognizing certain rather obvious parallels with her own case, went into action, an aroused Brünhilde.

"Mark and I could have wept with indignation over the treatment of our dear Katy by those beasts," wrote Kate Frederic's niece, Mabel Barr; and she thought Cora's help of Kate "so splendid." A fund for "the babies"? "Nothing could be more practical." But how strong sympathy seemed for "the other side." That appeal in the newspaper was amazing!

Mrs. Barr, whose husband, Mark, was no relation of Robert Barr, was referring to an appeal broadcast in a London newspaper by the friends of the lawful Mrs. Frederic, who looked upon Kate as a usurper, and, rallying to the cause of the widow and the orphans, had formed a committee. Frederic's death, the advertisement stated, "left his widow and four children entirely without resources," rendering necessary "this appeal to his friends and the public on their behalf." It was desired to make provision for the education of the two boys, aged ten and twelve. For the girls, seventeen and twenty, it was hoped "some occupation might shortly be found." The widow's need, meanwhile, was pronounced "urgent." "By the terms of Mr. Frederic's will the English royalties and copyrights of his works are left to his widow, but this possible source of revenue is so heavily mortgaged that it must be some considerable time before any income, however small, can be looked for from this direction."*

Not a word about the three other children, who, being illegitimate, did not exist for those dear "friends" who had rushed into court to have Kate jailed on the manslaughter charge. The appeal was signed by the editor of the *Daily Chronicle*, Mr. W. J. Fisher, as "Honorary Secretary and Treasurer," a fact which strongly suggests the *Chronicle* as the paper in which the appeal was published. Sidney S. Pawling also had associated himself with the committee as co-trustee. The rest of the long list of signers—aristocrats, clergymen, M.P.'s, and individuals prominent in the publishing world and the arts—reads like an index to the social register. When Cora suggested to Mr. Fisher that a portion of committee funds be released for the support of Kate's three young children,

---

* From a printed circular, "The Late Harold Frederic," distributed by the friends of Mrs. Frederic and published simultaneously in a London newspaper. Its appeal for funds is followed by an impressive list of signers, together with the name of the officers and trustees administering the Fund. Frederic's American copyrights and royalties were left in his will, of which Judge Alton B. Parker was executor, to Kate and her children.

that gentleman became smitten with a common form of legalistic paralysis. "We, the executive, dare not divert any portion of it [the Fund] without the sanction of the Committee and the subscribers."

Cora, who had sheltered Kate at Ravensbrook as soon as she was released on bail, promptly sat down and wrote to the signers one by one, presenting her side of the case, and in the majority of instances was successful in obtaining donations. For, as the dramatist Arthur Wing Pinero* put it, reducing the matter to a somewhat verbose nutshell: "It is a pity that, when the original appeal . . . was made, an ample and explicit statement was not put forward of the whole sum of the human legacy bequeathed by Mr. Frederic to the world. In matters of this sort the question of legitimacy or illegitimacy stands for little, the money should have been apportioned fairly among all those who are equally helpless." Or as Hall Caine† summed it up, "A man's children are his children, and that is all that remains to be said on the subject."

In this painful dilemma it was kindhearted Jack Stokes who came forward with a proposal to set up another committee, with Cora and himself co-signers of all checks drawn against committee funds. To distinguish between factions, on Stokes' advice Kate now took one of her family names, conferring it on the children and discarding her maiden name of Lyon—by which she was, nevertheless, persistently known to those who took "the other side."

But in the controversy that raged through London, feeling in some quarters was fully as intense over Kate's Christian Science views as her morals. Frank Danby Frankau, an agnostic old gentleman "anxious to do more for the children of this love union than

* British actor-playwright, best known for his play, *The Second Mrs. Tanqueray*, which was hailed as a daring example of social realism and acclaimed by its admirers as the best English drama since *The School for Scandal*.

† Sir Thomas Henry Hall Caine, British author, who lived on the Isle of Man. He wrote many novels on Biblical themes, which like his somewhat sensationalized tales of Manx life enjoyed great popularity from the last decade of Queen Victoria's reign up to World War I. A number of his novels were dramatized and had equal success as plays. One of these, *The Christian*, was occupying the limelight when Hall Caine was a guest at Brede Place, causing Crane to confer on him the deflationary sobriquet of "Christ on the Mountain of Man."

could be measured by a small subscription" wrote: "I did not seek out my poor friend at the time of the inquest—because of her association with Mrs. Mills, with whom I am personally acquainted —and who I *know* to be a thief and a liar and whom I *believe* to be also a constructive murderer—as I could not trust myself not to say this in public, and *prove* the major part of it—I stayed away. [How fortunate that he did!] But Kate's errors of judgment and their fatal consequences, cannot blot out in my eyes her brave and womanly life with Harold Frederic." He only hoped the children might be brought up "away from even the shadow of the hideous superstition that destroyed their father."

Mrs. Julia Field-King, a Christian Scientist who gave six pounds to Cora's fund, was equally positive that "Miss Lyon," for whom she had "a most loving regard," was not truly of the faith. "Had Miss Lyon been a Christian Scientist, Mr. Frederic's household would have been quite differently constituted. . . . God's edict is —We must reap what we sow—then the way out of undesirable reaping is to cease sowing, and that is what Christian Science tells us how to do."

George Gissing,* who had reaped the social punishments meted out to those entering into a union outside wedlock and later suffered in an unhappy marriage, and to whom Stokes had revealed "all that ought to be told about this sad affair," wrote:

* English novelist, whose most successful work, artistically and financially, was *New Grub Street* (1891), in which the grinding poverty and bitterness of the struggle to rise from the ranks of modern journalism to a position in literature are pictured with grim realism. Gissing himself remained to the end of his life a dreamer overwhelmed by the realities of daily existence. He compensates by conferring on his gentle scholar Ryecroft (*The Private Papers of Henry Ryecroft*, 1903) a quiet fulfillment at the end, longed for but never attained in his own career. For a short, bluntly stated but sympathetic, account of Gissing's struggle see H. G. Wells' *Experiment in Autobiography*, pp. 481-493. See also Gissing's letters to his family (London: Constable, 1927).
Cora received from Gissing, after Stephen's death, a letter warmly eulogistic of Crane and his work (No. 290 in the Columbia University Crane Collection). The two men had exchanged letters, and Gissing hoped to meet Crane. He had been one of the contributors to "The Ghost" and a signer of the autographed program, but owing to his residence in France at the time was unable to be present at the play's performance during the Christmas house party.

Head of Harold Frederic from Helen Crane's sketchbook. Columbia University Crane Collection.

I feel that everyone who has read with understanding and pleasure any of Frederic's recent work owes to *her* a vast debt of gratitude, that but for his true companion, his real wife, this work would never have been done. I cannot express the loathing with which I regard any man or woman who speaks slightingly of her. Surely it must be some solace to her to remember that she *did* play that part in Frederic's life—that she saved him and enabled him to do admirable things. Impossible that she should want for friends, so long as our world does not go quite brash and brainless . . .

Head of Cora Crane from Helen Crane's sketchbook. Columbia University Crane Collection.

Henry James, whom Frederic is said to have called "an effeminate old donkey who lives with a herd of other donkeys around him and insists on being treated as if he were the Pope," was a signer of the publicized petition; but he answered Cora's appeal with five pounds. "Deeper than I can say," he wrote, "is my commiseration for those beautiful little children."

But Conrad, who considered Cora "the only Christian in sight" in the whole affair, "exercising that rarest of the Creed's virtues:

that of charity," had little sympathy for the dead man or the mother of his progeny. "My admiration of your courageous conduct exists side by side with an utter disapproval of those whom you (in *your* own extremity) befriend."

Meanwhile, lost on the champions of morality in the hullabaloo over the Frederic case was a simple fact which did not escape Cora: that only the intransigence of the woman from Utica, New York, had stood in the way of remedying the wrong done the world by the illicit pair. Mrs. James Creelman, who in her husband's absence took charge of his correspondence, felt obliged to say, frankly, that she had "a great scorn for Kate Lyon and the evil influence she has exerted over a morally weak man"; and that she found "the irony of such a woman asking or expecting help . . . beyond credence after the deprivation she has forced upon Mrs. Frederic." Alice Creelman had no doubt that her husband's sentiments were identical with her own. Her letter, in the best style of outraged womanhood, late Victorian, roused Cora Crane to battle fury. Cora's reply:

December 30, 1898

Dear Madam:

I thank you for your reply to my letter asking for *private* subscription for the support of the three youngest children of the late Harold Frederic. In justice to their mother, let me say that she refused, absolutely, to join in a public appeal for help thinking, as I do, such an appeal in shocking taste. Nor did she have any knowledge, until yesterday when I wrote informing her, of *this* fund for the children.

The people whom you have heard "discuss this unfortunate scandal" are naturally, not the people one would look to for help. . . . The nasty taste that such a discussion would leave in their mouths would strike through to the organ which they use solely to pump blood—blood soured by lack of true charity—to the brain. One wonders if they think themselves Christians? And how they dare set themselves up as models of virtuous morality, when they have the example of Christ's loving kindness to sinners before them.

How can we judge another, we . . . so full of sin and weakness? And how can any creature knowing itself mortal lose an opportunity to be charitable in the true sense? Judging not!

To me, the supreme egotism of women who never having been

tempted, and so knowing nothing of the temptation of another's soul, set themselves up on their pedestals of self-conceit and conscious virtue, judging their unfortunate sisters guilty alike, is the hardest thing in life. If we women who are beloved and sheltered, would help those less fortunate of our sex to help themselves, (and this is not done by using a club or turning ourselves into shrews under cover of outraged innocence) the world would be a sweeter, purer place to live in and we ourselves . . . more worthy of happiness.

For the mere handful of the world's pigmies who do not leave as much trace of having existed, when their time comes to enter into the unknown, as a flower; these moralists swollen . . . with the knowledge of not having themselves sinned a particular sin, who rush to drag a dead man's name through the mire; to these poor souls scandal and the throwing of mud—*and* stones—is meat and strong drink. They roll it on their tongues as a sweet morsel, and the wine of it is the highest exultation they know! For those who have no charity I ask God's mercy: they are so poor a lot!

You say you are surprised that I should ask anyone to help Miss Lyon with the burden of her children. My surprise is, that people can visit the sins of the parents upon those innocent babies. If self-respect can come to mankind in proving their loathing of sin (and how can we judge the laws of God—by laws of state, or those of our theological brothers?) by not helping these children to bread and shelter, let them so get what comfort they can . . . with the knowledge of their own loved ones warm and fed. I have sheltered these children for five months in my own home and with my own name—and if all the world line themselves up to fight these babies, I will still shelter *them* and God will help me.

Yours very truly,
Cora Crane

I would say it is my wish to board the *children* with some very good Catholics in the country.

But while Kate Frederic was unsuccessfully seeking employment among the London publishing houses, friends of "the other side" were loudly proclaiming that her "abilities," her many friends and "rich relatives" rendered her need quite disproportionate to that of Mrs. Frederic. Cora had written to Sidney Pawling in the hope that he might find something for Kate with his firm, but the Heinemann editor wanted "time to think it over." Typical of Stephen Crane's curious ambivalence was his appeal, later, to the editor of the *Morning Post* for aid and employment for Mrs. Frederic—whose supporters had tried to have Kate put away on a murder charge!

Mabel Barr grieved "to think of all the dear Homefield things being sold." Cora had dug up several rosebushes from Homefield and sent them to her at Rosbrin, the Cheshire home of the Mark Barrs. Frank Harris* and a certain Mr. Lawrence [unidentified] —Mabel wrote Cora—were to have assumed the legal expenses of the trial, "but Frank Harris left without paying a sou and papa Lawrence was furious at having the whole bill to foot. . . . How small rich men can be."

Cora's own fortunes were at their lowest ebb. Pinker could place immediately a 3,500-word story by Stephen, but with no manuscript at hand they must wait for Reynolds to forward one from America. Then Cora suggested that, as a stopgap, she might write articles on her war experiences. Pinker, who had not known that she had been a correspondent, seemed highly pleased with the idea and suggested at once that she call on him in town; "we might discuss things." But before she could keep the appointment, Pinker had called on the editor of *The Wide World* magazine: "His idea is that you might take some of the most exciting incidents in your experiences . . . and write each one up in the form of a short story —making it as thrilling as facts will allow." The editor of course expected her to do one on approval; if it was to his liking, he would commission others.

Nothing came of it. Distractions and heartbreak pressed in from all sides; and the book for Methuen was still hanging fire. Pinker wrote Cora, on hearing of Stephen's expected homecoming, "directly Mr. Crane arrives, I think we shall have no difficulty in set-

---

* Irish-American author and editor of the English *Fortnightly Review* and *Saturday Review*. A witty poseur, braggart, and something of a charlatan, Harris managed to make himself the center of a brilliant group of younger writers which included George Bernard Shaw and Max Beerbohm, both of whom he later claimed to have discovered. Harris considered himself an intimate friend of Harold Frederic, but during the trial he defaulted on promises—behavior which seems wholly in character. For a lively sketch of Harris see Wells' *Experiment in Autobiography*, pp. 438-446; and Van Wyck Brooks' *The Confident Years* (New York: Dutton, 1952), pp. 239-263. A recent biography of Harris is Vincent Brome's *Frank Harris* (London: Castle, 1959).

tling up for his novel on satisfactory terms." If they could wait till then, Pinker would "be able to do better than would be possible under present circumstances."

6

"How DO you persuade anybody to do anything by cables and letters?" Stephen wrote an old friend, Mrs. William Sonntag, on November 28. "I am very anxious to have Mrs. Crane come to this country. Mrs. Crane is very anxious to have me come back to England. We are carrying on a duel at long range, with ink."

Near the time of their first parting, in Florida, Cora had written in her little red Manuscript Book: "We could not love in this world [Florida]. Something went astray with us." And now, in this long range "duel with ink":

> Are faithfulness, and love, and sweet grateful memories no good? Is it no good that we should keep our silent promises on which others build because they believe in our love and truth? Or is it good that we should harden our hearts against all the wants and hopes of those who have depended on us?

During those nine bitter-long months, alone with her thoughts, she must have become aware of their true position before the world. Even with her Stewart past all around them, not ten years away, England was safer than the United States. For until she and Stephen could produce those necessary evidences of legality—a marriage license and divorce papers—it would be folly to think of living in America; the past would follow them wherever they went. He, babe that he was, had not grasped this fact.

If Crane, while enjoying his wartime freedom in Cuba, secretly hoped that Cora would find some other willing cavalier onto whose shoulders his responsibility toward her might be shifted, there is no positive evidence that this represented his final wish. Such evidence as there is would seem to indicate that Stephen meant to remain with her: the letter to Dorothy Brandon of May 19, stating his intention of returning to England when the war was over, and a fiercely possessive jealousy of Cora, as we see it reflected in the "Intrigue" poems and subsequently in the will he made at

Brede Place. The theory that the last eighteen months of his feverish life—from the Cuban adventure to Badenweiler—is the record
of his failure to escape from the fatal clutch of Cora fails to take
account of personality tensions which were present long before
Cora came into his life and which Crane himself recognized but
was never able to resolve: those "colossal impulses more strong
than chains," whirling him in ambivalence toward self-destruction.
"I cannot help vanishing and disappearing and dissolving," he had
written Appleton's editor, Ripley Hitchcock, in 1896. "It is my
foremost trait."

Men like Stephen Crane always come back to the women whose
hearts they break, if for no other reason than that they cannot do
without them. Between Cora and himself there was, on his side,
affection and compatibility—much nonsense to the contrary; on
hers, reckless passion and a devotion capable of self-immolation
without counting costs: qualities which, were these two given
time and the willingness to discipline themselves, held all the potentialities for lasting happiness. That they were not given time
made theirs one of the tragedies of life's unfinished business.

About November 20 Stephen reached New York and made a
flying visit to Washington, where the anguish of politicians over
the lot of our troops in the Cuban war made one who had seen
men die without heroics retch with disgust.

I understand, now, that Congressmen and Senators rolled in august
pain by night and sat weeping by day. . . . This warhorse told me so.
He told me that he visited the War Department hourly on July First.
I asked him what good that did and he said it showed his interest in
the campaign. Nobody would believe in him. I can't believe in him
but it is true that I saw him.

At Las Guasimas, missing most of the battle, Crane ran five miles
to the coast to get help for his friend Edward Marshall, shot
through the back; sent off Marshall's *Journal* dispatch for which
his employers, Pulitzer's *World*, never forgave him; led the
stretcher bearers back to the spot behind the front lines where
Marshall lay propped against a tree, and ran back again with them
to Siboney. At Guantanamo, in the frying heat, he had carried
water to thirsty Marines, his little figure, festooned with water
bottles, laboring up the steep slope; and in dark of night, going

through the ambush of Spanish guerrillas who exchanged signals in the call of the wood dove, he carried messages to and from the outpost positions of Marine Corps commanders Major G. F. Elliott, Captain Charles L. McCawley, and Major Henry Clay Cochran. These men later recalled with affectionate pride the service Crane rendered them, and McCawley wrote: ". . . we regard you as an honorary member of the Corps." It got Crane officially mentioned for bravery. But more important, as he saw it, was to have won acceptance from such men as these, men who under impossible conditions of jungle, heat, and disorganization, remained serenely "intent on business."

So in this war fought under his own Stars and Stripes, he, the rabbit and the weed, "had been to touch the great death, and found that, after all, it was but the great death." He had met the Enemy —and acted right. And now he was, he said, "too tired to breathe." He wanted nothing but sleep. At Howells' home after a luncheon in his honor he fell asleep unashamedly on a couch. Garland, shocked at his appearance, had earlier advised, "Go into the country somewhere, and settle down, and get back your tone."

It seems certain that he did not go to Hartwood or Port Jervis. Despite letters date-lined from Hartwood—December 27, 28, and 29—a niece is positive he did not go. His brother Edmund's home at Hartwood was the permanent address he generally used when he was on the move, and it was probably the one he now named to some of his correspondents. A reason for *not* going to Hartwood would certainly have been his reluctance to face the family, until he could safely and decently introduce Cora as his wife. To certain of his friends, his agent, and very likely his publishers, the secret was out. He did not tell his brothers—though Ed came to see him in New York before he sailed—until, back in England, he learned of Cora's cablegram to William Crane.

House-hunting in New York and toying with the idea of buying a ranch in Texas, Stephen dallied, unable to come to a decision, missing old friends who had scattered and seeing much of newer ones—the music critic James Huneker, the painter Albert Pinkham Ryder. Then his mind was made up when, without warning, the all-powerful stick struck again, leaving more bruises. "For a mild and melancholy kid," said Huneker, "he certainly had fallen completely into the garbage can of gossip."

On November 23 he strolled into Delmonico's with Huneker. They had cocktails together. Crane was observed, and when they left a discussion began: Was it true that Crane had tried to get himself killed in Cuba? Somebody was incredulous. A notorious barfly named McCumber butted in: It was true, said McCumber. Not only that; Crane was dying of venereal disease, everybody knew it. Richard Harding Davis, dining in a corner, got up to escort the loudmouth outside, returned with a cut lip, and asked the men he knew at the bar to forget the affair. It promptly went everywhere. Howells was informed that the committee on admissions would blackball Crane if his name were proposed at the most eminent literary club in Gotham. Then one evening in December as Stephen was leaving the theatre with friends—Mrs. Sonntag, her seventeen-year-old son, and her cousin the Reverend Patrick Hart —a policeman shoved through the crowd, "asked if his name was Stephen Crane" and ordered: "Come 'round to the station, you drunken bum!" When Mrs. Sonntag, white-haired and on crutches, cried out, she was silenced with oaths. "That will be enough from you, you goddam French whore!" But for the priest's intervention Crane, standing rigid and silent, would have been manhandled and booked by the irate cop. This incident did not get into the papers, but young Sonntag was asked about it at school. "Someone," he said, "had sent out the word to 'get' Mr. Crane."

Stephen Crane was *persona non grata* with the New York police. Two-and-a-half years earlier, after Crane had insisted on appearing in court to denounce their treatment of streetwalkers, he had sent a long wire to Commissioner Theodore Roosevelt, which was read out to some of the ranking members of the force. The police neither forgot nor forgave. The theatre incident was followed by two more occurrences on Madison Avenue, when Stephen was set upon by an unidentified assailant. Then on December 20 he cabled Cora. And to someone else he wrote:

I am going to stay in England for some time. It seems that in New York, outside the immediate circle of men who know me well, I am some kind of Simon Legree who goes around knocking women into the gutter and then walking on them. If I was a grocery boy or a hired man or a bank clerk no one would give a cuss what I did. But I am a writer so all bets are doubled.

With the arrival of Stephen's cablegram Cora, with hardly a shilling in her purse, felt the Christmas spirit and sent an immense box of toys to Conrad's little boy, Borys. That week she wrote Edward Garnett, who sent her his essay on Crane which had just appeared in the *Academy*:

> From the Cooks tourist people, I learn that Stephen starts from Havana for home this week. We will let you know when he arrives and I hope you will be one of the first to welcome him. It will be such larks taking him to Brede Place. Perhaps you could manage to give us a day and go too?

Crane's abrupt return to the Cuban capital is unexplained. From the geographical standpoint, to go to England by way of Havana seems about as illogical as to approach the Arctic Circle via the equator. In Jacksonville, on December 28, hard up for cash as usual, he obtained fifty dollars by wire from his old friend Willis Hawkins;* and continued on his way to the fever-haunted paradise of fortune hunters and romance.

Cora, when writing Garnett, made no mention of the fact that Stephen had lingered a whole month in New York, seeing friends and enjoying himself, before making up his mind to return to England. In an earlier undated letter to Moreton Frewen—probably written about December 22—she likewise omitted any reference to Cuba, thus making it appear to Frewen that Crane was coming straight home from New York. "The horror of the last few months is almost at an end. Mr. Crane is in New York settling up some business affairs, but sails next Saturday week [December 31]."

This letter in Cora's hand, headed "Ravensbrook," oddly enough is written on Brede Place stationery which she must have ordered immediately after the first word of Stephen's earlier departure from Havana reached her, about December 1. Her housekeeper and cook, Mrs. Bryant—she wrote Mr. Frewen—was receiving wages up to January 27, but had been told she might leave by the

---

* The Western Union telegraph receipt for the $50 Hawkins wired Crane, dated December 28, 1898, Jacksonville (now in the Barrett Collection at the University of Virginia), disposes of any possibility that Crane was at Hartwood at this time.

twentieth if she wished, as the Cranes would be in Brede Place then. Some of the household were "going in" next week. Cora had sent to Brede "over three hundred very choice roses. One in particular, budded by a very prominent author" —whom one takes to be Ford Hueffer—she had had planted against the front of the house, sure that later on when the Frewens themselves were occupying the house the Cranes would "always be remembered by our rose garden."

Stephen, nevertheless, up to January 2 still had not announced the date of his expected arrival and Cora had heard nothing more since the cablegram of December 20. Conrad sadly remarked to Meldrum, "Mrs Crane still without news. I don't know what to think"; and Sidney Pawling, writing Cora on the same day, also expressed surprise: "I thought he would be home by now, as the money [from Heinemann] was sent some weeks ago."

At last, on January 10, Cora could write Garnett that she was "momentarily expecting a wire saying the ship which carries my dear one is sighted." The *Manitou* was due that day or next morning, and if time allowed she would go to Gravesend to meet Stephen. "We will go to Brede, perhaps on Thursday or Friday." She would wire, but would Mr. Garnett not stop in to see Stephen? She so hoped the storm they were having had not delayed the ship!

Robert Barr, held in town by bad weather and business, was not on hand to greet the returned bad boy. But how was the veal holding out, was there anything left of the fatted calf? Barr would also like to hear "what the master of the art of fiction" had to say for himself.

How long is he going to remain sane? Everything on earth is his if he mixes a little common sense with his genius. If not, he merely adds a unit to the long list of men of great power who were damn fools. I think you had better put him in irons, and see that he hasn't a loaded revolver when I get there, for I am coming unarmed except with curses. I am going to curse him up hill and down dale. . . .

PART TWO

(January, 1899 — June, 1902)

Cora Crane and Henry James at the benefit party, Brede Rectory Gardens, August 23, 1899. Gift of Henry W. Walters.

Brede Place: Ghosts at a Christmas Party

chapter 5

"ON TUESDAY afternoon [January 17, 1899]," Cora wrote Edward Garnett, "Stephen suddenly made up his mind to go to Brede, so off we went to Hastings." Driving over, they reached Brede Place after dark, ate a supper of ham and eggs beside the open kitchen fire, then tramped through frosty starlight to a cottage in the village where they put up for the night. The next day they spent exploring the old house. Stephen was "mad" about the place! He said that "a solemn feeling of work came over him there"; she hoped "the perfect quiet and the freedom from a lot of dear good people, who take his mind from his work, will let him show the world a book that will live." "His great difficulty," she had told Garnett in December, "is a lack of that machine-like application which makes a man work steadily." But for Garnett's judgment that Crane's powers might decline "when the picturesque phases of the environment that nurtured him give out," Cora had only the scorn reserved for the blackest of heresies. "The beautiful thoughts in Stephen's mind are simply endless!"

The house was "a pretty fine affair," Stephen wrote Sanford Bennett, "and Cora believes that Sir Walter Scott designed it for her. . . . We shall move in as soon as we can. I enclose 10 pounds. Do I owe you more than that?" Other debts must wait while he met his obligations to friends. A wire from Queenstown had gone to Conrad, another from Oxted with a draft for fifty pounds, all of which Conrad thought, "would be damnable bosh but for the fifty guineas which just saves me from battering my head against the walls."

With the dogs, the Cranes came on Sunday, February 11, to Brede Place and were "camping out," Cora wrote Mrs. Edward Pease, "till our things arrive. It is very jolly and we are happy"— though it seemed as if they "must wake up to find there is no 'truly Bweed' after all, as Barry says." The Frederic children, who had arrived first with their governess Mrs. Lily Burke, welcomed them with shouts. The young Frederics—Barry, Héloïse, and Helen— aged four, six, and seven, had been boarded with a Catholic family named Burke, who had a farm in Kildare where Stephen and Cora had stayed with Harold and Kate on the Irish trip. At Ravensbrook the eleven-year-old Michael Pease had fallen in love with an indifferent Helen, who soon went to stay with her mother in London and Liverpool. Cora sent Mrs. Pease the manuscript of a story Stephen had written for the Whilomville series, around the shy boy's unrequited attachment to the infant charmer; and thanked her for the gift of a warming pan the Cranes would have good use for in the drafty old house, "but you are always doing nice things for us."

"We love Brede with a wildness which I think is a little pathetic," Stephen presently wrote Mrs. Frewen. ". . . at Oxted we were enduring a great deal of bother and really we were too down-trodden to venture a word lest our friends heard only a moan." Here, in contrast, "the very atmosphere makes our heads lighter. I attack anew my infamous business of making a novel finished [*Active Service*] before March 30." The Cranes would "joyfully" accept her kind invitation to luncheon before Mr. Frewen's departure for America. But Stephen regretted his going as America was "wretchedly cold and disagreeable at this time of year and in this particular year." It was "good" of Mrs. Frewen to like the book, a copy of the American edition of *The Open Boat, & Other Stories* he had inscribed and sent to her from Oxted, "though it is not so much of a book that I should seek to mention it in this note" —but he personally liked it, "which is ever a thing a man can seldom say about his work."

Perhaps, for the first time since coming to England Stephen was happy in these surroundings, where he had a horse to ride; a fast canter around the little hundred-acre park before breakfast awoke memories of Hartwood. Not even the nagging of creditors could seriously upset his mood of content. In March he wrote

Moreton Frewen: "We have now been in the old house nearly a month and every day it seems more beautiful to us. Each time we catch a new view—notably when walking down from the village —we have new raptures." Friends were "astonished," and Stephen was "holding delicately in check two rampant students of old English houses and several journalists all of whom wish to burst into articles." He usually "let them bowl away, provided they allow me supervision of all things that are personal matters. For instance, an interviewer once declared . . . that in appearance I was very ugly and so when he came again I sent him away in tears." If he managed the *career* of the old house, probably nothing would be said "to annoy any of us aesthetically." His own friends, Garnett and others, he felt quite safe with, "but the ones I do not know so well frighten me a little." The weather was now delightful, "raw-gold sunshine"; he was finishing his novel rapidly in the room just over the porch. "I wish it were a better novel. I fear that in later years people who wish the house well will be saying that Stephen Crane did *not* write *Active Service* in the room over the porch at Brede Place. Would you name a day for us to come to London? Please."

Crane's letters to his landlord and generous friend, written at this time, support the conclusion that he was actually as much in love as Cora with "the wonderful old house." Warm, intimate, revealing, these letters speak of household concerns and the daily life at Brede Place. Hence both as evidence, and for the light they cast on the many-sided and always self-contradictory personality of a genius who so seldom revealed himself outside of his work, they are unique.

[April 10] We will be greatly delighted to have the supply of fresh mushrooms and will have spawn placed as you direct. All does indeed go well and we are comfortable in our isolation. . . . If you succeed me here next year, we will depart, at any rate, with a sense of a delightful sojourn. During these late heavy storms the whole house has sung like a harp and all the spouts have been wailing to us. It is rather valkyric. The servants are more impressed than we would like them to be and we have not yet found maids who will sleep in the house. We are expecting spring every moment. . . .

None of the locks and doors at Brede would stay shut, a circumstance of course wonderfully favorable to the prestige of the bloody shade of old Sir Goddard Oxenbridge. No servant could ever be induced to sleep there at night. The truth was that the old wooden latches, worn smooth and slippery, needed pegs to hold them. On his first visit to Brede Place, in April, Robert Barr slept in the "Gallows Room," but though conscious of drafts and eerie creakings and groanings was keenly disappointed that "the ghost was so unsocial as not to call." Barr's "disappointment" is recorded in some doggerel verses he sent his host and hostess after a later visit to their Sussex "castle"—"The Tiresome Ghost of Somberly Hall." Stephen, looking forward to a visit from the Frewens during the week of May 15, wrote Moreton Frewen:

If you can stay the night we will be very glad and can put you up comfortably. The ghost has been walking lately but we cannot catch him. Perhaps when the real Frewen sleeps under his roof he may condescend to display himself to all of us.

Stephen's swords and Mexican blankets, stored at Hartwood, were shipped over to hang in the entrance hall, with a captured Spanish flag he had brought back from Cuba. The long oak-paneled baronial hall, entered from the right, the core of the original house, now became the main living room. Although antique-hunting had not yet become a fad of rich Americans, Cora was clever at picking up odds and ends with which she managed to outfit a dozen rooms. The rest, including Sir Goddard's chapel, which the bailiff's family had used as a storage place for apples and potatoes, had to remain closed off. "I hasten to say that when you send anything down," Stephen told Mr. Frewen, "we shall store it in one of the empty rooms with our best care."

Cora's resourcefulness, a guest remembers, unearthed "a lot of lovely old four-poster beds" then doing duty as chicken coops; she "bought them for a song and had them rubbed down and fitted with mattresses." The dining room had a long refectory table, and such other oddments as a cricket bat and a Greek water barrel. But rushes on the stone floor, from the brook, brought smiles from the Peases at this modern aping of the Elizabethans; acidulous comment by Ford Hueffer and some of the "Indians" gave rise to the fantasy that the Cranes tossed bones to their dogs under the table—no less than thirty hounds! Lady Randolph Churchill was to find Stephen's manner at London dinners "over formal"; and it did not occur to the scoffers that rushes are more easily come by than Persian rugs. "A paradox established itself," Beer notes: "To some of his English friends Brede seemed a Bohemian stronghold while roaming Americans thought Stephen Crane in severe evening dress surrounded by formal gowns and black coats a most unhallowed spectacle, the Bohemian turned snob."

Conditions at Brede Place were certainly primitive according to present-day standards; but the longevity of those rushes and of the legends that surrounded them is noteworthy. A.E.W. Mason* writing to Vincent Starrett nearly a half century later—October 4, 1945—complains that "the house . . . had no proper plumbing or furniture"; and allegedly quoting Crane's physician, "he [Crane] should never have stayed" in it. Stephen, he adds, "was a great enthusiast and if he had been a little less 'Early English' just to suit Brede Place, it is possible that he might have lived longer. . . . You couldn't heat the place and the winter can be pretty harsh" (as though one would expect to find houses in Victorian England equipped with modern plumbing and central heating!). But Mason's hindsight was anticipated in Hueffer's memoirs, and in those of another Brede visitor, Karl Edwin Harriman. Hueffer's teary lament pictures the "ill-fated mansion . . . in a damp hollow . . . full of evil influences," and is answered in one word by Edith Richie (Mrs. I. Howland Jones), who also was there: "Rubbish! It [Brede House] stood high, looking down over a little valley where flocks of sheep cropped the good grass."

Dinner at Brede Place, according to Mrs. Conrad, was an affair of hazardous and peculiar uncertainty. The Cranes had inherited with the house a cook who indulged rather too freely in the bottle; a picturesque old coachman-gardener named Mack, with a long white beard and full of years, who bore a striking resemblance to Tolstoy; and a crotchety old serving-man, Heather, also given to little nips on the sly, who when required to let the dogs out—there were five—"would solemnly kick each one down the steps if no

---

* Alfred Edward Woodley Mason (1865-1948), British novelist and playwright. Mason was the author of a series of detective novels centering around the character of Inspector Hanaud, of the Paris Sûreté. Treading in the footsteps of Poe and Maurice LeBlanc, he became one of the early popularizers of the "whodunit." He also wrote one or two historical novels, and a life of Sir Francis Drake.

one were looking." As the Frewens had made the one condition absolute that the servants should go with the house, the Mark Barrs took the Greek, Adoni, until a place was found for him with the Pease family at Limpsfield. The cook, though a truly superior woman in her gastronomic art,

had often to be bribed to function in the evening with a bottle of brandy. The chances of dinner—at eight—were often very small, especially when there were many people expected. The cook would appear and announce in the most truculent tone that she was even at that moment departing. Cora Crane, at her wits' end for the moment, would wring her hands and appeal to Stephen. He in turn would give her one glance and solemnly ring the bell. Like clockwork the old butler appeared and handed a bottle of brandy to the thirsty woman . . . and an hour or so later a perfect dinner would be served.

The Cranes laughingly told their guests "modern improvements" dated from Elizabethan times. But to Hueffer and Sanford Bennett, who saw no charm in a picturesque old ruin equipped with ghost but lacking every comfort, the fact was not amusing; and Mason objected to the bats flying in at his bedroom windows before the candle was doused. Illumination was by lamp or candlelight; water had to be hand-pumped and brought in from outside; the house boasted only one indoor toilet; and most of the heat from the open fireplaces escaped up the wide-backed chimneys. But Cora's housekeeping arrangements had provided a laundry room where all the washing and ironing, including linen, was done by the "procession of really slatternly girls" Jessie Conrad objected to, chambermaids and scullions who appeared at the back door each morning and faded away at evening. The children had their own "dayroom" and "sleeping room." Hueffer mentions "beer barrels set up at odd corners, and barons of beef for real tramps at the kitchen door"— from which one gathers that the cook's disposition having been sufficiently sweetened on snorts from the brandy bottle, handouts were dispensed to the poor of the neighborhood in true baronial style.

But for the benefit of those who expect to find in the household setup at Brede Place the epitome of waste, it is worth noting that the rent of forty pounds a year to Mr. Frewen was somewhat less than half the sum owed for Ravensbrook; and even old Mack, with rather severe notions of upholding past grandeur, was critical of his new master for keeping so few servants! "We like Mack very much," Stephen wrote, "but he sometimes complains of the inconveniences, and sometimes longs for five or six footmen which of course we do not need."

Mrs. Conrad asserts that Cora had taken for her bedroom "the ballroom," an apartment so vast that the huge four-poster, on the dais intended for the orchestra, looked hardly bigger than a doll's bed. The other scant pieces of boudoir furniture were clustered around it, with two tall candles glowing amid acres of Stygian gloom. To Mrs. Conrad, with her own note of exaggeration, this was outlandish "theatricalism." In Cora's study—which Cora calls "the anteroom"—alongside her big desk with Stephen's photograph on it was a writing table for him, with a supply of pens and the legal-size sheets he preferred always ready if he cared to work there. Stephen worked all over the house as the mood struck him. His own study, "the porch room," had a couch for sleeping, useful when he shut himself in to work the clock around, turning out stories in hot succession which he slipped under the door for Cora to type and forward to Pinker. On the desk underneath a preposterous lampshade was a photograph of her in her war correspondent's field dress, inscribed "to me old pal Stevie" from "Imogene Carter." The study walls were his favorite red—but Cora drew the line at red lampshades. The windows looked down the park, with the church spire in the distance.

"The young barbarians"—Henry James' pet name for Héloïse and Barry—were turned loose to romp over the Brede acres. Cora planned to take them and the little Pease boys to see the Barnum & Bailey circus, then touring the continent, when it came to London; but the excursion was postponed when the Pease youngsters came down with colds. Jack Stokes had said, "Stephen must *not* be saddled with the burden of supporting this young family"; but now Stephen and Cora, hankering for parenthood, were thinking of adopting Frederic's little boy.

Cora had been corresponding with Judge Alton B. Parker, Harold's old friend in Albany and the executor of his will—later, Democratic presidential nominee opposing William Howard Taft—in regard to American aid for the three children. Now she made it emphatic that the contemplated adoption of Barry *must* be under

American law; she and Mr. Crane both wished it so. Judge Parker replied that he had found "omissions in the section providing for an acknowledgment of the parties, so it may not be taken in another country." Plainly an oversight. He had drafted an amendment to the statute "and delivered it to Senator Douglas who will press its passage. If it becomes law a legal adoption can easily be accomplished, if such be the desire of your husband and yourself and Miss Lyon."

But Kate proved reluctant to part with any of her children and the "legal" aspect—the Cranes' dubious matrimonial status—was a tougher nut than the good Judge ever imagined. So nothing, in the end, came of the adoption plans.

In March came a letter from Edmund Crane with "congratulations on your marriage. Give our love to your wife."

Stephen had told Conrad they waited to be sure Cora's husband was really dead before breaking the news to his family. Now it was "a relief" to have it over. What he may have told Ed in New York, in explanation of Cora's untimely cablegram, or if questions were asked at all, is not on record.

After the short greeting Ed's letter jumped to news of Hartwood, homely details that shone with the writer's natural simplicity and lighted a glow in the exile's heart. The blizzard driving across the pond and piling snow in drifts below the house; Ed's entrance into the ice business and the two ice-houses he'd built himself . . . "Beautiful ice, twenty to twenty-seven inches thick" and clear as glass. He'd fixed up his house some, wished he could see the house at Brede Place. "Our house could be stored in your big hall. When I become a wealthy ice dealer I will come over to see you." Ed was a justice of the peace now, but nobody called him "Judge." (He was also postmaster, storekeeper, lumberman, and a lot of other things. Steve had chosen Ed for his guardian when their mother died.) Will expected to get a bill through the legislature extending the deer season to a month and permitting hunting with dogs. Ed had two good English beagles and hunted a lot, especially the big rabbits in the swamps around Hartwood. "Your pony with a mate pulled the ice wagon last summer, and was very useful. It did not hurt his health or his spirits any, he is as gay as ever. . . ."

This was Stephen's little brown horse Peanuts, bought with

money from the sale of a story, the first thing he had ever owned. There was great excitement in the family over the arrival of Peanuts in a boxcar from Aurora, New York, where Stephen had gone to visit Elbert Hubbard; and in the will he made before he sailed in the Jonah-ship *Commodore,* Stephen directed that Peanuts was not to be sold. Now Ed said they were all fond of him, and Peanuts was up to all his old tricks, shying, jumping, cutting up with make-believe kicks. "We use him in all sorts of ways, snaking small timber, drawing the ice marker, plowing in team in light soil, hauling firewood from the shop, feed from the depot. . . . If you should ever want him come and get him, but if you do not, he can stay with us as long as I keep a horse. . . ."

With spring in the air, caressing the downs with soft light, blue and gold, Cora lived in an ecstasy which seemed like that of the awakening earth complete and shatterproof. There was one excitement lately, Stephen reported to Moreton Frewen,

a small accident of fire through the mistake of poor old Mack. I put it out with no particular trouble. I did not scold Mack at all because his heart was quite broken and the lesson itself was enough for him. He came grandly forward and confessed his part in it. It happened in the room over the porch which I use as a study. I only speak of it because of a chance that you might hear of it in some more exaggerated form.

Frewen undoubtedly had, for the rumor traveled that the Cranes had come near burning the place down through building fires too hot!

Stephen had told Nellie Crouse he never worked in summer, a "long lazy time to fool away." But now he was working with that "machine-like application" others besides Cora thought the situation demanded. "Of course, you will understand that although I say nothing to you of money matters," he had written Pinker on the eve of moving to Brede Place, "our affairs at this time are in a woeful condition."

Pinker then had just forwarded Methuen's contract for the new novel. The contract provided for payment of one hundred pounds on signature and another hundred on publication, royalties to start at the odd figure of 16⅔ per cent for the first three thousand copies, jumping to 20 per cent on the next three thousand and 25 per cent thereafter. But for serialization, Crane told Pinker, he expected to get "in the neighborhood of £600 for the American rights, but I would not know at all what to say in regard to the English serial rights." The buyers of the English rights would have to "come in consultation with the buyers of the American rights," but the latter would be "very docile." He knew his American market. He would *not* go on with the *Battle* stories—begun with Kate Frederic's research—objecting now that the time required for their preparation, would be all out of proportion to the returns. He had lost interest.

There had been an earlier blowup over payments with S. S. McClure, whom Stephen never forgave for keeping the *Red Badge* on ice for six or eight months; and now signs of increasing exasperation with the miserliness of others who had advanced him sums against future writings, that must some day be paid back, began to appear in Crane's relations with editors and publishers. How much of this may have been due to his increasing illness, who can say?

"Let me know when you hear from Meldrum as the idea of writing stories for the purpose of getting them buried forever in Scotland makes me very unhappy." He wished Pinker to "tell Meldrum that I am unwell so that he wont be indignant because I have not come to see him." The Whilomville series was resumed, "sure and quick money," but if "The Angel Child" were "not a good opening gun bury it in the heather i. e. send it to Blackwood." And would Pinker please tell him "when Mr. Meldrum was kind enough to loosen his talons on 'The Clan of No Name.' I think my relations with the Blackwoods is about the most expensive friendship I have yet devised." But now he was under the impression that "the Harpers do not count very well. . . . This looks as if they have got away with £3—or £4—of ours." His short stories, he noted for Pinker's benefit, were developing in three series: Whilomville, war tales, and tales of western American life. "It might be well to remember this. For instance if you could provisionally establish the war tales with one magazine and the western tales with another as the Whilomville yarns are fixed with Harper's, it would be very nice."

"I hope you keep that young man right at work all the time," was Robert Barr's warning to Cora, with the added advice to keep

Oriel window and porch entrance, Brede Place. The small room over the porch, with single window *en face*, was Stephen Crane's study. Gift of Henry W. Walters.

Stephen Crane at work in his study at Brede Place. The inscription is in Cora's hand. The photograph on the desk is of Cora as war correspondent. Courtesy Roger M. Frewen.

Stephen Crane in his study, room over the Porch Brede Place. Sep. 1899.

a good stout club handy. "Spare the rod and spoil little Stevie!" With poor Frederic in mind, Barr confessed to being worried himself by "a cringing fear that I may drop off suddenly and leave everything in a muddle." He was going to "WORK and get out of debt. I don't want no subscriptions got up for the family of RB. . . . I am impressed by the fact that a man without some little surplus of cash is a futile creature. . . . His name is Mud, and also Dennis."

Cora at this time was writing her story "Cowardice" and—perhaps for the Whilomville series with Harper's pressing Stephen to extend them—"The Lavender Trousers." The ferment of ideas boiling up around the question of women's rights also claimed her, though Cora was never a militant feminist in the strictly political meaning.

A decade later, in England, she might have been clubbed off the picket line and followed Mrs. Pankhurst and the others in the vanguard of the suffrage movement to jail. For in the years to come she was to learn much about the struggle for survival in a man's world that altered many of her earlier views. Now, however, there were matters of more immediate importance to her as a woman: the right to be mistress of her own life in choosing a mate; the twin right to a position of equality and the pursuit of her own interests within the marriage partnership itself. But she remained aloof from public agitation, probably, like many others, thinking it undignified. Of the dress reform movement, which Lady Randolph Churchill had championed in its early stages, Cora had written (in the London newsletters): "A great body of sensible women in England will let the cranks do all the hard work" and take the abuse. Dress reform she considered a "growing movement, sane and proper—this we can say . . . with due understanding that the world moves," but it would not set the world on fire for "the mass of women are aimed in another direction."

She must earlier have come under the spell of Lady Churchill, now, since her husband's death, living in semi-retirement. But Cora seems to have viewed with indifference the activities of the Primrose League, that left-wing offshoot of the Conservative party, fathered by Lord Randolph Churchill, with one-third of its membership from the distaff side, which continued to play a curious part indirectly in the growing movement for women's rights. Cora saw the average woman, conditioned from the dawn of history to men doing her thinking for her, as inexperienced and unprepared to assume her rightful place in the modern world. So the issue would best be settled not through politics, or the vote, but "by training the minds of the next generation of mothers." While Stephen, indifferent—like Linton in "The Squire's Madness"—sat patiently through conversations about "equality of minds and the public part in the world's history which would be played by the women of the future," Cora found herself among congenial company in the Society of American Women in London. She was invited to become an honorary member of the new organization.

The Prince of Wales, always with a keen eye for a pretty woman, had on his visit to the United States discovered the American Girl. They were "not as squeamish as their English sisters," he concluded—but more independent, livelier, and also better educated.

But some rather persistent attitudes toward Americans, particularly American women, which had flourished alike on the continent and in mid-Victorian England, had been dissected and turned on a rapier point in various short stories by the young Henry James—stories which caused their author to live for a while under a cloud. These notions also had given offense to young Lady Randolph Churchill, who never forgot on which side of the Atlantic she had been born. "The American Woman," she observed in her memoirs,

was looked upon as a strange and abnormal creature, with habits and manners something between a Red Indian and a Gaiety Girl. Anything of an outlandish nature might be expected of her. If she talked, dressed and conducted herself as any well-bred woman would, much astonishment was invariably evinced, and she was usually saluted with the tactful remark "I should never have thought you were an American." This was intended as a compliment. As a rule, people looked upon her as a disagreeable and even dangerous person, to be viewed with suspicion.

Now, however, times were changing. The charm of American dollars was competing with the sun of the royal smile in dissolving old prejudices; international marriages no longer were frowned upon. Indeed, the American wing of the smart coterie known as "the Prince of Wales' set" had for two decades exerted social leadership through the personalities of Lady Randolph Churchill, the Cuban-born Duchess of Manchester (Consuelo Yznaga, who was known as "the American Duchess"), Lady Paget (Minnie Stevens from New York City),* and Mrs. Cavendish-Bentinck. The influx of American women into Great Britain, some married to Englishmen, others the wives of American businessmen whose interests required them to spend a part of each year in London, was by now so large in number that these ladies had seen fit to band together ("organize" was still a dirty word in the aristocratic dictionary) in the Society of American Women in London.

The interests of the Society were strictly social and cultural, having nothing whatever to do with politics. Article II of its Constitution proclaimed its objectives to be "the promotion of Social intercourse between American women, and to bring together women who are engaged in literary, artistic, scientific, and philanthropic pursuits, with the view of rendering them helpful to each other and useful to Society."

In April, the De Frieses were guests at Brede Place. Lafayette Hoyt De Friese, an American and an old friend of Harold Frederic, was one of the partners in a firm of international lawyers with important connections in London and Paris, and from the moment of Stephen's coming to live in England had been one of his most enthusiastic admirers. It was De Friese who had sponsored the Cranes' social introduction to the American Embassy circle. His wife was one of the officers of the SAWL; and now Mrs. De Friese was urging Cora to be her guest at the Society's April 10 luncheon: "Mr. De Friese joins in asking you and Mr. Crane to come up . . . and stay overnight with us. Do manage it."

"Mrs. Craigie [Pearl Craigie, novelist and intimate friend of Lady Randolph Churchill, who wrote under the pseudonym of John Oliver Hobbes], Lady Henry Somerset, Genevieve Ward [American-born English actress and opera singer] will be with us," Mrs. De Friese bubbled, "and Winifred Emery is coming . . . on the understanding that she is not asked for a speech. I think Mrs. Hodgson Burnett is coming too. Sarah Grand [American novelist] has accepted for May 9th. . . . We haven't Mrs. Robert Barr yet." Did Cora know her and might she be got in? Barr answered for

---

* Not to be confused with the German-born Walpurga, Lady Paget, the friend of Ouida and author of several volumes of memoirs.

his wife when the subject was broached, that she was not a joiner and seldom went anywhere. Mrs. De Friese wondered if Cora would have an opportunity to interest Mrs. Frewen?

We are awaiting a reply from Mrs. Kipling. . . . So many people I hear are holding off to see what we are going to do, before they will make up their minds. We want the right kind of people. We want to make it all that a dignified feminine intellectual center of social culture should be. At any rate, our first meeting has done us credit.

In the bouquet of other illustrious names Mrs. De Friese jotted on the back of her letter were those of beautiful Mary Anderson, "our Mary," the darling of Broadway, who had successfully defied the wrath of managers and producers to appear in none but virtuous roles and quit the stage since her marriage to an Italian count; Elizabeth Robins, soon to join the ranks of militant suffragists and already the bold interpreter of Ibsen, afterwards hailed by Bernard Shaw as "Miss Hedda Hilda Wangel Robins, christened Elizabeth"; Mrs. Seth Low of Brooklyn Heights aristocracy; Mrs. McKinley Osborne, wife of the American Consul General.

Cora's enthusiasm in joining the SAWL was not dampened by Stephen's abomination of Mrs. Hodgson Burnett's *Little Lord Fauntleroy*, that menace to young males! And as for Miss Robins, her sympathies if not her pocketbook were offered in the cause of the Frederic children; she wished Cora "every success in your undertaking," only regretting that she had "already an object for my surplus, that has a prior and most imperative claim." The "object" of Miss Robins' "surplus" was no doubt the Women's Rights movement, in which she was already active.

The Society had shown itself determined to have only "the right kind of people." A curious provision of its by-laws empowered the Executive Committee to expel an elected Member with no right of appeal or show cause, and Section 2 of this Article penalizes by suspension for six months any Member guilty of the indiscretion of introducing a visitor "whose reputation or conduct be objectionable."

And now Cora, her sense of position quite undisturbed by her previous rebel transgressions, and with a genuine admiration for "the dear Queen," was thinking of presentation at Court! It would put the seal on respectability.

Mrs. De Friese, who being "on the list" could smooth the way, had been to the Embassy and reported the public relations secretary, Mr. Carter, absent; but she had seen Ambassador Choate's son, who was under the impression that "we could not present our friends." She had also spoken to General Osborne, she reported, who was not informed on the protocol governing that point but had been told by one of the aides: "It was not desired that we should go oftener than once in two years." Mrs. De Friese felt anyhow that Cora "would be safe in ordering an evening dress in white. If a vacancy occurred on the Embassy list you could easily get a train quickly"; or an English friend might present her.

It is a pity that we do not know whether the Court presentation ever actually took place. But perhaps some of the Cranes' English friends wisely talked them out of it.

2

HENRY JAMES, whom Stephen had met already in London and whose silk hat he had rescued when an overbold young woman poured champagne into it at a London studio party, was one of the first important literary figures Cora invited to Brede Place. The great man responded warmly, bidding the Cranes welcome to Brede but regretting that their arrival coincided with his own "first absence of more than a few days" from his recently acquired country home, Lamb House—a visit of several weeks to Italy. His return however would be "for a long straight stay" at home in Rye; he hoped theirs would be the same at Brede Place.

The Cranes and Mrs. Ruedy, "the good Auntie Ruedy," had paid a visit earlier to Pent Farm, which the Conrads rented from Ford Hueffer; and Conrad joked about the little Borys' restless nights afterward, when he and Jessie were roused by infant chatter of "the nice man" and "Ann-Anns"—the child's word for "aunties." The Conrads were expected at Brede Place in June, and Conrad wanted to know if they might bring his wife's younger sister Dolly, living with them at the time, "on account of the boy." Conrad described Dolly to Cora as "a young person with her hair down her back, and of extreme docility." He would take along his "dress clothes, and try to be a credit to you and Stephen"—an

Luncheon meeting of the Society of American Women in London at Victoria Hall in the Hotel Cecil, London, July 3, 1899. The original photograph is inscribed by Cora on verso, "For Mrs. Pease/ Compliments/ CC." Gift of Mrs. Nicolas Pease.

oblique allusion to the dubious pomp of the Brede setting, of which Conrad never approved. Henry James was solemnly shocked by Robert Barr's nickname for Stephen, "Baron Brede." But Cora, when she wanted to tease him, called him "the duke!" A duke who scandalized the old major-domo, Heather, by running down to greet arriving guests on the doorstep in shirt-sleeves and muddy riding boots. But "Duke" or "Baron Brede," Stephen went daily to the Pease home in Limpsfield because he liked to have himself shaved by Adoni—an indulgence viewed with disfavor by the austere Quaker, Edward Pease.

Stephen rode down to the park gate to meet the Conrads, on one of the two big white carriage horses, Glenroy and Gloucester —rechristened "Hengist and Horsa"—the radiant smile lighting his face. Of that day Conrad recalls, "it had really been given to me to see Crane perfectly happy for a couple of hours." Stephen was never so happy as when sitting a horse, "the one blessing of life." Guests gathered in the long hall watched him moving past the ivied windows where the white owls roosted, on one or the other of the huge horses that gave him, Hueffer said, "the air of a frail eagle astride a giant elephant." He liked horses, dogs, and babies, perhaps because communication with them did not depend on words, but was more subtle and direct. He spent hours stretched on the grass, a rug under him, watching Conrad's little boy learning to walk; and he announced one day, gravely, hoisting himself on an elbow to speak out of a long silence: "Joseph, I shall teach your boy to ride!" Another time, "Joseph, every boy ought to have a dog"; and when puppies sired by his favorite Sponge were born on New Year's Eve he presented little Borys with one of the litter. Often, he would sit in a window of the long room twanging a guitar and singing softly in a thin, but sweet, tenor voice some foreign song—Neapolitan, Jessie Conrad said, but it was more likely Mexican or Cuban. "He never varied his tune, but I always noticed an expression of serenity and quiet satisfaction on his face at these times."

Mrs. Conrad, and others, saw Crane "a changed man" since the Cuban episode. If Cora noticed silences that fell more often now, she did her best to cover them, sometimes telling "long, sentimental stories" which bored Sanford Bennett. Did she guess that his days were numbered? Only to Pinker did she reveal the fright shut in her moods:

I am so glad that you wrote him *not* to go to the Transvaal. His health is not fit for it. He had a return of Cuban fever while we were in Paris and he is in no physical condition to stand a campaign no matter how short. . . . Then he has settled down to his work so well and ought not to leave before Jan. or Feb. at least.

And afraid of having said too much, she added a postscript to this letter written in late September: "Please dont let Mr. Crane know I've said a word against the Transvaal."

The Conrads stayed two weeks. Another visit of the Cranes to Pent Farm, planned for August, had to be postponed on account of an influx of relatives and Jessie's neuralgia, which had sent her to bed "tearful and disappointed." For various reasons the visit never took place; and Conrad later confessed to staying away from Brede Place because of his dislike of some of the company Crane had there. Stoically, Stephen kept his temper before the "Indians" who sometimes sneaked past Cora's defenses, but he exploded to Pinker: "If you dont tell some of these lice that Cora and I aren't running a hotel I'll have to advertise the fact in the *Times!*" "How," he wanted to know of Sanford Bennett, "does it come to pass that anybody in England thinks he can come and stay with me before I've asked him and patronize my wife's housekeeping?" But Cora was more amused than insulted at being regarded as a kind of upper servant who ought to be delighted to be up at all hours to do eggs in a chafing dish and fetch bottles of wine. Of a journalist who had camped on them four days, undisturbed by Stephen's wry thrusts, she remarked with a wink to an English friend, "I always expect him to tip me!"

The Conrads were hardly out of the house when Stephen's brother Wilbur arrived from America bringing for a long visit their niece Helen, the daughter of William Crane, who had recently been made a judge in Port Jervis. Besides a real talent for drawing —her father said for "things concrete"—the eighteen-year-old Helen Crane showed a wayward defiance of parental controls manifested in secret correspondence with young men of whom her elders did not approve. Something of the sort had been tactfully intimated to Stephen and Cora. Will desired them to "exercise oversight" of Helen's choice of associates. He would pay board for her at Brede Place. He hoped Cora would be able to take her on sightseeing trips for she might "never have another chance

Cora in her "weird kind of
wrapper." Inscription in Cora's
hand.

mrs Stephen Crane. 1899. Brede Place

Photograph of Cora and puppies appeared in the article in *The
Critic*, March, 1901. Photographs courtesy Roger M. Frewen.

to see something of the continent . . . we will stand anything in that line, that is, of course, within reason." If clothes were needed, Cora was to get them and send him the bills; or if she needed money in advance, he would try to get it over by return mail. He wanted Helen to have a good time and hoped "she and Cora would be companions for each other."

On the same train from London was an energetic young American, Karl Harriman, a student at the University of Michigan and friend of Robert Barr, who had published a few short stories which had won favorable notice from literary critcs. Stephen met them in the high dog-cart pulled by Glenroy. Harriman was an enthusiastic worshipper of Crane's genius. Cora mothered him, and Stephen introduced him in literary circles; friendship quickened to intimacy during the weeks he came and went as a guest at Brede Place. But Wilbur Crane did not tarry long, perhaps finding the damps of the English climate bad for his asthma and the whole setup at Brede Place, with its curious mixture of formality and unconventionality—Cora's strange costume, the Greek sandals, and gold hair loose down her back—more than a little startling. Cora, noticing Wilbur's uneasiness, had tactfully suggested that they not dress for dinner: "Wilbur didn't bring his evening things." The three of them, and Harriman, traveled up to London to see Wilbur off and stayed over several days at a hotel in the city.

On July 3 Cora attended the monthly luncheon of the Society of American Women in London, at the Hotel Cecil. To the SAWL affair came Lady Randolph Churchill, no longer the reigning queen of that glittering *haute monde* of Mayfair politics and fashion which, while her husband's star was rising, had foregathered in the house in Connaught Street, but beautiful as ever and glowing with plans for a hospital ship to be fitted out with American aid and sent to the theatre of war in the Transvaal: a gesture of friendship between two great nations.

Mrs. Richie, Kate Frederic's elder sister, brought her pretty young daughter Edith to call on the Cranes at their hotel. The emotional, shy, nineteen-year-old girl fell promptly in love with the beautiful young Cranes, who petted her and called her "snubby" on account of her short nose. Then on the spur of the moment, Cora and Stephen decided to have a party at the Henley Regatta, July 4, and invited Edith. In Henley Stephen put them all up at the ancient little riverside inn, the Angel, whose stucco and timbers and thatched roof were hospitable to clumps of blooming wild flowers. Stephen was a gay host, wildly cheering for a little screaming, cursing ten-year-old coxswain who won the race for Trinity. From Henley Edith Richie went to Yorkshire for a long visit with a school chum, Florence Bray. But she had been only two days there when a letter arrived from "Mummy Crane" announcing a house party at Brede for the same crowd who had been the Cranes' guests at Henley; Edith must join them at once. Telegrams flew back and forth. Cora urged her to bring Miss Bray, who was persuaded to accept.

The brandy-tippling cook had finally departed, after repeated false alarms, and now was replaced by an excellent woman named Vernall, of Swiss-English origin, who had been Mrs. Richie's cook for ten years. Vernall's achievements in American cookery, learned from Mrs. Richie, found special favor with Stephen, who was suddenly homesick for the foods of his boyhood. His brother Will was sending over canned corn, with a gallon of good maple syrup promised after the spring running. Cora had asked for vegetable seeds to start a kitchen garden with the things Stephen liked; Will knew of some varieties of early corn that might come to maturity in spite of cool nights. Some of the corn seed was given to Mr. and Mrs. H. G. Wells, and when the Wellses later were asked how they had cooked it, Wells exclaimed, "Cook it! We didn't cook it. We cut it when it was six inches high and ate it for salad. Wasn't that right?"

A. E. W. Mason was one of the Brede house party; and George Lynch was there, a handsome, gay fellow who thoroughly enjoyed living up to his reputation with the fair sex as "that delicious madman." An old correspondent friend of Stephen's, Lynch was just back from China and the Boxer Rebellion, his luggage crammed with lengths of gorgeous silks and mandarin coats lined with sable and ermine which he distributed as presents. All were invited over to tea with Henry James at Lamb House, where Mrs. Humphry Ward was doing the honors for their host at the tea table and talk was of the Boers, Stephen dissenting:

People tell me that the South Africans and the Japanese can shoot like the devil and then tell me a couple of Guard regiments could whip them in a week. When a Yankee says such things he is bragging but I guess an Englishman is just lugging the truth from some dark cave.

If this was one of those moments that put strain on Cora's social tact, even Mr. James could forgive "the mannerisms of a Mile End Roader." Cora did not agree with Stephen's estimate of *Robert Elsmere* as "a lot of higgling rubbish" and the niece of Matthew Arnold was no "feminine mule," but next to Lady Randolph Churchill perhaps the best-known woman in England. Cora was interested too in the fact that Mrs. Humphry Ward's father, Tom Arnold, had followed his Oxford classmate, John Henry Newman, into the Church of Rome.

Then Karl Harriman went off to London with the gift of one of Stephen's manuscripts, other farewells were said, and Crane was back at his driven labors alone in the room over the porch. Once, Harriman said, Stephen remained in his room for three days, sleepless and complaining when Cora tiptoed in with food on a tray that even the slight sound, breaking his concentration, was like a brick hurled through a window. In that time he poked four stories under the door, and Cora ran them off on the typewriter for Pinker. He had "almost to meet his little grocery and butcher bill each week," he told the agent. But Lady Churchill had asked him for something for her new venture in magazine publishing, the *Anglo-Saxon Review;* and he was pleased. "It is not a commercial transaction."

Summer was gayer with young girls about. Henry James liked to listen to Edith Richie's singing when he came to call. There had first to be a solo number; then Cora would say, "Now let's have a concert!" and the five Brede puppies lifted five little black muzzles in song as Edith accompanied them all on the piano, James and the Cranes collapsing with laughter. Often when guests were staying in the house, late at night there would be a tap on Edith's door and Cora's voice outside, "Stephen wants some music. Slip into your dressing gown and bring your comb." They gathered first for a raid on the pantry. Then in the enormous old kitchen, the warmest place in the house, "with tissue paper over our combs and Stephen conducting with the toasting fork . . . we all would sing horribly and happily through the combs." And there was the time Mr. James came to call, when Edith and Florence were trapped in the drawing-room drying their hair after a shampoo! James, an odd figure in knickers and gaiters, bicycled the five miles over from Rye at least once a week. Once, on returning home, the Cranes picked up in their hall a visiting card with a scribbled note: ". . . had a dark foreboding it was you I passed ¼ of an hour ago in a populous wagonette. Will try you soon again. H.J." With no sign of his later misgivings, James had sponsored Cora's admission to the women's corner of the Mermaid Club. The Club rooms were lodged in the ancient Mermaid Inn at Rye. From Kate Cora forwarded him Harold Frederic's last novel, *The Market Place;* he read it, he told her, "with a lively sense of what H.F. might have done if he had lived—and above all lived (and therefore worked) differently!"

In July came Catherine and H. G. Wells, who probably met Stephen and Cora at Mrs. Garnett's during their Oxted year. When Wells obtained a divorce from his first wife, he and Miss Amy Catherine Robbins had dropped their early disavowal of the "Institution of Marriage"; for the back-fence warfare of landladies, neighbors, and tradespeople had, by the end of two years, brought their Shelleyan ménage to a condition of siege which made work all but impossible. In self-defense they got married. Wells, at this time, had finished *The Time Machine* and was writing *Love and Mr. Lewisham.*

That same July week end the De Frieses also paid another visit to Brede Place. "They are such fun, those two dear people," Cora wrote Catherine Wells—though her discovery that "poor little Mrs. De Friese" had left her handbag in the trap at Battle with card case, pocketbook, "gold and five-pound notes knocking about on the floor," caused anxious "visions of having to supply fresh diamonds, etc." The etiquette of that day made host and hostess responsible for guests' belongings, lost or stolen. But a wire soon revealed the handbag's contents intact.

That summer Stephen and Conrad bought a sailboat together. The arrangement was that Stephen should have her half the time at Rye: the rest of the time the boat, *La Reine,* was to be kept at Folkestone, which was more easily reached from Pent Farm. "I've just had a wire from my husband," Cora wrote in the same letter to Mrs. Wells. "They have started with the boat for Rye." She and Helen would go over after luncheon to stand on the dock and watch with shaded eyes for the white sail, though "it would be safer to take along a bed and a few ham sandwiches"—her private opinion—as the wind had died. Anyhow, she was "so glad the Wellses liked Brede Place well enough to come again. . . . It is very kind of you to ask us to stop at your place [Spade House, the Wellses' new home near Folkestone] on our way to and from France. We are likely to take advantage of it later on as I want to take Helen to Paris."

On August 23 a garden party fête was held in the rectory gardens of the ancient and beautiful little Norman church of Brede Village: a joint benefit in aid of the parish and the District Nursing Association. Lady Adeane, escorted by her husband the Admiral, officially opened the fair. Next came a rather flowery and long-winded oration from the Vicar eulogizing the ladies of the parish who had gotten up the affair; and then the crowd of several hundred who had paid their one-penny admission proceeded to have a jolly good time, "hoppers rubbing shoulders with aristocracy," according to the *Southeastern Advertiser's* write-up, "in a total absence of class lines that would have gladdened the heart of a socialist." Cora's rummage booth was one of the main attractions. Stephen in straw hat and white flannels lugged potted plants for feminine purchasers to their waiting carriages. Helen Crane and young Cyril Frewer, the Vicar's son, took part in the singing. But the star feature of the afternoon's entertainment was the fortune-teller's hut where dark-eyed Edith Richie, in gypsy costume, dispensed charms and love potions and forecasts—with all of the customary hocus-pocus—to rustic couples. To her extreme discomfiture Henry James insisted on remaining all afternoon at the side of the shy girl, a kindly but superfluous sorcerer's apprentice. George Lynch was there too, all smiles for the ladies, snapping photos with his camera at sixpence a shot. He caught one of Mr. James with the sun in his eyes, clutching a half-eaten doughnut. When thanking Cora for "the strange images" she afterwards sent him as souvenirs of the occasion, the Master of Lamb House protested:

No, surely it can't be any doughnut of yours that is making me make such a gruesome grimace. I look as if I had swallowed a wasp, or a penny toy. And I tried to look so beautiful. . . . But don't show it to anyone as H.J. trying.

With her parents' approval, it had been decided that Helen Crane was to be sent that fall to a girls' school in Lausanne, Switzerland, which Edith Richie and her sister Mabel Barr had both attended. Helen adored her Uncle Stephen, who had played games with herself and her sisters when they were youngsters in Port Jervis, and who had presented her with his stamp book. The newer attachment to her Aunt Cora was all that a perplexed and worried father could wish. But the ties of affection did not keep Helen out of trouble. Some kind of misdemeanor was discovered before they got her off to Switzerland, of which nothing is known except that Helen's transgression was followed by a full confession to her Aunt Cora somewhere in the course of which tears were shed; and that a letter went off by the next post to the new judge in Port Jervis. "I should be almost overwhelmed with this trouble," wrote Will Crane, "if I did not feel that you were bearing my burdens for me." He had only praise and gratitude for Cora's handling of "the late episode . . . which must have been mortifying as well as painful. . . . She is now on probation. I leave it entirely with you how the lessons are to be brought home." Cora suggested an allowance for spending money, and Will left the amount to her judgment. Then, worried lest Helen get into more trouble at school with "no good friend to protect her," he inquired what Cora thought of writing her "a straightforward letter of advice . . . call things by the right name and warn her that an indulgence in her indifference to the property rights of others might possibly land her in the police courts? . . . You would, of course, write in your tactful way, but it might be a point of view altogether new to her."

The next letter brought a disclosure which had come round about, the young man's sister having told somebody who told somebody else that Helen was not keeping her promise "not to correspond with any man without my knowledge and consent." Will now desired Cora to send to the miscreant girl "and charge to me a copy of Addison's *Spectator*"; he knew of "no reading that inculcates a love of truth more effectively." Unless it was Fenimore Cooper's *The Deerslayer*.

Stephen had liked Jack Stokes' "kind padre," who came to lunch at Brede Place, and Father Roe had a strong influence on Cora, for whom the realism of the Roman Catholic faith and the drama of

Henry James holding one of
Cora's celebrated doughnuts
at the garden party, Brede
Rectory, August 23, 1899.
Gift of Henry W. Walters.

Edith Richie in gypsy costume at the fortune teller's
hut. All garden party snapshots were taken by Ste-
phen's friend George Lynch.
Gift of Henry W. Walters.

its ritual had long exerted a powerful attraction. So now Cora sought counsel of kind Father Roe; and Will, who "came near overlooking one of the most important parts of your letter," replied that he had "no objection to your bringing influence to bear upon Helen to make her a Catholic." It would be unfortunate to make her "a bigot," but he saw little danger of that "for . . . if you had been a bigot you would not have married my brother Stephen."* His own notion was that true religion is the essential, and the form under which one worships is largely a matter of circumstance, not important.

Correspondence pyramided; but somewhere in it all Cora extracted a promise that Helen's peccadilloes should remain a secret between them, and that her own letters on the subject be destroyed. Will wrote to say her request had been complied with, and now he thought it best to confide to Cora a secret never hinted to anybody: he had sent Helen away to get her free of her mother's influence. A "good" woman, faithful to her husband and children, but for a year or two—he had noticed with a deep concern— she was—unwittingly—cultivating in the girl a disposition sullen and revengeful. When Helen did wrong, he said, her mother usually made the first contribution. Knowing Cora to be a good and wise woman, he would be grateful to her as long as he lived "for the loving interest you take" in Helen's welfare; and he signed himself, "Your affectionate brother."

In September, when Stephen set forth to take his niece to Switzerland, Cora and Edith Richie accompanied him as far as Paris. Mack drove the four of them in the big wagonette to Folkestone where they stayed overnight with Mr. and Mrs. H. G. Wells. There was music and fun after dinner. Catherine Wells accompanied Edith at the piano; and then they all played animal grab, Stephen roaring like a lion, Wells barking like a dog, and Cora a twittering canary. Cora and Edith lingered in Paris, staying at the old Hotel Louis le Grand while Stephen made the journey with Helen to Lausanne. Some of the time George Lynch was with them. They met other friends too, and when Stephen rejoined them two days later there was a gay round of lunches, dinners,

* Mr. Hoffman sees this letter as evidence of Cora's becoming a member of the Roman Catholic Church (see Hoffman, pp. 114-115 n.). I find nowhere evidence in support of this conclusion.

theatres, cafés-chantants, and sightseeing. Cora and Stephen wrote post cards home to the dogs, and got small pieces of candy from penny-in-the-slot machines to mail back.

Stephen, part of the time ill with malaria, shut himself in the little Parisian hotel bedroom to write. His American publisher, Frederick A. Stokes, was urging him to complete the Cuban war sketches, on which Stokes probably had advanced him money in New York. Hard pressed on all sides in his precarious juggler's game of keeping too many projects going at one time, and lashed by the eternal need of cash, he received a letter from Pinker which filled him with the idea that he had "written a story and then absolutely forgotten it as I often do." The small hotel was turned upside down in frantic search; and back home at Brede Place he sent off a confused telegram to Pinker, followed by two more anxious notes: "I cannot express how worried I am. . . . I can only remember writing one story and I would almost bet the two titles cover one story. We may be making a hideous blunder. Please find out."

There was no missing story, only the hallucinations of fever. Cora was frightened, but dared not show it. "Before I had finished the article for Lady Churchill," Crane wrote Moreton Frewen in Ireland, on September 26, "I was obliged to take my niece to Switzerland to school, and on my return to Brede Place I had a slight attack of Cuban fever and am still seedy."

We are getting along happily at dear old Brede [the letter continues], the ghost is behaving himself though the doors open in the same uncanny way. As to Mack leaving us; the old man found it too much out of the world for him. He missed his usual talk at the tavern we think. We were very fond of him and he seemed fond of us but when he said that he thought he had better go we did not try to keep him. You see it is impossible for us to keep all beer and drink under lock and key and the old man was tempted two or three times to take a bit too much. With lamps and the open fires it gave me an anxiety for the safety of your old house. You will remember we had one fire though this fact had nothing to do with it; it took place at 7:30 A.M. You have been very kind to me about rent. I've had a hard year of it settling my affairs which are nearly in shape now. I have taken advantage of your kindness to keep you waiting until almost the last. Next month I can send you a cheque. Will it be convenient for you to wait until then? I hope this next year to do more for the place than

I have been able to do this. We hope to see you down here the next time you come to England for, at least, a day and night and then we can talk of many things. My wife encloses two snapshots for Mrs. Frewen.

Then, at breakfast one morning in October, Stephen suddenly said to Cora, "Edith has never been to Ireland. Let's go to Ireland." He had begun *The O'Ruddy*, and needed to recharge his senses and his memory with live impressions of that trouble-torn country. In London, says Miss Richie, there was a big party at the Frewens where the Cranes were lionized. Next morning, consulting an old timetable, they missed their train for the Irish boat. More parties, lunches, teas, dinners followed. "Everyone wanted to entertain the Cranes." Three mornings in succession the train was missed! But they were all young, enjoying themselves, and time seemed unimportant.

In November William Dean Howells was in London and was seen by Henry James, from whom Crane may possibly have learned of his arrival. Stephen had not communicated with Howells since the summer of 1896, and there is nothing to indicate that Howells was ever a guest at Brede Place. But Stephen, who had not forgotten his indebtedness to the great editor and critic who had warmly befriended him in the lonely uphill days in New York, must now have journeyed up to town to see him. Cora was with him and, catching Howells in a jovial mood, she made a sketch from memory on the return to Brede Place, "Mr. Howells enjoying a joke." Then adding on the same sheet a humorous drawing of a fruity maiden, with caption, "My furst gurl"; another of the dog Sponge, and two more untitled, she wrote on the back "Scribbles by Cora Crane," and presented all five to Edith Richie as a souvenir.

3

. . . THE one thing that deeply pleases me in my literary life—brief and inglorious as it is—is the fact that men of sense believe me to be sincere. "Maggie" . . . made me the friendship of Hamlin Garland and W. D. Howells, and the one thing that makes my life worth living in the midst of all this abuse and ridicule is the consciousness that never for an instant have those friendships at all diminished. . . . I do the best that is in me, without regard to cheers or damnation. When I was the mark for every humorist in the country I went ahead, and now, when I am the mark for only 50 per cent of the humorists of the country, I go ahead, for I understand that a man is born into the world with his own pair of eyes, and he is not at all responsible for his vision—he is merely responsible for his quality of personal honesty. To keep close to this personal honesty is my supreme ambition. . . .

Crane, of course, was thinking of his art when he wrote this from England—probably near the end of 1897—to the literary editor of the Rochester *Post-Express*, John Northern Hilliard, a boon companion—according to Hilliard—during his early days in New York. Conscious of overstatement in the last sentence, verging on smugness, Crane was careful to add that he made no claims for himself in respect to honesty. "I merely say that I am as nearly honest as a weak mental machinery will allow." This aim in life seemed to him "the only thing worth while," and though a man was sure to fail at it, "there is something in the failure."

Something, indeed; only he did not perceive that it is a dangerous thing, sometimes, for a man to claim even that much. For honesty, like truth, is not a matter of purely subjective relationships and, when private scrutiny is the only test, is all too easily manipulated to the secret ends of necessity, greed, ambition, self-love, or simply the perpetuation of habits. Now living incredibly beyond their means at Brede Place, with little idea or regard for practical economies, the Cranes could not, or would not, curb their expenditures. And so Robert Barr's excellent advice about mixing common sense with genius went unheeded. Both Stephen and Cora were of the opinion that any piece of paper with words and Stephen Crane's name on it possessed currency value equal to coin of the realm.

Crane had hardly stepped off the boat from America when creditors pounced: the butcher and the grocer, the Oxted Dairy, innumerable others lay in wait with judgments. The rent of £91 for Ravensbrook—a full year—had not been paid, nor had the repairs specified in Crane's written agreement with the landlord been made. Immediate payment of £40 on account was demanded by the landlord; the rest, plus repairs, before Lady Day (March 25). A sum of £98 was owed to Whiteley's department store—the

Scribbles by Cora Crane

Rev. G. Ernest Frewer with Mack ("Tolstoy") Gift of Henry W. Walters.

this drawing, by Mrs Stephen Crane, is the property of Edith Richie

Five drawings in crayon or soft pencil on a single sheet by Cora Crane. The inscriptions are "Mr. Howells enjoys a joke," "Spongie, before!" "Copy Nico Turgmann," and "My furst gurl." The other inscriptions, on verso, are also in Cora's hand. Berg Collection, New York Public Library.

Macy's of London—most of which was for the unpaid balance on the purchase of a piano. Solicitors for Whiteley's notified Alfred T. Plant (Moreton Frewen's own representative in legal matters, to whom Frewen, with a kindred feeling for fellow sufferers in duress, now directed Crane) that £40 of this amount must be produced immediately and the balance in thirty days, otherwise their client's instructions were to proceed in bankruptcy. Pinker, to whom Stephen now confided the "woeful state of affairs," wrote, "the matter appears more serious than you thought, and I confess that I do not see a way out of the difficulty at the moment."

There was £40 coming from *Harper's* for a Whilomville story. Outside of that, Stephen's way was to enlist help from Pinker and the London representative of Frederick A. Stokes, Mr. Dominick, plus a loan of £100 from William Crane, which arrived barely in time—just before Lady Day. Stephen spent a long, exhausting day in town with Dominick, who "also bravely offered to go and stand in the breach." Dominick would have no hesitation in giving plaintiff's solicitors to understand that Stokes & Co. would come to his assistance to some extent at least, but wished him to write a letter "setting forth an acknowledgment of a little temporary mortgage upon the royalties of my four Appleton books vis: *The Red Badge, The Little Regiment, Maggie,* and *The Third Violet.* . . . It is Dominick's idea that this letter should be addressed to you and remain in your hands." He followed this up five days later—on February 9—with an appeal to Pinker for a personal guarantee of the rent sum, the other solicitors having expressed themselves satisfied with this arrangement.

Of course I dont want to let you in for any strange game but this seems to me my *only* way clear. Really your position would be simply that of a buffer-state. I hesitate to ask you to do it. . . . If you think you can stand it do so and God be with you.

This will enable me to move almost at once to Brede and get a fair chance at myself.

Again, he enclosed another Whilomville story and requested £30 by next post, "I need it badly." On February 16 he sent Pinker "a rattling good war story," for which he asked "cheque for £40 so that I will get it on Sunday morning." Then, on that Sunday, he sent off to Pinker "a whacking good Whilomville story":

and I am agitatedly wiring you at the same time. You are possibly able to forgive me by this time for the way I put upon you. I must have altogether within the next ten days £150. . . . But, by the same token, I am going to earn it. . . . £40 of my £150 have I done yesterday and today but for all your gods, help me or I perish.

Portions of these sums from Pinker were forwarded to Alfred T. Plant to stand off this and that one of the creditors—at least one of whom had chased Stephen all the way from Cuba! Reynolds wrote, in April, of a strange man who had called at his office in New York with a draft against Crane to the order of Diaz Gonselos & Company for $305.88. The long-suffering and extraordinarily amiable Pinker now was bombarded with appeals to rush money for deposit to Mrs. Crane's account in the Oxted Bank, to Mrs. Crane's account with Brown, Shipley & Company (London bankers) and to send other amounts to meet overdrafts or to satisfy some local merchant on the point of bringing suit. In the light of today's practice both these banks displayed a remarkable leniency—or laxity—in the matter of overdrafts, which they allowed to run on for as much as three weeks after the first warning. Cora and Stephen were constantly shifting funds back and forth, taking from the right hand to give to the left. Cora must have £35 "*at once* . . . as today I have had to draw that for one of his [Stephen's] accounts and I'm overdrawn now"; or £50 was needed for Mr. Crane this week: "He simply must have it. I enclose a letter from our solicitor. . . ." Or again it was £40: "The matter is so very urgent and important. . . . If this cheque [bill] . . . is not paid these people will issue writ—at once—and give us no end of trouble. . . . Now please wire me on receipt of this 'all right' if you have sent £40 . . . so that I may be sure that this troublesome bill is paid." Were there any doubt of Pinker's being able to get the other £150 Mr. Crane must have, she begged him to notify her at once "and I will come up and see what I can do borrowing on some of his stuff. Mr. Crane is now engaged in fighting his last creditors and they can be fought only with money." Still another appeal, also "urgent," had "nothing to do with my former request for £20—to enable Mr. Crane to take a few days holiday. This would be to take his niece to Lausanne where she is to go to school and to stay a few days there." Pinker was implored to "move Heaven and Earth—and publishers—to get every pennie [sic] you

Week-end guests posed at the main entrance of Brede Place in July, 1899. Standing, left to right, are Lafayette Hoyt De Friese, Stephen Crane, Mrs. De Friese, Cora, and Mrs. H. G. Wells. Wells is seated at right. Gift of Henry W. Walters.

Stephen Crane at the entrance to the Smugglers' Passageway, Brede Place, during the Garden Party, August 23, 1899, held for the benefit of the parish and District Nursing Association. Gift of Henry W. Walters.

can. The wine man must be satisfied and Mr. Crane must have a change or I fear he will break down and we can't have that." Of course, they both understood that Pinker "probably" had advanced them money not yet collected.

> Please do not think we do not quite appreciate this kindness. . . . It must be painful to you now but in the long run you will benefit as there *is* a market for everything Mr. Crane writes as you know. This is rather like promising golden streets to the good boy in a Sunday School class who wants the streets of mud today, but you are more certain of good results than the Sunday School lad.

And then came a demand from Crane for £30 to be sent to Ireland. Pinker and Plant meanwhile, each with a chattel mortgage on Crane's future, struggled on, keeping up assurances that all would eventually be well; and Stephen, with that fatal optimism—born of mistrust—which always overtook him at all the wrong times, wrote cheerfully to his agent of "a story with which you can have good game. . . . We like it a little. . . ."

We! He consulted Cora now in everything, and depended on her altogether for typing. The Greek novel, now at 48,000 words, he was confident would be his most successful book. But he had only just waked up to the fact that for some years he had been "allowing over half of my real market to languish without any of Stephen Crane's stories . . . a lot of newspaper syndicates in America which have made me personal requests to help fill their pages." And now here was "a double extra special good thing ("The Upturned Face"), only 1,500 words, but he was "wonderfully keen on it" and was sending a copy to the great actor, Forbes-Robertson, "in an attempt to make him see that in a thirty-minute sketch on the stage he could so curdle the blood of the British public that it would be the sensation of the year, of the time."

Then in a flash of the old independence so dear to every artist's soul—that condition of caring tremendously and wholeheartedly for something intangible—he was dead set against doing a Christmas story for Tillotson's, a syndicate "For supplying the Newspaper Press with Special Articles and the Works of Popular Novelists." Once when Mark Barr, who was an industrial technician, said of an experiment in higher mathematics, "You see, I cared so much," Stephen burst out:

That's it, Mark! Now that you've said it always remember it. You can never do anything good aesthetically—and you can never do anything with anything that's any good except aesthetically—unless it has at one time meant something important to you.

He had never written a story of the kind specified, "a seasonable story," and he would not begin now; Cora must say so to Pinker. She was handling most of the business correspondence.

He swung back and forth between extremes of exaggerated euphoria and cynicism. When a son was born to the Mark Barrs in September he sent the baby "a cheap mug"—of solid silver—"from me to him." His hopes for the little boy entering a world of strife and trouble echo the old mood of his poem about the heart-eater; but the tensions are no longer held in balance, the muscles of being have relaxed into flabbiness:

> You know me about writing letters.
> I cant do it. Your letter to me
> I *drank*. But—
> Anyhow, it is all the boy now.
> The boy! May the time-of-his-life
> rock him gently in ease and may
> the cradle spill only enough to
> give him those shocks which inform
> men, inform men that everything is
> already well-combined for their des-
> truction and that the simple honest
> defeated man is often a gentleman.
> Rubbish—Salute for me our
> dear Mabel.
>> Yours ever, my dear boy
>> S. Crane

In October Stephen had come near breaking with his American publisher, Frederick A. Stokes, over a misunderstanding concerning a cable, and but for the timely intervention of Robert Barr would have done so. Barr wrote him a long, frank, tactful, and most understanding letter counseling moderation:

Let Pinker handle all the business, and that will please Stokes, please you, and above all it will please Pinker. . . . You are all right when you stick to the pen, and are apt to be all wrong when you meddle with business. You are too much like Edgar Allan Poe.

But even Pinker's patience was wearing thin and on October 24 he sounded a warning:

I confess that you are becoming most alarming. You telegraphed on Friday for £20, Mrs. Crane on Monday makes it £50; today comes your letter making it £150, and I very much fear that your agent must be a millionaire if he is to satisfy your necessities a week hence, at this rate. . . . Mrs. Crane says I have "probably advanced money to Mr. Crane that I have not myself yet collected." As a matter of fact, this sum, at present, is £230. I mention this to impress you less with the obligation to me than to yourself. There is a risk of spoiling the market if we have to dump too many short stories on it at once. . . .

Pinker, nevertheless, would "try to manage *something* during the next ten days or a fortnight," by which time, the peremptory note in much of Crane's correspondence with both his agents had dissolved into a rather pathetic wail: "Please write me at some length about various stories and in particular always gladden my heart when you have news of a sale." He reminded Pinker of an instance when he had not been informed until proofs arrived. "It is only a matter of a few pounds but anyhow it was pleasant to know it and I might have had the pleasure earlier."

4

THE quality of their need rendered them imperious, and Cora Crane was certainly not the first woman to overestimate her husband's genius, or the size of his purse. Worshipping every line that issued from Stephen's flogged and faltering pen, Cora complained to Pinker that she could not understand the English publishers' rejection of certain Crane stories "while printing the rot they do." Mr. Reynolds had pleased them very much with his quick placing of these stories, editors had a lot to learn, "and the firm of Pinker are the people to teach them." Stephen "grumbled" to Pinker about "stagnation" of the English market; and Cora bullied him to "give editors to understand that two weeks is the limit to keep Mr. Crane's copy. Please make this your fast rule for all of Mr. Crane's work. Editors have always subscribed to this for me, when I have been disposing of Mr. Crane's stuff."

Forgetting that it was "not a commercial transaction," she asked whether Pinker couldn't make John Lane—publisher of Lady

Churchill's magazine—pay up for the £50 due from the story to the *Anglo-Saxon Review*? And McClure, who owed for the last story—a balance of £5 to Stephen's credit on McClure's books besides—was "just playing the artful!" But with Pinker's warning, in October, against flooding the market, which Crane considered "extremely wrong," Cora really hit the ceiling:

> Now Mr. Pinker, how could you say to Mr. Crane not to dump too many short stories upon the market for fear of spoiling it? This is a fatal thing to say to a writing man. Particularly to Stephen Crane. And how can you think so with an utterly un-spoiled and vast American market? Harpers and the Saturday Evening Post and one story to McClures are the only things sold in America *now* and you could sell a thousand short stories of Mr. Crane's there if you had them.

Thanks to Kate Frederic's research, the *Battle* stories were again "sure and quick money"; and now Crane had begun a new series, the Wyoming Valley tales. *Active Service* was issued by Stokes in America that fall of 1899, with a dedication to the kind man who had befriended the Cranes in Athens, Mr. Eben Alexander, from whom now came a sad letter replying to one from Cora. It brought news of the death from typhoid fever of his youngest son. His wife and married daughter also had been at death's door. Alexander now had a professorship at the University of North Carolina and was living with his family at Chapel Hill. Proud of the dedication, he thanked Stephen for the copy of the book received some time before. It had, he said, been a year of trouble, "and we are so unused to it. . . . I write in this way, partly because I cannot think of other things yet, partly because I know you and Stephen like me, in the goodness of your hearts well enough to feel sympathy in our sorrow."

Cora had written William Crane of the "return of Cuban fever in Paris," and Will laid it all to drinking coffee. Then someone frightened her, and Stephen was angry in a note:

Please have the kindness to keep your mouth shut about my health in front of Mrs. Crane hereafter. She can do nothing for me and I am too old to be nursed. It is all up with me but I will not have her scared. For some funny woman's reason, she likes me. Mind this.

He wrote to an English friend, George Wyndham:

What do you know about the Black Forest . . .? I mean as a health resort? The truth is that Cuba Libre just about liberated me from this base blue world. The clockwork is juggling badly.

With autumn closing in, they hung on to Edith Richie. Who knows what sinister and unbearable truths might have jumped out of the box had they suddenly found themselves alone with each other? Mrs. Ruedy had sailed home to America in June. Summer guests, too, had flown off with the swallows. Memories sharpened as the days grew shorter.

Cora was corresponding with Agnes Crane, Helen's sister; and in one of her letters to their father, she suggested that he send Agnes over to join Helen at the Rosemont school the following year. Will had written in September a chuckling account of the strong impression made on some Peck cousins—their mother's people—by their recent visit to Brede Place. The couple were "busy telling Port Jervis about it. We didn't have to say a word." But the proposal to send Agnes met with a chilly response. He couldn't afford it, he said, adding,

we have very good schools here. . . . Please allow me to say that there is a false quantity in some of your letters . . . to Helen, when you say that Port Jervis could not teach her this or that. . . . Helen was so indolent in her studies, careless in her choice of associates and so persistent in her ways, your invitation came as a godsend. She needed a tremendous moral and intellectual awakening and I think she is getting it.

Will did not think Stephen should pay his own expenses to Lausanne. But the "awakening" was proving a costlier experiment than even he had anticipated. For now it seemed, Helen had used the money sent for board and tuition for other purposes, borrowed from her school friends, and on top of that got thirty Swiss francs from the proprietress, Mme. Eytel-Hubbe—on the pretext that it was for her Uncle Stephen! After an angry letter from Madame, "He not only left her without any pocket money, but borrowed from me through his niece the sum of 30 francs which he has not repaid"—Will's only comment was that he had repaid the sum himself, but said nothing of all this to Helen. "For it would be an unpleasant matter to stir . . . Madame did not feel amiable about it when she wrote."

5

EDITH RICHIE (Jones) says that the idea of a Christmas party at Brede Place originated with Stephen. "We'll have all your family here and your friends and our friends. It will be your party! We'll have a ball and a play." When Edith and Cora asked, "What play?" the answer was, "Oh, you two can make up something. And I'll get a lot of people to send in a scene or a line or a word you can work into it. Then we can say they wrote it."

The play, announced by Crane in a note to H. B. Marriott-Watson,[*] was "some awful rubbish" he had written around the Brede ghost. Most of the writing was actually done by Crane himself, but there were nine other collaborators, all of whom were distinguished literary names. Owing to this mixed authorship, *The Ghost* has been called "a literary curiousity unrivalled." *The Southeastern Advertiser's* write-up (January 5, 1900) described the piece as "a combination of farce, comedy, opera, and burlesque." The time, 1950: as the curtain rises, the poor frustrated phantom is complaining about his ill luck and lack of recognition by the tourists visiting Brede Place, who no longer believe in ghosts. This is followed by a catchall burlesque of characters borrowed from the works of the ten collaborators, interspersed with songs and dances reminiscent of *The Mikado* of Gilbert and Sullivan. In Act Three, despite their disbelief, the crowd of tourists is paralyzed by the sudden appearance of the Ghost at midnight, who sadly enters upon a recital of his autobiography while being heckled and constantly corrected by the caretaker. In the year 1531, he mournfully recalls, he was "sitting in that very same room, consuming six little Brede boys, and washed down his meal with an appropriate quantity of beer. This overcame him, and whilst in a stupor four courageous Brede men entered and sawed him asunder." At the end of his tale he disappears and returns presently to make the rounds, hat in hand, his fee to each bus load of tourists being "two bob." The piece concludes with a grand chorus and dance.

A. E. W. Mason, who at one time had been an actor, consented to

---

[*] Henry Brereton Marriott-Watson (1863-1921), English editor, novelist, and playwright.

take the part of the Ghost—adding with wry intent, that Henry James ought to be "compelled" to act in the production: a double reference perhaps to James' famous ghost story, "The Turn of the Screw," and his unhappy experience as a playwright. In order "to make the thing historic," Crane invited Marriott-Watson and the other contributors each

to write a word—any word "it," "they," "you," . . . and thus identify themselves with this crime. Would you be so lenient as to give me the word in your hand writing and thus appear in print on the programme with this distinguished rabble.

Besides himself, Mason, and Marriott-Watson, the "distinguished rabble" included Henry James, George Gissing, Joseph Conrad, Edwin Pugh, Rider Haggard, Robert Barr, and H. G. Wells.

Robert Barr, who hated crowds and "rather shunned" his fellow man "when he is in a dress coat," begged off from the house party. James, Conrad, and Rider Haggard also stayed away and Gissing, who had wanted to meet Crane, sent regrets from France, where he was then living.

Mason, chief collaborator, produced a draft for the last act of the play, to which songs were added, and was helpful in numerous other ways. Cora prevailed on him to act as stage manager and director, and also to supervise the ordering and construction by a firm of London carriage builders of a capacious, smart-looking omnibus to be used in transporting guests from the railroad station at Hastings to Brede Place. It was a winter of exceptional cold, ice, and heavy snows. As early as September 23, Mason was writing that he would bring along "an ice axe and cut steps through the park." A snowplow he thought would not be necessary.

Preparations for the party were begun three months ahead, and as the holiday week drew near, the old house resounded with a gay hustle and bustle. Copies of the play script had to be typed for the actors by Cora and Edith Richie, music copied, new lyrics written for the songs they were going to use. Edith worked hard at painting scenery. Extra servants were hired from London, and an orchestra, and cots from the local hospital. Cora ordered dozens of iron brackets made by the village blacksmith, each to hold two large candles, which, as they burned down during the ball, dripped wax over the backs of guests and the dancing couples. Guest rooms were made ready for the married couples; but as there were not enough habitable rooms to provide paired accommodations for sixty people, latecomers had to separate and bunk in with others in two of the vast cold, unused chambers now thrown open and converted into dormitories—one each for men and women. Guests who could do so were asked to bring their own bedding. The H. G. Wellses, who arrived early, were lucky in getting one of the bedrooms. Every evening the names of dinner partners, written on cards, were placed conspicuously near each guest's bed. The whole house was festooned with ropes of holly and ivy. From the hand of the ever dependable Vernall, more than fifty plum puddings, sauced and burning with holly sprig in the center, made their appearance at the Yule board in the three days of feasting and festivities.

Mason came down to spend Christmas Day with the Cranes and help with final arrangements for the play, before the house party assembled. Eight people sat down to Christmas dinner. The other guests probably were Mr. and Mrs. W. F. Richie—Edith's parents —and the Mark Barrs. The menu, hand-copied by Cora and preserved in a scrapbook, consisted of Stephen's favorite dishes: a typical American family dinner with holiday trimmings:

> Xmas dinner 1899—Stephen Crane—Author—8 people.
> Roast Turkey, stuffed chestnuts, giblet gravy
> Sweet potatoes, mashed potatoes
> Sweetcorn, stewed tomatoes, cranberrie [sic] sauce.
> Plum Pudding, Hard Sauce
> Minced Pies, Pumpkin Pies
> Nuts, raisins, apples, oranges, figs, dates.
> Coffee
> Champagne, Claret, Green Mint.
> > Brede Place, Sussex.

The cast arrived on the day after Christmas. The following afternoon, after a brief rehearsal in the morning, a trial performance for the school children—really a dress rehearsal—was put on in the Brede Hill Schoolhouse. The main performance took place on the following evening, December 28, and one local newspaper account said it was much enjoyed "in spite of the prevailing epidemic and bad weather . . . by those who accepted Mr. Crane's invitations to see the performance." The *Southeastern Advertiser's* more detailed write-up noted that there was no admission charge, "the whole of the expenses being defrayed by Mr. Stephen Crane, including an addition to the stage, which he has since presented to the School. Mr. J. F. Smith kindly gave his services as stage carpenter." "A treat," was the *Advertiser's* judgment of the play and the performance, for which all who saw it had "every reason to be thankful to Mr. and Mrs. Stephen Crane."

Catherine Wells at the piano furnished accompaniments for the songs and dances. Cora was the prompter. "It was a dreadful night," she wrote, describing the affair to Mrs. Frewen; but an appreciative audience had given proof of its willingness to be frightened by the Ghost's recital of his "horrible" tale, with groans and cries of " 'oh! and oh my!' . . . It was lovely." Their facial expressions entertained her, "as much as I've ever enjoyed anything in my life"—but though Mr. Frewen was "good enough to say not, I think . . . that some of the old women thought it horribly immoral."

But for C. Lewis Hind,* who made one of the party, *The Ghost* performance was driven from memory by "the agony of getting to Brede Village." There had been a thaw, with thunder and lightning and sluicing rain. The juicy condition of the roads made hard going for the handsome new omnibus, guests having to get out and push.

Lewis Hind, with eyes only for the "bevies of beautiful American girls" he was introduced to at the dance the next evening, remembered *The Ghost* as "an awful play." But the *Manchester Guardian* (January 13, 1900) declared it a pity that this "remarkable piece of literary patchwork has been allowed to waste its sweetness on the Sussex air," and coyly hinted that "a good many people would rather read it than Paolo and Francesca"—Stephen Phillips'† trag-

---

* C. Lewis Hind, editor of the *Academy*, a literary weekly published in London. Hind recorded his recollections of the Christmas house party in a section devoted to Stephen Crane in *Authors and I* (London and New York: John Lane, 1921), pp. 70-74. For a concise biographical sketch of Lewis Hind, see H. G. Wells, *Experiment in Autobiography*, pp. 432-433.

† Stephen Phillips (1865-1915), British poet and dramatist. Phillips was one of the group of avant garde writers which at the turn of the century included the English Decadents, and others under pre-Raphaelite or French Symbolist influence, whose rallying point was the *Yellow Book* magazine edited by the American expatriate, Henry Harland. *Paolo and Francesca* was produced at the St. James Theatre in 1901.

The ghost: "I am the ghost o I dont admit this because I am proud o I admit it because it is necessary that my indentity should be established o My identity has been disputed for many centuries— how many, I forget — anyhow, it was some time ago o It is difficult to be a ghost here o I would like to have an easier place o Tourists come here and they never give me a penny although I had my last pipe of baccy two hundred years ago and I drank my last pint of bitter in '53 o * * Ha, a noise! Perhaps some terrible tourist! Will I fly? No; despite my constitutional timidity, I will stand my ground o

(Enter tourist with white whiskers and his wife o)

Tourist with white whiskers: "Now, you see, my dear, there is no such things as ghosts o Really there is not o It is all a superstition o There is no such thing as a ghost o

The Ghost: (approaching unnoticed.) "Aw — — pardon?

Tourist with w w (jumping) Beg pardon?

Ghost   Oh, nothing o Only I thought I heard you denying the existence of ghosts o

T. with w.w. (excitedly) Well, you did o I can prove to you mathematically that it is impossible —"

Ghost (holding up his hand) I —

First page of the manuscript of "The Ghost." The handwriting is Stephen's except for the last few lines which are in Cora's hand. Courtesy Roger M. Frewen.

edy in verse which had recently appeared in the *Yellow Book*. Complaining of the dearth of good plays offered to London theatregoers, the *Guardian* writer—spoofing his readers a bit—felt that managers might do worse than turn to the Sussex-born "piece of literary patchwork" to fill the gap. So, too, thought Moreton Frewen, who tried unsuccessfully to get the play put on in London.

H. G. Wells remembered the whole party, except for the ominous red ending, as "an extraordinary lark." As the great open fires roared up the chimneys, Cora's hostess talents shone to best advantage in the setting she loved. The ancient rooms ablaze with candlelight and echoing with holiday spirit must have frightened the owls from their perches in the ivy outside chamfered windows. The guests "revelled every night until two or three, and strolled down towards noon to breakfasts of eggs and bacon, sweet potatoes from America and beer." Once, Crane in the small hours abortively attempted to teach some of the men to play poker, which no one took seriously, and was sharply annoyed with Wells for chattering over schoolboy reminiscences during the game.

On Friday evening, December 29, was the ball. Henry James, standing at his garden gate in Rye in the late afternoon, called a facetious warning to A. E. W. Mason driving past in the dogcart, that he might find one or two actresses in the crowd at Brede Place and had better look out—he might get caught! Stephen, who had danced badly with Lily Brandon Munroe at Asbury Park, now went through a lancers with Mrs. Pease to the tune of *Run Away Girl;* a barn dance with Edith, the guest of honor; and waltzed with her sister, Mabel Barr, as the little orchestra brought from London squeaked and thumped out *The Belle of New York*. He had another dance with Marriott-Watson's daughter, and two more with fair samples of those "bevies of American girls" who had enchanted Lewis Hind. Mason remembers that "a tremendous fall of snow" kept away most of the local people who had been invited, "perhaps just as well . . . for H. G. Wells . . . invented a game of racing on broomsticks over the polished floor, which I think would have staggered the local gentry if they had turned up."

When the party had broken up for the night and all but one or two of the guests had retired to their rooms, or dormitory shakedowns, Stephen picked up his guitar, softly strumming as he liked to do with his cheek close to the strings.* Whose was the shoulder he suddenly fainted against has never been told. But along in the wee hours Cora knocked on the door of the Wells' room; Stephen had had a hemorrhage from the lungs and tried to conceal it from her. Wells, who had had tuberculosis himself at one time, got out the thermometer he always carried in his vest pocket, then mounted a bicycle and rode off "into a drizzling dawn along a wet road to call up a doctor in Rye."

If Stephen was not on the doorstep next day to speed the parting guests, Cora made excuses; the house party was scheduled to break up anyhow after the ball. The Mark Barrs, the Richies, and young Frederick Bowen stayed over. Stephen wanted people there on New Year's Eve "to keep Cora from seeing spooks." He saw the Old Year out, and at midnight called a toast to the new century— over a mathematician's objection from Mark Barr that the century had not begun yet.

* Beer says it was a violin (p. 234), and Berryman repeats this (p. 250). Mrs. Conrad, in her "Recollections of Stephen Crane," says that Crane in relaxed moments often strummed a guitar, but in her later book, *Joseph Conrad and his Circle*, she has him playing a violin! One finds nothing in the memoirs of friends or associates of his youth to suggest that Crane ever played the violin, the most difficult of all musical instruments, and I strongly suspect the "old violin" of being a romantic invention of later letter writers.

chapter 6

LUGGAGE went astray, other things got left behind in the shuffle when the house-party guests scattered on their various ways. Cora must have spent a good part of the next day packaging forgotten possessions for return to their owners as tragedy and trivialities jostled one another in the domestic hurly-burly of Brede Place. The courtyard was choked with people and relics of the morning after: dried holly wreaths and ivy garlands tossed out on the ash heap, phalanxes of "dead soldiers" waiting to be carted away. The shabby procession of menials, swollen to necessity's use, traipsed in and out the rabbit warren of cellar passages on their way to the laundry where mountains of soiled linen piled up. All this work of clearing away the debris went forward while Stephen lay abed upstairs in the red study, sunken and silent. But he would not keep to his bed after strength returned, deceptively soon with the stoppage of bleeding, and next day was about again, obdurate in refusals to see doctors or listen to advice.

"I send your pillow slip," Cora wrote Catherine Wells; "many thanks again for the things you let me have. We are at work and just beginning to feel alive again after the Flue [sic]." The "prevailing epidemic" offered a convenient explanation of Stephen's illness, which like the ills of royalty or heads of state must not get noised about. "Edith [Richie] left us Tuesday last [January 2]. Her brother [Ford Richie] goes soon, then we shall have a long spell alone." But young Frederick Bowen was staying on at Brede Place till all danger of recurrent hemorrhage was past. Cora felt the need of a man's steadiness, and Fred Bowen, a sensitive and gentle youth, was strong in devotion to the Cranes. "One thing we have resolved upon," she briskly added, with forced cheerfulness, "Never will we have any sort of a party without the Wellses—we shall drag them of [sic] their death beds if we've a party on!"

Only the long room downstairs had been made habitable when Ford Hueffer drove over in his dogcart from Winchelsea, attracted by rumors of Babylonian orgies, which amused him and blew piquantly about the Sussex countryside. The Cranes and their visitor sat having tea and muffins before blazing logs in the "great room with warm shadows and rather good bits of furniture that Mrs. Crane had picked up," and "talked composedly" of the recent house party. Hueffer was reminded of the tea hour at Henry James' Lamb House. When he left, Stephen followed him, white-faced, out to the arched porch steps and gripped his arm, "his avenger's face lit by my cart lamps in the January darkness."

"Mr. Hueffer, you have been intimate with me in several places. . . . Now tell me on your honour. . . ." Had Hueffer ever seen him drunk, or drugged, or lecherously inclined, or foul-mouthed, or even quarrelsome? Had he ever heard any housemaids' gossip? In any particular or on any occasion?

"Poor Steevie," Hueffer sighed—blowing his nose in his memoirs —"poor dear fortunate youth!" Hueffer, of course, had never heard a word against him. "If it did not seem so fantastic I should be inclined to say that I am certain that he was as pure in heart—and almost as naïve—as his mother. . . ."

Robert Barr wrote to a friend that Mrs. Crane was "so incensed by the nonsense talked about the New Year party" that Stephen was taking her home; they were sailing in February. "England has been kind to Stevie in many ways but some of his cherished friends have said things too carelessly about his most generous but not too formal hospitality . . . and he is subject to a kind of jealousy that knows how to hurt him worst."

There was talk again, for a night, of buying land in Texas and living in the open air; then a new scheme of going to Gibraltar. Would the Rock lend endurance to the shot rabbit, to the weed cut down? Pinker thought nothing could be done with the Gibraltar scheme, but hoped to give Crane "a better one"; and Barr, who had not been a guest at the house party, thought it was "all over with the boy, he might last two years."

They did not sail. A fresh avalanche of bills and threats from out-raged creditors rolled in on them in the wake of the Yule party. Crane now screamed to Pinker, January 5, that he must have money immediately or find a man who could get it for him. Cora's tone was milder. She tried hard to make light of his illness, writing to Pinker on January 2 that Mr. Crane was in bed but keeping at work; some money was due from Stokes from *Active Service*. If these large sums, which ought to come from Stokes and for serial rights, could be gotten in "it would put Mr. Crane straight. But as it is we have to keep begging you to put cheques in bank all the time. I dont know what Mr. Crane would do without your kind help through these long days of trying to get straight, but I'm sure you feel that in the long run he will prove his appreciation of your simply sav-ing him from going smash. Again I have to beg for £20. . . ." She promised more chapters of the new novel—the Irish Romance which was to become *The O'Ruddy*—by the end of the week; and begged Pinker to let them know Stokes' answer by wire, as every moment saved would mean so much less worry for Mr. Crane. "Above all things, please do not get out of patience with these con-stant demands for money '*at once.*' "

It is nearly impossible to make anything of dates in much of the correspondence of this time with Pinker. Cora, whose time sense was as erratic as Stephen's, often misdated letters, supplied only the day of the week, or omitted dates altogether. Now time went un-clocked, days rushed together or lagged in dreadful apprehension. The picture comes clear only by comparison of the letters with Pinker's replies and the dates he, a careful businessman, recorded.

About January 4, receipt of twenty pounds was acknowledged, with a further request for thirty pounds to be sent "*without fail* on Monday" to the Oxted Bank. It was, Cora explained, to meet checks already returned and credit would be gone if they bounced a second time. Now too she was overdrawn at the London bank, and wired Pinker for another thirty pounds to be deposited with Brown, Shipley. Next day, "4:30 P.M.," Pinker's promised wire hadn't come but she hoped he had managed to do as she asked yes-terday; if the money were not deposited, the Bank might close her account. On the seventh at last came a wire from Pinker, but not the one they were expecting. Cora wrote:

Mr. Crane intended no threat and will keep all engagements made with you. He does not understand your telegram . . . and it has quite upset his day's work. . . .

It was again the old story, Crane needed a lot of money this month—at least £150—"and he is trying to earn it, and had no doubt that you would not help him, until your telegram. . . ." But one can hardly blame Pinker if he drew the line at footing the bills for the Brede house party! The Cranes must know whether their agent could be counted on to raise money as needed, so long as he got the stuff to sell; and Pinker already up to his neck in the broth, must have felt his only chance of ever getting out was to keep Crane going, and trust to luck. His reply:

January 9, 1900

I have this morning paid into your credit with Messrs. Brown, Shipley & Co. a cheque for £30. I am sure it is not necessary for me to tell you that you and Mr. Crane may always count on all the help I can give, but as you know, the demands on my help have been greater in extent and persistency than was ever contemplated, and I was therefore very much surprised to receive Mr. Crane's letter of the 5th. As you and he think I misinterpreted it, let me repeat what he said:—

"I must have the money. I cannot get on without it. If you cannot send £150 by the next mail, I will have to find a man who can. I know this is abrupt and unfair, but self-preservation forces my game with you precisely as it did with Reynolds."

If this did not mean what I took it to mean, I am at a loss to understand it. However, I am glad to have your assurance that Mr. Crane did not threaten any breach of our Agreement . . .

Then Cora on the tenth: "Mr. Crane says he had no idea of putting any of his work in any other hands than yours. . . . Mr. Crane is very faithful to any agreement [she could write that now!] and he appreciates the fact that you have advanced money upon stories before you received payment for them yourself." Would Methuen advance £100 on the Irish Romance? Several more chapters would be finished by Friday. Should she come up to town on that day bringing what was then finished of the novel—or could Pinker see Methuen and say that they now have, or can get at any time, the manuscript for the war stories? Would they advance £100 at once on the Irish story? "If they will do this they can send contract for

Mr. Crane to sign for this book—and for the next one for which they are to pay £200. . . ." Or did Pinker think it would be better to drop the Irish Romance and write some short stories in order to raise this money? Mr. Curtis Brown, an old friend of Mr. Crane's, "of whom you doubtless know, is anxious to buy a book from him and says that he will give a bigger price than anyone. . . ."

She could almost make herself believe in "the next one." For she, who was without common fear, now dared not look back—or ahead into the abyss of sorrows that would be her lot on earth without Stephen.

So more and more guests came "to keep Cora from seeing spooks": the Frewens, De Frieses, Colwells. Commander J. C. Colwell, U. S. Naval Attaché, had read with admiration and chuckles Stephen's story, "The Revenge of the Adolphus," in which was described the exploit of an old harbor tug (the *Three Friends*) in one of the sea fights of the Spanish-American War; and, probably at the author's request, had made corrections in the use of nautical terms. In the last week of January, through interested neighbors, a luncheon was arranged in Stephen's honor at Fairseat, High Wickham, the Hastings home of Mr. Tommy Parkin, a local magistrate, ardent bibliophile and warm friend of authors. Another governess was procured for "the young barbarians" when Mrs. Burke had to leave, through the generosity of a kind-hearted manufacturer of linoleum, Mr. John Barry (also a visitor at Brede Place), who paid her salary. Cora attended the monthly meetings of the Society of American Women in London, taking an active part in procuring new members and speakers. The garden party fete of the previous summer had owed its brilliant success largely to the participation of Brede House and its guests. So now Cora was making plans, placing advertisements and holding committee meetings for another charity bazaar to be held on August 1 for the benefit of needy families of soldiers wounded in the Transvaal. The Vicar thought August a better month than July, "as there is always a lull in work then, between harvest and hopping." He hoped she would carry the project through, it would be *very* popular. But the bazaar this time would be held at Brede Place, instead of the Rectory gardens.

Lady Randolph Churchill's hospital ship *Maine*—called after the American battleship sunk in Havana harbor—would soon be bringing back the first shipload of wounded from South Africa, and

Stephen's brother Will had looked in vain for their names in the long list of patrons. Then posters announced a concert on February 6 in the Brede Hill schoolroom, in aid of the Yeomanry Hospital Fund. " 'A London Crowd' and 'Bugle Calls' will be given on the Gramophone kindly lent by Stephen Crane, Esq., Brede Place." The affair was "gotten up at a moment's notice," but the audience was "delighted" by the gramophone, the singing of Mr. Richie, Miss Marriott, and others. The *Southeastern Advertiser's* account mentions in particular two songs sung by Miss Héloïse and Master Barry Frederic, aged six and five—"I Had a Black Dolly Called Topsy," and "Bonnie Dundee"—which "called for loud applause." When the children applauded back, thinking it expected of them, that brought down the house.

But the clockwork was "juggling badly"; and Cora's off-calendar timing poses a question of dates. Her letter to Mrs. Frewen giving her own version of *The Ghost* performance (see p. 224) speaks of the concert, but is dated "Jan. 16th, 1900": "I sent you two county papers, one with the account of the 'Ghost', isn't it funny!, and one with notice of the little concert." She retained duplicates for her scrapbook. But the first of these clippings, a column and a half with caption in large type, "Theatricals at Brede," bears underneath this heading a notation in her hand: "South Eastern Advertiser, January 5th, 1900"; and the second, a short paragraph about the concert, uncaptioned, is dated by her, "Feb. 17th, 1900." Her letter to Mrs. Frewen begins: "We were disappointed that you could not come to us the first of the month and we trust that you will not forget us at the *end* of January."

The *Advertiser*, like most weeklies, probably came out several days ahead of the date of issue; and the concert announced for February 6 may well have been postponed to the following week on account of weather conditions. The Frewens' visit to Brede Place probably took place early in March. It thus appears that, owing perhaps to the increasing emotional strain she was under since Stephen's collapse and which she must keep hidden, the events of these two months had become jumbled together in Cora's recollection and she therefore twice wrote "January" when she must have meant February.

How splendid, she finds it, that the Frewens are going to plant trees and shrubs at Brede Place.

We often say: "oh, if we could only replace every tree that has been cut in the Park," and we have said: "We must plant an avenue of oaks to mark our time," then we are forced to say: "We can't do it now," and publishers are behaving so badly at the moment that now we say: "Well, we must plant *one* oak to mark our time."

And echoing Stephen's delight in the weird harp-like sounds made by the house during a thunderstorm, she remarked that Brede Place "gets on some people's nerves, but I don't believe we have any, for we love it most when 'the children cry' and the house rings as if it were filled with telegraph wires." She hoped for a wild night "so that you may really enjoy it," hastening to add, lest their guests be frightened away, "we will make you comfortable and warm, but it's very jolly to sit by the fire and have things moan and hum, particularly if you have someone to tell good ghost stories. Does this sound childish?"

"My dearest girl," wrote Kate Frederic (letter undated), who had just come in and found a letter from Cora. "*What* is the matter with Stephen?" She could not tell from Cora's note. But whatever it was, the dear boy was sure to throw it off at once; and God would be good to Cora, who had been so good to others. Kate apologized for not having "Solferino" ("The Battle of Solferino") further along, but would "heave away at it like mad." Lippincott had asked Stephen to do two more of the Battle pieces "in order to make a more presentable volume"; and Kate wanted to know if he were "well enough to go over what I write? Do you mean me to work it up in a *finished* state for the magazine?"*

Crane talked and smoked less now, and went for no more rides around the park on Glenroy and Gloucester, but worked on doggedly. To a gentleman meeting him for the first time at Mr. Parkin's luncheon, he had seemed tense and uncommunicative, with the strained, white look of nervous exhaustion. The man was dying. But as in the case of Surgeon Gibbs ("War Memories"), dying sometimes took a long time; and you couldn't quit; and Cora must

---

* From this correspondence with Kate Frederic it appears that, in addition to research, her work on some of the *Battle* pieces involved actual writing, to the extent of full-fledged collaboration, a fact which went unacknowledged by Crane but which, I am told, was common knowledge in Kate's family.

not be frightened. The spirit hovering on the borders of two worlds retreated to a place of remoteness, shut in indifference. "I'm just a dry twig on the edge of the bonfire," he had told Willis Clarke, a young man who had visited him in November at Brede Place. Dominick's views regarding a title for the Cuban war sketches—Dominick who had valiantly stood in the breach—mattered not at all, he was "only surprised that Methuen found occasion to agree with him on any point." He roused himself to ask Cora to write Pinker "to try to get £100 from Lippincott for American book rights [for the Battle articles] and to get it *now*, telling them that's the reason they get it so cheap." He reminded Pinker, "Remember the 12th [February]. I must have a good sum on the morning of that day. . . . Please wire me on Friday night but state the words ambiguously because my post-master is my grocer." And again on March 24:

Please send a cheque to A. T. Plant, 18 Bedford Row, Grey's Inn for £22 before Wednesday or a bailiff will be here and also deposit £20 to my wife's a/c at Brown Shipley, and send the enclosed wire. This does not include the £15 which I asked from you today.

The novel (*The O'Ruddy*) stood at 61,000 words, and although "extremely doubtful about my prudence in writing it at this time," he expected it would "pull me out much more than even." Would Pinker take his note for £100?

Helen Crane was looking forward to Easter marking her deliverance. She was being taken out of the Rosemont School to go with her aunt and uncle to St. Helena. But she was also communicating to her Aunt Cora feelings of an opposite nature, clumsily disguised and no doubt intended to pull wool over the hostile eyes of her jailer, Mme. Eytel-Hubbe, whom she now quoted as saying: "What makes your aunt act so, and why didn't you write her and say you want to stay until June?" But how glad she would be, to get away from the school and Madame! "She cannot say I do not study, because I do. In French I have got along very quickly and I am first in German and also draw better than any other girl here. . . ." Cora had seen to it that Helen had dancing and violin lessons, as "extras." But a wheedling missive, this, filled with complaints and sly innuendo bearing on the single subject that the writer was "simply in rags" and must have a few things to look respectable. Helen found it "im-

H. G. Wells during one of his visits to Brede Place. Gift of Henry W. Walters.

possible" to make something for the bazaar in August, too busy with her studies. Why of course, she could travel to Paris alone, but wanted no more sight-seeing outside of the shops . . . and a trip through the Morgue!

Twelve hundred miles out in the Atlantic west of Africa, along the sea lanes to Brazil, lay the rocky island of St. Helena where the beaten Napoleon was exiled after Waterloo. A garrison and a Boer prison were there now. What ghoulish impulse led Crane to this desolate spot with its gloomy associations of extinguished glory, captivity, and defeat ending in death, it is hard to imagine. Now at any rate, he proposed going there to write political articles on the Boer question for the New York *Journal*, the London *Morning Post*, and the *Daily Chronicle*. Cora and his niece would go with him. Friends thought, or pretended, that his health might benefit. The owner of the *Morning Post* was Lord Glenesk, whose son-in-law the Earl of Bathurst was commandant of the garrison at St. Helena; at least, life would not be dull for the girls on that isolated rock!

Judge Crane had consented to Helen's going with them if the cost were about the same as to continue her in school. Her year abroad had been "rather a severe drain, but we wish her to have some advantages and have not begrudged the expenses." Cora had written Will already of Stephen's hemorrhage and the need to get him out of England into a drier climate; her brother-in-law invited them both to visit him at Port Jervis "and stay as long as you can." April 3, Will was "overjoyed to hear of Stephen's improvement"; then he abruptly turned to financial matters: *

Stephen paid me $500.00 on account of $1,250.00 which he was to pay me for a one-eighth interest in Hartwood. He has no deed and even hasn't a contract which, however, makes no difference. Now if he does not wish to complete transaction, the situation is about like this: I credit him with $500.00. I charge him with various items, including the £100 which I sent him in March, 1899, and he is still in my debt $155.27 at this date.

Of course, I do not expect him to pay this until he gets ready. I am merely setting forth the business situation of the Hartwood transaction.* If he is able to think of business matters kindly show him this letter and I think he'll concur. . . .

In the whirlpool of her emotions the effect on Cora of such a letter, at such a time, may be imagined. But so swiftly were events closing in now, hurtling toward crisis, that she probably never had an opportunity to show Stephen the letter, or to speak of it.

On March 31 she left for Paris to meet Helen, arrived the next day, and found awaiting her there a cable from Stephen with Corwin Linson's address. Stephen had only just learned of Linson being in Paris, and wanted Cora to call on him. Worried lest she and Helen might run short of funds, Stephen also wired Pinker to rush £30 over to Mrs. Crane. Cora and Helen spent two happy days in the shops of the Rue St. Honoré making brilliant additions to the girl's

* He is referring to the Hartwood Club, a fishing and hunting resort started in 1893 by William H. Crane on a 3,500 acre tract located in the hills above the Minisink Valley, some twelve miles from Port Jervis. As stated, Stephen never finished paying for his "one-eighth interest in Hartwood." Judge Crane, one of the largest stockholders in the corporation, had induced his brother Edmund to come to Hartwood as superintendent of the farm and estate, but Edmund Crane moved back to Lakeview, N.J., in 1900. The Hartwood Club is today a flourishing and exclusive private resort, with a handsome clubhouse and some eighteen "cottages"—or more accurately, two-storey "mansions."

wardrobe. Then on April 3, they returned to their hotel to find a cablegram from Vernall, Cora's faithful housekeeper and cook: Mr. Crane had had two hemorrhages and did not wish Mrs. Crane to be upset; Vernall was sending the cablegram without his knowledge. Cora and Helen caught the night boat. . . .

2

FROM Paris Cora sent cablegrams to Hoyt De Friese, Moreton Frewen, and to Will Crane in Port Jervis. She asked the De Frieses to obtain from the American Embassy the name of the most eminent lung specialist in London, and to take charge of arrangements for getting him down to Brede Place—above all, to lose no time! Later in the week she wired their Embassy friend J. C. Colwell, the Naval Attaché, asking his advice in procuring a male attendant.

Katherine De Friese arrived at the Embassy the next morning— April 4—before it opened. She reported the young chief aide, Henry White, much worried over the time that had elapsed since Crane was stricken before his examination by a specialist, feeling the responsibility in the case of a man of such world fame heavy on the Embassy and himself alike. Mr. White wrote a note of introduction for Mrs. De Friese to Dr. J. T. Maclagen, the physician he recommended, and sent along a clerk to bring back a report. He also directed Mrs. De Friese to a nursing home, where she arranged for a nurse to go down on the same train with the doctor, who would have to remain overnight at Brede Place for his train connection back to London. On reaching her own home in St. James Park, Mrs. De Friese found another telegram from Cora, from Brede Place, with the encouraging news that Stephen was a little better.

For Cora, the next four days rolled up into a foggy nightmare of weariness, anxiety, heartbreak. She had had no sleep except short naps. She had had to give a check for fifty pounds to Dr. Maclagen, but "he was so encouraging that I am glad." The Solferino battle article she would have up to Pinker in a few days—it was partly typed—and she enclosed a copy of a note she had written to Lippincott's London representative, Mr. Garneson, asking him to send a check to Pinker or deposit it with Brown, Shipley, to meet the check given to Dr. Maclagen of 9 Cadogan Place. "I dont think they will hestitate as it was a matter of saving Stephen Crane's life."

Pinker did not see it that way. He was much put out that Cora had gone over his head in the matter of the fifty pounds for the Solferino article, writing Lippincott herself. Cora controlled her feelings: "Now Mr. Pinker, it was a matter of life and death to have the Specialist down. I could not leave any stone unturned." Pinker might not have gone to his office on Friday or Saturday, she *had* to write Lippincott; but she had written the agent at the same time, enclosing a copy of her note to Mr. Garneson. "One cannot stand upon ceremony at such a moment. Pray forgive any seeming lack of courtesy to yourself."

On April 7, she had written pressing Pinker to let her know whether serial rights for the Irish novel had yet been sold. "If Mr. Crane should die I have notes of end of novel so it could be finished and no one will lose—if that thought should occur." Now she was glad she could tell him, "my husband seems a little better today. He had a quiet day and night with no hemorrhage, and takes his nourishment well." His illness nevertheless would be a long one, the expense great. The two nurses alone were costing £2.4.6 each per week! She hoped Mr. Crane would be well enough to dictate the rest of the other Battle article, the last of the series, so that she might get the £100 due for book rights from Lippincott. She reminded Pinker that his draft, the £30 sent to Paris, had not reached her, and supposed it had been returned.

Friends showed their affection in messages that cheered and comforted. Moreton Frewen rejoiced in the news of Stephen's improvement: ". . . please God this desperate load of anxiety will be resolved. . . . That such danger and distress should have overtaken him and you under our old rooftree is a matter of sadness indeed to us both." His wife, he said, had telegraphed him from Ireland: "If there is anything I can do you will be sure to let me know." A. E. W. Mason stood ready to drop everything and come: ". . . it must have been a terribly anxious time for you, no doctor next door and not even H. G. Wells' thermometer." Robert McClure of the publishing house, old scores forgotten, also offered to come down to Brede if he could be of any help to her.

Cora's Aunt Abbie Holder—Mrs. Cates—had seen by the newspapers that she must be very anxious about Mr. Crane, but as there had been nothing in the last few days she took that to mean that he would recover. "I hope so I am sure. I think from your letters that you are quite happy and hope you will see many happy days together yet." Cora was fond of both her aunts, her mother's people—her nearest living relatives—and seems to have been writing to the two old ladies more or less regularly since coming to live in England. She sent snapshots of Stephen and Brede Place to Aunt Abbie, in Massachusetts, and one of herself with a lapful of puppies. Her aunt begged her to write, when she had time, "all about your troubles and tell me the particulars of Stephen's illness. With love to you both I am your affec'ct Aunt Abbie."

To the dismay of Cora and Ford Richie, the news had leaked to the London press, then flashed across the world. Thereafter, the big dailies on both sides of the Atlantic blossomed forth with regular bulletins on the condition of Stephen Crane's health. The Associated Press representative in London, Walter A. M. Goode, an old correspondent friend of Stephen's, was instructed by his chief, the European manager of AP, to get reports telegraphed from Brede Place to "Associated, London." As they could not prepay charges, Goode explained, "I am going to ask . . . if you will be good enough to let *me* know . . . and allow me to forward you the necessary sum for a daily telegram until my old friend is out of danger." Along with the presidential race and the fate of the Boer republic, Crane was front page news.

Face to face with such sobering realities as the illness of her adored Uncle Stephen, the awful imminence of death itself, Helen Crane was rapidly outgrowing her teen-age delinquencies. She now took over the task of answering correspondence, a great help to her overburdened Aunt Cora.

Sanford Bennett hurried over from France. He found a weary and desperate woman pacing the long hall, "lashing her skirt with one of his [Crane's] riding crops. She broke out into a frantic denunciation of herself for allowing so much entertainment at Brede." The first and only time since this latest crisis that Cora had given way to emotion, at the sight of Stephen's devoted friend she broke down, sobbing. Bennett spent "a ghastly quarter of an hour. . . . But she showed her courage," he said.

Now, in response to Cora's wire, Fred Bowen came again to stay two weeks at Brede Place, until Stephen was pronounced out of danger. Cora and young Bowen, a technical engineer, had some while earlier entered into a joint business arrangement respecting an improved type of army canteen which Cora had invented—probably inspired by her experiences with thirst and impure drinking water in the Greek war. The *Memorandum of Agreement* stated that Cora had "made a new and valuable discovery or invention relating to the construction and manufacture of canteens and filters," and that Frederick L. Bowen had contributed improvements on her design. They agreed to patent and put their product on the market, sharing profits equally; Bowen was to undertake all the business of merchandising in England and abroad, and "to keep account books." Moreton Frewen, sniffing fortunes to be made, with his usual zest interested himself in procuring financial backing for the enterprise. Whether this proved to be another of Frewen's "splendid crashes" is not on record, but the *Agreement*, drawn by Mr. De Friese, survives as testimony to the extraordinary range and versatility of Cora's ingenuity.

There was also a matter of Rumanian oil properties and "an influential man"—Moreton Frewen—to whom Cora seems to have introduced Fred Bowen's father, an entrepreneur seeking capital. It was a venture in which the elder Bowen apparently lost heavily, while others cleaned up. But the "influential man," was not among those to reap the profits.

She now felt the whole of existence, with all the resources of her loving heart and fierce determination, centered on the preservation of Stephen Crane's life. Whatever the state of her own hope, financial worries must not intervene to retard Stephen's recovery. The old note of command came back into her correspondence with Pinker.

It was primrose time and never had Brede Place looked more lovely, with rivers of gold and pink flowing down the slopes, new leaves budding, roses bursting into bloom, the ragged old orchard trees a mist of pink bloom fountained on azure skies. The nightingales sang deliriously; and it seemed to friends that with warm breezes and all this juice and joy and dazzle about, health must come back to the invalid too with the rising sap. There began to be talk now of Stephen's "wiry" and "strong American constitution," which had pulled him through so many earlier crises.

Cora, too, half believed in this myth: ". . . the doctors think Mr. Crane much better. They say if he can pull through to Thursday without a hemorrhage—ten days—he will be out of danger. The doctor said to him today, 'in three weeks you can work!' " "Wonderfully good care" had pulled him through; and "Dr. Skinner [the physician in Rye whom Wells had roused up in that bloody dawn with a summons to Brede Place] says that the trouble seems only superficial, not deeply rooted."

Mark Barr wrote from Paris, where he was installing linotypes for the International Exposition: "I have heard what a brave fight Stevie and you made and it is what your friends would expect, dear Cora. . . . Stephen, all my cigars!" And H. G. Wells, an expert on hemorrhages: "I'll bet an even halo . . . that hemorrhages aren't the way you will take out of this terrestrial tumult." Hemorrhages were from every point of view a bloody way of dying; Wells knew of few "more infernally disagreeable." But what business had Crane in the Valley, confound it, not mid-day yet and his work "well started," but only just begun?

Stephen was permitted to see letters now, Cora wrote Pinker and Wells, "but nothing that could possibly worry him." As soon as he was strong enough she and Dr. Skinner would take him up to London for another consultation with the specialist "as to the best way to care for his health in future." Then they wanted to get him to Bournemouth for a stay among the pines." . . . Of all places Bournemouth, where the canonized shade of R. L. Stevenson was enshrined in a yellow-brick cottage on the edge of Alum Chine! . . . Cora asked for a check immediately. "This is such a critical time now—every post delay will make his temperature fly up—so please do your very best." She was thinking of subletting Brede Place—furniture, linen, servants, horses, carriage, everything. Would Pinker, if he heard of likely tenants, direct them to her? Myra Haggard—wife of H. Rider Haggard, the author of best-seller romances—"so very grieved to hear such a sad account of your husband's health," promised to do everything possible to interest friends wanting a place for the summer if Cora would send particulars as to rent, etc.

In this move of letting Brede Place, which must have had the approval of their landlord Moreton Frewen, Cora was clutching at any straw to lighten the financial burden. Judge Crane, though "greatly alarmed and grieved over Stephen's condition," feared that he could not help with money at present. On April 13 he was still "troubled"; he read the news in the papers every day but found this "unsatisfactory" and would like "frequent reports." If the trouble was tubercular, Stephen should leave England and come to the United States. "You and your wife will be welcome at our house for as long as you care to stay." Pleasant here, he added, except in winter, "then you can, if you wish, flit southward with the birds." On April 21, he was sending Stephen a book by Dr. Buckley, "one of Father's old friends," *A Consumptive's Struggle For Life.* The good doctor as a young man had suffered from hemorrhages, until he began the use of Dr. Howe's breathing tube. Will recommended highly both the book and the gadget. "Stephen can tell you I have blown on Dr. Howe's tube over twenty years, and I am sure it has done me great good." He wanted Helen to stay another year in England. . . . "This morning's papers say that Kimberly has not been relieved. You would be surprised to know how passionately the American people disapprove of England in the Transvaal matter. Nobody favors her, excepting the great financial interests and a few of *our* Tory newspapers." Judge Crane was an ardent Democrat and Bryan-ite. Then on May 10: "We are grieving over the situation; but I really cannot send money in any amount to make it worth while at present." Port Jervis was 460 feet above tidewater, and Hartwood 1,600; Will thought they might easily do worse than come to America. "My wife would love to nurse him back to health." The invitation was "not given lightly."

In interesting contrast to this well-meant but useless advice was the offer from their good old friend, Eben Alexander, of a home in his house at Chapel Hill, where the air was just right, "for as long as you like." With money coming in from books already published, and practically no expenses, Stephen might soon get on his feet financially. "We live in utmost simplicity, but I don't think either of you will mind that. If I had money I would send enough in two minutes. . . . But I have only my salary. You two would add practically nothing to our living expenses." Writing in haste, the kind old diplomat-professor feared he had not made himself clear. "But you and Stephen will understand. . . . We shall be as glad to have you as if you were our own children."

But Alexander's letter arrived too late. The agonizing journey to the Black Forest had begun.

Meanwhile, the sick boy's thoughts traveled back to his ancestral past and the earlier Stephen Crane from whom he got his name. As though seeking to be reconciled with the gentle ghost of his father, he dwelt much on him who was "a great, fine simple mind"; and his mother, the ardent religionist with the voice like Ellen Terry's, he saw now as less "narrow than most of her friends," the rescuer of "fallen" girls and their "accidental babies." Stephen lay abed reading at random his father's sermons, and occasionally dictating lines for a story or parts of the Irish novel: the ironist casting up accounts with life lived and musing on the holy show some people made of it. The drawled words came whispered now, speech was an effort. "Men," he wrote, "have never much deserved Christ and Buddha, because they went to work and changed the teaching of generosity into a teaching of roars and threats. I can not be shown that God bends on us any definable stare, like a sergeant at muster, and his laughter would be bully to hear out in nothingness."

Cora forwarded to Pinker Stephen's dedication of *Wounds in the Rain* to Moreton Frewen. And then one day—April 21—in the interim before the shadows deepened, Crane summoned the solicitor Alfred T. Plant to Brede Place and made his will: a new will—canceling the earlier one he had made in Florida—in which, legitimacy hanging in the balance, he recognized Cora as his wife.

3

Boy he was, and remained, to the end of his life: hopelessly impractical, bedeviled by centripetal involvements with the warring impulses of his nature; increasingly bitter at his own dependence on others for a solution of his personal difficulties; spinning out of fever and illness mirages of self-delusion and grandeur.

Without laboring comparisons, certain parallels between the stormy history of the Cranes and the Stevensons—Louis and Fanny —can hardly escape notice, beginning with the central fact that Stevenson and Crane were each involved with an older woman not yet divorced. Both of these women were of superior mental powers, cultured, energetic, managerial, unconventional, and by masculine reckoning more attractive than beautiful. The Darwinian ideas that were revolutionizing the century into which the feudal lord of Vailima and the squire of Brede Place had been born, plunged them from boyhood into moral conflict, whence issued the challenge of their genius. Both were iconoclasts, in pursuit of vastly different objectives through the medium of their art. In Crane's impatience with Stevenson's "velveteen romanticism," his abomination of the Stevenson myth, was perhaps more than a hint of self-justification and buried guilt in respect to Cora—calling to mind the youthful Stevenson's righteous blast against the supposed lecheries of the apotheosized Burns.* Whereas in Victorian times in extra-marital relations the feeling of sin traditionally abided with the female, under the pressures of the double life they were caught in it was Stephen—reversing the usual order of things—who suffered most from guilt complexes. Not Cora. Not Fanny. There the parallel ends, as Stevenson enjoyed a better break from the powers that be and from his own Calvinist conscience than the unluckier Crane; for at the end of the Stevensons' first year together Fanny's divorce came through and he was able to make an honest woman of her. But it is also worth remembering that while the truant fourteenth child of dead parsonage parents was cadging small loans from Garland, Acton Davies, and a host of anonymous associates of potato-salad days in New York, many thousands of pounds sterling from a well-to-do engineering father had gone to support the truant Scot on his difficult climb to successful authorship and fame, until his thirty-eighth year—the year of the elder Stevenson's death. Robert Louis Stevenson died at forty-four; Stephen Crane was to die at twenty-eight.

In justice to Cora, it must be said that she had not a drop of Fanny Stevenson's cattiness. Perhaps she had not remained long enough with either of her previous husbands in those two unhappy marriages to become a frustrated woman, as were so many of her contemporaries, including Fanny. A frustrated woman was just what Cora had always refused to be; and in their working association she was under no sort of compulsive need to impose her own literary judgments upon Crane, as Fanny had sought to do with Stevenson. If more ruthless than Fanny Osbourne in her assertion of independence when husbands failed to satisfy her woman's needs, of heart, sex, or mental compatibility, she was also less self-enclosed in her interests; and she possessed a sense of humor which Fanny unfortu-

* In "Some Aspects of Robert Burns," *Cornhill,* November, 1879. Stevenson was writing this holier-than-thou essay denouncing the amorous strayings of the Scottish bard and declaiming against hypocrisy, at the very moment of becoming most deeply involved in his liaison with Mrs. Osbourne.

nately lacked. "I'm always talking of myself," she once remarked, "but it's a subject of real interest to me!"

From motives of chivalry Crane could be obsessed with rescue of street-walkers, or of talented unfortunates with psychotic leanings like Amy Leslie. But his curious streak of Puritan conformism reared up in these last days, who knows whether at the touch of scandal or some recessive memory from the family religions? It exerted an influence on the making of his will, with peculiarly disastrous results.

An attorney, knowing nothing of the tangled divorce situation which kept them from marrying or of Crane's compulsive need to make up for the privations of his starved youth, which kept him on the verge of bankruptcy, finds this will "designed out of a feeling of obligation. Cora was the recipient of an obligation, rather than of a bounty. It is *not* a bounty, dictated by feelings of tenderness toward her, or the love of his heart. The will reflects these contradictions and vacillations of the man himself. It also indicates certain delusions about himself, and what he had to leave."

William Howe Crane and Alfred T. Plant were named co-executors, and trustees, for the United States and England respectively. Under these separate trusteeships, Crane directed his American Executor to remit to his English Executor "all moneys arising from the sale of my real estate in America and from the collection and conversion of my personal estate," except what may be required for payment of debts. Plant was then empowered to invest funds transferred from America and all other estate money remaining after payment of English debts in government securities, investment stocks of any British colony, mortgages of any leaseholds in England or Wales, etc., and was likewise directed to pay income from residuary trust funds "to my dear wife" during her life or widowhood. If Cora remarried, income and corpus of the residuary trust were to pass to his relatives, one-half going in trust to his namesake Stephen, Edmund Crane's baby son born a few weeks earlier, the other half to be divided equally between his brothers Will and Ed.

One would like to know Judge Crane's feelings on first reading this will; they would make interesting copy for the Recording Angel. For the only thing that looked like "real estate in America" of which Stephen Crane at this time could possibly die possessed was the one-eighth interest in Hartwood—which his brother said was based on a verbal promise, never fulfilled, that netted Stephen a debt of $155.27! As for the rest, situate in England or Wales, etc.— no mention of Ireland—it existed nowhere outside of his expanding imagination.

Anyone of the legal profession, schooled in wills and trusteeships, recognizes that when a man begins to pile up something to leave, especially if he started from nothing, that is the time when the desire to dictate and control from beyond the grave takes hold of him. Stephen wanted to forbid Cora's marrying again, whether because he didn't trust her judgment and wished to protect her, or out of feelings of jealousy and distrust. Had not jealousy and disillusion, the sad aftermath of unsuccessful courtships, always played a negative part in his attachment to her? And Cora was not yet thirty-five. He devised a punishment if she remarried: he disinherited her. It was only a life interest he settled on her under the trust, but if she married again it wasn't to be even that; it would all stop. He cut her off.

And then on the same day—April 21, 1900—he added a codicil.

It appears from this most curious afterthought that on reading over the will before signing it, Stephen must have felt that he had treated Cora too harshly. He must also have felt that the end was not far off. In the codicil he gives her trinkets: his jewelry and household furnishings, his wines and liquors, plate, glass, linen, china, books, pictures, plants and garden tools, his horses, carriages and saddlery. These things do not come under the trust, but are given to Cora outright. He does *not* give her his real estate, stocks and securities (which did not exist). But he does direct that the income from literary earnings should not go into the trust, but outright to her. Then he ties it down again with a stipulation that if she remarries, the trust created for her under the will would terminate and the property go to his brothers and his nephew. The will was witnessed by Dr. Ernest B. Skinner, and Stephen's nurse, Miss Charlotte Edith Gardner.

"Every sin is the result of a collaboration," Crane had written at the conclusion of "The Blue Hotel." Ironically, it was, in this instance, for this will of his was to become an accessory in Cora's downfall.

4

IN SPITE of Crane's visible emaciation, no one yet seemed to realize that the whole Brede Place extravaganza was coming to an end. Doctors continued optimistic, and the London specialist, Dr. Maclagen, wrote Cora on May 2 that he "would not readily take a hopeless view of his case." The week before, Stephen had been moved to a room downstairs, from which he could be carried out every day into the warm sunshine. The lung had healed over. He had had an abscess that was very painful and still "not finished with"—Cora told Pinker—but otherwise he was getting on wonderfully well, the danger from hemorrhage quite over. But now the doctors said he must have a sea voyage. Could Pinker get some English paper to pay expenses for Mr. Crane and herself to St. Helena and back, and a month there? Stephen could send back interesting letters.

H. G. Wells had seen an item in the *Academy* about Crane's illness, and on April 13 he wrote Cora asking for news of his condition; a week later he wrote Stephen. Cora replied April 25, speaking frankly to Wells—it was such a relief to unburden herself to someone in whose discretion she trusted. "Stephen is not up to letter writing so I am answering your very cheerful letter to him," she wrote. The lung trouble seemed over; but she was so anxious about him! The doctor after an examination that day had pronounced the right lung

> entirely unaffected. The trouble is that this dreadful abscess which seems to open from time to time in the bowel—or rectum, makes him suffer the most awful agony. And it takes away his strength in an alarming fashion. . . . So he is very weak. Then the *fever* (Cuban fever) comes for an hour or two each day.

In the last week the chills seemed to have stopped; he hoped within three or four weeks to go on a sea voyage. "Write to him when you can. Sick people have fancies that their friends neglect them . . ."

John Foster Fraser, M.P., whose admiration for everything Crane wrote had begun with *The Red Badge*, which he had read "while stewing aboardship on the Beluchi coast," hoped newspaper accounts of Crane's illness were exaggerated. He had found Crane "not looking well" when the Frasers lunched at Brede Place one Saturday in March. "I thought then that I would like to get you astride a bicycle and take a jaunt through a country of moorland where bread and cheese and ale is all you can get to eat and where the inhabitants never even heard of Stephen Crane!" Remembering that Stephen had expressed a desire to visit the Houses of Parliament, he proposed that the Cranes and the Frasers meet in London on May 3, when Parliament would be sitting again. Mrs. Crane could go with Mrs. Fraser to the Ladies' Gallery. The next evening he hoped they would be the Frasers' guests at the Whitefriars Club for the Club's annual ladies' night. But if Crane, with his well-known aversion to female novelists, wished to avoid them, the two couples could "sit at a modest table and be as secluded as you like." As to the glories of old manor houses, "If it weren't for you Americans," exclaimed the hearty gentleman in a postscript, "I believe we gor-darned Britishers would never realize we had anything to look upon!"

The owners of Brede Place, too, perhaps were of the same mind. Clara Frewen, who had already made known her intention of undertaking restorations, wanted the work to begin as soon as possible. Cora recommended the architect who had done the earlier repairs. Anxious to secure the commission, young Mr. Harrison Cowlishaw, the brother-in-law of Mrs. Garnett, was sure "it is entirely through your kindness and influence that this has been brought about"; Mrs. Crane's warm invitation to stay at Brede Place while work was in progress would be "very acceptable." In the press of other concerns, Cora found a moment to write to the Commons member from the Northiam-Hastings-St. Leonard's district—Mr. Brookfield—about a job in the London post office for a former Brede employe.

Then suddenly, hope evaporated; friends showed anxiety. Henry James rushed up to London on a rumor that the great Dr. Trudeau of Saranac was in the city, and wildly cabled to America for softshell crabs to tempt the invalid's touchy appetite. James' love of the boy, whose stripped utterance of "shockers" he did not understand, was genuine, his respect for Crane's talent and literary judgment evidenced by manuscript after manuscript he sent him with requests for criticism. Florence Bray wrote inquiring if there were any Yorkshire dish she could send—did Stephen like honey? Edith

Richie sent Easter eggs from Rosbrin. The Frewens, grown skeptical of Bournemouth and St. Helena, now urged the high Alps: Switzerland, or the German Black Forest. Moreton and Clara were writing to their intimate friend the Duchess of Manchester, who had lost two daughters from tuberculosis, about the celebrated Nordracht treatment in the Black Forest, and the Swiss sanitarium at Davoz of which the Duchess had particular knowledge. Clara Frewen's younger sister, Lady John Leslie, obtained from the Duchess and relayed to Cora all the necessary information about getting to Davoz: itinerary, train schedules, fares, etc. A mutual friend, Mary Cranshaw, wrote to Moreton Frewen: "Here is Consuelo's description of the cure . . . that costs less and is much more cheerful and less cruelly severe on the patient than Nordracht. Do think of it." The Duchess, she said, would write to Dr. Doughty, head of the Swiss sanitarium, "and get Mr. Crane taken on *special terms*." The Duchess herself wrote from her home at 45 Portman Square:

My dear Cora . . . I think Mr. Crane would be very comfortable at Davoz. It is the Nordracht cure without the brutality. You could not get anyone in at Nordracht under six-eight months. I am not even sure Dr. Doughty has a vacancy . . . but if you decide I will write and bring the case before him. Affec'y yours, C.

Doctors disagreed: Skinner strong for a sea voyage, Maclagen opposed to moving Crane anywhere for at least two months. Then around April 30 he suffered another collapse; and Dr. Skinner, who five days earlier had pronounced him out of danger, abandoned hope.

Cora did not give up, writing Pinker: "Mr. Crane is no worse and the right lung holds out, only, this change must be made without delay. We will go to some small inn in the Black Forest." A nurse and the doctor would go with them, a *very* expensive journey but "a matter of life or death and it must be done."

Just how expensive was made clear in her next communication, a few days later. "There is another consultation tomorrow—which means fifty guineas cash." But a valuable life could not be saved by pinching pennies or pounds. There was a chance of arresting the disease, or even of a cure, by going to the Black Forest for the Nordracht treatment. Dr. Mitchel Bruce—whose connection with the case is unexplained—had been the one, Cora afterwards told Moreton Frewen, who favored the Black Forest over the Duchess of Manchester's preference for Switzerland.

And was there again astral interference from the shade of R. L. Stevenson, who some fifteen years earlier had been a patient at both Saranac and Davoz? When told he looked like the long-haired Stevenson, Crane's reply was, "I hope I outgrow it!"

"Now I give you an outline of what has to be done," Cora wrote Pinker. He is carried on an air bed on a stretcher to *Rye*. There an invalid carriage will take him, the nurses, one doctor and myself, to Dover. Here we rest for one or perhaps two weeks at the Lord Warden Hotel . . . then a deck cabin to Callis [Calais] & there an invalid carriage awaits us." It would cost *sixteen* first class fares—but there was no change of trains from Calais to the Black Forest—and would mean " £100—to get there and I must have this within a week. Now you know the situation." Once more she begged Pinker to try to find a tenant for Brede Place, "even if they pay running expenses only for two months until I can pull matters together again . . . he has a chance to get well & live for years if we can get him out of England."

Cora was probably right. But Crane himself was the horse that shied at the hurdle. Stevenson, to all appearances nearer death than Crane when Fanny took him in charge, had lived with the disease arrested in the mild climate of the South Seas, to die fourteen years later of something else. But Stephen, on his own confession, had no wish to live on into middle age. His disregard of earlier warnings and his stubborn refusal then to see doctors, belies any willingness to submit himself to the health disciplines the tubercular must live under to recover or hold the disease in check.

Cora no longer tried to conceal the truth from friends, or to choke back feelings that must be kept hidden from Stephen behind a smiling face and calm exterior. "Mummy Crane, God has fooled doctors before," wrote the grieving girl Edith Richie, after Cora's wire of May 1, to the Richies, "and He's going to again. Don't, don't, *don't* believe them!" Hoyt De Friese, "broken-hearted," scrawled on the back of a letter to Cora from his wife: "Seldom in my life have I found such affection for *anyone* . . . and now to lose him in his very youth! I can't realize or believe it." Just back from Paris, the De Frieses wanted to hurry down to Brede Place without stopping to unpack. Cora should not bother to think of food or drink or a place to sleep, "I only want to see you all." Later in the month came Mark Barr, who only just peeped in the door of the sickroom but "wanted to rush in and grip Stevie's hand till he swore!" And Conrad: "What awful news you are giving us! And yet people given up by the doctors have been known to live for years." Conrad had stayed away from Brede Place, "not wishing to bring my barren sympathy and my helpless sorrow only to hinder you who are fighting the battle." But he would go to Dover, as Cora asked.

Conrad was now heavily in debt to his two publishers, in arrears with his work, his future already in pawn. These circumstances—he wrote—forced him to refuse another appeal of Cora's frantic need. "You can't imagine how much I suffer in writing thus to you. I have been almost distracted since I had your letter. Won't Stephen's relations come forward." Conrad could write no more. "I feel too unhappy."

Stephen's relatives not only did not come forward, but his brother William declined *any* financial aid. Cora appealed to Moreton Frewen. Mr. Frewen wrote immediately to J. P. Morgan, Sr., who had been away on the Continent but replied cordially—May 18—that he would be very glad to see Mr. Frewen about Mr. Crane at any time, either at his Hyde Park home in Prince's Gate or at his office. Mr. Frewen meanwhile had twice called on Alfred T. Plant, at Plant's office in Gray's Inn; and May 5 Plant wrote Cora: "I . . . can only say that it was at Mr. Frewen's express wish that I asked you for the list of debts, as he was most anxious that this trouble should be, if possible, removed. . . ." Frewen had written directly to Dr. Skinner, Plant said, and was doing all in his power to aid her. The "trouble" was an action to recover a small sum—the Vicar termed it "most cruel"—which had recently been brought against Stephen Crane by one S. App, a local merchant. Whether this, or any portion of debts outstanding, was ever assumed by Moreton Frewen is not known, but it is certain that he had involved himself both intimately and generously in the tangled financial affairs of the Cranes. By some remarkable wire pulling, the Associated Press man Walter Goode obtained fifty pounds from Andrew Carnegie.

A. E. W. Mason dropped Crane a delicately worded hint about applying to the Royal General Literary Fund for aid—in the form of a loan if he wished—to tide him over financial worries while his illness lasted. J. M. Barrie, a member of the committee administering the Fund, had suggested to Mason that something might be arranged, and Mason was now suggesting that Mrs. Crane should write making formal application. But time had grown too short.

Friends lauded Cora's courage. Details clogging the preparations for departure left no time for brooding over useless and enervating feelings, even had she been so inclined. Always the woman of action, she called personally on the Ambassador, Mr. Joseph H. Choate, who made a special effort to waive passport regulations. Ordinarily, passports were issued only at the Embassy, "but under the exceptional circumstances" the Consular Agent at Dover was directed to proceed to the Lord Warden Hotel to receive the sworn declarations, which would then be returned and forwarded to the Lord Warden from the Embassy.

For Stephen, the miserable struggle with debts had almost ceased to matter, but he had Conrad on his mind: a gentleman poor and proud, with a young child and a wife not strong. Garnett thought it not likely that his writing would ever be popular "outside the ring of men who write." The day before quitting Brede Place to begin the long journey, from which there would be no return, Crane dictated a note to Sanford Bennett, the last letter he wrote: "My condition is probably known to you. . . . If Garnett should ask you to help pull wires for a place on the Civil List for Conrad please do me the last favor. . . ."

Late frosts and cold winds did Crane no good. On May 15, Cora wrote Wells from the Lord Warden Hotel at Dover:

> We got Stephen safely here today. We rest here one week and then if I can arrange it and all goes well, I take him on to the Black Forest. Dr. Mitchel Bruce said one lung is all right so far and that there is the chance of recovery—I should say, the chance of *life!* The doctor and two nurses have to go with us. The wound needs constant care [Crane had undergone an operation for a fistula]. I've done all mortal can do and I hope!

The old Lord Warden, where the Empress Eugénie and the dead Prince Imperial had waited for the last Napoleon, made the weary skeleton smile: "Hope she liked the carpet!" he whispered. As meals in the hotel were expensive, the nurses were fed outside, and

Cora, trying to stretch English pounds to Badenweiler, skipped as many as she could. ". . . I know that the wife often went without," Jessie Conrad reported later.

From Vernall came a letter to Helen Crane at Dover. "The children"—Héloïse and Barry—were "looking better," and going to the Vicarage to tea next day. Would Mrs. Crane like to sell the pigeons in pairs?

The Vicar won't have them. All the doggies are well and send lots of kisses. How is dear Sponge? [Helen and the favorite dog had gone with them, to cheer Stephen.] I did feel sad after you had started—it is so sad and lonely here now. Dick Russell [Jobmaster] has just fetched the high dog-cart away, the horse [Glenroy] has got a nasty flesh wound but is getting along all right so far. The flowers are looking lovely in the garden. All sends kindest regards. With much love to all I remain yours very respectfully Vernall.

So sad and lonely! Henry James bicycled over from Rye with a party of friends a day or two later, "to show them the face of the old house; but the melancholy of it was quite heartbreaking. So will it, I fear, always be to me." He would not utter hopes which might be futile, but thought continually of his young friend, adding with a parenthetical Jamesian stutter, "and as it were, pray for him." To Badenweiler he sent Cora fifty pounds which he begged she would view as "a convenience . . . and dedicate it to whatever service it may best render my stricken young friend. It meagrely represents my tender benediction to him."[*]

Conrad, ill himself, "dragged to Dover"; and never got over that last sad glimpse of the wasted figure lying on the narrow stretcher-bed, the feeble voice, "his wonderful eyes" fixed on the white ship sails drifting past the open window—seawards. Henry James had arranged to come, but was prevented by the sudden arrival in the morning's post of "a mass of proofs to be instantly attended to."

Who was to finish *The O'Ruddy* was a question that obtruded, like a fading echo of this world's din. Cora, writing Moreton Frewen from Badenweiler, quoted Stephen as saying: " 'There are only two men who could finish The O'Ruddy. One is Kipling

[*] Berryman (p. 238) first noted this gift of fifty pounds, along with a note: "I've money, and moreover I care." But Berryman had not seen the letter of June 5, and the quotation is apocryphal.

& the other is Robert Barr. Kipling would have the style and Robert Barr the humor.' So when Robert Barr," Cora's letter continues, "came to see my husband at Dover he read the MS. & thought it equal to 'The Three Musketeers.' " Barr, too, thought Kipling the only man to finish the book, but—Cora wrote—"we said 'no' and so it is that Mr. Barr has the MS., 65,000 words." But Moreton Frewen also seems to have had Kipling in mind in connection with Crane's unfinished novel, for Cora's letter continues:

> Yesterday when your letter came my husband said: "Say to More-ton Frewen that it will ever be my joy to follow his wishes in every way. Tell him that if Robert Barr finishes the O'Ruddy and if Kipling goes over the book . . . I shall be glad. Robert Louis Stevenson left in his will that Quiller-Couch was to finish his book [*St. Ives*] and the world calls it *his book* (R.L.S.) and I shall be happy if my book goes through Kipling's hands.

Cora, at Stephen's urging, had written Barr from Dover about the completion of *The O'Ruddy*; and Barr, who had been away in the States since February, telegraphed to Stephen his reply: a re-fusal. Cora, he said in the telegram, was "the logical one." The wire was followed on May 17 by a letter in which Barr also recom-mended for the task young Stewart Edward White, "a coming man" with a first novel just accepted by McClure. It would be "ab-surd," he argued, for him—only "a commonplace plugger"—to attempt to finish a novel of Stephen Crane's. With almost any other man, except Kipling, he would have the cheek to try it. Stephen however wanted Barr, and judging him too ill to be refused, Barr promised.

Stephen dedicated the novel to Cora. But for reasons not known, when *The O'Ruddy* was issued three years later it appeared with-out the dedication Cora forwarded from Dover to Pinker on May 20:

> May—1900/Brede Place/Sussex/England
> To/My Wife/Stephen Crane

Robert Barr reached Dover on Saturday, May 19, and remained four days with Crane to see him off to the Black Forest. When Barr had finished his reading of *The O'Ruddy* manuscript, Stephen, with a glance toward Cora hovering anxiously near, said to her, "Can't you understand, there are times when men like to be left alone together?" In the fusty old Lord Warden, Barr's efforts at cheerfulness failed dismally; Crane stopped him with a wink. But it wasn't bad, he told his visitor while Cora was out of the room, substituting a metaphor for the word no one uttered, "when you come to the hedge—that we must all go over. . . . You feel sleepy—and—you dont care." Just a little dreamy curiosity, a confusion of worlds.

H. G. Wells had come from Folkestone to see Stephen, and intended coming again, but with Barr there Cora put him off, writing Wells on the 20th that the nurses advised against Stephen seeing anyone before starting on the crossing to Calais.

> Best for him to be quite alone tomorrow, so I must ask you not to come & I *am* sorry. I will write you of our journey. . . .If ever a good book or a magazine turns up send it to us in the wood [the Black Forest].

The crossing, which possibly was delayed one or two days by Crane's increasing fatigue, took place on May 24. To break the journey, they made a stop-over of two or three days at the Hotel Trois Rois in Basel, on the Swiss border, reaching Badenweiler in the German Black Forest probably sometime in the afternoon or evening of May 28.

Stephen's room on the second floor of the Villa Eberhardt, one of the buildings of the sanitarium,* had a pleasant view of the garden where fruit trees and flowers were blooming, surrounded by dark, pine-covered mountains. The small villa on the edge of the Forest was costing them—Cora wrote Moreton Frewen—90 marks a week (about $22.50). For an additional 2.50 marks a day they had a German cook, who also did cleaning and laundry. It was "difficult to get any woman as they would rather work in the fields. We live very simply. One big item is washing. Sometimes Mr. Crane's bed is changed 3 times a day." The journey from Brede Place to this villa had cost £150. "It seems awful!" At Basel they had bedrooms

---

* Dr. Edward Livingston Trudeau was the originator of the cottage type of sanitarium for the treatment of lung tuberculosis, and co-discoverer with the German, Dr. Robert Koch, of the means of isolating the tubercle bacillus. The institution at Badenweiler where Crane died was, like others of its kind in Europe, modeled after Dr. Trudeau's Cottage Sanitarium at Saranac Lake, in the Adirondacks. See his *An Autobiography* (Doubleday, Page, 1916).

on the top floor of the hotel and went out for most meals, but were charged an additional six marks per day "because we did not take all meals in house and everywhere it's 'pay extra' because of my husband's illness."

Stephen stretched out a listless hand at intervals to pat the dog Sponge, who remained constantly near his bed, and dictated to Cora notes for *The O'Ruddy*. Cora corrected proofs as she sat beside him, and dashed off frantic and somewhat incoherent communications to Pinker, bombarding the agent with questions: What about serial rights for *The O'Ruddy?* Had Pinker seen Robert Barr yet? Why didn't he put it in Reynolds' hands for the U.S.? *She* could sell the American rights herself—having in mind Curtis Brown's offer—"and I simply *must* have money for Mr. Crane." The rest of the time, sleepless or dulled in the stupors of exhaustion, she gave to outwitting Death with plans for a *Life* of Stephen she herself would write; and as though straining by force of will to hurl back the inevitable and keep hold of the life fast sinking before her eyes, she put down notes on the beauty of his physical appearance, the beauty of his character as she and others had known it. And to Moreton Frewen she poured out her grief in a long letter written on June 3:

I've only sad news to write you. There seems little hope of cure. The fever seems the thing that cannot be conquered. It is not due alone to the lung but is the remains of the yellow fever and the Cuban fever. Dr. Frankel [Dr. Albert Fraenkel, head of the sanitarium] cannot see why the lung trouble was not discovered [diagnosed?] when Mr. Crane was examined in Dec. He will not take responsibility of Mr. Crane's case alone so I've consented to a consultation tomorrow with Professor Brueiler [?] of Freiburg, to whom Dr. Mitchel Bruce wrote and through who's advice we came here. I wired you but have received no reply. There is nothing for me to do but to consent to consultation. Dr. Frankel said that Professor Brueiler would ask only about 125 marks. My husband's brain is never at rest. He lives over everything in dreams and talks aloud constantly. It is too awful to hear him try to change place in the *Open Boat!* I nearly went mad yesterday & the nurse gave me some drug which made me sleep for hours, so I'm fresh again today. He worries so about his debts and about our not being able to live here. So I told him yesterday that I had £300—cash—& since then he has been satisfied. I think

where Stephen Crane died

Last photo taken of Stephen Crane with his dog "Spongie" –

Inscriptions in Cora's hand. Both photographs courtesy Roger M. Frewen.

it is really worry about my future. So I do everything possible to ease his poor tired mind.

About the book, *The O'Ruddy*, she was writing to Robert Barr to see "what he is doing." Would Frewen see "if Kipling will do this for the book? Kipling is a friend of Robert Barr's. My husband also has 2 or 3 acts of a war play finished." She would try to get "some good man" to finish that, too. Any financial result from either the book or the play "would not be for a year at least." But she clung to a last hope that "if Robert Barr *and* Mr. Kipling say they will finish it it ought to bring a £1000—for the American and English *serial* rights alone. Mr. Crane expected £600—for American serial rights." She thanked Frewen "very much for the £25. . . . It is too dreadful to *have* to think or write that if God takes my husband from me I shall not know what to do. What shall I do! I can't write more about it."

Later that day or evening she wrote again to Moreton Frewen, a short note saying if it were possible to put "the Filter" [her own invention of an army canteen filter] on the market, that seemed the best way to get money; and added a single sentence, from which Frewen must have discerned the whole truth: "Stephen is not quite clear in his mind tonight."

Then on the afternoon of June 4—as noted in the spotty diary Cora kept of these last days—after severe hemorrhaging, Crane was given an injection of morphine "which went immediately to the heart," and he sank into coma from which he never emerged. The end came at three o'clock in the morning, Tuesday, June 5.

5

THE Whitsuntide holiday made complications, but as nothing in the short life of Stephen Crane had ever been otherwise, he was in death running true to form. All London was on the move, the holiday exodus had left the city nearly empty. The Frewens, De Frieses, Walter Goode were away, Robert McClure abroad, and but for the checks of Henry James and Moreton Frewen, Cora might have been without funds for the weary and heartbreaking long journey back. Luck was with her in catching Robert Barr, who, advising cremation, offered to go at once to Badenweiler or to meet her at Dover. Alfred Plant, having perhaps communicated with Pinker, telegraphed that he had no funds on hand and strongly advised "temporary funeral at Badenweiler."

To the compounding of these troubles, maddening delays piled up at the other end. The Germans, philosophically disinclined to hurry matters involving death, had to be exhorted in telegrams to move. The doctor was not on hand to issue the death certificate; a telegram was sent off; and Dr. Albert Fraenkel replied by letter on June 12 that he had issued the death certificate an undisclosed while after receiving Cora's wire, and the day after *that* had dispatched to Mulheim "the burying man" to obtain the government seal on the necessary papers, whence this gentleman had proceeded to the United States Consulate at Freiburg with a request to forward papers to the British Embassy in Berlin. "So I think all will be executed in the most rapid and best way." Cora meanwhile was wildly cabling Ambassador Choate, who in turn cabled the Berlin Embassy instructions for the American Consul at Freiburg to go personally to Badenweiler. Her funds were so depleted by this time that she had no money for visas; the Consul had personally to lay out these sums and collect later from the estate.

Friends were opposed to bringing Stephen's body back to England, on account of the expense. Moreton Frewen hoped Cora would "defer that sad removal until at least his brother has joined you"; and Mason, who had had firsthand experience of the difficulties involved in transporting his own father's remains across borders, added his opposition to the rest. Plant wired again:

FREWEN STRONGLY OBJECTS TO REMOVAL. IT WILL UTTERLY RUIN PROSPECT OF FUND [The Royal General Literary Fund] AND CANNOT BE PAID FOR OTHERWISE. MUCH BETTER AWAIT BROTHER'S ARRIVAL.

But Judge Crane had changed his mind about coming over; and they reckoned without Cora's determination.

To Cora Death was not an abstraction but a condition overwhelmingly real and present in the material sense. When the breath left the body the spirit had not gone far; but although she struggled hard to believe with Kate Frederic that Stephen was not lost to her, writing Linson he was "only gone upon a journey which I will take one day, so that we may be together again to work and live under the new conditions," her faith did not sustain her and she could take little comfort from it. So powerfully rooted was her attachment to the physical body, none of this belief in a hereafter, orthodox or heterodox, could overcome her horror of the body's destruction. Mason and the others thought Stephen would "just as soon sleep in the Black Forest." But Cora, like the widow of Hector fallen upon the plains of Troy, could not leave the body of her beloved to lie in alien soil, comfortless and unmourned with funeral rites. Influenced by these relics of paganism, she perhaps felt such things were necessary to the soul's peace in the hereafter.

Under the strict quarantine law the dog Sponge's re-admission to Britain presented a minor problem. Cora viewed it as major, and so gave rise to comment and innuendo of an unflattering sort which circulated widely. Jessie Conrad was stuffily scandalized by her appeal to Plant, in the same telegram telling of Stephen's death, to make arrangements for the dog.* For some reason Cora also wired Sidney Pawling, the Heinemann editor—who may have had connections with the Ministry of Agriculture—and Pawling replied: "Agriculture cannot make exceptions. Have tried hard. Might arrange if dog started for America within a very few days." None of all those brilliant people understood in how literal a sense, emotionally, the dog was now a link with Stephen.

Judge Crane had taken steamship passage for Germany. But he must have changed his plans on receipt of Cora's cable that the end was only a matter of hours—a useless journey perhaps, from his point of view. On June 5 came a message from Port Jervis: "Passage cancelled. Money this afternoon." Two days later Will wrote, his pen dripping clichés, that he had several times taken pen in hand but was stopped "because I could not think of anything . . . that would fit the situation." All of Port Jervis was "in mourning . . . the village claimed him as one of her sons." The matter of Helen's return was also giving him concern. He took for granted that "Stephen's wish was to be buried in our family plot at Elizabeth, N. J." In a letter of June 9 he was "quite clear" that Helen should come home with Port Jervis friends sailing from Liverpool on July 1; Cora was to furnish travel expenses as far as Liverpool. They would

* According to Mrs. Conrad, noted for her exaggerations, the telegram read: "God took Stephen at 11.5, make some arrangement for me to get the dog home." (*Joseph Conrad and His Circle*, p. 75)

be delighted to see Helen at home and—an afterthought—"we want you to visit us, if you come to America. I am deeply grieved that I did not see poor Stephen before he died, especially as I know how he wanted to see me."

Somehow, the dog with them, Cora and Helen reached Dover on the ninth and were met there by Robert Barr. Cora must then have gone straight to Queen Anne's Mansions, St. James Park, London: a smart but conservative family hotel where the De Frieses, Edwin Pugh, Mason, and other friends resided and Cora herself put up on her visits alone to London. From this address announcement cards, handwritten by Helen, for her Aunt Cora, were sent out:

> Mrs. Stephen Crane has arranged that friends of her late husband's may see him to say goodbye, at the mortuary 82 Baker Street on Thursday between the hours of 3 and 5 o'clock.

H. G. Wells could not bring himself to look upon the final overthrow: that exhibition of the body lying in state at the mortuary. He regretted having "failed" Cora. These things affected him "so darkly." But in the last few days he had been very much with Stephen—"the ample portion of him that will not die"—writing an article asked for by *Harper's* in which he had "tried to say without exaggeration and without cant the essential greatness of his work."

Henry James, who had learned "the miserable news" from the papers, could write only what Cora must already have been saying again and again to herself: "What a brutal, useless extinction—what an unmitigated unredeemed catastrophe! I think of him with such a sense of possibilities and powers!" If Cora returned later to Brede Place, and there were a chance of seeing her, he "would greatly value it."

On June 17 Cora sailed with Stephen's body from Southampton on the North-German Lloyd liner *Bremen*, accompanied by Helen Crane, Sponge, and another of the dog favorites from Brede Place, Powder Puff. There was a service in New York City at the Metropolitan Temple, on Seventh Avenue near Fourteenth Street, conducted by the Reverend Dr. J. M. Buckley, assisted by the Reverend Dr. S. Parkes Cadman. This Dr. Buckley was the same who had been the friend of the dead author's father, and was himself author of the dusty work, *A Consumptive's Struggle For Life*. Interment was in the family plot at Elizabeth, in what is now Hillside, N.J.

With her bright-gold hair gathered in a bun at the nape of her neck, her lovely blue eyes and fresh complexion, an aura of cosmopolitan glamor clinging about her even in black mourning garments, Cora must have seemed a figure out of another world on the Main Street of Port Jervis and in the sleepy little village of Rio, in Sullivan County, where Edmund Crane's family were spending the summer. As the babies, little Stephen and his twin brother, had developed whooping cough, the family was camping out in the country. Cora came up to the camp in the hills to see them. Stephen's nieces found her "a lovely companion as she wandered with us girls in the woods at Rio." Sitting down to rest on the pine needles, they started a game of story telling, each one contributing a chapter. When it came the turn of Agnes Crane, Agnes introduced a pair of ghosts who "were living in a cemetery on the tombstones." Cora's quip, "A good solid diet!" drew shouts of laughter.

The warm, simple affection shown her by the Edmund Cranes went to her heart. And if Cora felt herself a misfit in these rustic surroundings, her native poise did not desert her in the ordeal of being exhibited to hosts of visiting Crane and Peck cousins as "Stephen's wife." She charmed them all!

Little rip tides and sharp undercurrents developed, nevertheless. Cora's observations to Brother Will on the paucity of cultural opportunities in Port Jervis—with respect to Helen and Agnes—perhaps still rankled; and someone let it be known that she was to blame for keeping Stephen writing when he should have been resting. As a peace offering, Ed gave her Stephen's old scrapbooks. An elder sister, Helen Hamilton, a minister's wife, loaned her Stephen's baby pictures and some early photographs—which she never returned. The girls were impressed by Aunt Cora's knowledge of clothes and fashions. But some older women in Port Jervis circles, in cast of mind near relatives of a "feminine mule" who once roused all of Stephen's "bloodthirst," criticized her appearance everywhere in the same costume: a princess style mourning dress of black nun's veiling, smartly cut, with a full skirt. It was her only frock.

Cora, Cornelia Crane (Will's wife), and Helen Hamilton had procured a hotel bedroom in New York, where the three of them, who had arrived early on the day of the funeral, were resting before the service. Cora walked over to the mirror and looked at herself in the glass. "If Stephen could only see me now—" she exclaimed, gazing at her reflection in "widow's weeds"—"how he would laugh!" The remark seems to have shocked her "in-laws."

The William Cranes, whom she visited next, may have offered her a home with them which she had the bad grace—or good sense —to decline. In any case, the great-granddaughter of George Howorth would hardly have found conformity more endurable in Port Jervis than in Boston or under the Stewart family roof at 73 Harrington Gardens. And now to throw herself on the charity of Stephen's brother who had "grieved" but had not helped—unthinkable!

Cora once wrote that she found "common people not at all interesting, they only think of things to eat, and heaven and three acres and funerals." Her reaction to the religious fundamentalism of "common people," though uttered only to her journal, must now have contributed nothing to mutual friendliness or understanding:

> Remember the shriek of the village choir
> Before Jehovah's awful throne—
> Ye nations bow-wow-wow
> with sacred joy!

Toward the end of her four weeks stay in the United States Cora attempted to see Judge Alton B. Parker, who from the American side was representing Kate in the settlement of Harold Frederic's tangled affairs. Cora seems to have been unable to keep the appointment with Judge Parker at the Manhattan Club.

Then the nineteenth of July saw Cora sailing back to England to take up life again in that broken and abruptly dismantled world in which, without Stephen, so many memories pitilessly lived on. With her went a friend, Mrs. Brotherton, about whom even less is known than of Mrs. Ruedy. They took lodgings in London at 47 Gower Street, at which address David Belasco presently was writing to Cora, on July 28, disappointed at having missed her that very day by only five minutes. Belasco, then leaving for Berlin, would not be back in London for two or three weeks but could say

very definitely in advance that I will undertake the dramatization of your brilliant young husband's new story *The O'Ruddy,* as well as his former book, *The Red Badge of Courage.* May I hear from you again soon?

chapter 7

FINAL judgments as to Cora's influence during the three and a half years she and Stephen were together I leave to the Almighty and those who delight in standing angels on the point of a needle. Human nature being what it is, an egregious bundle of erring complexities and contradictions, very nearly anything under the sun may be made of it or its actions, according to the particular axe to be ground. The wives of geniuses are especially liable to misrepresentation from biographers of genius, who tag them as shrews, prehensile busybodies, she-devils of frustration if they show signs of an IQ slightly above a cretin's—a phenomenon Stevenson's able biographer, J. C. Furnas, amusingly terms "the Livy Clemens complex."

Certainly it is arguable that as Cora put no checks on Stephen's compensatory wastefulness expressed in meaningless hopitality, or on the graver waste in repeated exposures of his frail health to the senseless adventure of war, she did him no good. But it may also validly be asked: What illumination follows from insisting that a man ought to be somebody other than he is, or his work somebody else's? The declaration of independence implicit in Crane's words, "I am too old to be nursed," was surely not lost on Cora! Her eager possessiveness was directed toward making herself important to him in other ways, important without interference: the organizer of his household; hostess to his friends; a not always silent partner in the increasing drudgery of his literary productivity—typing and proofreading manuscripts, answering letters, fulfilling the thankless role of buffer and go-between with agents and publishers. Then, like the angel with the flaming sword, she stood guard over his study door to fend off shyster intruders and others who would waste his time. Whatever her improvidence, and mistakes, Cora did try to bring order into Crane's dislocated and disorganized life. And she brought much else: warmth, gaiety, kindness, and humor, and above all, that sense of intimate support every artist needs for doing his best work.

> It is the theatrical and literary view of life which makes it so unintelligible. The only real road to wisdom is reached by the path of personal experience. . . . I feel like one having started out upon a journey which led for a while through pastures green and waters still. Then suddenly to have lost the turning—henceforth the desert and the darkness of loneliness forever.

The words echo Stephen's philosophy of the individual. But Cora might have been thinking of Daisy Miller, or of a lesser known figure out of another of Henry James' early stories: Mrs. Headway, in "The Siege of London." For this was the period when the young girl rebelling against conventions and the older woman with a "past," both, were objects of scandalized attention in the plays of Ibsen and Shaw and the novels and short stories of James' early and middle periods; when the realistic version of the woman pursued by her past was popularized on the stage in A. W. Pinero's heroine, Paula Tanqueray. Cora's protest here is directed against the retribution which overtook these heroines of fiction, and which accorded not at all with her ideas of reality and social justice.

It is easy to see Cora Crane as one more in the covey of Jamesian prototypes of Daisy Miller and Mrs. Headway. But the comparison comes a little too patly, and those who may be tempted to misapply it would do well to bear in mind that James himself—he, too, had lived in Boston and "incredible New York"—saw considerably more in the characterization of his witty and charming adventuress storming London society than the bare theme of Mrs. Headway's story implies: "People don't change their natures; but they change their desires, their ideal, their effort. This incoherent and passionate protestation was an assurance that she was literally panting to be respectable. But the poor woman, whatever she did, was condemned"—by the serried phalanx of her opponents—"to be only half-right."

Not even the impeccable Richard Harding Davis or her worst

enemies (of whom Davis perhaps was one) ever questioned Cora's devotion—"extraordinary," Conrad called it—or her faithfulness to Crane during his lifetime. But it cannot be shown that her motives were entirely selfless. Love is seldom disinterested, and when the romantic passion—even the most pure—is subjected to near scrutiny, first among its components is likely to be found a whole complex of desires and needs not limited to the sexual, to which the lover has attached as object the beloved. Stephen had been the instrument, thus far, of her salvation, which appeared to Cora— romanticist that she was—in the twin guise of redemption and social rehabilitation. Conscious, therefore, of all that she owed to him —her own Prince Myshkin—in terms of personal happiness, her sentimental indiscretions to Corwin Linson perhaps may be forgiven "It is such a joy to me now," she wrote, picturing for Linson Stephen's happiness at Brede Place, "to remember that his last years here were so filled with comfort; comfort bought by work." His life, too,

> so filled with good. We had the two children of Harold Frederic you know, and there was always some poor-in-luck or health chap staying with us. Sometime I hope to tell you about Stephen's charity—and no one, not even himself felt it to be charity. His character the last year was wonderful! He could see all things clearly. His mind was too wonderful to stay here, and that is why God took him. On this subject I cannot write quite coherently.

She confided to her journal: "I had clothed a lay figure with drapery of honesty and golden truth and was satisfied that it was my ideal." But Linson's friendship she wanted as "a material thing. . . . It will help to keep tighter the bonds which his going into the beyond before me cannot alter."

On her black-bordered stationery with the monogram "CC" in the center, she thanked Hamlin Garland for his appreciative article in the *Saturday Evening Post*:

> So very few people understood Stephen or even knew him. I want you to read his books still to come out and if *you* could review them, particularly *Wounds In the Rain* it would mean so much to make his work live! I feel sure that *you* will see how much better work there is in this book than in *The Red Badge of Courage.* Then—*The O'Ruddy* [,] which is to be published later on—is really splendid work. I feel sure that my husband's *best* work was done the last year of his life. *He* thought so.

Crane had always found it necessary to see in each of his later novels and short stories an advance over earlier work. The inferior *Active Service* was no exception; and he always underrated *The Red Badge*. For her own reasons, Cora was equally sure it was so. She wanted, she told Garland, "to write a little book of Stephen's life"; it would have little commercial value. Might she use any of the facts mentioned in his article? It had been "a great disappointment" that Garland had not come to Brede Place. "Stephen said that he supposed you had reason to believe that he had neglected you and so did not care to reply." She hoped "to settle in a tiny house in London. But ways and means are a puzzle just now."

2

A PUZZLE indeed. On the eve of Cora's sailing for the United States had come a kind and sympathetic note from Moreton Frewen. He and Plant would watch over her affairs until her return to England, then "we will talk over your plans and future and see what is best to do." He was sorry to say now that he had met with a refusal from Kipling, having expected "another answer."

Moreton Frewen did not let Rudyard Kipling go unmindful of the favor done him when success and fame were strangers to the shy, bespectacled youth in India—in the matter of *Plain Tales From the Hills*. Now viewing Cora's need as an opportunity to collect on the old debt, he approached the king of storytellers with a suggestion that he assume the task of finishing Stephen Crane's novel, *The O'Ruddy*. Crane and Kipling had never met, but Crane had read *The Light That Failed* before writing *Maggie;* his young enthusiasm for Tolstoy as the greatest living writer was for a short while transferred to Kipling; and when Kipling was stricken with pneumonia in New York after his flight from Vermont, during the winter of 1897, Crane cabled anxious hopes for his recovery. He must have been overjoyed when Robert Barr wrote him after dining with Admiral Dewey at Monte Carlo that the hero of Manila Bay "admired two literary men, Stephen Crane and Rudyard Kipling." Now Kipling replied in "a pleasant, appreciative letter," but declined Frewen's appeal:

My own opinion is and I hold it very strongly that a man's work is personal to him, and should remain as he made it or left it. I should have been glad to have done him [Crane] a kindness, but this is not a thing that a man feeling as I do, can undertake.

Rider Haggard had had one of his novels produced as a play by David Belasco. It seems not unlikely that he, or Mason, who also had old contacts with the theatre—his last novel, *Miranda of the Balcony*, was soon to be adapted for the American stage with Mrs. Fiske in the leading role—had given Cora a letter to Belasco which was left at the producer's Broadway office sometime during her stay in the United States. Belasco's communication to Port Jervis had caught up with her at 47 Gower Street; he also acknowledged from Berlin, August 6, Cora's telegraphed reply of July 30 and was "deeply sorry" that their meeting had miscarried. "I would be very glad if you could tell me at once whether, on my return to New York, I may announce the arrangements to dramatize your husband's books—*The O'Ruddy* and *The Red Badge of Courage*." The veteran impresario's sure instinct recognized the value to book sales and packed houses of such timing, a brilliant follow-up after the recent phenomenal successes of his London season:

there will surely be an unusually keen interest in my future plans. . . . I am most desirous to see the manuscript of *The O'Ruddy* as soon as possible, as I should advise taking that up before *The Red Badge of Courage*—for the reason that already we have had several war plays, and I believe in offering the public a change until interest in the war drama shall have had time to revive. . . . I want you to believe, my dear Mrs. Crane, that you will have all my best efforts and best work.

There followed a hectic flurry of letters and telegrams. Cora wrote Pinker from Brede Place, where she was then occupied with the heartbreaking business of moving out furniture and other belongings: "I am returning to town tomorrow late and want you to be good enough to send to 47 Gower Street a typed copy of *The O'Ruddy*—Dont fail as I am seeing someone about it being dramatized." On August 3 she was back in lodgings and hopefully prodding Pinker, "Is it not good that both the *Red Badge* and *The O'Ruddy* are to be dramatized?" But she must have money for her landlady and the movers. Then redoubled pressures from Belasco brought renewed appeals to Pinker to produce a copy of *The O'Ruddy*, "even if we have to take it away from someone else."

The czar of Broadway was unused to being kept waiting. Even

before seeing the manuscript he already saw the novel in production, "a great success both artistically and financially." Would Cora go at once to the office of his London agent Miss Marbury,* in St. Martin's Lane, and see a Miss Wooldridge about the final arrangements? He had instructed this lady to give her a contract on the most favorable terms. Or would she prefer to meet him in Paris on the sixteenth or seventeenth of the month, at his expense, and fix matters there?

Again, luck was against her by a hairline! Had she accepted Belasco's invitation to meet him in Paris, Crane's name might have been blazoned in lights on Broadway and much else, later on, might have been different. The producer often wrote his own plays, or adaptations, and had the meeting actually taken place, in this instance he would no doubt have produced a play script himself or assigned one of his authors to do so. A Broadway success would have kept Crane's name alive on both sides of the Atlantic, and possibly would have sent book royalties zooming to a level that might well have provided for Cora, without recourse to the desperate means of the last shadowed years. The Ifs, however, were in control of the situation; and Cora did not go to Paris. She signed a contract in London "allowing him [Belasco] to show play to managers without my seeing it, if this would avoid delay in production. From Paris Belasco skipped off again leaving a trail of addresses.

The immediate problem of *The O'Ruddy* had been to lasso one of the manuscript copies then out in circulation. But there were other snarls. Cora, as early as July 3, had been in correspondence with the American agent Paul Revere Reynolds, regarding dramatization of both novels. Reynolds at once raised the question as to *The Red Badge* of whether Crane's original contract with Appleton did not also include dramatic rights; and expressed the view that "the new romance . . . could not be dramatized until it had been brought out as a book and had a success as a book." Then on July 21: "I understand that the dramatic rights on *The Red Badge of Courage* are in my hands to place." He was in consultation then on the matter and would be glad if Cora would give him authori-

* Elizabeth Marbury, dramatic agent, for many years well known on both sides of the Atlantic; a New Yorker by birth, a vigorous personality, and ardent champion of the career woman.

zation to proceed. But Reynolds' coolness toward the new novel may have determined Cora to keep her own counsel regarding Belasco's overtures. When she presently informed him that she had signed a contract for dramatization of both novels, his only comment was, "I understood you wished me to sell the dramatic rights of *The Red Badge of Courage*, and I was trying to sell it."

Delighted with the Irish novel's beginning, Belasco wrote enthusiastically from New York. Eight months later his enthusiasm had given place to irritation:

I wrote you a long and important letter asking you when you thought the book of The O'Ruddy was coming out, and stating that I would then arrange for the play accordingly. I presume you never received it. . . . Kindly let me hear from you to enable me to formulate my plans. One thing is very certain—I can make no arrangements until the book is published.

Ill luck pursued her with *The O'Ruddy*, but the fade-out of the Belasco negotiations was a mortal blow. Robert Barr had written concurring in Kipling's refusal, but offered a counterproposal. On going over complete chapters and the sketch Cora had given him, based on Stephen's notes dictated to her in the last days of illness, he found the sketch "so vague and incomplete . . . it gives little guidance for another." Barr thought Cora the only one in the world who could finish the story,

and thus I come back to my original idea. You know better than anyone else what he had in mind . . . and when the story goes forth as by Stephen Crane and Mrs. Crane people will take that collaboration as the right and proper thing.

Would she do it, he would edit the manuscript and make suggestions; "also, if you like, I will take it down to Kipling . . . and will endeavor to get him to go over it as well."

If this was a polite way of passing the buck, there can be no question of Barr's sincerity. But, contrary to much that has been adduced as desire to put herself forward, Cora Crane never thought of herself as a writer, and her low opinion of her few literary ventures must have been somewhat colored by Stephen's ridicule of female authors. Far from wishing to compete with her adored one, had not her whole effort been dedicated to creating a setting in which *he* would shine? She even thought it injurious to "a normal man's" pride for a wife to undertake activities to earn money independently. (By inverse reasoning, Donald Stewart's predilection for spending her grandfather's money presumably was *not* "normal." Cora had the American point of view regarding the husband's financial responsibilities to his wife and family.) Of the unfinished story "The Squire's Madness" which she completed for publication—a little more than half of it her work—she wrote G. H. Perris, the literary agent:

By the word "finished"—I mean that I "conceived" the finish . . . I trust it is not *too* bad! I worked so much with Mr. Crane, and knew his work so well that it is not difficult to picture the ending of his stories —but of course to attempt to finish them as *he* would have done is impossible!

A novel, too, was something else again; she probably felt that the very thought of a woman laying hands on his last novel must have been enough to raise Crane's ghost.

Her next appeal was to H. B. Marriott-Watson, who had been among the first to draw attention to Crane's work in England with an article on *The Red Badge* in the *Pall Mall Gazette*. Watson, too, felt the task beyond him; and Cora now turned to A. E. W. Mason. Mason had thought, if she had no "other views," of proposing himself for the job nobody else apparently wanted, but had seen that "Barr was going to do it." At that time he could have begun work immediately. Now—the end of August—other commitments would force a postponement until November.

Meanwhile . . . I fancy it would not be wise to let it get known that Barr, having splashed about finishing the book, is not doing it . . . lest people should be rushed into the idea that it was passing round.

A man of naturally generous impulses, Barr seems to have shown himself in a contrary light at times—at least, in the opinion of Mason. "A funny fellow," Karl Edwin Harriman later remarked to Cora, "though why he does some things that he does I have never been able to tell."

A year went by; the publishers Frederick A. Stokes & Company were becoming impatient. Mason wrote from North Africa that he could not fix a date; he was in trouble with the manuscript and advised Cora in a postscript, "I should just let the story go out as Stephen's I think, if I were you. . . . A short note saying that the latter part has been completed by another hand will meet the case. . . ." But Stokes issued press notices. Then an article appeared in Miss Jeanette Gilder's magazine *The Critic* (March, 1901) announcing Mrs. Stephen Crane's plans for completing and publishing her husband's unfinished works, and naming A. E. W. Mason, to whom "pressure of other work induced her to assign the task" of finishing *The O'Ruddy*—that bugaboo novel!

The fat was in the fire. Mason, a successful purveyor of romantic potboilers, may have had honest doubts—as Harriman did—about the wisdom of Crane, whose genius was impressionistic, and whose emphasis was perpetually on the conflict between ideals and reality, in trying his hand at a long picaresque novel.* Anyhow, red-faced and in deeper than he bargained for, Mason issued a blast from Cairo—without having seen the offending notices. A slow worker in his own writing, he would be no faster in finishing Stephen's novel, while desiring "to do what I possibly could for Stephen's memory." Cora, he thought, did not fully appreciate the difficulties, although—with another dig at Barr—"from Mr. Barr's not undertaking it" they should be easy of realization. Miss Gilder's rather lame paragraphs he dismissed with a blunt disclaimer: "I simply believe that the value of these paragraphs before the issue of a book is very much over-rated. . . . The fact that the publishers press for copy is not the important thing. . . . I give

---

* Mason's memory of *The O'Ruddy* episode—forty-five years later—plays him odd tricks! Writing to Vincent Starrett on October 4, 1945, he disavows any connection whatsoever with finishing the novel: "As to *The O'Ruddy*, during that last spring he [Crane] asked me to read it. He told me its history. He had begun it, scoffing at some of us who were writing that sort of romantic tale, but, as he went on with it, he got bitten by the theme and the treatment and the period, and was enjoying himself writing it. I read it very carefully. I think there must have been, even at that time, a suggestion or hint that if he did not come back, I should finish it, but of that I can't be sure. Certainly I read it carefully and inclined to realize that this was not his pigeon at all. However, I think I told him that he must get well and finish it himself. After he died, Cora wrote to me and asked me to undertake it. I didn't, for although I guessed that Stephen's affairs were not very flourishing, I did not think that *The O'Ruddy* would add either to his estate or his reputation. It was a little time afterwards that Barr finished the book and justified my reluctance."

with a very willing heart my work. . . . I remain unmoved by the
paragraphs or by Mr. Belasco—by the way, why does he not think
of a finish since he is so eager and in so desperate a hurry?"

Occupied now with plans for his own forthcoming play *Miranda of the Balcony*—which lasted only a few weeks at the Manhattan Theatre in New York—Mason no doubt wished himself out
of the whole mess. He had not been aware, he told Cora, of "what
The O'Ruddy meant to you. . . . I rather thought Stephen's brother was seeing you through. . . . I forget now who it was but I was
told that you could have stayed in America with that family until
all the business . . . was settled." The Literary Fund he thought
had "acted upon a similar belief," a natural one, "and I still think
Stephen's brother is the one who should help besides us." On
Cora's account he was "really very sorry," the more so that she
had not let him know of her financial straits. He would have suggested that "someone quicker" should take over the work, and
was "still quite willing to agree to that."

On paper willing; actually, it would seem, Mason would neither
turn loose nor get on with the job. Cora, frantic at the thought of
more delays, was now coaxing and pleading. When she was about
to sail again for the United States at the end of April, 1901, Mason
wrote that *The O'Ruddy* would be finished "very soon now."
Next, it was promised for the following September (1901). But
one year later the deadlock was broken only when Frederick A.
Stokes & Company finally took matters into their own hands.

The innocent third party to these ructions was Karl Harriman.
Since the publication by Harper's of his volume of short stories,
Harriman was beginning to make a name, and, like many another
who has come up in the world, was anxious to do favors instead of
receiving them, especially to those who had shown him kindness
in a less prosperous era. His devotion to Crane's memory amounted
to veneration. Nor would he ever forget Mrs. Crane's kindness to
the young stranger who had arrived at Brede Place looking as if
he might justly be "expected . . . to steal the spoons." "Now Mrs.
Crane, here is what I want you to do . . ." Harriman had "a nice
little friendship with the editor [Miss Gilder] of a literary monthly of large circulation and the highest standing. . . . I want to write
for an early issue something *about you*. . . ." He wanted photographs, a short biography telling where and when Cora had met

Stephen, details of her "travels and adventures, etc.," particulars as to her present plans, "for I know you must write. . . . Also tell Mason to write me concerning *The O'Ruddy*, how it is progressing and all about it. . . ." A young man who clearly understood the value of publicity.

So all this, and more, appeared in the article written by Miss Gilder from notes furnished by Harriman: photographs of Stephen in Ireland, of the Cranes at Brede Place; announcements of Cora's intended *Life* of Stephen, of stories she was finishing for publication; other stories, her own, yet to be written, and a novel "well in hand" dealing with the American Revolution, ". . . in which she will introduce historical personages from whom Stephen Crane was directly descended." And lastly, a somewhat doctored travel resumé containing the extraordinary statement, for which God knows who was responsible, that Cora "went through the Cuban war with Crane at Santiago!"

Stokes & Company notified her (April 29, 1902) that they would "attend to the completion of the story in the best manner possible in the circumstances." Shortly before Mason came in on it, Mr. Frederick Stokes had approached Judge Crane about naming Robert Barr for the task, but met with a flat refusal from Barr himself. Now to the intense relief of everybody, after the ruinous delays, Barr reconsidered. And so *The O'Ruddy* finally was completed, in July of 1903—three years and one month after Stephen Crane's death.

It is painful to record that Barr, who had been so true a friend to both Cranes through so many earlier vicissitudes, now demanded payment of 220 pounds before he would surrender the manuscript. "I think he is behaving abominably in the matter," Alfred Plant wrote Cora,

as he knows perfectly well we have no money and the arrangement I made with him was that he should have the serial rights for publication in "The Idler" [magazine co-founded with Jerome K. Jerome, in which Barr still retained an interest] as payment for his work upon the book.

Plant threatened action to compel Mr. Barr to carry out his agreement with the executors of Crane's estate. Publication of the book followed in October—by which time, adversity had done its worst to Cora.

3

HAD she, like Ouida or George Sand, whom she so much resembled in her prodigious energies, been able to carve out for herself a career in literature or journalism, her story might have had a happy ending after all. But George Sand had a private income, and literary talent does not often come to fruition as a marketable commodity overnight. Ouida had prepared herself from childhood for a literary career, and a best seller at twenty-two made possible the channeling of her astonishing energies into the stream of popular successes which poured from her pen almost to the end of her life.

Stephen Crane left debts amounting to almost one thousand pounds (then about five thousand dollars.) Outside of royalties and copyrights, there were no assets except the unfinished manuscripts and unpublished works on which Pinker expected to realize—he told Plant—a sum not less than that amount.

And so Cora, hounded by estate creditors and beset for the means of daily subsistence, had neither leisure nor the mental composure necessary for creative work. "I say you can write," replied Lewis Hind, Stephen's friend and editor of *The Academy*, "but can you make money by writing? That is . . . the question . . . you really want me to answer. To make money by writing is to study the market, and to offer the kind of goods editors and publishers want." He saw no reason why she should not succeed. "Many do but it is a long, uphill task, and demands great self-confidence and industry." To Cora, scarcely a new thought. "All sorts of information comes to me of Stephen's struggle before the Red Badge success," she wrote Louis Senger; and to Hamlin Garland, "I am of the opinion that it is criminal for people to write who know nothing about it—but one must live, and I must work to live."

So she went at it, finishing some of Crane's stories, and turning out others of her own that she must apologize for to Garland, Linson, and Senger. "Woefully bad" they were, still—what else had she now to turn to? A little encouragement from friends, Karl Harriman, Mason, and Poultney Bigelow who said, "You have an effective style," was enough to persuade her that it was what Stephen also would have her do. "The Squire's Madness" and "The

Man from Duluth" were finished and given to G. H. Perris, Bigelow's London agent who advanced her ten pounds on each before
disposing of these stories to *Crampton's Magazine*. Then heartened
by this mite of success she plucked up nerve to show to Robert
Barr her own story, "The Lavender Trousers," originally written for the Whilomville series, but not included when *Harper's
Magazine* published the series. Now that those tales were about to
be issued in book form, might not "The Trousers" go in? And
why not offer the story to *Harper's Bazaar*, which had asked Stephen for six more on "the angel child" theme? Barr gave his opinion categorically: as a story it was good enough to stand on its
own merits, Cora's picture of an American village and its mores
well done, "but not as a Whilomville story." Those tales simply
could not be duplicated.

Early in September a long story of her own, "José and the
Saints," was finished and sent off for criticism to Poultney Bigelow—the popular American author-lecturer on politics and travel
then with his wife and daughters in the Swiss Alps. The Bigelows
were newer friends who had visited the Cranes at Brede Place in
the spring of 1900. The friendship, which possibly owed its existence to Cora's membership in the Society of American Women in
London, of which Mrs. Bigelow also was a member, seems in this
instance to have been chiefly with Cora. They were a breezy pair.
Edith Bigelow, working on a play she thought "not very good and
would come to nothing," possessed an instinct for drama off-stage
that doomed her to endless victimizations by housemaids who
turned out to be either alcoholics or else in the family way. "P.B."
boiled with enthusiasms and dislikes. Son of an ambassador, he had
had the same tutor—at Potsdam—as the future German Kaiser
William II with whom he continued in lifelong friendship. He had
been expelled from a minor diplomatic post in Russia, in 1892, for
political writings which gave offense to the Czar. Among his pet
abominations were Harold Frederic, whom he accused of lying and
plagiarism, and Theodore Roosevelt, whom he publicly denounced
as a tinhorn politician in the Spanish-American War.*

* When Poultney Bigelow died, at the age of 98, the New York *Herald-
Tribune* said of him in an editorial, May 29, 1954: "All his life he stayed an
individualist, ready to battle for his beliefs and prejudices—the first not always popular, the second, many and strong. Always he was ready to go against
the tide and swing an able and pugnacious paddle."

Whatever else "José and the Saints" may have been, it was no doubt overpraised by the ebullient Mr. Bigelow. The story was never sold, and the manuscript is lost. "Out of sight," "P.B." exclaimed. "It made me creep—it has just arrived and I have devoured it. . . . I post it at once to be re-typed in two copies and I shall do my best." Lewis Hind's conservative judgment is probably nearer the mark. "I think the story . . . shows that you can write, and that you can treat a powerful subject powerfully, but there is too much description, and it needs pruning." He was in favor of circulating it, but held out little hope of acceptance. "The fiction public, as a rule, do not want unpleasant or horrible tales."

This familiar tune came wafted across the water also from Bigelow's American agent, John Russell Davidson, to whom Bigelow sent copies of "José" and other samples of Cora's work. Davidson, too, found the story "too gruesome for the present editorial frame of mind on this side of the Atlantic." The *Traveller*, *Strand*, and *Pall Mall Gazette* said "nice things"; the *Graphic* considered it "good and powerful," but dared not print it. Cora snorted to Perris: "Rubbish, the public can't want all love and milksop!"

But "love and milksop" could be successfully turned by the imagination of a Ouida into flamboyancy and *brio*, hence into gold sovereigns. Cora had none of Ouida's instinct for what the Victorian novel-reading public wanted of fiction as entertainment, and when she tried to base herself on realism she became imitative. "The Lavender Trousers" eventually was returned by Davidson as "lacking strength," while the much inferior "The Red Chimneys" was sold to a Chicago syndicate. The prose-poem sketch "What Hell Might Be," that bitter confession of disillusionment composed in the dark days of Stephen's rumored desertion, was bought by the *Smart Set*. The magazine *Truth*, said Davidson, would like to see more of her work.

Of the remaining stories it is not necessary to say much. "Elbridge Carter's Dream"—the title a curious mélange of her "Carter" pseudonym and the Elbridge-Holder family name—belongs in the same category with "The Lavender Trousers," but is in some respects a better story. Both are echoes of Whilomville; and in both the women sewing for the heathen, the men "hearing little of the outside world, sunk to the level of one desire, more food and more rest," are projections of Cora's own antipathy to the cramped horizons of the American "Main Street." But the two stories reflect no regional characteristics; Cora's Whilomville might be located anywhere east of the Mississippi or north of the Mason-Dixon line. In both the note of protest is so generalized it barely escapes the stereotype. Her own final judgment of "The Trousers" was that "it seems like dough that wants working up."

Most of the fiction pieces show little sense of formal structure, and the tendency to overload with description is common to all. But her description is usually alive, with excellent use of sensory detail, particularly of color, the best of it suffused with poetic and symbolic meanings. When free of Stephen's influence she uses color, not in his manner but in strong splashes reminiscent of the painter her father was. The story "Cowardice," a horror tale written around the Brede ghost (poor old Sir Goddard Oxenbridge), has good atmoshpere, a good feeling of rising excitement, more relaxation, as well as stronger action than some of the others. A story leaning heavily upon atmosphere, it achieves an effect of plausibility and also reveals an excellent ear for dialect. With so good an ear, it seems odd that when reporting the speech of people out of her own familiar world the result is so often lifeless and wooden. (But this is also true of Stephen at times: for woodenness and artificiality nothing can outdo the way the people talk in *Active Service!*) "Cowardice" was eventually sold to the Northern Newspaper Syndicate. The theme of the story is "the human heritage of cowardice." Its treatment, though marred by technical immaturity, evidences an alert sensibility capable of formal development. But far and away the best of the lot, though unsold, is "An Old World Courtship," a "genre" story fully alive. It has charm, tenderness, a sensitive and authentic understanding of rural English types that makes it seem a pity she did not do more of this sort of thing.

"Arundel Castle" and "The 17th Regiment of Light Dragoons" are both fairly good examples of nonfiction narrative, the latter an historical account of an Irish cavalry troop which fought on the side of the British in the American Revolution. This piece may have found its way onto paper in preparation for Crane's novel dealing with the Revolutionary War, which never materialized. But Cora's Tory leanings in "The 17th Regiment . . ." at odds with her caustic Americanism in the London newsletters, would certainly have given offense to the Yankee patriotism of Stephen. Exhaustive research must have gone into the writing of the Castle piece, an account of the building of Arundel Castle, its architectural history, its moss-growth of legend and anecdote together with a history of the families holding the lands and titles of the Dukes of Norfolk from the time of Alfred the Great. They had been for many centuries the leading Catholic family of England. Too largely a straight factual account, unshaped, to be of interest today, it was probably acceptable enough for the journalistic standards of the time and compares very well with Stephen's account of the New Orleans Mardi Gras written for the Bacheller-Johnson syndicate. But neither "Arundel Castle" nor "The 17th Regiment" was ever sold. American editors, Davidson reported, fought shy of such material. In England local historians were a dime a dozen.

Outside of Sunday editions the woman's column was not yet a regular feature of the American big circulation dailies, and in Victorian England did not exist. Yet that is where Cora might have succeeded. The London newsletters indicate a nose for what goes into a column housewives like to read; the article on Greek lithographs extends her readability to other areas.

4

ARRANGEMENTS for the charity bazaar at Brede Place were necessarily given over to others: the Vicar and Mr. Frewen. It took place presumably as scheduled, on August 1, and Cora was there—but not now as mistress of the house, only as a week-end guest. She slept for the last time in her own bed in the big, dark room. The ghosts rollicked all night. Next morning she watched the vans move off with her furniture and belongings, and came back and wrote in the Visitors Book: "August 2nd, 1900. Sun, wind and time but color it, strong, solemn grey—Brede Place in 1899—laughing (silently) at the puny lives of men." But she did not sign it.

Cora's "lack of pounds, shillings and pence" had already begun to be acutely felt. We find her, nevertheless, coming to the rescue of friends worse off, with a private sale of "Chen things" George Lynch had collected in his wanderings over the earth. The "delicious madman" once more was on his way back from China after "a simply immense time" in New York, where he had been lecturing and writing articles, putting up for a month at the Waldorf and dining in every house on Fifth Avenue. He landed with only just enough left in his pocket to buy himself a drink at the Queenstown Club. "How good and kind of you to think of helping me like this," wrote warmhearted Mary Lynch, "and George also will be so grateful." But Cora remembered how it had felt to be left high and dry, her man off to a war on the other side of the world.

A group of art connoisseurs and well-heeled friends was invited down for the sale, Cora's farewell to Brede Place, at which Mary Lynch deemed it best not to be present for fear "it would make things awkward for you and your friends." George showed his gratitude by inviting Cora to lunch in town, "and if I have no money to pay the bill I will photograph the proprietor!" "Poor Stevie's" memory he had found "still spring-green throughout America—his friendship a passport."

Stephen's name on the lips of friends who had loved him laid open the wound. A young man who had visited the Cranes at Brede Place with his sister and a college friend, whose mother had known Stephen's parents in Newark, ran into Cora one day in Regent Street. Cora stopped to ask for his sister who, unknown to her, had died suddenly on the same day as Stephen. When the young fellow blurted it all out, Cora exclaimed, "Oh, your poor father!" remembering that the young girl had been the idol of a worshipping father; and there in the street she simply burst out crying. "No one can realize how great my loss is," she wrote Hamlin Garland,

> or how difficult it is to fight for an existence which I dont want. But my faith bids me believe that we shall be together again. Our life was too beautiful, too full of work and sunshine not to be continued, under new conditions perhaps, but still I am sure that I shall be with him again.

"Poor darling Cora," wrote Jessie Conrad, "I would like to see you. I think you are sure of our sympathy." Cora must come to them for a visit and rest. The check she enclosed was sent at Conrad's request, and he would "send again as soon as possible."

Henry James, who had written in support of Cora's application for help from the Royal General Literary Fund, was not optimistic about the chances of success, owing to the Cranes' status as Americans, "that is, alien . . . and not long domiciled in England." An appeal to H. G. Wells, presumably for a loan, was somewhat sheepishly refused. A less tactfully worded refusal brought a cry of protest from Cora, followed by an embarrassed explanation from Mrs. Arthur Pinero, the playwright's wife. "Believe me, I deeply sympathize with your great sorrow," wrote Mrs. Pinero, "and I never for one moment imagined you desired charity."

But harder on spirit and flesh, this battle for life unwanted, than watching a man die. "Life," she remarked now to her journal, "is just one long struggle against misery, with the certainty of being beaten in the end, only some of us are beaten in the beginning."

Was this an admission from one who had never accepted defeat, that her own life had gotten rather badly off-track somewhere near the beginning? In the United States, a woman with a certain amount of nerve and push could succeed in competition with men, even beat them at their own game—as she had reason to know. But now she, who had striven so hard to undo the mistakes of the past, found herself in this England, where she chose to live and where such things were not expected to happen to a "gentlewoman," abruptly thrown on her own resources too far in advance of her time.

On August 28 Cora was writing to G. H. Perris, "I am sending my friend Mrs. Brotherton with the ms. 'finished' of three stories of my late Husband's, Stephen Crane." She begged he would do his best with them—and advance her five pounds:

> I have just had a terrible run[-in] with the woman who keeps this place [47 Gower Street] and must leave today. I am short just £3.10 in paying her. These things and kinds of people are new to me and I am unfit to go out or I would have come personally to see you. [Cora at this time was ill with gout.]

She wrote again on the same day,

> I have qualified your form of receipt for the story *The Squire's Madness* [one of the three] as I cannot believe you offer only £10 —for *all* rights. I need the money . . . & so if you think that is all you can offer for both American & English *serial* rights, I will accept the £10—but I cannot let you have book rights as well.

If time permitted, she was sure Mr. Reynolds could get more for the American serial rights alone.

Then on September 11, "too ill to go out today," she could not come personally to see Perris but had asked Mr. Richie (Ford Richie) "to take this to you," enclosing "four short things of Mr. Crane's." Would Perris buy them outright, or let her have an advance of ten pounds? And send check by the bearer, Mr. Richie; this would be a *great* accommodation. And would he make the check payable to Mr. Richie so that it might be cashed at once? She would return a receipt. Illness had prevented her answering Perris' two communications of August 28; she begged him in postscript to do something about the enclosed cablegram from Reynolds inquiring whether Crane's story, "A Desertion" which Reynolds had just sold to *Harper's Magazine*, had been previously sold in England. "Can you straighten this? I cannot afford to cable again."

October 23: she was "unexpectedly called upon to meet an obligation today" and needed five pounds; would Perris advance it and "try to get some money in by the first of the month," she would be "very, very glad."

November 19: "Please give Mrs. Brotherton a ck. for six guineas. I hate to ask but I'm at my wits end over being dunned by a man who wants £7." Did Perris think he could place *Great Battles of the World* book rights in England? A book of short stories, and English *serial* of *The O'Ruddy?* "Please answer so that I may show letter to the Executor [Plant] of my late husband's estate."

Cora's business connection with G. H. Perris, at first limited to her own work—to which Pinker anyhow was indifferent—was one of those things in her life determined by the pull of circumstances. There is nothing to indicate that she planned, or wanted, a break with Pinker; the Nemesis whose long shadow now lay across her path resided in the portly figure of Judge Crane.

In the situation with the Estate, relations were already showing signs of strain. Plant followed a more liberal line of administration in granting priority for widow's maintenance over the claims of estate creditors than did Judge Crane. And one can hardly blame Pinker if by now he had had enough! Repeatedly, his hands were tied by Cora's exaggerated ideas of the high prices Stephen's name could still command in the literary market. From her original demand of £500 for book or serial rights to *The O'Ruddy* she had come down perforce to £300, but when Pinker presently backed up her refusal to go further the opportunity was lost to sell to an American publication, the *New Magazine*.

Reynolds, too, was having his troubles with Cora's intransigence. Stokes would not risk more than £50 on *Last Words*, the volume of Crane's unpublished stories Cora was now putting together. Reynolds also considered this all the book would stand, "a rather heterogeneous mass of matter" and on the whole much below Crane's standard. But Cora held out for £100, with the result that *Last Words* never appeared in an American edition. Perris finally unloaded it to the English house of Digby, Long, for £50; but even he ultimately despaired of selling some of the pieces serially.

> I think that one obstructing influence must be the prices which have been asked and obtained . . . in the past and which have created a sort of tradition of expensiveness, which cannot be maintained now that his personality is not behind them.

Cora probably had been evicted by her landlady when she got behind in her rent. But before quitting 47 Gower Street for an interim stay at 22 Montague Place she was house hunting, counting on a lodger or two to help meet the rent of £70 a year; and with a naïveté one can only call staggering in view of the fact that, perhaps on Plant's advice, she was already weighing the transfer of her business dealings to another agent, she had given Pinker's name as a reference to the real estate agent! The first house she did not get, being unable to meet the requirements for "doing it up." When another was found, apparently better suited to her slender resources, she again turned to Pinker—on August 25—adding with a touch of "angel child" coyness:

> My friend who is going to live with me is almost out of patience at our not getting settled . . . Please say the nicest possible things you can. I saw your letter to the other agent which as he said, was 'perfectly satisfactory'.

Whether Pinker came through a second time does not appear, but Robert Barr did so handsomely:

I have known Mrs. Stephen Crane for years . . . If I had a house to let, I should be delighted to have a tenant at once so careful and so honorable as Mrs. Crane.

Noticeably in a state of extreme agitation, attributable no doubt to a combination of illness and the situation in America regarding the estate—besides the troubles with her landlady—Cora had written Pinker the day before her second appeal for a character reference to the real estate agent, asking to see the book contracts:

> I am going to see if all obligations of the estate cannot be paid off quickly so that the executors work will be finished. I understand, that in contracts, money from royalties from the above firms are [sic] to be paid to you but I must know how I stand before I can do anything. Please let me hear from you [about the stories being offered to Harper's] so that the English edition [*The Monster & Other Stories*] can be gotten out at once. Mr. Plant will agree to anything of the kind of which I approve.

But she must make everything clear to her brother-in-law, so that a quick settlement of the estate could be arranged. "Do try to hurry your countrymen Mr. Pinker. Please think how very distressing all this is to me and how I long to be settled and to get to work doing what I know my dear one would have me do."

There was an interview of some kind on the twenty-seventh, which was followed next day by a note abruptly putting an end to business relations with Pinker:

> I explained my position to you yesterday. And so I must ask you to return me all the MS. and the verses to see what I can do with them personally. I have instructed the boy to bring them with him.

Although this step has all the marks of action taken in haste and repented at leisure, it is hard to believe that Cora could have embarked on it without first consulting Plant, Crane's English executor, who quite possibly considered it a desirable move toward freeing the estate from the encumbrances imposed by the American executor, Judge Crane. Plant, at any rate, wrote Pinker in October: "I must again urge you to do your utmost to dispose of serial rights of *The O'Ruddy* as it is most important that I should pay the creditors a dividend with as little delay as possible"; and again on December 19, asking for the surrender of "all contracts and papers in your possession." This request was denied in an undated letter from Pinker to Plant, of the following day:

As you are aware, I advanced money to Mr. Crane on the security of the contracts and Mss. which I hold, and I scarcely think I can give up all controls and papers until my account is settled.

Cora meanwhile had lost no time in sending Perris the few stories of Stephen's she had finished herself: "The Squire's Madness," "The Man From Duluth," and probably also "The Surrender of Forty Fort"—one of the Wyoming Valley series. Would *Cassell's Magazine* take more of the series, if she did them? She had notes. A long story, "The Fire Tribe and White Face," she tried to induce Frederic Remington to complete. Remington, the artist whose pictures of horses, Indians, and cowboys first inspired Stephen with a longing to see the West—and whom Stephen later knew as a war correspondent in Cuba—would do "anything in reason" for Crane's widow, but feared she could not "find a man who can carry Crane's master hand through so mysterious a scheme as the Fire-Tribe story. . . ." Cora did not venture to look further.

Perris with an eye to profits made unusual demands. Cora replied:

It would be impossible for me to sign a contract giving you the exclusive rights in my late husband's (published) works. We will leave the contract until I come to see you. . . . I shall go over what manuscripts you have . . . and send the stories for you to sell for me, but of course you will not charge me 15%. 10% is the usual rate everywhere.

She was careful to let Perris know that "Mr. Pinker has a few things yet, which go to the Estate and which must therefore remain in his hands." Also, that money from the sale of the Wyoming Valley stories should be paid to Plant, as those stories she had turned over to the estate.

On November twenty-third Cora was again needling Perris:

I want you to use every effort to sell the English serial rights of *The O'Ruddy*. Methuen has book rights here, Stokes & Co. in U.S. Mr. Reynolds has the serial to sell in U.S. Mr. Pinker has had it . . . but has done nothing with it. I have given my word [to Plant] that you are the people who will work the hardest to place this

O'Ruddy serial, also the English book rights of *Great Battles of the World.* . . . At present you have two book rights to sell, one long serial and a lot of short things. Do your very best with them at once.

What emerges from this jumble of correspondence is that Cora rather unjustly blamed Pinker for letting slip *The O'Ruddy* sale to the *New Magazine;* and that she was now at loggerheads with Judge Crane's administration of the American end of the estate. A letter from Paul R. Reynolds dated May 14, 1901, highlights her grievances against Judge Crane:

Remembering that I paid to Judge Crane some money that I received for a story from the Cosmopolitan entitled "The Great Boer Trek" I asked Judge Crane, as executor of Mr. Stephen Crane's will, if he had any objections to my paying such money to you. He replied that while he is not prepared to say he objects, at the same time he does not consent. . . . You will see that if I paid this money to anyone but the person who has legal authority to receive it, I may render myself personally liable for the amount of such money.

Cora had some thought of going to America in February to have it out with her brother-in-law, a course strongly favored by Reynolds. Judge Crane, now established in New York City as one of the partners in a prosperous law firm with offices on lower Broadway, told the agent he would be glad to "discuss matters with Mrs. Crane." Reynolds, in turn, would release money to Cora "as soon as he consents." But "matters," meanwhile, continued on the downgrade:

In a letter dated August 21 (1900), Will had promised "cooperation" but could not possibly send money then. "I have given you my promise and it will be kept, if I'm alive."

In November, Will again brought up the subject of Hartwood: Stephen had paid only $500 on his investment and Will had returned this sum to him "about April 7, 1899." This he would not like to consider a gift, as he had borrowed it and still owed it. "But you may rest assured, my dear sister," Will wrote, ". . . your interests will be more than safe in my hands."

The presidential campaign then in full swing, Will was on the road for several weeks stumping for Bryan. Though still "your affectionate brother," the correspondence now had an edgy note.

Will had received "absolutely *no* clippings," and had heard nothing about the clock. Had Cora actually sent it? He knew of no "things" or books of Stephen's left behind in Cuba, or sent her in his care by Charles Michelson—Crane's old friend on the New York *Journal* with whom Cora had been in correspondence.* Or did she mean the unsold copies of *The Red Badge* Appleton had released to the estate under the terms of Stephen's contract? He had no desire to be "technical"; if Cora wished some of them and some of the original *Maggies*, he would send them as soon as the *Maggies* could be obtained from Appleton. When the clock arrived, it was shown to a clockmaker who pronounced it a Ticehurst, "the grandfather of them all." A coat of Stephen's also had been received. Then Will wanted autographs, some of Stephen's and two more of Harold Frederic. If Cora were satisfied with the inscription for Stephen's tombstone, he would have it put on:

STEPHEN CRANE, POET—AUTHOR
1871–1900

"Puff" was well and fat. They all hoped to see Cora in February, it was so much more satisfactory to talk things over.

But Cora postponed her departure. Reynolds meanwhile had sold the American rights of *Last Words* to Henry T. Coates & Company, of Philadelphia, for $250. Cora, anxious to have this money

---

* The saddlebags Crane used in Cuba had been left behind, for whatever reasons, with Charles Michelson. After Crane's death Cora wrote Michelson, who replied July 8, 1900: "The saddle bags and contents will be sent to you immediately. Among the things you will find an autograph battle hymn, probably written while your husband was in Cuba. I sent a copy of this to the Pall Mall Magazine [*Pall Mall Gazette*]—which I see now I should not have done. Will you kindly keep me advised of your address in order that I may forward to you the check the magazine will doubtless send if they publish the hymn. . . ." This was "The Battle Hymn," which Daniel G. Hoffman calls Crane's "longest and most ambitious attempt to define in verse the significance of combat." (*The Poetry of Stephen Crane*, p. 158.) There is no record that the poem was ever published, although the absence of any mention of it in Cora's correspondence with agents suggest that it may already have appeared in the magazine to which Michelson sent it,—presumably the *Pall Mall Gazette*. Two copies, one typewritten, the other in Cora's hand, are in the Columbia Collection—with a note likewise in her handwriting: "The ms . . . has just been discovered in saddle-bags used by Stephen Crane during the late war with Spain."

paid directly to her, wrote Reynolds on April 26 (1901) begging him to do his utmost to get it for her, "as I shall land in New York without money and must send money back here to save my things. I also want to go directly to Ky. where I am to spend the summer."

Last Words, by what supreme irony, was the rock they split on. Why the book never appeared in the United States is conjectural; but getting wind of the estate imbroglio, the publishers after paying their money may have gotten cold feet. Reynolds anyhow, on receipt of the check from Coates & Company, wrote again to Judge Crane requesting permission to make payment—less his commission—directly to Mrs. Crane. The exchange of correspondence between them continued through summer into fall, and by November a note of chilly warning was detectable in Judge Crane's epistolary style: he had written Mrs. Crane that she'd better consent that the moneys in Reynolds' hands be paid to him. Mrs. Crane had not replied. Will reiterated that "under the circumstances" the amount should be paid to him, and Reynolds might take "this letter as my agreement to indemnify you against any further payment to her."

Reynolds, no mean scrapper himself and no quitter either, seems to have stuck to his guns. He replied with some sort of challenge, which drew from Judge Crane a detailed and strongly worded exposition.

As the duly qualified executor of the American branch of his brother Stephen's estate, Will now charged that Mrs. Crane had gathered up from various sources, and particularly from the brothers and sisters of the deceased, various unpublished stories in manuscript; and that she also obtained from newspaper files other stories of Stephen's which she put into the hands of Mr. Plant, the English executor, as the property of the estate. Plant sold the English rights, and Mrs. Crane filed with him a claim for her services in getting this material ready for the printer. She brought the same stories to the United States and put them into Reynolds' hands for sale. Will was in no doubt that they were the property of the estate, and that the proceeds of the sale which had been approved by the American executor should therefore be paid to him. The claim that Mrs. Crane filed with the English executor presumably was for the entire value of her services, and the one hundred dollars paid to her with Will's consent would be credited upon that bill. Cora might make her claim to the estate for services rendered, but Will could conceive of no theory by which she could claim to be the owner of these stories, or to be entitled to the proceeds of Reynolds' sale of them.

Will saw an excuse for legal hairsplitting in the fact that Stephen had received a sizable advance from his American publisher Stokes for *The O'Ruddy*, left unfinished at his death. He might be held to account for the whole, or a portion of this sum; and in order to protect himself he must be able to show that he had waived none of the rights of the estate.

William Crane's closeness in money matters did not pass unnoticed in family circles. A niece says that William bought up his brothers' shares, Stephen's among them, of certain Pennsylvania coal stock left by their father, at a fraction of its value. His skinflint behavior in this instance leaves little room for doubt that he seized upon the issue of *Last Words* to make of it a test case in his dealings with Cora.

But did not the language of the will, in the codicil, clearly reserve all income from royalties and copyrights to her—specifically excluding it from coming under the trust? So Cora thought; and Plant, who had drawn the will, seems to have proved no match for his American confrere in the subsequent duel over legalistic verbalisms.

Judge Crane's letter of November 11, 1901, had the desired effect of shutting up Reynolds, now left with no choice but to bow to the authority of the American executor. And then the horse Peanuts stepped into a hornets' nest. Peanuts had run up a board bill!

Will had written on August 21, 1900, that his brother Ed claimed $129 due him, at a rate of board fixed by Stephen himself before Ed began using the horse; and that Ed was willing to keep the horse for the bill, but that if he gave up the horse he would make that claim against the estate. Will was in favor of letting Ed keep the horse. Then Peanuts, who had been the pet of the entire family, was sold. Cora protested. Will could see that she had been "misinformed," and supposed his brother would "explain the transaction." Edmund Crane did so. But knowing nothing of Cora's circumstances, angered and hurt by her demand that the money from the sale of the horse be paid to her, he burned her letter which he did not answer; and so ended all communication between them.

The circumstances which brought about the sale of Peanuts were these:

In an accident when the whiffle-tree broke loose and fell on his heels, Peanuts became frightened and ran away, endangering the lives of Ed's wife and several of his children. "He ran, he bucked, he reared, he jackknifed," one of Edmund Crane's daughters wrote later, describing the incident which terrified them all. "With one of his lunges forward he separated the wagon tongue from the wagon. It struck in the road and broke in two. . . . I can still hear my mother moaning, 'Oh, my babies! Oh, my babies!' " And so, rightly or wrongly, Ed felt that the safety of his family thereafter made it necessary to get rid of Peanuts, whom Stephen had directed should not be sold.

Some three-and-a-half years later, on January 12, 1905, came another even more astonishing communication from William Crane, the last Cora was ever to receive from any member of the Crane family. Will wrote that his brother Ed had filed a claim against the estate for $52.28, "the balance of the bill due for board of Stephen's horse, and $13.33 interest on same for three and one-half years, making $65.61 in all"; and to make the gesture of petty vengeance look holier, Will explained that the bill would be outlawed by time if Stephen had not been continuously out of the country for so long before his death. Before accepting the bill, he would "inquire into its merits and let you know."

But the board bill episode is contradicted by Edmund Crane's own words on the subject of Peanuts to his brother Stephen in his long letter of March 2, 1899. And if the tone of that letter, simple, straightforward, and warmly affectionate, is to be taken as representative of the man himself—the favorite brother Stephen had chosen for his guardian—the whole business of the board bill must be written off as certainly not inspired by Edmund Crane, if he even knew about it, and wholly out of character.

On June 16, 1903, William H. Crane as "one of the executors" of his brother's estate filed with the Surrogate of Orange County, New York, an accounting showing moneys received by him in the amount of $1,312.28; and bills paid, $785.61. These latter included $500 to himself, advanced against funeral expenses; thirty cents "expressage on books"; and forty-four cents "freight on Maggie." There was also his commission of $57.80 and a credit balance of $31.13 which he was allowed by the Court to pay to himself out of any assets which might later come into his hands—a sum he continued to collect year after year. Out of moneys received, $500 was forwarded to the English executor, A. T. Plant. Deponent declared that "the moneys stated in said account as collected, were all that were collectable"; that he still had in his possession "the interest of the said Stephen Crane in his late father's library, which interest is of nominal value"; also "twenty-seven copies of a book . . . entitled "Maggie," which I have not sold for the reason that I could get no offer for the same, although I have offered to sell them to several booksellers."

Since an executor's accounting is always placed on file with public records, Will may have felt that the formality of submitting a separate accounting to the other legatees—his brother Edmund in particular, as trustee for little Stephen—could be dispensed with. Cora received none either. Will did not like to be "questioned" about such details, it made him angry, Edmund said; and his "tight" administration violated no rule of law.

No investigation of the "marriage" was possible through ordinary channels—of records, that is. But did William Crane, the shrewd lawyer, put two and two together and come to his own conclusions? What might he have learned from the correspondents —any who did not keep silent out of respect for Stephen Crane's memory? When the court order and citation for the probate hearing was finally issued by the Surrogate on December 8, 1904, Cora was not named as Stephen's wife, only "one of the next of kin."

Previously, on September 14, Will had addressed a letter to Cora at her Aunt Mary Holder's New York City apartment, requesting her signature on a "consent and waiver, which if you will sign and return, I shall be able to make some progress in the matter of my account." It would commit her to nothing "excepting to the approval of the account on file of which you have a copy." Cora did not sign the waiver, but wrote to the Surrogate petitioning to have royalties paid directly to her instead of to Judge Crane. She was supplied with the legal forms, which she filled out and forwarded by mistake to Appleton, the publishers, only to have them returned as not "in legal shape." "They should be made out and certified by the Surrogate himself, and sealed with his seal." This done, Appleton would be glad to transfer the account to her name. She wrote again to the Surrogate, her letter date-lined from Aunt Mary's apartment December 31, 1904: "I am now in Georgia—but the above [is] the permanent address."*

Events must finally have convinced Cora that she was in a losing battle with William Crane. Writing Plant from Florida—July 9, 1905—she closed the book, remarking that she thought Plant should ask Judge Parker to look into the matter. "Judge Crane has not acted as a gentleman should. . . ."

5

A HOUSE in London possessed the advantage over lodgings, in Cora's view, of enabling her to resume the social contacts on which her precarious future so largely depended. In journalism, or any other type of employment, she must count on help from friends.

South Kensington was a neighborhood of colleges and museums. Its nearness to the Serpentine and the gardens where fashionable London promenaded or rode in carriages at the favorite noon hour was an added attraction for the American tourist. The location, Cora hoped, would fit in with her plan of letting the first-floor suite—bedroom, sitting room, and bath—with *pension*, to an American couple or a single man. She had a maid who could valet, she told Perris, and look after a gentleman's clothes. Garland, Linson, and others of her correspondents were urged to pass the word along. She begged pardon for asking, "but I must leave no stone unturned."

So she made a virtue of necessity after her forced exit from 47 Gower Street; and some of her old buoyancy was back when, early in September, she and Mrs. Brotherton moved into a little house at 6 Milborne Grove, The Boltons. Undaunted by her dis-

* When Cora wrote this letter to the Surrogate, she had already been back in Florida for two years. The casual reference to "Georgia," as though she were on a visit there from her Aunt Mary's house, conceals both the fact and the reasons for her return.

covery of "what hard work manual labor is"—no one knew until he tried it for himself!—she saw herself now banished from "the delicious land" of imagination "into which idle folks with little to do retreat. . . . One learns fidelity from work."

The house in Milborne Grove was but a stone's throw from the Stewart family home at 73 Harrington Gardens! But no ghosts walked; or at any rate, since they had not intruded on her life with Stephen she perhaps by now accepted their proximity as harmless. Old Sir Donald had recently died, and Norman come into the title. But there had been no reply from India to her last appeal in regard to the divorce.

To those in America who had sponsored Stephen's struggling talent Cora wrote, begging them to put their recollections to paper for use in the *Life* she was planning. Howells responded with a tender memoir. Irving Bacheller recalled his enthusiasm, and his wife's, on first seeing the manuscript of *The Red Badge*. "He went to Mexico for me," Bacheller added, "and came back with the longest revolver I ever saw." Louis Senger, Stephen's boyhood chum from Sullivan County days—a cousin of Corwin Linson— had offered help with the *Life*. Would Senger write her now "about this work we want to do?" She wished he might come to London in the spring, "for us to revise and finish the book together. . . . This address will find me for years to come, I trust."

But the little book still did not get onto paper: it had to be laid aside while she did other things to earn money. Stokes would make no advance without seeing the completed manuscript. Illness was added to the other torments, and her eyes were giving trouble. "Dear little woman," wrote Mrs. De Friese from Mexico, "do take care of your eyes and dont use them too much while you are physically run down."

Publishers were careless about sending proofs. Cora complained to Perris when "The Squire's Madness" appeared without proofs having been submitted to her, "The mistakes are simply endless!" Over *Wounds in the Rain* she exploded to Pinker:

> Please make Methuen understand that their contract is with *me* now & that when I ask for proof . . . I intend to have them. . . . I've always done my late husband's work of that kind as you know.

And with a flash of the old imperious manner she reminded Pinker that it was customary for publishers to submit jacket designs. She also wanted to see the dedication page and would be obliged if Pinker would see to these things; otherwise, she must see Mr. Methuen herself "and this I do not like to do."

But while the dogs of trouble snapped at her skirts that winter life was not all work and worry. Mabel Barr, Edith Richie, and Florence Bray paid a visit in December to the little house in Milborne Grove. The four of them and Mrs. Brotherton, who seems to have been socially liked, were invited to a studio tea, "with only a few people," said their host Douglas Sladen, "but there is pretty sure to be somebody interesting." Cora was in with the studio set, and soon there came another invitation from Hal Hurst, who did "charming pictures very like . . . the popular American Gibson girls." To Cora's own Sunday evenings in Milborne Grove came artists and literary people, musicians—a violinist who had the same teacher as young Kubelik, just then creating a furor in London— and a sprinkling of titles. Lewis Hind, Edwin Pugh, the Princess Kropotkin were guests at these affairs.[*]

At a small reception in December her "little house was a crush." Cora described this party in a letter to Agnes Crane, Edmund's daughter, who for more than a year had been a steady correspondent. The guests this time, she told Stephen's niece, included Lady Randolph Churchill, now Mrs. Cornwallis-West; the Frewens; Mr. and Mrs. Walter Crane, "the great artist," and their daughters; Mrs. Parvis; Mrs. Ronalds, the celebrated society beauty and friend of the Prince of Wales; Lady Hamilton; "and heaps of other distinguished men and women. They all know it's a question if I get my next meal or not," she added, wishing to impress upon Agnes the fact that in England "there is no distinction between rich and poor if they are nice people."

---

[*] Jan Kubelik was a world-famous Hungarian violinist and composer, great-uncle of Rudolf Kubelik, orchestra conductor who has appeared with the New York Philharmonic.

Edwin Pugh, English novelist and magazine writer, was one of the many friends from Brede Place days who later wrote in appreciation of Crane's work. (See the London *Bookman*, LXVII [December, 1924], 162-164.)

Princess Kropotkin was the wife of Prince Peter Kropotkin, Russian geographer, author, and revolutionary. Kropotkin, an anarchist, had been associated with the Nihilist group but later turned against the methods of terrorism. Exiled from czarist Russia, he spent most of his later years in England, returning to his native country after the revolution of 1917. Best known in the United States for his *Memoirs of a Revolutionist*.

Cora got Poultney Bigelow to speak at one of the luncheons of the Society of American Women in London, and handsome George Lynch, who discoursed on his experiences in China. The ladies were charmed. But holidays were a dark time, and Christmas brought ghosts of the year gone by with its terrifying changes. "It makes me sad because I cannot send a good Xmas box to you all," she wrote in the letter to Agnes,

> but it's impossible this Xmas. Last year at this time we were so gay and happy at Brede Place. You can fancy how miserable a time this is for me. I am ill with a bad leg. The doctor says it is the result of shock and general misery and worry which has culminated in my weak spot—my gouty leg! However, I hope to be better soon. Now my foot is high in the air on a pile of pillows. . . .

The Frasers invited her to spend Christmas Day with them. "There will be nothing livelier than the company of our two selves," Mrs. Fraser assured her; and Cora accepted, knowing that if she remained alone on that day she would weep her eyes out. "Remain in the world if you wish to forget," she wrote in her diary, "do not go into solitude. . . . Solitude is the nurse of all passions, because in solitude there is no standard of comparison." Perhaps she had not yet sounded the depths of psychological truth in that observation, but before another year closed in she would touch bottom. "I cannot send you an unmeaning Christmas cardy thing," wrote Catherine Wells, who wished "very sincerely that the New Year may give you some days of brightness and hopefulness, and happiness among your friends." Henry James acknowledged her Christmas card greeting echoing "words of woe" over the "rather ghastly business. I can well imagine how little of anything but heaviness it must have had for you—in the dark and dreary town and with little but ghosts at your fireside."

Agnes Crane, at the impressionable age, showed a desire to be initiated into the mysteries of good manners and the social arts. "Your Uncle Stephen wanted to give you a year or two at school," Cora reminded her. "Perhaps some day you can visit me and see things for yourself." She was delighted with Agnes' "very nicely worded letter," and much interested in hearing about her studies. "If I were you, I would not try to do too much . . . when you have so much else to learn. . . . The poor old piano and violin are murdered so," music, she thought, was "best left alone, unless one can seriously study and has a real talent for it." But it was "splendid" that Agnes was learning shorthand.

> Read good books and add constantly to your vocabulary. In ordinary conversation so few words are really used, but nothing will give you a better foundation for an education than a big vocabulary & proper pronunciation.
>
> . . .
>
> Our winter has not set in yet, the leaves are all off the trees, but you know that here the grass is always green. We do not have the heavy frost and snow, but then we miss the glorious reds and golds of the leaves in Autumn; here they go into soft yellows and browns with very little red.
>
> You ask if the poor people and the rich separate in England— No. Wealth makes less difference here than in any country in the world. But *Class* distinction *does* make a difference. For instance, a servant is always a servant. A servant marries a servant and their children and grand-children are servants. They have no chance to become anything else and they do not see the need or feel the need of any different life. That is one class. Then there are the tradespeople. People who keep the shops (stores). They are another class, both here and everywhere in Europe. Unless they are great manufacturers they are not received by what is called the "gentry." In America, a new country, all the conditions of life are different. It's a wretched life for any man, no matter how much wealth he may have if he is not in business. . . .

Was Cora, writing thus to Stephen's niece, thinking perhaps of her henpecked young artist father whose life had been made miserable by the acquisitive instincts and mercenary ambitions of a self-centered woman? Of Stephen's years of struggle too, in New York? Although her picture of rigid class lines no longer holds true over most of the earth's surface today, it illuminates her preference for life under that system in Victorian England—where "the grass was always green."

> Here the gentlemen have estates to look after, or they are Barristers, or Doctors (not Dentists; a Dentist is not in any better social position than the barber from whom he has taken the trade here.) They go in for Parliament. In America our rich men don't do their duty toward the government. They do not bother themselves with

politics and that is the reason that we are laughed at by all the
world, for our dishonest politics and men who hold office. Here,
though goodness knows there is evil in . . . public life, the men
who hold positions are so rich that they can have no interest in
being anything but honest. Just think, a Judge in England, every
Judge, gets $50,000 a year . . . the same as the President of the
United States. This is to place him far above any dishonesty &
usually, too, he is a rich man. Then the Gentlemen go in the
Army, the Navy, and the Merchant service. And the Civil list,
that is the government positions in India and all the vast British
colonies, take many of them. Then there are men of letters and
artists. Once one has a good social position and only by being of
gentle birth can this be obtained, no matter how poor one may be
it is never lost. In America it is different. When people lose their
money they seem to vanish from the earth. . . . All you Crane
children should be very proud of your good blood, and you should
try in every way to be well bred, and gentle.

I am so glad to hear about little Stephen. What an adorable infant he must be. I long so to see him again, and his other half. . . .
Please give my love to all and wish them a happy Xmas & joyous
New Year for me. Write to me as often as you can and I will try to
answer any questions. Your loving aunt

Cora

Mary Anderson, the actress, now the Countess de Navarro, was a
member of the Society of American Women in London. She and
her husband, "Tony," were beloved friends of Henry James. Cora
—who understood the interest, real or vicarious, which women
readers had in a wider life almost as well as she did that of their
husbands who had looked for it at the Hotel De Dream—wrote to
the celebrated stage beauty proposing an interview at her country
home in Worcestershire. The Countess responded with a warm
invitation (absent-mindedly addressed to Mrs. Walter Crane), enclosing train schedules. Cora at once communicated with Curtis
Brown, who though still London manager for the New York *Press*
was then in the first phase of launching his new literary agency.
Stephen's old friend and editor had been a guest at Brede Place,
and relations continuing of the friendliest, brought his wife and
daughters to dine at Milborne Grove. "If the Anderson thing turns
out as you hope," he wrote, "there ought to be a lot of other things
that could be done, and also one or two things in the literary
agency line."

Curtis Brown's enthusiasm for the Anderson article had induced him to offer the high rate of two pounds per thousand words— double the price paid by the New York *Press*—with "a bonus if the article is suited to general use and is sufficiently illustrated." He hoped Cora could manage a camera. "My syndicate pays cash on acceptance." He outlined questions: "If she has unusual views on any topic whether on the bringing up of babies, decay of drama, or making pies, get all possible on the topic to the exclusion of other topics." Then the interview unfortunately had to be postponed to suit the Countess' change of plans. Curtis Brown wrote again, on February 13, wishing Cora luck "and a pleasant journey to Madame Navarro's." But this time there was an accident of some sort, in which Cora suffered injury. Mrs. Brotherton sent apologies, Mme. Navarro was graciously distressed:

We waited lunch for her, and sent a fly to meet her and were sorry when she did not come. . . . Will you tell her with my kind regards and many regrets over her sad accident. I'll be so pleased to see Mrs. Crane another day.

Tomorrow never came! First the Navarros were away from home while workmen and painters had possession of their house. If Mrs. Crane would write again in a fortnight and propose another date the Countess would be "most happy." A fortnight hence Cora would be on the high seas. But she did not give up easily; in the time remaining, an interview in town might still be arranged. To this suggestion Curtis Brown was lukewarm. "Your personal impressions of Madame Navarro and her home" he felt would be necessary to round out the article, otherwise it would lose much of its value. "Can't we look for one of the Duchess' interviews on modern English and American Society instead?" The Duchess of Manchester, equally famous for her beauty, warmth and wit, shared the modern views of Lady Randolph Churchill in favor of a rapprochement between the two countries.

It is not known whether Cora ever had a press interview with the Duchess of Manchester. But an illustrated article by her on the Society of American Women in London seems to have been bought by Curtis Brown's International Publishing Bureau; a copy was sent to Reynolds for the American market. Someone had told Brown Cora had "thought a little" of going into the agency business herself. In February he wrote:

If you are really considering it, dont send the letter (enclosed) to Mr. Pugh, for I have broached the subject therein to him, and wouldn't for the world approach anyone with whom you might make arrangements for yourself. Of the authors with whose American rights I should like to deal, several are doubtless known to you personally, and if you could capture them for me, I should be glad to divide the meagre spoils.

Edwin Pugh seems to have been the only writer she captured for Curtis Brown's agency. Poultney Bigelow probably stood by his agreements with Perris and Davidson; and Conrad wrote that "any change as to disposal of my work" would be impossible. "I am bound in too many ways." But Conrad was "so really and truly glad your work finds space and recognition. No news could have been more welcome." Cora must come to them for rest, as soon as the weather improved a little.

Clement T. Flower, an artist known to Robert Barr, was to do a portrait of Stephen. He had exhibited at the Royal Academy and had excellent connections with the Chapel Studios in Hertfordshire. Cora hoped Judge Crane might order the portrait; Will thought otherwise. When the silence from overseas became embarrassing she wrote Flower,

> to be quite frank with you, I cannot pay for it until the estate is quite settled and that seems months off. . . . It is causing me simply endless worry and it is so unnecessary, but the fact remains. Now if under these circumstances you are willing to undertake the portrait I shall be glad to have the "head."

Flower, agreeing, asked for a photograph, a coat of Stephen's, any and all details Cora might write him as to color of eyes, hair light or darkish brown, etc. When the photograph reached him the artist decided to paint a larger portrait "and present you with the extra size, as it would be so much nicer to have the hands in." This meant that he could not get it finished in time for this year's hanging, but would send it in next year. He would like to arrange an appointment to show her the picture at the studio before she left for the United States. This letter, written on the day Cora sailed, followed her to America. No trace of the portrait has come to light. In all probability it was never paid for and so was retained by the artist himself.

One evening that spring Cora ran into an old friend, the young girl Vere, dining with her uncle at one of the smart restaurants. Vere had just returned from a visit to her parents in India.

I began to hear a familiar voice at the next table. And, lo, there was Mrs. Crane in a black lace frock with Lady Randolph Churchill and some young men. . . . When she recognized me she ran over to our table and made a lovely American fuss. I had lunch with her several times.

Cora frankly admitted to Vere that she was "not panning out" as a journalist; she had turned to writing bits of advertising for some smart shop. Years later, when Vere knew all the gossip, she wrote: "I do not know how she lived and do not care. She was 'on the level.' She was plucky and gay and kind."

Earlier, in December, Cora had told Perris,

> In thinking over what Mr. Radford said to me, I can't quite see *what* he meant by saying "it can't go on; this hand to mouth business." Perhaps he does not understand that all my late husband's estate is mine, but that until the small estate is settled I cannot draw any money—hence my present difficulties.

As she saw it, it was all as simple as that! The unknown Mr. Radford may have been her landlord, or the agent through whom the Milborne Grove house was rented. Cora had written Pinker also, during the period of house hunting:

> Please say to anyone inquiring for reference that I have all income in all countries from my husband's books and plays, etc. You will know what to say.

Now she wrote Reynolds, going on record for the third time that *she*—not the estate—was the owner of all rights to the income from Crane's manuscripts:

> Will you please say to Henry T. Coates and Company of Philadelphia, that I own the exclusive book rights of the book of short stories which I am selling to them. Mr. Crane never sold book rights of short stories except those sold to Harpers by yourself. They published stories first in their magazine and then in book form.

She had supposed matters would be settled quickly, and that in the interim she would be able to borrow money against the estate as needed, for living expenses. Now she was learning that sometimes the law moves at the speed of a glacier. "The little words, 'give me,' scare away friends as the cry of the hawk does the chickens!"

But not having yet grasped the meaning of William Crane's attitude in his handling of the estate, she was looking forward to Helen's arriving to spend with her another summer in England or the Swiss Alps. The Bigelows were staying at a pension in the Zimmerwald, and "P.B." wrote singing the praises of the delicious food, good rooms, wonderful air; and he needed a secretary.

By April, however, Cora must have known that she was beaten —for the time being anyway. She would go to America and sit it out while the estate remained in chancery, telling all of her friends that she expected to be back in England by the end of next year.

Moreton Frewen wrote from Ireland: "I think you are wise in your decision. I believe if you get a quiet year out there," in the country in Kentucky he hoped, "not in Louisville or any of their horrid towns . . . it will do you more good than anything." It was just the rest she needed "after the awful strain of the past year." He gathered from what Plant told him that after an interval her financial affairs would be likely to recover. He hoped so, for "such worries as yours spoil all good work."

Her mind made up, Cora with her usual vigor set about preparations for departure, saying nothing to Perris yet of the move she hoped—and believed—was only temporary. She had let her maid go. Arrangements were undertaken through Plant for subletting Milborne Grove, on which she had a two-year lease. The house was let furnished. Hoping to realize an extra sum toward her passage money to America, she placed with a London art dealer several items from a small collection of works by contemporary artists which she and Stephen had assembled at Brede Place—a Beardsley among them. But the dealer reported no luck with the Beardsley, the best offer he had being for "a sum quite insignificant," reproduction rights included.

Moreton Frewen sent twenty pounds, and asked for news later "on how the world is treating you." If matters did not improve he would give her

a letter . . . to one or other of my senatorial friends in Washington, they would find something with a reasonable salary attached . . . in the

Treasury, or one of the other of the Departments. . . . Dont please give me any charge on the rent of your house, if times turn out well later on you can return me this tiny loan.

What line of steamers would she take? The Atlantic Transport would carry her comfortably. He knew the president and would write him, and might also be able to get her a railway pass to Kentucky: "the more dollars you arrive with . . . the better."

Cora wanted Conrad to keep one of the Brede Place dogs, Tolstoi, but Conrad replied that he could not have the dog at Pent Farm. Escamillo, Stephen's gift to little Borys, had gotten them into trouble already chasing chickens and sheep; one dog on the place was all that an aroused farm bailiff would stand for. Escamillo was the puppy Pizzanner, so named on account of his odd legs which splayed out in all directions—Cora said, exactly like the legs on an old-fashioned grand piano—now grown up and re-christened, a Toreador. So the unwanted Tolstoi found a home with a former neighbor and kindred dog lover, Mrs. Forbes-Bentley of Bay Tree Cottage, Beckley.

To the Society of American Women in London Cora made a gift of the captured Spanish flag Stephen brought back from Cuba, which had hung in the entrance hall at Brede Place. "A most precious relic," wrote the president Mrs. Hugh Griffin, "we shall all be proud of possessing." Cora imposed the one condition that were the Society ever disbanded, the flag must then be returned to the United States government.

Friends grieved to lose her from their midst, but already they looked forward to her return next year. Thursday evening, April 25, when all were invited to a "farewell" at Milborne Grove the little house was jammed to capacity. The Princess Kropotkin was kept away by a severe sore throat which she had "had to poultice." The Prince was in the States. If Cora were not sailing that week, might the Princess visit her the next day, or any other afternoon during the week? "I shall be disappointed if it is too late to go to see you, but if I am to bid you farewell without seeing you," she wrote, "let me express to you a sincere wish that an active life in the States might appease your great sorrow . . . and bring you some bright days."

A rather stiff little note had come from Henry James, "fast

down" at Lamb House. He wished her "a prompt and fortunate journey," adding,

I am afraid your recent stay in England has not had much convenience for you and I can't help congratulating you on your decision to bring it to a close. That America may· be easier for you is the hope of yours very truly.

It was H. J.'s dismissal, not without a sigh of relief. Not much escaped "the old man." Perhaps he had always known the facts of Cora's past and kept them to himself. He had loved "Stevie" dearly, and it was all very well while the poor boy was alive, but there were limits to what the friends of a dead author could reasonably be expected to swallow.

Wednesday, April 25, Cora wrote Perris: "I am obliged to go suddenly to the States. Please give any money for ms. in your possession to Mr. Plant." Her own unsold stories she wished returned to her; the address after Saturday: Owensboro, Kentucky.

Had creditors suddenly threatened action and Plant advised leaving without delay? Three days later, in a calmer tone she wrote again to Perris:

I am so sorry that I cannot come to see you personally before I sail but it is impossible. Now about the £17 advance on the MS., you said you could value my work in collecting, re-writing and revising the book of short stories [*Last Words*] at £50—to be paid me by the estate. Mr. Plant wants you to value the work, if you can value it at £50 and will let me know, we can arrange to have the £17 paid out of that money. And that will leave the MS. free to sell as Mr. Plant directs.

The passenger list of the Hamburg-American liner *S. S. Pennsylvania*, sailing April 28 from Southampton, carries the names of *Frau Stephen Crane* and *Frau L. Brotherton*. And—cream of all ironies—*Fraulein Marie Anderson!*

6

IN THE eleven months since Stephen's death, Cora had been too busy to have a breakdown. Now grief, fatigue, the letdown after crisis engulfed her, and like a deep-sea diver when the pressures are suddenly removed, she was feeling "the bends."

What was she doing in the next ten months? And whom was she with in the little town of Owensboro, Kentucky? Facts are meagre or missing altogether.

Some of the "guessers" have her staying with the Richie family —on no firmer evidence than Mrs. Richie's supposed Kentucky origin. But Mrs. Richie and her younger sister, Kate Frederic, both were born in Oswego, New York; and this theory is refuted by Edith Richie's own statement that she and her parents returned to America in 1902—one year after Cora's final departure from England. They never saw Cora again. Moreton Frewen, an active correspondent, makes no reference to the Richies, who were old friends; this would have been unpardonable rudeness in a Victorian gentleman, were Cora then domiciled under their roof. There is left only Mrs. Brotherton, of whose antecendents and place of residence absolutely nothing is known.

Upon her arrival Cora stayed briefly in New York with Aunt Mary Holder, moving there from the Ashland House. She presented herself one morning at the office in West Forty-third Street of Major Henry Clay Cochran, one of the Marine Corps officers Stephen had known in Cuba, who had left the service to go into business. Cochran in a formal note presents his compliments to Mrs. Crane,

and begs to express his profound regret that owing to absence from the city he did not get her note till late last night. If Mrs. Crane still desires a pass to Florida and will inform him of the steamer or route by which she would like to travel, he will endeavor to procure it this afternoon.

Her plans were nebulous, her mind spun around like a feather in the wind. But she did not then go to Florida; and Moreton Frewen, in July, rejoiced that "after all your vicissitudes you got safely down to Kentucky."

Energetically trying to pull wires in Washington, he had heard from Vice-President Roosevelt who, despite his "warm regard for poor Stephen . . . did not appear sanguine that he could be of use to you." Frewen urged her to go there herself "when Congress comes in Session. . . . You might get something rumunerative." On September 30 he wrote advising another try with Roosevelt, who in the meantime had become President on the death of McKinley: ". . . in the position he now finds himself he would probably further your interests." Then on November 24: "We are indeed sorry to hear so poor an account of you; but I hope that physically and financially better days may be dawning . . . and if courage will pull you through your future is assured." He was "likely to sail for your side" within a fortnight, and would be in Washington himself before Christmas. "I will look over the ground and let you know how matters are." Cora had left a mantelpiece at Brede, "still there awaiting a buyer. I venture to enclose you £5 and if I sell it for more I will send you the balance."

How much did Major Cochran know, or surmise, of Cora's Florida past? How much might have leaked out through the grapevine to official circles in Washington? The outcome of Moreton Frewen's inquiries is unreported, but his generous efforts bore no fruit.

And now while the future looked ever more dark a letter followed her around the world through that ghost-filled gloom, to Kentucky. The letter, postmarked from China, was from her brother-in-law Sir Norman Robert Stewart, now a major general with Her Majesty's forces in India.

Getting no answer to her first communication—from Florida— Cora had written again from England, six months after Stephen's death—evidently on January 10, 1901—renewing her appeals to Norman to obtain for her an interview with Donald Stewart in regard to the divorce. But whatever this reply brought her now, of good or ill, had come too late:

Pekin, 7th March, 1901

My dear Cora:
    Yours of 10th Jany reached me last evening. Now before answering this one request you have made me let me explain matters. As you know, I went home in '96 on 3 months leave, [to be divorced and remarried] at the end of which I returned to India leaving Tiny in England. After a stay of 5 weeks I again went home in October and did not go back to India till *May 1898* when I found yours written, as well as I can remember, November '96. All that time I was under the impression you had ceased to write and when I got your letter nearly 2 years after it was written and you had not attempted another, made up my mind you had come to the conclusion it was better to forget we were at any time connected by marriage. Of course during the time I was in England I saw a great deal of Donnie and learnt how absolutely

hopeless it was to attempt to bring you and he together. So when I found your letter on my return it seemed to me wiser to remain silent. I cannot treat your last in the same way. You say you hear I am coming home soon and ask if I will let you see me. In the first place I dont think there is any chance of getting out of this abominable country in the immediate future; and secondly, Tiny is waiting for me in India and as I had only seen her for three weeks in '99 (when I went home on two months leave) since April '98, you can imagine how keen I am to go to her and at last settle down in the nice place I am stationed at in India and which she hasn't even seen yet as she only went last November so as to be nearer me . . . By last night's post I also heard from Tiny and in her letter she said "Surely you wont think of going home before I have seen our house and opened out all the nice things I have brought out to furnish it." So any thought of going home this year, in the event of our getting out of China, is over. I am pretty sure to go home for short leave *next* year and take her and my small boy with me. The latter is a ripping little chap just three years old last month. If you have anything to say to me put it in writing and you may accept my assurance that it will be treated "with honor." When I was at home and saw how truly useless it was to do anything towards bringing you and Don together I tried to forget he was married and as I have told you previously divorce seemed to me the only wise step left. As I am writing about my own brother you will I know treat my letter with sacredness. I have stood by you all along in spite of never having seen you but at the same time it would not do to have my name in any way mixed up in your affairs, however if I were at home I would certainly go and see you without concealing the fact from Tiny, if I did conceal it from the members of my family for I know Donnie would resent it and it would only lead to family jars. I feel sure Tiny would be only too glad to befriend you . . . I dont like writing any more as I am not certain how long you will be at the address you give. . . . I wonder what you are doing in England? I hope you are staying with friends and your life is not too lonely. . . .

Although Sir Norman's communication arrived only just as she was leaving England, Stephen then a year in his grave, Cora seems to have been no less anxious to shed the marriage tie which had been a sword of Damocles above their heads. So from New York or on shipboard she wrote a third time, throwing caution to the winds and laying all of the facts on the table. The reply came addressed to "Mrs. D. W. Stewart, 6 Milborne Grove, The Boltons, South

Kensington, London"—the address she must have given with the expectation of returning to England:

Bolarum

17. 10. 01

My dear Cora:

Yours of 6th May duly reached me just before I left Pekin and fairly took away my breath as your previous letter enclosing Mrs. Crane's card did not make me in the least suspicious of your having changed your name. We wont say anything on this point. You have had an unhappy life and it is not surprising that you jumped at the chance of happiness which might have offered itself again and I am for your sake truly grieved to hear it lasted for so short a time. About meeting Donnie I dont see how I can help you, separated as we are. I know it would be useless to write and ask him to have an interview with you, because he has already told me that he wrote to you on the subject. If I were at home and you and he also it might be quite different. Anyhow I would do my best for you. Tiny and I hope to get home next August but only for 3 months unless I make up my mind to retire which is not at all improbable. So perhaps after all we may meet, but you know this must mean a certain amount of deception as I have already explained to you. I have got your address and when anything is settled about our going home I will let you know. Tiny would I feel sure do all in her power to make your life happier, but like myself she would have to act a more or less deceitful part as she does not wish to go out of her way to offend my people and you are sensible enough to see this. I dont quite understand whether you *married* SC or not. If you *did* marry him you ought to be very careful of your secret for a very large circle of your friends must only know you as Mrs. Stewart! You want to know whether I am still your friend, why *of course* I am. Donnie told me his version but I dont think he went into particulars with the family generally. I have always defended you because you have never been bitter and have never written an unkind word. Whatever your married lives were you have completely cut adrift now from each other and my advice to you is "forget and never wish to meet." Is the London house your own? Curious you should be so very close to Harrington Gardens.

Let me know all about your plans and whether you intend to stick to America or not. . . . I wish I hadn't to address you as Mrs. Crane, but will doubtless get accustomed to it. Goodbye and God bless you

Norman

While in Pekin I saw a great deal of General Adna Chaffee and the Americans and made many friends among them. One a Captain Bel-

COWARDICE.

BY MRS. STEPHEN CRANE.

It was in '95, the month of August, that I went broke—stony. No money to buy colours or bread either for that matter, and without a shred of an idea, beyond that of a sign painter, how to use colours if I had suddenly fallen heir to enough money to purchase them by the ton. I was not only penniless, but I was stale, and I knew it. The noise of town offended me. The narrowness of life there; the never failing flow of meaningless commonplaces which one must listen to and accept as wit; the unceasing, useless babble from lips of self-satisfied parrots; all these things had tired me into a state bordering upon melancholia. I moved through the days as cluminally, mentally, as a tortoise, with life the shell clinging to my unwilling back.

I decided to leave London and to bury myself amid the solitude and mists of the Sussex marshes. I had wanted to "do" the marshes in black-and-white for years. So I sold my few sticks, and the whole, three pounds seventeen shillings and seven... of three lights, still grasping in the stone edges bits of coloured glass—the arms of the Bluebeard. Then priest's room, a secret cupboard behind the oaken panels of linen-fold, and with staircase burrowed in the four-foot wall, leading from high in the chimney down into the subterranean passages beneath the house. Here, in Cromwell's time of cassock-hunting, the household priest could escape to safety. Next to the tower-room above the dungeon, with the spot of blood upon the floor which neither soap and water or the footprints of ages could wear away. It is in this room, when the wind is high and the night is wild, that the cries of children are heard; children killed and eaten by Bluebeard, who, it is said, "lived upon human flesh, with a particular relish for that of infants." Through the gloom of long passages I wandered, from empty dusty room, the windows choked with ivy, to empty room, no two upon a level; from floor to floor, through shadows, and up and down unexpected staircases, the caretaker's voice

"Cowardice," by Cora Crane, from the *Nottinghamshire Guardian*, October 4, 1902.

lairs, war correspondent, knew Stephen Crane very well and spoke so nicely of him. Of course I did not mention you and you may trust me with your secret. . . .

In such a complex of loyalties, the sincerity and forthrightness of this statement from an English gentleman who was in the fullest sense a product of the Victorian era is remarkable; and so it must have seemed to Cora. But saddest of all words in the language: Too late! Now Cinderella was back in the kitchen, the Prince lay dead under a stone in the cemetery of his people; and Cora found herself, all of a sudden, a woman with neither marital nor social status. And no longer young.

The autumn months saw her, so unused to vacillation, divided and shaken by crisis. From New Orleans she wrote Perris, on December 2, of "trying to recover from a bad cough in this mild climate," having been "so ill"; she was returning to Owensboro next week expecting to find there a letter from Stokes, the publisher. If the letter reached her it brought no good news; matters with *The O'Ruddy* were still hanging fire and the estate eternally deadlocked.

Had she drifted down to New Orleans on account of her health or for other reasons? She was, at any rate, coming to a decision, "the best way to earn my salt, and something to sprinkle my salt upon." Pleasure was the one sure thing which could always be counted on for conversion into dollars, with an ever-expanding market of which she had abundant and cynical knowledge; and the best thing in the world was "a healthy frame, steeled sinews and strong nerves; better still a quiet conscience with them."

She is next in Jacksonville, receiving mail sent in care of a local banker who had been a firm friend from the early days of the Hotel de Dream. Word reached her there from Alfred Plant—on June 13, 1902—that her tenants were vacating the house in Milborne Grove. Plant thought it his duty to warn her that "the various Kensington Creditors are very angry, and will certainly commence proceedings as soon as they hear you are in England."

And was the last small whisper of conscience now effectually silenced? She found nothing "delightfully wicked"; Byron she thought, was

> wicked enough but not at all delightful to himself. . . . Sin is easy only because it meets with such very general encouragement. . . . This is our misery, we always deafen our consciences and say: Look around—others are no better than we.*

"The future," says Paula Tanqueray, just before taking poison, "is only the past entered by another gate." Cora had once horrified a group of people at Brede Place during a discussion of Pinero's play, with her blunt declaration that the play's tragic ending was "false and exaggerated"—unfortunately betraying to her audience, it seemed to Sanford Bennett, that she knew "too much about life." But now she knew that not all the tricks in the dramatist's bag can equal the cruelty of life itself. Society takes vengeance on those who break its laws or flout its mores, usually in the form of excommunication; now society, she felt, had pulled the rug out from under her. Then fie upon their excommunication—she would throw it back in their faces! She would brazen it out, and henceforth show the world what she thought of its hypocritical morality and gold-plated respectability.

* Stephen Crane, in "The Blue Hotel," had said, "Every sin is the result of a collaboration."

PART THREE

(May, 1902 — September, 1910)

"Hattie/ Edna/ Self/ and/ 'Teddy'/ St Aug—/ 1907." Inscription in Cora's hand. Courtesy Columbia University Crane Collection.

The Court

chapter 8

IN the Pullman cars waiting on sidings at the Jacksonville Terminal before the last leg of the journey to the coastal playgrounds, tourists gasped, and wondered what catastrophe had struck here. Lonesome chimneys, skeletons of burned trees thrust up starkly from acres of scorched rubble. An area of nearly two square miles, the oldest part of the city, had gone up in the big blaze of May 3, 1901. But two blocks over on Ward Street most of "the line" had not burned: a fact that raised an outcry and an investigation from which, however, the Fire Department Chief and his lieutenants emerged unsinged. And when, on a May morning one year later, a short, blonde, determined woman alighted from the train in the Union Station a new metropolis of brick and concrete was already rising from the ashes of the old wooden city.

Cora Taylor's movements in the next twelve months are obscure, save for the fact that she was buying property and borrowing money to erect a building. A warranty deed dated May 28, 1902, records her purchase from one Helen L. Johnson and husband of the southern half of Lot 1, Block 3, Division "B" in the district known as LaVilla—the southwest corner of Ward and Davis Streets—for the sum of $1,000. Five days later the northern half of Lot 1 also changed hands, by conveyance from M.S.G. Abbott and wife to Cora E. Crane, widow, for $1,500. Then on May 29 she gave a mortgage of $700 back to Helen L. Johnson on the property conveyed, as part of the original purchase price, payable on or before three years at eight per cent interest; and likewise, on the same date and same terms a mortgage of $700 to Mr. Abbott. Thus it appears that the cash sums actually put down totaled $400 and $800 to the Johnsons and Abbotts respectively.

Where did she obtain the money for these down payments?

While Cora was "stoney broke" her old friends would not let her down, and in the city were some who may have come silently to the rescue with small loans or gifts, which in unfriendlier circles would be represented as "touches." The banker in whose care Cora was receiving mail probably loaned her up to a thousand dollars. Her diary for the year 1907 shows that she had notes, possibly dating back to this time, in each of the leading banks. But a personal loan is one thing. The officers and directors of these banks must have turned pale at the thought of the scandal if it became known that they had used their depositors' funds to underwrite a business proposition with Cora Taylor's name on it; for the principal required to float her undertaking she had to go elsewhere. She would always be "Cora Taylor" in Jacksonville.

There are in every city, large or small, mysterious birds of prey whose flexible interpretations of the law pass unnoticed by the authorities, to whom they are occasionally useful. To one of these, a character by the name of Charles C. Butler, with a ramshackle office on a sand-lot back street, Cora now had recourse. We should like to think she gulped over the deal, but it was sink or swim, and Cora had made up her mind that she was going to stay afloat. Butler loaned her $8,800 at eight per cent: a sum then sufficient, or nearly so, for the construction of a two-storied brick building of fourteen bedrooms, parlor rooms, ballroom, kitchens, dining room, and an annex with eight additional bedrooms.

The fire, which was transforming the physical appearance of the city and bringing prosperity in its charred trail, ushered in other changes less desirable and not immediately visible to the naked eye. On "the line" itself, syndicates controlled by a "silent" owner or partner in a company, who replaced the old-fashioned proprietors with a hired operator, male or female, were already making their appearance. There was also an influx of Negroes. Ironically, with the adoption of the first local Jim Crow law in 1905 the number of Negro "cribs" and white establishments employing colored operators increased noticeably. These developments, of course, were but reflections of a widening trend repeated in city after city with its red-light district, until the prohibition era when sporting-houses began to be replaced by call girls.

Cora now found herself right up against the syndicates. "He that toucheth pitch shall be defiled therewith." But bolstered by her sense of position, that protective coloring of ancestral roots which had come to her from the Howorths and the Holders, Cora pooh-poohed any such probability in her own case. She retained perfect confidence in her ability to set the tone and the style, regardless. She would always keep the personal touch, and have nothing to do with "vulgarity." At "The Court," as the new place was christened, everything would be held to the same level of quiet good taste which had been her greatest asset in the success of the Hotel de Dream.

So the handsome and substantial building of red glazed brick and smooth stone trim now rising on the corner of Ward and Davis Streets, with its carefully trimmed grass plots, umbrella tree and privet hedge, must have been a sight to cause wonder—and headaches!—up and down "the line." It is not hard to imagine the feelings of her old adversary across the street, Lyda de Camp, who on account of it was obliged to smarten up her dingy place and presently move into new quarters; and to others, who doubtless looked with a sour eye upon its aesthetic attractions, the mistress of the Court seemed to give herself the airs of royalty. Other than "Lyda's," the Court's formidable competitors were Belle Orloff—known as "Russian Belle"—and side by side in the next block east, "The Senate" and the "New York House."

Although Cora paid off the two mortgages to Abbott and Mrs. Johnson as soon as the loan from Butler was obtained, things had not gone well at the outset. The opening of the Court for business was delayed by the architect's refusal to surrender the building until he had received the full amount of his fee. Costs, as usual, probably exceeded specifications. Still, without the architect's certification to health and safety regulations, a requirement for all buildings used by the public in whatever capacity, she could not take possession; and on February 19, 1903, the architect, W. B. Camp, filed suit against her. Her lawyer, Halstead E. Bowden, successfully defended her in this action and on May 4, 1903, the case was "dismissed in open court."

Matters did not end there. The contractor, Marion Dickman,

also decided to go to court with an action of assumpsit, "a suit for money owing to the plaintiff by the defendant growing out of some contractual relation"; and one other who had furnished building materials likewise threatened suit. Cora was feeling the pressure of the wall at her back. "Very well," she countered, and coolly looked down her gun sights, "If you wish to have your name in the papers along with mine, go ahead!" The gentleman did not; and Marion Dickman, too, changed his mind when D. C. Campbell—replacing her attorney, Bowden, who had moved to another city—filed pleas denying the original indebtedness and pleaded payment. Cora swore to the truth of the pleas and the case was settled out of court.

Very likely, the court took a practical view of matters in regard to the pending suits, based on the clear relation between defendant's income potential and ability to pay, and ordered the building surrendered. At any rate, the victoria soon reappeared on the streets—albeit without the coachman in livery. This time it was a vehicle hired from the livery stable, but still a red flag to Cora's creditors. She was called names unfit for the lips of ladies and gentlemen. She did not take kindly to abuse; and when a post office clerk took upon himself the defense of public morals by withholding occasional pieces of her mail, the retort uttered to her diary was unflattering to "southern chivalry."

From England, meanwhile, were heard other rumblings and warnings. In a series of politely worded communications her solicitor, Alfred T. Plant, reminded her that rent and taxes on the Milborne Grove house had gone unpaid since the tenants left. Plant had had "a rather stormy interview" with the landlord, who was about to attach her furniture. Harrod's, with whom the furniture was stored, also considered it their right to be paid. Plant asked for twenty-five pounds for both debts; Cora sent him ten pounds for the landlord. The Kensington creditors, too, were pressing Plant. Cora finally sent another draft for nine pounds, which was less than the amount due Harrod's; and enclosed a list of goods to be shipped in care of the Lincoln Safe Deposit Company of New York, with whom she had arranged for the things to be received and moved down to Florida. The rest could be sold, "and whatever they bring can go towards paying for the carriage."

She wished to know if Plant had received any money from Judge Crane yet for the sale of *The O'Ruddy*? And had he ever received the one hundred pounds from Stokes which was to be paid on delivery of the manuscript? All of this correspondence with Plant, dragging on into the summer of 1905, was addressed to her at Aunt Mary Holder's apartment in New York City.

Of the furniture, a few old pieces in bad condition were to go separately to a New York firm of cabinetmakers for repairs: two clock cases, a long bench, a hall seat and oak chest, and one small carved chair. Cora now heard from these people that one hundred and fifty dollars would not cover the cost of repairs, and they could guarantee nothing: "We find the pieces in the worst condition imaginable, many parts missing, and if it was the intention of somebody to have broken them so as to make them useless, all we can say is that they succeeded."

It seemed like the last straw! But these few broken sticks, the manuscripts and the rest of the furniture from Brede Place—and memories—were all that remained to her now of England and her dream of happiness with Stephen Crane. She was determined to have them.*

With the Court in operation came a short breathing spell as it began to draw in money, so much money that the vulpine cupidity of C. C. Butler, the ward heeler and usurer, was instantly inflamed by the prospect of lush pickings. Butler already had his hooks in property in LaVilla. He now decided to increase his holdings by annexing the Court and, to that end, on the foreclosure of Cora's mortgage.

Fortunately for her, her new legal representative was a gentleman who could swap blow for blow and keep going. David C. Campbell's introduction to the local bar had come with a sensational murder case in which he was associated on the side of the defense with a veteran criminal lawyer, who won for their client a dramatic acquittal, since which time he had become known as a hard slugger. His rise had been rapid. In the slugging that now ensued, Campbell's punches cut the wind out of his opponent and Butler took a licking. The case was "dismissed upon Written Stipulation and agreement"—September 26, 1904.

* The long bench found its way into a Jacksonville home, as did other pieces, when furnishings from the Court were auctioned off after Cora's death.

Two years later, when Cora fell behind with one of her interest payments, Butler tried it again, and this time without going to court succeeded in tacking on $1,191.40 to the mortgage principal—payable in ninety days. This was actually an independent second mortgage, but the odd amount and short term indicate that it probably represented an increase added onto the original principal —Butler's revenge, perhaps, for the settlement out of court. When Cora presently raised the money to pay off this new debt Butler, suspecting that Dave Campbell was already negotiating for a transfer of the first mortgage to a New York concern at a lower interest rate, was determined to block any such move and refused her satisfaction. Cora notes in her diary—January 29, 1907:

> Saw Butler about satisfaction paper—did not sign it and threatened me. Would shut me up. He is a dangerous old snake.

So Butler in the last move had her over the barrel, and intended to keep her there. But a personal friend and client of the Court, no less a one than the State Prosecutor, comforted her with the advice, recorded in the same entry, to "tell Campbell tell Butler to go h—!" Similar assurances, in milder language, came also from her good friend the banker, "it's all right. Campbell looking after interest."

Despite these troubles, by 1906 Cora Taylor's affairs were prospering and she was able to add to her real estate. In May of that year she purchased for $2,200 the corner lot facing the Court on Ward Street, paying $1,000 down and giving a mortgage for the balance. On this lot was a stable in which was housed a brand new victoria, recently purchased from a local firm of carriage builders —McMurray & Baker. On the other half of the frontage stood a frame building, 915 Ward Street, which Cora presently rented to one Mildred Bates for $30 a month. By the next year her investment had almost trebled in value, and she refused an offer of $3,000 for the half of the frontage on which the stable stood.

Sweet, indeed, her new security must have seemed to her after the years of darkness and struggle, concluded with these hard-won battles! And in the midst of it all, she suddenly knew how tired she was. In the autumn of 1904 Cora acquired for $750 two ocean-front lots at Pablo Beach, eighteen miles southeast of Jacksonville, on which she planned to erect a comfortable, roomy, two-storied frame house with wide screened porches. No cash payment was involved in this transaction, the property passed to her by conveyance upon her assumption of the mortgage encumbering it to John E. Hartridge, trustee.

The Florida East Coast Railway ran four daily trains, with additional Saturday and Sunday excursions, to Pablo, the seaside summer resort of Jacksonville's working-class population. One mile away at Atlantic Beach, where the fashionable well-to-do had their summer homes, Henry M. Flagler had built and opened in 1901 the last of his great chain of coastal hotels, the Continental.

August, 1905, saw the construction on Cora's beach lots of "Palmetto Lodge," which she maintained during the next three years as a seaside annex of the Court. Here too, as at the Court, she had her own apartment set off from the rest of the house: sitting room, bedroom, kitchen, and bath; and here she relaxed in enjoyment of the sea bathing. Long black stockings and skirts below the knees were still a part of the conventional bathing costume; but to protect her fair skin from the sun Cora kept her arms well covered with a scarf tied around them, and wore a wide shade hat secured under the chin by an elastic band. Taking with her, in a hired vehicle, small parties of her girls and their young men friends, she spent long summer days picnicking and crabbing at the jetties six miles away, where the broad river wound and meandered to the sea. Returning home at sundown, they brought with them huge quantities of crabs.

2

With "Miss Cora's" firm hand on the reins, life at the Court and at Palmetto Lodge moved along in the placid "family" groove Ernest W. McCready had found so congenial at the Hotel de Dream, the one major difference being that girls lived on the premises. The service no longer included meals served to transients, as a regular thing; but supper parties where champagne flowed and quail was the featured delicacy continued in popularity, and the price of beer remained one dollar a bottle.

The girls were mostly plump, gentlemen liked a hefty armful; and they probably put on weight with the bountiful meals Cora fed them. She later concluded that forty-five to fifty dollars a week for the table was "too high!!!"—a sum then equal to at least three times as much in terms of the present-day dollar. The regular "staff" at the Court averaged thirteen, but it varied from time to time, with girls often away on long trips with gentlemen and the not infrequent marriages, to which "Miss Cora" gave her blessing. She still believed that a girl's best chance in life lay in discovering the right man, and marrying him, and to that end she exerted herself to see her girls well "launched," and she did not forget to send orange blossoms to the brides.

Most of these girls came from poor families, from isolated tenant farms in the hinterlands of west Florida, south Georgia and eastern Alabama. Most were in the very early or middle twenties, with faces unlined and good-humored, though all looked older than their years. The majority could barely read and write. Cora probably did her best to encourage them to self-improvement. The library from Brede Place was kept under lock and key, but the bookcases in the lounges at the Court and Palmetto Lodge were stocked with an assortment of the latest popular works, and novels in profusion, which were available to the girls or to clients with the injunction on flyleaf:

> Please return to book case in sitting room so that others may enjoy / Cora Taylor[*]

But the two fat, well-thumbed post-card albums which remained always out on the table in the lounge rooms suggest tastes running more to comics and "minstrel" cartoons from the era of Moran & Mack (a minstrel team famous before World War I).

The fame of the Court had traveled, and to Cora's girls it was

[*] This inscription also appears in an album erroneously attributed to Cora Taylor, owned by the late Henry W. Walters of Jacksonville. The album consists mainly of cartoons by J. R. Williams, and many examples of sentimental doggerel. Copyright dates on the cartoons and verse are of the period of the Whitehouse Hotel and after—name under which the Court was re-opened when the property passed to a syndicate, one year after Cora's death. (See Appendix Four.) The scrapbook may have been started during the last year of Cora's life, at which time she turned over the management of the Court—but retained control of the business—to her housekeeper, Edith Gray. The above inscription is duplicated in a copy of Hardy's *Jude the Obscure* (London, 1896), and cited in a letter from Vincent Starrett to J. Blanck, 1944—now in the possession of R. W. Stallman.

literally—and unsentimentally—"home." They sent back post cards at regular intervals from the vacation spots where they sojourned with their gentlemen, and these scrawled messages were all much alike:

Dear Miss Cora/ This is the way I am going to look [picture of an enormously fat "Billikins"] when you see me and no kidding/ that is going to be real soon for I am so anxious to get back home. Lots of things to tell you. Write soon. Would love to hear from you. Edna.

Dear Miss Cora/ Wish I were at "the Court" so I could get a good square meal [picture of goat leaning over fence eating man's straw hat]. Love/ Louise

Louise, who seems to have drawn a stingy "date," writes again to ask if Number 12 or Number 14 (rooms at the Court) is vacant, she may "need it soon—unless the weather is too hot at Jax." And homesick Edna longs for jazz music: "Sounds good to me/ The music at the Court" (Picture of man leaning out of theatre box applauding minstrel and band).

Old Point Comfort (probably no significance in the name) was a favorite resort of "vacationing" couples, but post cards came from Middle Western cities, and others as far away as San Francisco and Vancouver. One girl who had spent six weeks in Ohio with her friend extolled the delights of horseback riding; she sent snapshots of herself and her escort, both rather stiffly and uncomfortably sitting their mounts and grinning self-consciously, but happily, into the camera.

Cora kept a watchful eye on the goings and comings of her girls, and while this was probably not unconnected with business, she worried about them, too. The girls were expected to check in and out between the Court and Palmetto Lodge, and once when two of them failed to do so, Cora sighed to her diary, "Ray and Nita took French leave for Gainesville for a night." Another girl, Baby Allen, "left without goodbye."

"Miss Cora" mothered her favorite clients, and to them also the Court was "home." The young men who came there reported to her, the same as the girls, when away on pleasure trips, or when job changes brought about transfers to other towns. Wrote one young fellow from Atlantic City: "Hello Ma / This is what the

San Francisco earthquake did for me. I am a good boy now. Hope this finds you and children well and happy. Son." In postscript he added, "I'm on the water now." (Cartoon shows man astride a street sprinkler.) "Son" wrote again from Washington, D. C., "a regular blizzard raging here today" and wished he were "in Jax."

This post card correspondence must have furnished prurient thrills to the peeping Toms in the post office, and certainly contributed to the weed crop of rumors crediting Cora with an illegitimate son. (See Appendix Three.)

In an age in which sex without love is regarded with a callousness that would have horrified the Edwardians, it must again be stressed that Cora Taylor, notwithstanding her occupation, never to the end of her life accepted that separation as natural. Her assertion to the contrary we have already had in her own words, uttered to Stephen Crane: "Even when love is so base as to be only a thirst for pleasure it seldom dies with the first embrace, and who can say he possessed the entire woman in one night of love?" How far she now deceived herself with the rationale that the Court and its facilities offered to the lonely and frustrated something to enable them to continue life's struggle, it is hard to say. But the testimony of various eyewitnesses who prefer to remain anonymous indicates that she actually tried, if with dubious success, to send the men who came there back to their homes and families in better shape than she found them. A gentleman who indulged in a three-day spree in the pleasant confines of the "Senate" while the business of his law office went to pot, and who was finally traced there and brought home in the same soiled evening clothes in which he had escorted his wife from the theatre three nights earlier, would have been sold no liquor at the Court. A saying attributed to Cora— which may have been apocryphal—defines her attitude toward overindulgence: "The Court is for the needy, not the greedy."

A member of the Jacksonville Police Department, who as a young rookie coming on the force was assigned to patrol the red-light district, bears witness: "Her place was well run. Never any rowdiness there, she didn't allow that. I don't recollect a single arrest—but there were plenty of others down the street!"

A local undertaker: "She was a woman of great dignity and personal magnetism. She did a great deal of good, she helped many people. More than was ever known or talked about. Any time she heard of a poor family in trouble, Cora Taylor's hand was in her pocket. But of course, she could be hard and rough—with anybody she thought wasn't worthy—"

She could, indeed. In the diary—January 9, 1907—we find this: "Sent Pauline to jail." On the twenty-first she wrote to the proprietress of a sporting-house in New Orleans "that Harriet Taylor was a beat"; and on February 19, "Put Florence Ray out / beat me out $37.50."

Cora's acquisition of post office box 480 marked, in a sense, the burning of her bridges: except letters from England, most of her mail now came to her directly instead of being forwarded from Aunt Mary Holder's in New York. She continued to hear from Kate Frederic, who was in Chicago with her three children having hard scrabbling for "the daily oof" (Kate's word for the means to live); and who, had she known what Cora was doing then, would have been heartbroken. Kate would never forsake the friend who had stood by her in her own need, but her pure spirit must have shuddered. Once Cora sent her two dollars; and Barry, whom she had wanted for her own little son, a post-card photo of the Brede puppies across which she had written: "This is when we were babies—Spongie's children!" In September, 1904, she sent the Frewens a copy of *The O'Ruddy*, with a letter, and Mrs. Frewen, "so gratified and delighted that the . . . last chapter ends at Brede," replied in the same month (September 27) from Ireland:

How can I thank you. . . . I enjoyed reading the O'Ruddy more than I can say—and remember poor Mr. Crane was working at it, when I came to stay with you at Brede. We used to sit after dinner in his study upstairs and I remember how very great was my interest in some of the details he told me of the plot—which you were then typewriting for him—and now I find it all so beautifully told with his powerful "way." But—dear Mrs. Crane, I had no idea that *you* wrote so beautifully.

I was thrilled with excitement over *your* story ["Cowardice," which Cora had sent her with *The O'Ruddy*]—and your description . . . and recognized all the landmarks in and out the dear old house—and everything.

Well—I have been hard at work here the last two years and I hope you would approve of all I have done—though of course we have to go very slowly on account of the expense—and do so much that does not show—such as strengthening floors and ceilings, etc. I *did* buy the oak

room you took me to Rye to see—and it now lines the porch room or—
Mr. Crane's study—and really looks beautiful!

I have no photographs with me here, but when I get back to
Inishannon* I will send for some more—and perhaps someday you will
come across the sea again and come to us there and see it all again—for I
know how dear the old place must be to you and that your memories
dwell there much. . . .

In the same mail was a letter from Moreton Frewen, who had
read "with gladness and sadness too" Crane's last novel. "It is so
nice to be in touch with you again. We have often talked of you
and your dear man when at Brede. . . . I like the book very much—
as indeed you know I liked all his work." And how were the fates
treating her? Was life at all easier? He hoped to be over soon in
the States, to find her in New York "and hear all you have done.
. . . Old 'Gloucester' [Stephen's horse] is you will like to know, still
with us at Brede—a most faithful old servitor he is. Mr. De Friese
I now and again see. A very pleasant man . . ."

And so—in the bewildering maze of contrasts and contradictions
and subterfuges that her life had become, she who had for a short
while been "Mrs. Crane" now threaded her way among the ghosts
and the gargoyles as best she could. Her day usually began with a
trip to the post office. Then, after she had collected her mail, there
was shopping to be done—for wallpaper to redecorate rooms at the
Court, for shoes and hats and a thousand small personal things.
(The provisioning of the Court was attended to by Cora's housekeeper.) There might also be a visit to the bank to deposit money,
to see after a note, to "put papers in safe box"; and the morning was
likely to be concluded with a call at the office of her attorney, D. C.
Campbell, in the old Law Exchange Building on Main Street. The
eyes of Campbell's young clerk bugged out at the appearance of the
woman all of Jacksonville was talking about, seated in an armchair
in the private office smoking a cigarette, whose voice and speech
lacked nothing in courtesy and whose style of dress and general
manner suggested affluence. Quite different was the impression
registered on the legal minds next door, who bluntly informed
Campbell that he must "get rid of that woman" or find another

* The Irish estate of the Frewens in County Cork. It was burned to the
ground in 1906 during "the troubles."

office. "Why, shucks," the lawyer blandly replied, "I can't afford to get rid of her. That woman's business pays me a thousand dollars a year!"

Cora had hocked her rings, one a small but good diamond, to pay debts, and later redeemed them from a pawn shop in New Orleans. But as the size of bank deposits varied according to business, let the diary now speak:

> January 17: Beautiful day. Went shopping. Bum business. Took doggies out.
>
> January 18: . . . Shriners Day / Wrote Macy for shoes. Not so good as last Shriners Night / House closed at 4 A.M. $126 beer / $20 wine
>
> January 26: Beautiful day. Had a miserable night with my cough. Slept late. Drove in afternoon. . . . Letter from Emily / wants to call / coming south with Mother / $137 bank
>
> January 29: . . . $325 bank. Minnie's man here, very nice chap. . . .
>
> February 15: Note due & int C C B [Butler]. $1191.40 Paid
>
> February 22: Washington's birthday. Dull day. German Amer braves [the Germania Club of Jacksonville, a German-American society]. . . .
>
> March 2: . . . Hattie and I shopping. . . . Deposit Fla Nat Bank $585
>
> March 24: Summer day. May and Stella to Pablo. . . . Bum biz. Deposit Fla Nat Bank $167.47
>
> May 17: Shriners night. Worst ever had. Tampa Shriners here. Did not go out. Hattie and Mabel came up from Pablo.

The usual program for the afternoon was a drive in the victoria to Riverside, where the dogs were turned loose for a run in the little park or along the river bank: Sponge, who had been Stephen's favorite at Brede Place, and Hatson, an upstart of unknown origins. Besides these two there were Bon-Bon, Pill-Box, and Lamb Chops who did not live at the Court but were placed in charge of Owen Wingate, a hack driver at Pablo regularly employed by Cora Taylor.

Sometimes, with one or more of the girls, there were outings to St. Augustine where they patronized the Turkish Baths, enjoyed dinner on the train, and had their photos snapped in front of the Old City Gates seated in a high automobile "Miss Cora" had hired to drive them about. The new excitement over motor cars was in the air! The birthday of Hattie Mason, Cora's capable twenty-three-year-old housekeeper at the Court, was celebrated with mint juleps and, as a special treat, an auto ride in the evening.

Birthdays were never allowed to pass unnoticed at the Court; there was always a cake and a party. The girls received presents of wrappers, garters, small jewelry, a silver water set, electric fans —the latter a summertime necessity in the days before air conditioning. For the banker's son, one of Cora's special friends, whose anniversary fell on the same day as George Washington's, there was a party with champagne.

Always a lover of the theatre, Cora attended matinee performances at the local playhouse, the Duval. She mentions *The College Widow* (February 23), which she dismisses as "not much." Marie Cahill in *Marrying Mary*, the following week, drew more enthusiasm: "Good support and enjoyed show." Was she conscious of the ripple among the audience, whose attention was focused on the box where the mistress of the Court sat with her retinue in dignified but conspicuous splendor? A young girl recently graduated from the local high school, who was hostess to a group of her classmates in another of the boxes, noticing the constraint and odd twitchings which seemed to interfere with her friends' enjoyment of the play inquired the reason, and was told that "only women of that class" occupied boxes at the threatre.

When Jacksonville's first movie house, the Grand Theatre, opened its doors on Forsyth Street, "Miss Cora" accompanied some of her girls to the afternoon show usually once or twice a week. "She was very nice about it," says the owner of the now defunct theatre (who rented the building from my grandmother). "She came to see me and asked what to do. She wanted her girls to see the show, and she didn't want any disturbance in the audience. I said, just don't all come in in a bunch—and don't all sit together."

3

UNDER the licensing system "the line," until about the year 1913, had always been wide open, and some of the stories told of it reflect an element of Rabelaisian gusto somehow drearily absent from today's wickedness.

It is recorded that an august political body, at the conclusion of its meeting in Jacksonville, sought relaxation and diversion by going "down the line"; the mayor himself, a very tall man, headed the procession "clutching under each arm a 'soiled dove.' " Some while later the veteran J. E. T. Bowden, who had twice held office and had also been mayor of LaVilla in its days as a separate municipality, challenged the crusading incumbent Van Swearingen, who had under pressure closed up the red-light district, by running on a platform of open friendship for "the line," and won handily. Bowden climaxed his campaign with an election eve address to the voters in Hemming Park, in the heart of the city, at which he caused girls from the district, dressed in scarlet tights, mounted on horseback, and carrying red lanterns, to parade round and round the Park while a delighted populace whooped and applauded.

But perhaps the peak of carnival entertainment came with the visit of Carry Nation, who paused in Jacksonville on one of her hatchet-wielding swings across country. "The irrepressible disciple of the hatchet descended upon what she termed the 'demonocracy' of Jacksonville last night," is how the Florida *Times-Union* article described it (February 14, 1908):

and conducted one of her tirades against sin. Mrs. Nation went unannounced, and as was expected, she was not welcomed at many of the resorts.

Early in the evening Mrs. Nation called up the *Times-Union* office and announced that she would visit the "red light" district and asked that a reporter be sent along in order that the worst of the resorts might be pointed out to her. She also made a declaration of her intention to the *Metropolis* [evening paper, edited and published by W. R. Carter] and at the appointed hour three newspaper men were seen [making their way to the Windle Hotel to join her.]

Accompanied by Mrs. Bateman, matron of the Central City Mission, and another prominent local temperance leader, and escorted by [the] three newspaper reporters Mrs. Nation left for the scene of her intended crusade.

The newspaper men, in their hack, led the way, and the first resort to be visited was the 'notorious' Court, which takes rank with the largest and most palatial of these houses. The public had evidently got wind of the visit, for when the vehicles came to a halt in front of the resort there were at least a couple of hundred boys and men with gaping mouths, eager to see Carry Nation and what they thought would prove to be a knock-down-drag-out raid.

The figures of "Lt. Morgan of the police force and Sheriff R. F. Bowden and his force of deputies, or somebody that looked like them, were discerned by the newspaper men in the darkness of the night." The doorbell was rung, the door opened, and "Mrs. Nation followed the newspaper men inside. The inmates were taken unawares, and Mrs. Nation's reception at first was just the reverse of cordial. However, Carry, not to be outdone, ascended the stairs to the upper floor where she lectured as she went from room to room."

The party, as they emerged from the Court, had to push their way through a rapidly increasing crowd of curiosity seekers. When the carriages were reached, not without difficulty, they moved on to Belle Orloff's. " 'Russian Belle' as she is familiarly known," was not in when they arrived—a circumstance the writer of the article judged "fortunate" for Carry—for when she did appear "she proved a match for the famous smasher." A colloquy ensued, and they left, Carry shouting from the departing hack denunciatory epithets at Belle of "demoniac" and "Jeptha's daughter!"

The last stop was at the New York House, where Carry met with some success. "The inmates of the house evidently considered her a curiosity, but when she began to talk" it was soon apparent that she was making headway. "At this juncture Mrs. Nation requested the newspaper men to leave the room, and closing the door of the ballroom . . . she lectured for a quarter of an hour to the girls." Her words must have made an impression, for girls emerged from the room "bowed in shame and weeping." Then "with tears streaming down her cheeks" Carry took leave of them, "thanking the inmates for the kind treatment and consideration shown her and her party."

One can only regret "Miss Cora's" absence from the Court during Carry Nation's memorable trip "down the line" (she was probably away at Palmetto Lodge), for it may be supposed that she would have gone even "Russian Belle" one better in besting the six-foot Carry before the latter could get in a word or a single blow.

But vice is never picturesque. It is only as we see it in retrospect, colored by time's elisions, that it presents itself occasionally in a grotesquely humorous or softened light.

Wednesday, March 6, a "fine day but coolish"—Cora noted in her diary—was a day of tragedy on "the line." "Great shock! Jean

Raymond killed herself this A.M. at 111 Davis St. Poor Jean! Poor foolish Jean!"

Jeannette Raymond, evidently a friend of Cora's, was according to the newspaper account of the suicide "usually of a cheerful disposition"; but, since she had read in the society columns of the arrival in Palm Beach of her wealthy former husband, whom she still loved, she had brooded over their estrangement—and taken poison. She was found dead in her room, and on the bureau a note addressed "To those I love, Venie, Edith and Hazel [inmates of the small house she operated]: I just can't help it." The next day, Cora received a telegram from Jean's husband (who was presumably well acquainted with the Court) asking her to take charge of the body. She went to see the undertaker and "stood good," turning the rest of the funeral arrangements over to "Venie" Beckett. At the funeral parlor she was much affected by the sight of "the young man's body who killed himself after 10 days of married life." The body had just been brought in. "Terrible sight."

The diary continues with a brief note that on March 11, a beautiful day but windy, Jeannette Raymond was buried "in my lot 156 Woodlawn, beside little Mabel Atkins." The next day, Cora ordered the lot at Woodlawn Cemetery cared for up to "one year from date. No word from Jean Raymond's people yet" since the wire from her husband. Two weeks later, a lovely warm day, Cora hired a brown horse and "went round the road to Mabel and Jeannette's graves in Woodlawn." Having paid for annual care, she was furious at finding the graves neglected and the pansies she had planted on them herself dying for lack of water. She sent Easter cards and money to two people whose names are indecipherable, "paid Hattie to date," wrote Jean's husband and sent him the bill for the funeral. (He never replied—and Cora Taylor footed the bill.)

"Little Mabel Atkins," twenty years old, who died from the effects of poison (June 25, 1903) swallowed two weeks earlier—"by accident," the newspaper said—was one of three others to whom Cora gave burial when no relatives came forward to claim the bodies. Mabel Atkins was perhaps one of her girls. Lottie Quesenberry, twenty-eight, was an inmate of 915 Ward Street, which was known as the West End House and operated by Cora's tenant, Mildred Bates. Brooding over her life of shame, Lottie

Quesenberry drank poison on the street and collapsed in a drug store, where, holding a handkerchief over her mouth, she had gone to ask a drink of water (February, 1908). Of these four lost creatures, the only one to die a natural death was Hattie McCullough, another of Cora's girls, who died at the age of forty-three from a ruptured gall bladder (September 19, 1907).

It is easy to assess Cora's actions in these instances from either extreme, the sentimental or the cynical, but human nature usually admits of no such black-and-white interpretation. Counterposed to her horror of death as the finite end was her Christian faith in divine mercy. But these suicides utterly demolished her theory that life in a well-run house of prostitution was to be preferred to the miseries of sweatshop labor, or existence behind a store counter.

4

"La distance n'y faut rien; il n'y a que le premier pas qui coute," Cora had written in her Manuscript Book—quoting Voltaire, who in turn was repeating one of Madame Du Deffand's *mots*. ("The distance is nothing, it is only the first step that counts"—her translation.)

In Cora's own case, anyone who did not know that the first step lay somewhere far back in the mists would be strongly tempted to see in her marriage to Hammond P. McNeil in New York on June 1, 1905, the principal factor in her subsequent decline. For on that day Cora's life entered the shadows, and there was to be no halt thereafter in her downhill slide.

Her downward course was not inevitable. But in the light of past experience it perhaps became inevitable, given the influences external and internal which had molded her character during the impressionable years, once the checks and balances imposed by her adoration of Stephen Crane were removed with his death—as Crane himself in a moment of clairvoyance had foreseen. By the time she arrived in New Orleans, ill and desperate, she had made her choice, though not without a severe and shattering struggle. She then set about hardening herself to the point of absolute ruthlessness, a thing necessary for survival in the world she had elected to return to. That she never wholly succeeded is indeed a large part of her tragedy, rendering her sufferings the more acute; for therein lay her Achilles heel. She could not steel herself against her memories of Crane—her life with him and the people they had known. Nor could she wholly suppress her own personal qualities of warmth and generosity and her need for love.

In these years in Jacksonville we see her turning a hard surface toward the outside world, especially the upper ranks from which she had fallen, while at the same time holding onto her own private image of the position she had previously occupied and even exaggerating it to herself and others. She permitted herself no looking back, and no introspection; her inner life dried up and what remained of it, except in occasional brief flashes, was completely sealed off. This seems most sharply reflected in the diary of 1907. The bareness of the entries here contrasts, significantly, with the discursiveness and range of her interests in the earlier notebooks. There is little opportunity for the interpreter to penetrate her feelings directly, for the very reason that she was trying so hard not to have any.

But now that her circumstances had improved, and pressures relaxed, memories fought with her determination to forget and the need for love once more took possession of her. "No woman forgets who has not someone to teach her forgetfulness," she once wrote, with the self-delusion which came so easily at times.

Hammond McNeil was superficially a personable young man, attractive, good looking, of medium build, twenty-five years old and the scapegrace son of a family of prominence in Waycross, Georgia. (Hattie Mason, housekeeper at the Court, also came from the vicinity of Waycross.) His occupation appears on the marriage license as "railroad conductor"; but not long after becoming the husband of "Cora Crane, widow," McNeil became the proprietor of the Annex Saloon, located in the Everett Hotel annex. Whether Cora set him up in business does not appear, but as this was a socially disqualifying trade in those days, it seems safe to assume that his proud family did not. A diary entry (March 30, 1907) suggests that Cora gave McNeil money from time to time: "Paid Hammond $45 Pablo from Private acct."

Had she been able to accept McNeil as a passing fancy, she might have come out of the affair with a good deal less emotional damage. As it was, she must needs love him—or think she did, which comes to the same thing while the illusion lasts; must mother him, and then put the seal on her own ruin by marrying him.

With today's knowledge of psychopathology Hammond Mc-

Neil's alcoholism, his crazy jealousy and pistol swagger, would be recognized for what they were: symptoms of a personality badly out of joint. And a worried family might, perhaps, have had the intelligence to place him under treatment in time to avert a multiple tragedy. But families in those days were even more given to hushing things up and thrusting skeletons back into the closet than they are now. If there were an aunt who tippled or took drugs it was never mentioned. To undergo the "Keeley Cure" was tantamount to disgrace; and a "bad actor" in the family was just a throwback to "Old Adam!"

"Bad actors," as history shows, have often possessed unusual charm. But whatever the spell that McNeil cast over Cora, his alcoholic excesses could hardly have been completely unknown to her at the time of their first interest in each other. It is perhaps a measure of how far her judgment had been blunted, if she imagined it within her power to cure or hold these tendencies in check.

McNeil insisted that the marriage should be kept secret "until her affairs were settled"—that is, until her retirement from business—and Cora complied, meanwhile retaining full control over the affairs of the Court. Since she had no legal status as Crane's widow, and Donald Stewart no longer counted, she cheerfully wrote down "second" under marriages—for the license—and gave her age as thirty-six, taking off five years. They had gone to New York together—and Cora insisted on being married in a church! So the ceremony performed by the Vicar took place in the Episcopal Chapel of St. Chrysostom's, with only one witness present. Aunt Mary Holder (if she was still living) seems, for whatever reasons, not to have attended the wedding.

McNeil subsequently stated on the witness stand that he had known Cora Taylor about a year before they married, but had known her "personally" only four days (the period of their stay in New York); and that he had married her while they were both "on a spree in New York." He also stated that he had no knowledge at that time of "the character of the place she operated," or that "she was an immoral woman." Which was too much even for the defense lawyers!

On their return to Jacksonville, a room seems to have been set aside for McNeil's use at the Court, where he apparently spent a

The Court. Columbia University Crane Collection.

good deal of time after hours. "When I closed up at night I usually went down to Cora Taylor's place and set down a while." Neither of them seemed in any hurry to "settle" Cora's affairs, which were increasingly prosperous. But by 1907 quarrels were erupting and McNeil's drinking showed no signs of tapering off. The diary furnishes the only available light on their domestic relations:

> January 23: Cold clear day. Feel very badly little sleep with my cold and cough. Did not go out. Got mags [magazines] and "Prisoners" and "The Viper of Milan." H home for his dinner / expects father. Hattie came go Pablo with Will. Remained in my rooms at night. Did not go in parlors. . . . H father came. . . .
>
> January 30: . . . Hammond phoned me he was going to ride—to meet him Edwards [Edwards Half-Way House, a restaurant and gambling resort on the city outskirts, frequented by the sporting and racing set] so Hattie and I went. . . . Hammond came home paralyzed drunk at 9 PM. Disgusting. Shirt undone and pants half down. My life is not living with him.

From these indications, trouble started with McNeil's drinking, and on February 2 he seems to have threatened Cora in some manner. "Told H insurance must protect me." She wrote to him, and speaks of going several times to see him at his place of business that month. Then on March 3:

> Pablo. . . . H came on 2 train but did not come to house until luncheon over. Rose and Ned Sloane, Stella and Elsie came—girls went bathing. H stayed overnight. So did Stella who had company RR boy H P.
>
> March 18: . . . H and I good terms again.
>
> March 24: Calm. Lovely day. . . . H went Dixieland [a popular recreation park in South Jacksonville] and home. We dined together.
>
> May 19: Pablo. Lovely day. Had good sleep. H came on 10 AM train / had nice morning alone.
>
> May 21: Nita got breakfast and I worked hard all day long. . . . Sent H eggs and devilled crabs. . . .

But a more serious flare-up occurred in April, this time over the "railroad boy" Harry Parker, a youth of nineteen of whom McNeil was violently jealous.

Parker, who seems to have transferred his attentions from

Stella to Mabel Wright—housekeeper at Palmetto Lodge—was just at the age when the young male seeks to impress the world by opening his mouth. Flashing a roll of bills, he boasted that he had it "from his girl"—who he implied was "Miss Cora." Perhaps he dreamed of conquering the woman many men desired, before his approaching marriage to a plain Miss White. Anyhow, he seems to have been flattered by Cora Taylor's casual notice and anxious to attribute to it a fictitious importance, representing himself to others as the royal favorite.

To any but a disordered mind, Parker's loud-mouth brag would have seemed ludicrous; but McNeil had got it in his head that Cora's interest in the "fresh" boy was something more than maternal. So when Cora, Hattie Mason, and Hattie's young man failed to return from an outing to St. Augustine on the evening they were expected, McNeil interviewed one Conductor Smith at the depot the next morning. Had he "seen any of the folks?" Smith, an old fuddy-duddy, had a grudge against Parker, his baggage master on the Pablo run, and had recently succeeded in getting him fired. He made much now of the roll of bills, adding that Parker had invited him to make one of the party bound for St. Augustine and had told Smith confidentially, "he was with Miss Cora." Parker's or Smith's, this was probably a lie, but more than enough to inflame McNeil who jumped aboard a train, Smith tagging along. The two of them made straight for a sporting-house known to Smith in St. Augustine, where they collected more tales from "the landlady," an adder-tongued woman whose motive in doing Cora Taylor an ill turn was no doubt economic. Parker, she said, had talked to one of her girls and "told her different things." "I heard she was married. What became of her husband?"

McNeil believed it all and told Smith, "It looks like Parker is with Cora"; and the conductor, realizing that his mischief-making had gone too far, became flustered. They hung around in St. Augustine waiting for the evening train, on which the party was to return from Daytona where they had gone that morning; but when it came in there was no sign of Harry Parker. Walking through the train with Smith, McNeil encountered Hattie's young man who told him, "The folks are up in the parlor car." McNeil made a violent scene in the car, charging Cora with intimacy with Parker, to which she burst out, "It's a lie!"

History loves ironies, and history was repeating itself in melodrama when Cora telephoned McNeil at his place of business next
day and informed him that she had telegraphed his father to come
to Jacksonville, "HAMMOND IN TROUBLE," and signed the message,
"CORA MCNEIL."

"If you did that, then I am going to tell my father the whole
thing!"

Actually, McNeil was in such a fright at the mere thought of
having at last to face the consequences of his own actions in respect to his marriage that he took to his bed with a temperature and
summoned a doctor. Cora went to his room in the Everett Hotel
that evening with Hattie and tried to reason with him, protest-
ing her innocence, but McNeil turned a deaf ear. When she
asked whether he wished her to remain within call during the
talk with his father, he coldly rebuffed her. There is no way of
knowing how much, or how little, McNeil told his father in that
interview. But Cora was not introduced to Hammond's father before he returned to his home in Waycross.

Early the next morning, as alleged in the defense testimony, before the departure of the elder McNeil, Harry Parker came to the
son's room, which he entered without knocking. "Mac, I hear you
were looking for me in St. Augustine yesterday," he is reported
to have said. "If you had found me, I'd 've fixed you—with this—"
Then he allegedly pulled a gun; and McNeil told Parker, "I'm married to that woman. I want you to stay away from her!"

Parker promised he would. McNeil then went out and bought a
gun; and it was only a question of how long, after that, before the
trigger was pulled.

Parker continued to see Mabel Wright, and on the evening of
May 30 had supper at Palmetto Lodge. McNeil, who had an-
nounced his departure for Indian Springs, a popular Georgia health
resort, suddenly turned up at the railroad station, coming from
Jacksonville, a few minutes after the other train pulled out taking
Parker back to the city. At the station also were Cora and Hattie
Mason, looking for a gramaphone which was coming by Express.
That night, while they were playing the gramaphone, Cora several
times laid her head in her arms, sighing, "Oh hell."

"Playing for your fellow?" McNeil taunted her.

The remark precipitated a violent quarrel, Cora having warned him to mind his own business; a scuffle followed, and the threat from McNeil: "After what you said, you are as dead as in your coffin!"

Next morning, before catching the early train to town, he left a note with the Negro maid, Alice Campbell, to be given to Cora. This note was never produced in court. But the defense story claiming that McNeil's return to Pablo four hours later was for the purpose of discussing divorce considerably softened his threat to kill Cora: "My feelings for you are as dead as if in the grave. I never had any friend except my mother."

Alice Campbell testified that when McNeil returned and questioned her, "Had I seen Mr. Harry Parker and Miss Cora together, I told him no. . . . He said, 'Well I am going down and I am going to kill them both, then I am going to New York and you can have my dog.'" McNeil later denied making any threats. "I had better sense if I was going to kill anybody [than] to make threats before a Negro."

The picnic at Mayport Hattie and Mabel were planning for May 30 was postponed until the following day, after a telegram from "Miss Cora" that she "was coming down." So at 7:30 on the morning of May 31 the party set off up the beach in a carriage driven by Owen Wingate. At the Hotel Continental they got out and went inside to send wires: one from Mabel Wright to Harry Parker, which "Miss Cora wrote out for her (Mabel did not write well); and one that Cora, on some rash impulse of retaliation or abortive humor, dispatched to Hammond McNeil:

I HOPE YOUR TEARS WILL KEEP MY GRAVE WATERED

In Mayport, they spent about an hour and a half in the rear of Floyd's saloon— "there was no place else to go," in those days— where the town marshal set them all up to a round of drinks, and "Miss Cora" one more. Then proceeding toward East Mayport they met Harry Parker on the road, walking, and in a hurry to catch the train back to town. They let him take their carriage, and continued walking in the broiling heat. When the carriage presently returned with Parker, who had missed his train, they opened the lunch basket and invited him to picnic with them.

Mabel Wright was on the front seat of the carriage, Parker standing beside it playing with her foot, Cora and Hattie in the back, and Owen Wingate was leaning against a tree eating a sandwich when McNeil drove up, jumped out, and came toward them exclaiming in the best stage manner of insulted honor, "Ah, I have caught you at last! I am going to kill you both!"

The first to catch sight of McNeil, Mabel said, "Here comes Hammond"; and Parker came around to the other side of the carriage, grinning cockily. "What's the matter with you, Mac?" he said; and as Mabel jumped out, McNeil warned, "Stand back, Mabel, or I'll kill you too." Then taking a step backwards he fired four times, and the cocky smile was wiped from Parker's face. At the second shot, Parker fell to the ground.

Cora cried out when she saw McNeil, "He is going to kill me!" and jumped behind Hattie Mason. Mabel became hysterical. Then Cora ran to Parker, and taking his head in her lap told the others to bring ice water, and ordered McNeil's driver, Willie Wilkerson, to fetch a doctor from Mayport. "Must I do it?" Wilkerson asked, turning to McNeil, who answered, "Don't do anything." (This was changed on the witness stand to "Do everything you can.")

The fatal bullet had entered the base of the brain. Cora sat holding Parker's head in her lap, and bathing it with the ice water, until a half hour later he died.*

McNeil's only sign of nervousness after the shooting was in picking up the wrong hat. His victim's.

5

THE LIGHTNING bolt in July that tore off a corner of the roof of Palmetto Lodge, badly shocking two of the girls who had to have medical treatment, was symbolic. Everyone was feeling the reaction from the horror of recent events; everyone except the slayer

* The single piece of evidence brought forward at the trial that was damning to Cora was her diamond ring, which was taken from Parker's necktie by Justice Greenberg after the shooting. Whether she had foolishly loaned him the ring to gratify a schoolboy whim, or however he obtained it, cannot be known. But if she were at all worried that it might be brought up against her, as a motive in the shooting, she had ample time to remove it before the arrival of the Justice with the doctor from Mayport. She did not.

of young Harry Parker, who at no time evidenced either emotion or remorse.

McNeil was lodged in jail, and Cora, ill most of the summer, suffered from a ghastly combination of sleeplessness and terrible dreams. She was careful to cut from her diary all of the pages relating to the Parker murder, and the differences in April which had preceded it; but on July 9 she wrote, "Feel awfully sad today. Life is not worth living."

On the twelfth, her birthday, she was up early after a "horrible night and dreams." But the girls gave her presents: Hattie and Mabel "a beautiful set" of silver knives and forks; Nell a carving set; Nita a tray and silver chocolate service. Fred Puckhaber, the caterer, sent "two fine cakes"; Ray, "three dozen American Beauty roses from Philadelphia"; Rose presented her with a dozen silver teaspoons; and Fern, a pillow she had worked herself. They all arrived on the two o'clock train, surprising her, with several old friends of the male sex in tow. "Also one professor. Doggies decorated with my colors." After the little celebration, in which everyone was making a special effort to be gay, Cora left with some of the others to spend the evening at Puckhaber's house in town.

On that day also, papers were served for the preliminary hearing in McNeil's case, and a cry escapes her as she notes it down, "six weeks since H P funeral!" Harry Parker had allegedly been the support of a widowed mother. Cora bought a lot in Woodlawn Cemetery for him, for eighty-five dollars, and the other burial costs, including a headstone, also were borne by her.*

The next day, July 13, Hammond sent for her to come to the jail. She also saw Campbell, her lawyer, who showed her a letter from Hammond's father, W. A. McNeil. We can only guess at the contents of this letter, but it probably had something to do with the visit to the jail; for although "feeling ill," Cora spent the whole afternoon of July 18 with Mr. McNeil, who now showed unusual interest in seeing her.

Here the diary jumps to August 29, when Cora went to Pablo

* Celia E. Wilbur, mother of Harry Parker, filed suit in the Circuit Court for Duval County on May 26, 1909, against Hammond P. McNeil for $50,000 damages, charging that the son was the sole support of his widowed mother at the time of the killing. But Mrs. Parker having meanwhile remarried, the suit got nowhere.

with Hattie "after very tiring day." Hammond followed on September 1, having been admitted to bail in the amount of $3,500 and
released from the Duval County jail, over the prosecution's objection that "the facts in the case did not warrant it." Hammond returned to town the following day, and Cora was alone until the
arrival, in the late afternoon, of W. A. McNeil for a stay of five
days. The next day, "showers and lightning afternoon," she was
busy putting up pickles. Then on September 4 the father and son,
Cora, and Mabel Wright made a picnic excursion by wagon to the
jetties, where they caught 175 crabs but were driven home early
by a heavy rain storm. The day after, she was up before five, making "katsup" and writing letters. McNeil was drinking again and
she anxiously notes, September 22, that he came home from fishing
at the jetties at 4 P.M., "Drunk!" It rained steadily for two days;
she remained indoors "doing mending," and "wrote English
letters."

And on October 13 she writes, "Last Sunday with babes at Pablo
for some weeks." The next day she visited her dentist, saw Campbell "and gave him power of attorney," and "left hurriedly" by
train for Savannah where she made connections with the through
train for New York.

> October 19—at sea. Sailed from New York SS "Finland"—Red Star
> Line—with Hattie 3 P.M. Fine weather—not many passengers.
> Rate $54 to London—we bound for Dover. Went bed early. Fine
> big cabin.

What is the explanation of this "hurried" departure, followed
by the sea voyage?

Subpoenas were about to be issued for the indictment of McNeil
in the shooting of Harry Parker. At the coroner's inquest on June
7, and again at the preliminary trial hearing on August 13, Cora
had refused to testify against her husband. But the key witness was
Hattie Mason, whose testimony at both hearings was damning and,
if repeated when the case came to trial, would almost certainly
convict McNeil. Mabel Wright's testimony was shaky, she proved
responsive to pressure; and Willie Wilkerson, held as "an accessory
before the crime," was of course completely subservient to the
defense. Owen Wingate stuck to his story that McNeil had said
he intended killing both Parker and Cora, and had continued firing

after Parker fell. Hattie could not be shaken, and with Hattie out of the way Wingate's word alone would not be sufficient to send McNeil to the chair. No one, of course, would believe the Negro woman.

We cannot know the specific nature of the deal offered Cora, on that afternoon of July 18, by the elder McNeil when he saw her alone. But McNeil's family were mobilizing their combined influence to get him off and there seems little reason to doubt that a proposition was made to her then that she get out of town, preferably out of the country, taking Hattie with her, and remain away until the trial was over; and that the proposition included some vaguely worded promise, as to her own future, that "everything would be all right."

What sort of future with Hammond McNeil Cora could possibly have envisioned is again a question unanswerable. But that she, like his family, wanted his life saved, and that she believed that by removing Hattie from reach of a summons she was also saving her marriage, seems equally certain. The motives of the human heart are devious, as well as complex. At any rate, the line she had earlier drawn as to the impossibility of consorting with a murderer was now dangerously blurred in her scheme of values.

Although the coroner's jury had returned a verdict of "willful murder" (Parker was unarmed, with not even a pocket knife on him at the time of the shooting) and the State announced its intention to "prosecute vigorously," the outcome was never in doubt. In the code of that day a crime involving a man's wife was excusable, and an abstraction called "honor" was at stake, which though it might be synonymous with ego was nevertheless of more importance than the reputation of a *demimondaine*.

With each postponement obtained by the usual court maneuvering, the defense gained not only time but valuable publicity. The young man was given a tongue-lashing in the newspapers! Through "bad company" he had "disgraced his family and shocked his friends"; "a young man of handsome appearance" and prominent connections, who "dresses in good taste." And while Cora Taylor, "his alleged wife," was called "keeper of a disorderly house" and "woman of the under world," the killer and his victim both were represented to the public as the unwitting dupes of this notoriously evil Jezebel. The defendant's elder brother, W. D. McNeil, a lawyer in Macon, Georgia, was associated in the case with the defense attorneys; and the public was treated to the sport, at that time not unusual, of witnessing a State's Prosecutor in a criminal case pitted against his own brother and former law partner, who headed the team of defense lawyers. It is an interesting fact that the plea of self-defense was denounced by the trial judge, Hon. Rhydon M. Call.* The defense attorneys then filed a "Request for Instructions Relating To Self-Defense," and won an agreement for information from this source to be inserted in the Judge's charge to the Jury. So it was upon that premise of self-defense, over the Judge's protest, that step by step the defense built its case. The case did not come to trial until December 2, and the trial lasted only two days. Great was the rejoicing and backslapping when the jury, after being locked up all night, finally brought in a verdict of acquittal. "Without exception," the reporter of the Florida *Evening Metropolis* announced, "it is said that the arguments in this case were the best under the circumstances made in this court for years."

But Cora Taylor, throughout that feverish summer while the case was pending, must have been reading the papers with mixed feelings.

At sea the weather, though cold, was fine and the ocean like a pond. But Cora's sleep was continually disturbed by bad dreams: there was one about Hammond and Hammond's dog. And her head, too, had "not ceased aching." Still, on the first day out she managed to finish two novels, *The Lady of the Decoration* and *Beau Brocade*; and commenced a letter to Hammond. They soon ran into heavy seas, "very beautiful," and there was excitement one night when the sea smashed in their cabin porthole, spraying Hattie's bed. Cora was invited up to the bridge for little chats with the Captain; and she watched, fascinated, the exchange of wireless messages with other ships. One day there was a fifty-five word message which brought news of a panic in Wall Street, and improvement in the health of the Austrian Emperor Franz Joseph. Cora with her usual zest entered fully into the life of the ship, conversing with the other

---

* Parker was unarmed, and no weapon of any kind was found among his effects. McNeil claimed that he was being "choked" when he fired the second shot, and that no shots were fired after Parker was on the ground.

passengers, who were "simple, and funny, and nice"; and in between promenades and deck conversations she polished off Mrs.
Humphrey Ward's *Marcella*.

The landing at Dover on October 28 was accomplished with
some difficulty, the ship's bow stove in. In London they put up for
the night at the Charing Cross Hotel, where Cora had stayed with
Donald Stewart at the time of their marriage—how long ago it
seemed, how many lives away! There was a light fog next morning,
and after tea in the rooms she went straight to Cook's in Cockspur
Street and thence to Ludgate Circus, where letters and invitations
from Mrs. Pease and the Conrads awaited her; also a letter from Mr.
De Friese, whose wife was in America. She looked in on Westminster Abbey "and enjoyed it first time in my life"; then to 47
Gower Street, her old lodgings—where there must have been a
different landlady now!—where she got a sitting room and bedroom for thirty-five shillings a week. "Bus to Charing X—lunch
Gatti's—cab to A & N [Army and Navy] stores. . . . Moved to
Gower Street. Sitting by fire now and very comfy."

Sightseeing with Hattie, whom she put through the paces, she
came upon a discovery which, though it no longer mattered, was
still a shock:

> October 31: Tower of London and City. St. Paul's. Went into
> crypt and saw brass to Sir Donald Stewart and his son. (My hus-
> band Sir Donald William Stewart died Africa Gold Coast* in
> 1905. I did not know he was dead. Poor old Don!)

And then she decided to go to France for a few days:

> November 4: Noon train to Folkestone and boat to Boulogne—fine
> passage—had stateroom—crowded train to Paris. Was ass enough
> to go in carriage "For ladies only"—8 women and 1 grown kid!
> Paris at last. Customs all O.K. Drove to Hotel St. Petersbourg
> Rue Caumartin.

In the Bon Marché she "spent money" recklessly for a coat, hat,
underclothes, etc.; then "drove in Bois" and stopped at the Café de
la Cascade and the Chateau Madrid. November 6, "not good day,"
they motored through fog in a "magnificent" car to Versailles. "In

---

* Cora was mistaken. Donald Stewart, who was then governor of the
British East Africa Protectorate (now Kenya), died at Nairobi.

Palace until 1 P.M. Then to Hotel des Reservoirs—Famous. More Royalties and celebrities have lunched here than in any hotel in the world. Back to Palace. . . . Saw State carriages, Petit Trianon and the Grand Trianon—too wonderful and charming to describe." But Robespierre's portrait was "like W.D. McN of Macon, ugh!" The Paris trip ended with a visit to "Napoleon's Hotel des Invalides," and the Palais Royal where she "bought trinkets. Books!" And back in London:

> November 9: Fine day. Lord Mayor's Day. Wrote H and then went out to see show—made friends with Bobby [policeman] and he put me in front row. Stood for 2 hours—best show in years. Then got cab and rode, not through, but over crowds. King Edward's birthday. Home for tea—out for walk and home for dinner, dead tired. Wrote H and sent papers.

Meanwhile, in spite of these agreeable distractions her thoughts turned anxiously toward affairs in Jacksonville. She wrote every day to Hammond, and had written Campbell, but still was without word of any kind.

> November 11: Fog in A.M. . . . Went to A & Navy stores and bought thick walking shoes, spats, 3 prs., slippers self—and shoes and slippers for Hattie—also veils and goodies to eat, then home. Fog too bad to go out later. Sat up reading until 1 A.M. Worried about H—and no letters yet from Nellie [her housekeeper now at the Court]. Cable Co. says still registered "Brede London."

Hattie was ill with a cold next day and Cora, feeling "wretchedly," cabled both Nell and Campbell. Then at last, she had a cable from Campbell saying he had sent five letters to "Brede London— of all the asinine things!" So once more she wrote Hammond; and she also wrote the postmaster of London about recovering her letters, which were promptly forwarded to her in Gower Street. She noted in her diary the fact that it was "four weeks tonight" since she had left Jacksonville.

Mr. De Friese came to take her to the theatre, where they saw Marie Tempest, and to supper afterwards at the Carlton. He wished he might "see lots and lots of you," but kind friends hardly ever left him an evening to himself and week ends usually had to be spent playing golf with MP's or "one of His Majesty's judges." His letter closed with "All good and sweet things to you. . . ."

The next two days were spent seeing friends and driving about the Sussex countryside. Hattie, who for the purposes of social intercourse had become "Mrs. Barrett," was probably with Cora on this trip. They motored over from Battle in a "good car" to Beckley where, over tea with Mr. and Mrs. Forbes-Bentley at Bay Tree Cottage, Cora seemed more concerned at the behavior of the dog Tolstoi than worried about the possibility of malapropisms or incriminating *faux pas* on Hattie's part. "I think he thought I would take him away from these people he loves. He is very wonderful to see. His hair, curls and ropes, almost drags on the ground." Then motoring back "through lovely Sussex lanes" they spent the night at Battle, and for dinner enjoyed fine mushrooms:

> Bed. Feathers under, canopy over. Funny old waiter. "George Hotel" old Wagstaff dead, son runs inn for mother. Must tell Hattie about garters sometime . . . Willie's legs!!
> November 15: . . . bought postals and saw church and B.A. [Battle Abbey] . . . drove to Bodian Castle—saw ruins—to Hawkhurst for lunch at the old "Queens" where bowling green, pheasants and old furniture etc. are just the same as when I was last here. On through Northiam—saw church, "Queen Eliz Oak"—Brickwall to Rye. . . . walked to old church, Town Hall . . . to Mermaid Inn—my club—had tea there, then walked to Ypres Tower, looked over moors. . . . Dined in sittingroom and took 7.38 express to town. . . . Wrote home. No letters from US. Wrote Hammond.

In Rye she had "walked past Lamb House" without going in, for in reply to her inquiry had come a curt little note from the Master "to say that I am at present in London, so that a call at Lamb House will not find yours truly." But some of the sting must have been taken out of this rebuff by Jessie Conrad's warm greeting presently: "If you will come and see us here we will give you a proper big welcome and I will undertake to say Escamillo will be a delight to you." So Cora and "Mrs. Barrett" set out from St. Pancras Station at noon, on a day of black fog, to be met at Luton by "little Prince Borys" waiting with a victoria. It was a twenty-minute drive to Someries, "a heavenly old farm" in Bedfordshire with a "beautiful walled garden," the new home to which the Conrads had recently moved from Pent Farm, in Kent. She found Jessie "fat and an invalid with her knee. Borys a fine lad of 9—and the babe [John Conrad] beautiful, 15 months. Conrad just the same." After a "good lunch" Borys picked her violets, and took snapshots.

But with no further news from Jacksonville, the suspense was becoming unbearable:

> November 18: . . . Court supposed to convene at Jax! . . . Went to A & N stores, bought sheeting and books. Mrs. Pease came at 5 P.M. As dear as ever. . . .
>
> November 23: . . . Lunch at Frascatti, walked Oxford St. Cab home —dined home. Letter from Campbell at last. *Dominus providebit*
>
> November 25: . . . cold and fair. Went out to A & N stores—drove to Boltons, looked at my old house—to 73 Harrington Gardens and thought what a fool I had been—to Fuller's for tea—to Liberty's, ordered frock. . . . Letter from C. Frewen offering me Brede Place for Thurs. night—from Mrs. Coombe offering 3 days, Mrs. Scott-Stokes photo of children. . . . Oh, such a dear letter from Mrs. Frewen.

Cora did not spend Thursday night at Brede Place however, as the Frewens were to be away at a shooting party over the week end, but she probably caught them at home early in the afternoon of November 28. "Very much touched" by Cora's "charming letter" which followed this visit, Mrs. Frewen wrote to say "how much pleasure it gave me to see you again—and [I am] so pleased that you approve of my improvements!" But she herself was not at all pleased with "the knobs in the arch room! The design and idea was quite different, but I was obliged to be in Ireland when it was done—and was horribly disappointed. . . . The wood arches should have been made much heavier, and instead of horrible little knobs there should have been the old flat carved heraldic Plantagenet roses." The cost of changing just now was prohibitive, but "some day I hope it *will* be done! . . . I am so glad you noticed it, as you have such perfect taste and had we had time I would have pointed out several other things, too, which must have struck you and told you the reason why! ! !"

The day before the visit to Brede Place, Cora and "Mrs. Barrett" had tea with Mr. and Mrs. H. G. Wells at Spade House. Mrs. Wells had "heard of her marriage." Cora had earlier looked up old friends in the Society of American Women in London, and now to shake off ghosts from overseas, whose insistent clanking pervaded her dreams, she suddenly decided on a motor trip to Ireland and Wales, on which she had as a third companion the Society's vice-president, Mrs. Dietz Glynes.

They left Monmouth for Landclower, Wales, in a streaming rain, but had "good crossing" on the Irish steamer. "Nice cabin. Interesting to see them put car on board—shipping rates in G.B. [Great Britain] very cheap compared to US. Took train for Wexford car on flat train. . . . 'Whales' Hotel—nice dinner, sittingroom and good bedroom—but no featherbeds in Ireland!" Then from Jacksonville came news which upset her profoundly.

> December 7: *My darling Spongie died!*

From Wexford they started about ten o'clock in the morning for "Derregarvan," most of the time in a pouring rain:

> Lunched at "Devonshire Arms"—old inn—nice Irish lad waited on us. Off again for Youghal—arrived about 6 P.M. Dinner in nice private sittingroom. Funny old waiter got us post cards and told us about Father O'Neal being flogged in 1798—& the monument, etc. To bed early. I little knew I was losing the dearest and best treasure I had, my old faithful dog!! This will always be the reproach of my life & it is surely a punishment.

Progress next day was interrupted when the car broke down on a mountaintop seven miles from Bandon, their destination for the night. Cora and Hattie shed their fur coats and started walking, leaving "Mrs. D. G. with the car." At the end of a two-mile hike they got into a farmhouse where "a very kind old Major asked me first thing, 'Are you married?' I said 'yes,' he said, 'Oh, I'm sorry, if you were single I'd be courting you!' " The people at the farmhouse sent a man into the field to catch the "jenney" which was then harnessed to a very high, springless cart, with only straw in the bottom for a seat. The Devonshire Arms in Bandon proved to be "a horrible old stone barn . . . with darkness profound! Got them to take horses and go after motor—cold supper . . . and bed when car came in."

With the car now out of commission indefinitely, Cora persuaded Mrs. Glynes to return by train. December 10 was rainy, and she "did not sleep at all." They got into Paddington at ten o'clock at night, and Cora took a four-wheeler straight to Gower Street, where three cables were awaiting her. But she could think of nothing else now but the painful severing of one life from another, of these obverse halves of herself, borne in upon her with the dog's death—the dog she and Stephen had both loved:

> I've paid dearly to lose him while I was away . . . and I will always believe he died of a broken heart. Went out again and cabled Nell to have him buried in metallic casket in Court yard until I returned.

Another bad night, "Very very sad about loss of my Spongie, poor old man to die without me by him"; and then she suddenly decided to go home, and took passage on the American liner *New York*. Cora and Hattie shared the railway carriage to Southhampton with a young Englishwoman, Mrs. Romero, who was going to join her American husband in the States. The mother of the bride begged Cora to "look after" her.

December 14 was "sunny." Cora and Hattie had a "fine large cabin—writing desk, chiffonier, two basins, and large bathroom—very comfy."

> . . . Mr. Campbell should receive letter of 3rd and cable "Safe" if it's all right for Hattie to return.
> December 15: Fair—bit rough at sea. . . . Tea in cabin. Mr & Mrs. Mitchel, W. Gordon, Miss Emerson, Mr. Fabian . . . at our table next captain's—very nice people. Read "The Broken Road"—and Mason's new book, "The Furze," queer Devonshire moor story.
> December 16: Everyone ill yet—ours the star table . . . never miss a meal—still rough. Read "The Stooping Lady," "Irish Neighbors," "The Brushwood Boy." . . . A woman from California—a Miss Byrne—affords much amusement—wears a Turkish fez and waterproof—and says she is a rich American called back on account of panic [the financial panic of 1907]. Called on Mrs. Romero.

The next day continued rough, but Cora was "on deck just the same & of course to all meals. Only 4 women to meals most of time. H & I, Miss Emerson, Miss Byrne." The Captain was "charming." There were also "two nice doctors on board and two couples with ducky babies." The day after was cloudy, but the sea now quite calm off the Grand Banks; and she had better rest.

> . . . Read "The Secret Door," and began "Shadow of a Dead Man" and "Women in War"—rotten both of them.

December 20: Woke up 5 AM. Made 437 [miles] to noon, don't expect to be in before Sun. Sent Marconi message to Nellie, told her phone Hammond. $5.33. Mrs. Romero gave tea party in her cabin—2 gents and 4 ladies, very nice. Captain's dinner.

In New York it poured rain all day. Cora and Hattie remained in their pleasant rooms at the Cumberland Hotel; and the next day, December 23, they left at noon for Jacksonville by rail. "$42— almost as much as going to Europe—quite as much counting tips and meals." But a gentleman from Jacksonville got on at Washington and took her in to dinner; and the next morning the three of them were joined by another old friend at breakfast. The train was three hours late, and they arrived at eleven o'clock at night, "dead tired." Cora notes, more than a little wistfully, that Hammond did not come up to welcome me"; but the girls had punch, gifts, and flowers waiting, "very nice."

December 25: Nice dinner. H & father in afternoon. H brought me flowers.

After the tragedy of her son's death Harry Parker's mother had remarried, and now Cora received a letter and a "beautiful" Christmas present (word indecipherable) from the man she refers to, erroneously, as the dead boy's "father":

Hammond's kid brother working for him—secretly married to actress!!

Some of life's bad jokes were too much even for Cora. The day after Christmas she was again ill, and wretched:

Wrote Hammond and he promises to do his duty toward me. Made up my mind to get out of this business and stick to him.

So the diary ends, with the year's end, on a "lovely day." And now, the decision taken, she feels "better in mind and body."

6

"WHAT IS life worth," she once remarked to her diary, "if we have not someone with whom we can share our sorrows and pleasures?" McNeil, a murderer, was not much to stick to. But even now her tremendous vitality was rallying for a comeback; and Cora was making plans! In Rye she had seen a wonderful old house with a garden, and a second storey projecting over Pump Street, which had captivated her fancy. So staggering up from the shocks life had dealt her the preceding year, and somehow believing that in these surroundings the face of ugliness might be changed to beauty as in the fairy story, and she and Hammond begin a new life together, she wrote to her friend Mrs. Forbes-Bentley inquiring about the house.

Mrs. Forbes-Bentley, who had gone over the house "very thoroughly," replied at length and in detail. "Charmed with its possibilities," she was only "afraid of biasing you in any way in case they [the owners] came to your terms and you regretted it afterwards." The sash windows, she thought, should be changed to casements

not the old *small* lead panes which darken rooms, but . . . the large *diamond* panes, which suggest a window seat. . . . The boarding wants seeing to, also some mortaring on a bedroom wall and things of this sort, and above all the beautiful carving requires tender care and *oil*. . . . It would make a delightful house if you have the things to put into it.

The entrance hall with wood paneling was "beautiful"; and in the dining room was a wonderful fresco which should have a silk curtain right across it to preserve it from the light. "I should love to see old furniture in this room with a roaring fire throwing up its lights." Behind this was a room with bad paper on the wall, but "a cheerful Philistine room!" The kitchen was "a nice light one." A pretty little conservatory adjoined the oddly planned back premises; and "the summer-house with its magnificent view should tempt you over to write, it could not fail to inspire." The grounds in the rear opened out "into the hanging gardens of Babylon! There seems to be a long, long garden reached by a succession of . . . staircases"—now so overgrown that one could venture no farther. "Of the *drains* of course I know nothing and had I inquired I should only have been told they were in perfect order." The bathroom was "very fair," though "planned in a peculiar way up a small staircase which leads to nowhere else—from the kitchen—so I should imagine it must have been a servant's room." The cellar, down a steep stairway, had "a fine groined roof, several arches—

just like a small chapel!" Wondering if she had told Cora "all you want to know," Mrs. Forbes-Bentley thought "the house would be *livable* with only little in the way of repairs, but with more money spent on it it could be made into a charming old world retreat. It's historic value, of course, is great and it would be nice if it fell into the hands of someone who would appreciate its associations—so far as they are known." One can only guess what the Master of Lamb House might have had to say on learning he was to have Cora Taylor as a near neighbor!

In the light of the transactions which later took place and the substantial sums which went into the pockets of others, there would undoubtedly have been enough from the sale or lease of Cora's real estate to enable her to live in retirement and modest comfort in England—where she longed to be—for the rest of her life. But it was not to be.

"Once a madam, always a madam," according to no less an authority than Polly Adler; and if escape must depend on the men in her life, luck was certainly not with Cora.

In the summer of 1909, Hammond McNeil formally entered suit for divorce. The preliminary steps probably had been taken sometime during the previous year. We cannot know just when the subject was first broached to Cora, for McNeil, after promising "to do his duty" by her, continued for some while to deceive her in regard to his real intentions, leading her to believe that things had been patched up between them. But in all probability, his determination to be rid of her antedates even the shooting of Harry Parker. For it seems clear that on that night in the hotel bedroom when they discussed Hammond's "trouble," the elder McNeil must then have made it plain to his son that all would be forgotten and forgiven *only* if he got rid of "that woman"; and had it not been for the impulsive act of the shooting which upset the apple-cart, Hammond perhaps would have needed little persuasion to leave his wild oats behind him—namely, Cora. Now, at any rate, he was ruthlessly bent on coming up in the world, at whatever cost to her. He had picked out a suitable girl to marry, this time a woman younger than himself as well as attractive, from a family of influence and means; and like Donald Stewart, he was determined to blot out of memory all trace of his previous marriage. An unusual provision of the divorce proceedings, when the final decree came through on October 18, 1909, was McNeil's stipulation permanently enjoining Cora from ever calling herself by the name of "Mrs. Hammond P. McNeil."

The bill of complaint charges "ungovernable temper, violence, and cruelty"; more specifically that defendant beat the complainant "many, many times with anything to hand"; and that in the final instance she struck him on the head with a shoe, opening a wound above the eye which required a surgeon's ministrations and three stitches. The spectacle of a fairly large man unable to defend himself "many, many times" from the physical assaults of a rather small woman—even such a hellcat as Cora was alleged to be—would ordinarily be a subject for laughter. But these charges were sworn to on behalf of the complainant by Mabel Wright, who meanwhile had left the Court for a house at 954 Ward Street; Edith Gray, Cora's present housekeeper at the Court; and one Bessie McPherson, a chambermaid. All of these witnesses testified that they had heard Mrs. McNeil say, "Yes, I did it, I would do it again, and I only wish I had beaten him to death. I have lost all respect for him—and I will never live with him again!" Bessie McPherson adds, that she had found Mrs. McNeil one day outside her bedroom "crying and very angry."

When she learned the truth as to McNeil's intentions, Cora must have been beside herself. She had refused to testify against this man who was a murderer, had sacrificed whatever remained of her reputation and allowed her name to be dragged through the mud in the newspapers, only to be double-crossed—bought off with a trip to England! Then tossed aside like a common jade; and those of her household whom she had trusted now appeared against her like so many Judases. She did not contest the divorce action. She went to pieces.

Retribution however was awaiting Hammond McNeil. Six years to the month after the killing of Harry Parker, he was shot with his own gun, in his own house at Pablo Beach, in a quarrel with his new wife during which he knocked her down and threatened to kill her. In the scuffle the gun went off, the bullet lodging at the base of the brain exactly as in the shooting of Parker. "It is stated by friends of the wounded man that on several occasions when he had been drinking heavily McNeil was known to have had a fancy for a revolver and took pride in showing his dexterity in handling a gun." The newspaper account describing McNeil as "a capitalist and liquor dealer, financially interested in various enterprises of this city," also stated that his father and brother "have been constantly at the bedside of Mr. McNeil [in the hospital where he died] since last evening."

But to Cora the lightning bolt that felled her, in the whole business of the divorce, must have been her final overwhelming realization that her life in these years since Stephen Crane's death had been an utter waste. Something of this mood is reflected in a letter undated, but certainly written about this time, to an unidentified friend about to marry, who may have been the banker's son:

My dear ———————

The little reminder of your friendship and my many wasted hours and lost fortunes, came to me yesterday, and while I see in them the same fascinating, living beauty which wrecks lives, ruins souls and desolates homes, yet to me they shall only be a keepsake and reminder that we have been and are—friends.

I am glad if your position is bettered, glad if you can manifest a strength of character sufficient to throw off old associations and avoid new ones of the same character, and resist the increasing temptations which life in such a place will surround you with. Make the woman who loves you happy and a true lover, rather than a source of prayers and care. Your disposition, your proneness to improper associations and the consequent evils thereof, is so similar to my own, that I speak to you as I know you would to me. Sometimes I try to imagine what there is in the future for me, but it is all a blank. Perhaps it is best so. . . . I cannot believe that my life is to be a mere existence and that I shall go on and on in the same old way and finally leave to the world . . . only the *space* which I occupy and nothing more. Don't you sometimes fall into reveries fringed with egotism and imagine that you are possessed of capabilities and talents which by the strength of constant effort, would develop and lift you into a more exalted position in life? I do frequently and though it may be only a dream, it is a pleasant one. . . . I am blue today. You must pardon my inflicting on you this letter. . . .

There can be no doubt that the rich aroma of scandal pervading the McNeil murder case had given a strong push to the reform elements in the closing of the red-light district. Public sentiment hardened against Cora Taylor; and some individuals who formerly had coveted admission to her inner circle now gave heed to the tearful recriminations of affronted housewives, and stayed away from the Court. Her business suffered.

Cora herself had changed very much in appearance during the last two years. Her face now had a hectic flush which neither sunburn nor her usual high coloring could wholly account for, and she had grown very stout. Some thought that she had taken to drowning her sorrows in the bottle, but she seldom if ever touched hard liquor, and Mabel Wright's sworn testimony in the divorce case contained the statement that "Mrs. McNeil drank only in the course of business, when people came in and bought wine."

In April of 1908 had come a note from Conrad thanking her "for the memento of poor Stephen" (some personal article, sent after her return from England), and "for this proof of your continued friendship for us both." A cheerful, newsy letter from Kate Frederic in Chicago reminded her once more, by contrast, that her own future was still "a blank." Barry, the delight of his teachers though "a good deal of a monk," had received his high school diploma. Héloïse was a "crank" about Latin, and longed to study Greek and Hebrew; Helen was winning scholarships at the Art Institute. "How is the present menagerie?" Kate wanted to know.

Ours is so limited by encircling dogs that some of its most brilliant inmates mizzle off. Winston L. Spencer Churchill was killed by a tomcat. Wilbur F. Wright and his sister Wilhelmina of Holland now occupy the arena of our affections without supplanting Margot, their mother, the sweetest of cats. . . . I'm going to try to get up a book of kitten-puppy verses for Christmas and get an artist friend to illustrate it—a baby book. . . . There's a bit of a lake breeze blowing through the heat today. Otherwise I'd like to find myself on an English down looking over the sea with all the long summer light, and nothing to make one think of weather at all! Still, Chicago summer with a lake breeze is not bad. Now it comes, cooler and cooler. . . .

Cora meanwhile was living in semi-retirement, and spending more and more time at Palmetto Lodge, no longer operated as a branch of the Court now but reserved for her own private use. Here she received her special friends and entertained a select little company at week-end house parties, to which invitations were still much sought after despite the murky cloud under which her name had fallen. Although she continued to manage the Court, she had given up her apartments there and moved into a suite in the Annex at 118 Davis Street.

Among the friends of happier days and lusher times who had not been driven away by the repercussions of scandal, was Ernest Christie Budd, a man whose declining star had a short while before ridden high in the heavens. The real estate firm in which he was a partner had played a prominent part in rebuilding the city after the devastating fire of 1901, and had made a great deal of money. Ernest Budd, born in Nova Scotia, had been a resident of Jacksonville from early childhood. Many people thought him "the brains" of the real estate combination, but a weakness for drink and playing the horses eventually brought about his downfall. He undoubtedly induced Cora Taylor to let him place small bets for her; and the catalogue of the Rancocas Stud Farm in New York State, found among her personal effects after her death, probably came there by his doing rather than hers. The burned child dreads the fire and Cora, who had become more cautious perforce in money matters in recent years, had no large sums to risk now. The marginal notations in three figures are certainly his own bets, the smaller ones perhaps hers.*

Ernest Budd had earlier found congenial refuge at the Court from one of those dreary marriages in which that period abounded. He was an attractive and sociable fellow, but his wife took a dim view of a glass of anything more potent than lemonade, of the two-step and even old-fashioned whist. From the beginning the marriage on both sides had been unhappy, but Mrs. Budd, like so

---

* A post card in the Crane collection at Syracuse University addressed to "Mrs. Stephen Crane, P.O. Box 480, Jacksonville, Fla." is in the handwriting of Ernest Budd—signed "Uncle Edward"—and appears to be a message in cipher having to do with racing bets, or purchase of stud shares:

New York, Feb. 10/10

Dear Cora

I wrote you as usual last week & sent "Reviews", all to Jax. I hope you are fully well now and happy. I expect your usual letter each day. Will write soon. Best love.

Affec. Uncle Edward

[At top, crossed] Very cold and severe winter here. So far no snow lately. Not seen Bro James as yet. Don't forget the check, please. Best to register it. Write about operation.

many other unhappy wives, was grimly opposed to divorce. Still, in spite of all the scandal, Ernest Budd wanted to marry Cora Taylor; and Cora seems to have been the only human being who could ever get him to stop drinking, even for a short while. What sort of compatibility there was between them, or how deep, may only be surmised; but finally, when his wife continued to refuse him a divorce, he moved his things over to the Court and stayed there. His wife had him arrested for nonsupport and hauled him back. Old friends began dropping him; his partner intimated that an embarrassing situation would be relieved if he retired from the real

Cora Crane's grave in the Evergreen Cemetery, Jacksonville, Florida. Gift of Henry W. Walters.

estate firm—much of the time he was in no condition to carry on business anyhow. Meanwhile, a fascinating and luxuriant crop of rumors concerning a child Cora was supposed to have "adopted" burst into bloom. Nobody had ever seen this child. But, of course, it was hers and Ernest's.

In January, 1910, Cora suffered a light stroke. Though she still retained full financial control of the Court, she now turned over the whole management of it to her housekeeper, Edith Gray. Only very rarely did she come up to town, and then it was only to see her doctor or her lawyer. She made a will leaving all of her property, both real and personal, to Ernest Budd, also naming him her executor. During this time, she evidently indicated to him or Campbell her wishes concerning her headstone.

Sunday, September 4, 1910, was a very warm day, hundreds of motor cars jamming the old South Jacksonville ferry as perspiring families waited in line, bound for a cool dip in the ocean. It was high tide, and a car which had lingered too long stuck in the soft sand in front of Palmetto Lodge. Cora had no guests that week end, she was alone in the house. Noticing the stranded car, she went out to offer help and the use of her telephone. They all pushed and got the car out. The sun was very hot. Feeling dizzy, she went back in the house to lie down—it happened so suddenly—and never regained consciousness.

Waves on the shore, how often she had lain listening to that sound rolling in from the borders of Infinity, and now as the darkness fell it must have been the very last sound in her ears.

Her lot in Woodlawn was filled up, and she was buried in the newer, adjoining Evergreen Cemetery. And so, among the quiet oaks and green vistas of St. Augustine grass, the tired heart and overstrained body of one who all her life "had lived five years in one" eventually found rest. As she had asked, there is a simple block of white marble:

CORA E. CRANE

1868-1910

The Problem and the Use of Cora Crane's Notebooks

AMONG THE papers, books, manuscripts, etc. that Cora Crane brought over from England and kept together until her death— now comprising the Columbia University Stephen Crane Collection—are her little red "Manuscript Book" and a small, worn, cloth-bound copybook which she called her "Memorandum Book." In these pages she left an intimate record which, however fragmentary and jumbled, and often extremely difficult to decipher, is the most important source of information we have about her relationship with Stephen Crane.

The use here made of the Notebooks in the text is always in conjunction with biographical facts, which they illuminate and help to set in chronology, even though Cora's entries sometimes are intelligible only in the light of certain previous knowledge. All passages quoted in the text without reference to their source are from the Notebooks. Long quoted passages in reduced type are indented when they are Cora's words or writing; those not otherwise identified are from the Notebooks. Quoted matter is frequently put into Cora's own mouth in the form of dialogue, a device in use throughout the book to give an effect of conversation in scenes. But since a biography is fact and not fiction, some limit must be set to the use of techniques borrowed from fiction, hence no attempt is anywhere made at interpretation of mental and emotional attitudes except as they reveal themselves in the Notebooks and letters. These limits have been strictly observed.

The subject matter of the Notebooks consists of Cora's own observations on life and people, her private feelings, anecdotes which amused or otherwise impressed her; random jottings which one takes to be travel notes; words and idiomatic expressions in French and German—even Greek and Turkish! There are emotional outpourings in what can only be termed execrable verse, best forgotten, of which Stephen Crane was apparently the inspiration; scraps of letters, also presumably written to him; and a perfect jungle of quotations from her wildly diversified reading. In short, anything and everything she wanted to remember and keep near her, whether the recollection evoked delight or heartbreak.

Cora must have been an unusually fast as well as omnivorous reader, for according to a later diary (1907) to read two novels in a day was nothing out of the ordinary. The quotations she set down in her Notebooks range over many countries, civilizations, and literary modes, all the way from Seneca and St. Jerome to Shakespeare, Dante, Ibsen and Omar Khayyám. Sheakspeare and Byron (*Don Juan*) maintain a strong lead. But among others who are quoted less often we find Coleridge, Shelley, Keats, George Herbert, Dickens (*David Copperfield*), Thackeray, George Eliot, Thoreau, Emerson, Tennyson, Matthew Arnold, the Brownings, Burns, Stevenson, Kipling, Victor Hugo, Goethe, La Bruyère, Hafiz, King Solomon—and one Philander Johnson. From the Scotswoman Joanna Baillie (1762-1851), poet and author of *Plays on the Passions,* she cites four lines whose juxtaposition to some of her own impassioned utterances to Crane suggests that they may have been repeated to him: "Will I live with thee? Will I not cheer thee? Wouldst thou be lonely then? Wouldst thou be sad?" All of these authors are identified by name, their lines enclosed in quotation marks. But Du Maurier's *Trilby,* the novel everyone was reading, must have made a deep impression on Cora, as the Memorandum Book lumps five or six quotes under the head of "Trilby bits/Pure Trilbyness." In it she undoubtedly discovered fancied resemblances to herself and Stephen Crane. Other *Trilby* quotations are scattered through her pages without identification. But a comparison with the novel text enabled me to locate all of these "Trilby bits" in the original Harper's edition (New York, 1894). Those appearing in Chapters One and Two are from pp. 335 and 339 of that edition.

In another category are numerous items from sources untraceable, which Cora put into quotation marks although she omitted the authors' names.

With the exception of the sentimental verses, which are unsigned, Cora frequently points to the products of her own authorship by the use of initials, "C," "C.S.," "C.E.S.," or "Cora." But in fully as many instances when she forgets to do so, the line jottings and paragraphs are clearly recognizable by the phrasing and character of the thought content as unmistakably hers.

Fragments and incomplete drafts of letters supposedly written to Crane, of which there are a good many, also are easily spotted. Sometimes she addresses him directly, though she is always careful not to refer to him by name: 'I am delighted with your letter, it seemed more like the dear one I knew and loved so well. . . .'' At other times she writes to herself, thinking aloud as one does in a diary. It is as though she were practicing here, putting her thoughts down and rehearsing what she would say to Stephen in the letter presently to be composed from these rough notes.

The existence in the Notebooks of these letter fragments— Cora's replies to Stephen Crane—is I think, despite all contrary claims, proof positive that Crane *did* write letters to her. The question is, Where are they? Berryman points to "three long letters written to Cora and now announced for early publication" (*Stephen Crane*, p. 300), which he later concluded were forgeries (John Berryman to Lillian Gilkes, October 29, 1954—in answer to my inquiry). The letters were to have been included in a volume of authors' love letters scheduled for publication in England, but the book was withdrawn. A well-known book dealer who afterwards sold them to an American buyer, has no record or recollection of the identity of the purchaser (Ben Abramson to Douglas M. Jacobs). It now seems quite probable, on the face of it, that the letters were genuine. But there must also have been others, ones that Crane wrote Cora from Cuba, for instance; and as she cherished every line and scrap from his pen, one can still hope that they may eventually turn up out of whatever attic or cellar hiding place they have dropped into.

Since Cora usually omitted dates, it is impossible to date Notebook entries except, as has been said, in relation to the main biographical facts. Beyond this, anybody's guess is probably as good as another's. Yet taking them in this context of events, we do find clues. The Memorandum Book, for example, clearly seems to come first, starting off with a long entry which looks like the beginning of a letter to Crane. This is the item, "I am delighted with your letter," etc., which I date from Crane's departure from Florida. It appears to fall somewhere in the interim between their parting and

Cora's arrival in London to rejoin him, a conclusion which gains support from the next few entries: fragments of two more letters to Crane, which are followed by a list of foreign words and phrases such as might be useful in conversation, and which certainly suggest preparations for their travels en route to the Greek war.

I do not believe any entries were made before this time. The jottings, quotations, reflections, outpourings which fill her pages all seem to have had their origin in that Niagara of feeling Crane awoke in her. So the Memorandum Book begins here, and ends with a fragment of another long letter to him beginning, "Of all the sweet letters you have written me and there have been many —none were so sweet as your letter of_____." The date here is tantalizingly witheld, no doubt for concealment. Coming between this concluding letter fragment and the one which stands at the beginning—possibly transferred from some earlier record—is a mass of those quotations drawn from her heterogeneous reading, personal observations, philosophising, etc. But mid-way through the book is a long passage recording an incident that happened during a break in a railroad journey undertaken without Crane: "When going to Venice from_____which is a fourteen hour ride, I decided to break the journey and rest overnight at Gratz." Gratz is a town in the Austrian Tyrol, so she was traveling westward to Venice, and the last letter marks the end of the painful separation he had insisted on after Athens—the second separation —which Crane himself abruptly ended by rejoining Cora in Paris before the specified month was up. Putting the pieces together, thus, the conclusion follows that the Memorandum Book covers a time span limited to Florida and the Greek war, and breaks off just before the arrival of the Cranes in England.

The Manuscript Book appears to belong chiefly to the Oxted period, although scattered entries clearly reflect Cora's mental and emotional harassments during the latter stages of Crane's illness at Brede Place, and the subsequent crisis which later brought about her return to Florida. The number and frequency of later entries, turning up as they do *in the first pages*, introduces a puzzling and complicating factor which perhaps may be explained by the fact that although the greater number of new entries were actually composed at Oxted, they were not recorded in the Manuscript

Book *until some while afterward*—probably after she moved from Brede Place to London. Her entry, for example, on page 3 undoubtedly echoes her grief and despair after Crane's death: "I feel like one having started out upon a journey which led for a while through pastures green and waters still. Then suddenly to have lost the turning—henceforth the desert and the darkness of loneliness forever." And a few pages along—Cora never numbered her pages—"The best way to earn my salt (and something to sprinkle my salt upon)", etc., certainly seems to point to the fateful decision of returning to Florida, which did not become final until the early months of 1902. Other passages near the beginning also hark back to the beginning of their intimacy in Florida, the arguments Cora must have used to allay Crane's scruples about her "past," while within a few pages of the end we find the only dated entries —two only. Both are from "Dec. '98," which for Cora was a time of acute mental and emotional upheaval occasioned by her pressing financial difficulties and Crane's prolonged absence from England. One of these items was obviously inspired by the Frederic case, then undergoing a ferocious airing in the courts; the other a cry of heartbreak, "My letters are one long inky howl!"

Numerous other references to unhappiness connect the Manuscript Book, in the main, with Oxted. But now another puzzle arises to confuse the sequence: Cora, for whatever reasons, at some later time transferred a part of the contents of the Memorandum Book to the Manuscript Book. Thus we find about half of the material from the former reappearing, in duplicate, in the latter. All of these transfers I have tracked down. But the significance, if any, of the frequent marginal notations appearing in both Notebooks —initials and abbreviations resembling editorial codings—still escapes me. These appear to be in Cora's hand, although it is just possible that they were added by someone else—perhaps in the period of sequestration of these papers before they were acquired by Columbia University.

One other factor which adds much to the difficulties of interpreting Notebook contents and determining their relevance to the various emotional crises confronting Cora Crane, is her habit of caution, consistently observed, of tearing out pages bearing on the intimate details of such matters. She did not wish her letters to William Crane, regarding the misdemeanors of his daughter Helen,

to fall into other hands. So, too, in the crisis over Stephen's return
to England, and in the last sordid business of her husband, McNeil,
and his shooting a man in cold blood: she tore out the pages which
might have revealed so much.

One further peculiarity of the Notebooks is the extraordinary
variations in handwriting, already noted. In the years they were
together Cora's handwriting took on a resemblance to Crane's at
times so marked as to be almost indistinguishable to anyone but a
handwriting expert. The problem of handwritings has been noted
in connection with the holograph manuscripts of the syndicated
London newsletters. I take friendly issue with Daniel G. Hoffman
on this question (see *The Poetry of Stephen Crane*, p. 228), finding it impossible to believe that Stephen ever made any entries in
Cora's diaries.

The Will of Stephen Crane

I, STEPHEN CRANE of Brede Place Northiam in the County of
Sussex Author hereby revoke all former Will and testamentary
dispositions made by me and declare this to be my last Will and
Testament.

1. I appoint my brother William Howe Crane of Port Jervis
Orange County New York United States of America to be my
American executor to administer my personal estate in the United
States of America meaning thereby all stocks and loans of Corpora-
tions created by the United States and by the State thereof and all
loans of any of the stocks of the United States or of any municipality created by any such State all Policies of Insurance and all
debts moneys and personal property due or belonging to me at the
time of my decease or which may become due or belong to my
estate thereafter not collectible by my English Executor by virtue
of the grant of letters testamentary to him by any of the Courts
of Great Britain.

2. I appoint Alfred Thomas Plant of 18 Bedford Row in the
County of London to be my English Executor to administer all my

personal estate to other than what is hereinbefore directed to be administered by my American Executor.

3. I devise all the real estate of every sort and kind situate in any part of the United States of America belonging to me or over which I have any power of disposition unto the said William Howe Crane In Trust without any more delay than is consistent with the realization of reasonable prices to sell or dispose of all the said real estate and of all that he may acquire after my decease in any way or manner at public or private sale with power to make good deeds of conveyance thereof in fee simple or for any less estate without any obligation on the part of the purchasers to see or be responsible for the application of the purchase money and with power as regards any real estate agreed to be sold in my lifetime to perfect the title thereto and convey the same to the purchasers thereof.

4. My American Executor and Trustee shall remit to my English Executor and Trustee all moneys arising from the sale of my real estate in America and from the collection and conversion of my personal estate in America except so much thereof as may be required for payment of my debts in America and the expenses of administering my estate in America and the receipt of my English Trustee for all moneys remitted to him as aforesaid shall be a sufficient discharge for the same.

5. I devise and bequeath my real estate and chattels real in England or Wales and all my personal estate other than what is hereinbefore directed to be administered by my American Trustee unto the said Alfred Thomas Plant (hereinafter called my English Trustee) In Trust to sell call in and convert into money the same at such times and in such manner as he shall think fit.

6. My English Trustee shall stand possessed of all moneys arising from the sale and conversion of my real and personal estate hereinbefore devised and bequeathed to him by my American Executor and Trustee as aforesaid upon the trusts following (that is to say) my English Trustee shall with and out of the same pay my funeral and testamentary expenses and debts (except such debts as shall be paid by my American Executor and Trustee) and shall invest the residue of said moneys with power for my Trustees from time to time to vary such investments and shall stand possessed of the said residuary trust moneys and the investments for the time being representing the same (hereinafter called the residuary

trust funds) In Trust to pay income thereof to my dear wife Cora Howarth Crane during her life or widowhood and after the death or marriage of my said wife In Trust as to one moiety or equal half part thereof for my nephew Stephen Crane the son of my brother Edmund Bryan Crane absolutely if and when he shall attain the age of twenty-one years and as to the other moiety or equal half part thereof in trust for my brothers the said William Howe Crane and Edmund Bryan Crane in equal shares absolutely.

7. I declare that my English Trustee may after the death or future marriage of my said wife apply the whole or such part as he in his discretion shall think fit of the income of the expectant or presumptive share of my nephew the said Stephen Crane in the said Trust premises under the trusts hereinbefore contained for or towards his maintenance education advancement and support and may pay the same to his parent guardian or guardians for the purposes aforesaid without seeing to the application thereof.

8. I declare that all moneys liable to be invested under this my Will may be invested in Government securities or any other stocks funds or securities authorized by law for trust funds or in the purchase of inscribed stock of any British Colony or on mortgages of any leasehold houses in England or Wales held for any term having sixty years to run at the time of the investment And I declare that the power of appointing new Trustees conferred by Statute shall for the purposes of this my Will be vested in my wife during her life And I also declare that my executors and trustees for the time being of this my Will may instead of acting personally employ and pay a solicitor or other person to transact any business or do any act requiring to be done in connection with the administration of my estate or to trusts hereby declared including the receipt and payment of money and that any executor or trustee being a solicitor or other person engaged in any profession or business may be so employed and shall be entitled to charge and be paid all professional or other charges for any business or act done by him or his firm in connection with the trust including any act which an executor or trustee not being a Solicitor or other person engaged as aforesaid could have done personally In Witness Whereof I have to this and the two preceding sheets of paper set my hand this 21st day of April one thousand nine hundred.

Stephen Crane

Signed by the above named Stephen Crane as his last will in the presence of us both being present at the same time who in his presence at his request and in the presence of each other have hereunto subscribed our names as witnesses.

Ernest B. Skinner, Bank House Rye Sussex
Charlotte Edith Gardner 8 New Cavendish St
Portland Place London

THIS IS A CODICIL to the last will and testament of me Stephen Crane of Brede Place Northiam in the County of Sussex Author which Will bears date 21st day of April one thousand nine hundred.

1. I give all my plate linen china glass books pictures prints wines liquors furniture and other household effects watches jewels trinkets personal ornaments and wearing apparel and all my horses carriages harness saddlery and Stable furniture plants and garden tools and implements unto my dear wife Cora Howarth Crane absolutely and I direct that as far as the law will allow my debts funeral and testament expenses shall be primarily borne by my real and leasehold estates whether situate in this Country or elsewhere.

2. I direct that all Royalties arising from my literary works or the dramatization thereof shall be treated as income of my estate and shall be enjoyed by my said wife in specie during her life or until remarriage. And in all other respects I confirm my said Will. In Witness Whereof I have hereunto set my hand this 21st day of April one thousand nine hundred.

Stephen Crane

Signed by the said Stephen Crane the testator as and for a Codicil to his last will and testament in the presence of us present at the same time who at his request in his presence and in the presence of each other have hereunto subscribed our names as witnesses.

Ernest B. Skinner, Bank House, Rye, Sussex
Charlotte Edith Gardner, 8 New Cavendish St. Portland Place

The Correspondence of William Howe Crane and Cora Crane with Paul Revere Reynolds in the Matter of *Last Words*

Cora's letters and the paraphrased letters of Judge Crane to Reynolds, below, are from the Clifton Waller Barrett Collection at the University of Virginia. Reynolds' reply to Cora of May 14, 1900, is in the Columbia University Crane Collection.

> *6 Milborne Grove/ The Boltons/ S.W./ April 16th 1901*
> [Dear Mr. Reynolds]:/ If you have not already sent me draft, please address me care Mrs. Holder—156 West 128th St. N.Y. City, as I am coming to America in a few weeks time. Please do not fail that I may get money for book of short stories then.
>
>   C. H. Crane

Her next appeal was more urgent in tone:

> *6, Milborne Grove,/ The Boltons, South Kensington,/London/*
>   April 26th 1901
> Dear Mr. Reynolds:/ I am sailing for America on the Pennsylvania Hamburg Line, on the 30th April. I expect to be in New York on the 10th [of May]. Will you please say to Henry T. Coates and company of Philadelphia, that I own the exclusive book rights of the book of short stories which I am selling to them. Mr. Crane never sold book rights of short stories except those sold to Harpers by yourself. They published stories first in their magazine and then in book form.
>
> *Please* do your utmost to get the £50—for me. As I shall land in N.Y. without money and must send money back here to save my things. I also want to go directly to Ky. where I am to spend the summer. I enclose a separate letter which can serve as contract and which you can send to Coates & Co.
>
>   Faithfully,
>   C. H. Crane
>
> P.S. The story which you sent to Mr. Stokes called Cowardice, I have sold all serial rights of to the Northern Newspaper Syndicate here.
>
>   C.C.

Cora's sailing date, for whatever reasons, was advanced to April 29. Reynolds meanwhile had received a letter from Henry T. Coates & Company expressing willingness to pay to him the fifty pounds agreed upon for the book of short stories, but raising the question of earlier copyrights. Reynolds replied to Cora on May 14:

I have received the advance of $250.00 from Messrs. Henry T. Coates & Co. After deducting my 10 per cent commission and $2.63 for postage charges and cost of telegrams to Philadelphia, etc., it leaves a balance of $222.37. Remembering that I paid to Judge Crane some money that I received for a story from the Cosmopolitan entitled "The Great Boer Trek" I asked Judge Crane, as executor of Mr. Stephen Crane's will, if he had any objection to my paying such money to you. He replies that while he is not prepared to say he objects, at the same time he does not consent to such payment. You will see that if I paid this money to anyone but the person who has legal authority to receive it, I may render myself personally liable for the amount of such money. I, therefore, suggest that you see Judge Crane, who is now permanently settled in New York . . . and straighten the matter out with him. As soon as he consents I shall be glad to turn the money over to you. I hope that this will not put you to trouble and to serious inconvenience. Judge Crane said he should be glad to talk the matter over with you.

Cora answered the next day:

> Ashland House/ 15th May 1901
>
> Dear Mr. Reynolds:/ Your letter just recieved [sic]. I am glad to hear that you have cheque for the book of short stories. I will write to my brother in law Judge Crane and I cannot see what objection he can have to this money being paid to me. The book-rights belong to me, the work of revising and collecting was done by me to some stories almost written by me. You recieved [sic] ms. from me and so of course I hold you responsible for the amt. re-cieved [sic]. You will please hold cheque until matter is settled.
>
> Very Sincerely,
> Mrs. Stephen Crane

We do not know whether the interview suggested by Reynolds ever actually took place. He shortly received a letter (June 21, 1901) from Judge Crane saying that he had written to Cora asking her consent that the $150 be paid to him as executor of Stephen's estate. On July 13, Judge Crane requested a list of the stories that made up Stephen Crane's *Last Words*, wishing to see if it was identical with the contracted English edition.

On October 21, Judge Crane refused to give his consent to Reynolds' paying Cora the $122.37 balance, saying that he had learned from the English executor that the same stories, under the same title, had been sold in England and that Cora had not made claim to their ownership but had filed a claim for compensation for her work in getting them into shape. He promised to write to

Cora, giving her the information gained from the English executor.

The sum in Reynolds' hands had by now become $122.37, in lieu of the earlier figure of $222.37. Whether Reynolds had out of kindness made himself responsible for an advance of $100 to Cora, or whether this amount was owed him against earlier advances is uncertain, but the letter of November 11, below, seems to point to an advance to her. The next communication from Judge Crane was dated November 6 and restated the remarks of the English executor on *Last Words* and the fact that Cora had merely filed claim for recompense for her services. He advised that he had written Cora "that she'd better consent that the money" be paid to him. Because she had not answered his letter, he recommended strongly that Reynolds pay him the amount, adding that this letter was to be taken as his agreement to indemnify Reynolds against any further payment to Cora.

On November 11, probably in response to some challenge from Reynolds, came a more detailed version of the position now taken by Judge Crane. Cora had gathered a number of Stephen's un-published stories from his brothers and sisters and from the files of various newspapers. The rights for publication were sold in both England and America. Because these stories were the prop-erty of the estate, there was no doubt that the proceeds of the sale should be paid to the American Executor, Judge Crane him-self. Cora had been paid by the English executor for her services, and the $100 paid her by Reynolds was to be credited upon that bill. She had no claim whatever to be owner of the stories nor any on the proceeds of the American sale. He attempted to justify his position by remarking that he might be obliged to account for the advance Stephen had received on his unfinished novel, *The O'Ruddy*.

Obviously, in this letter of November 11 Judge Crane is con-testing not only Cora's claim to ownership of copyrights, but like-wise to any portion of the corpus of Stephen Crane's estate—whether with knowledge, or surmise, that her connection with Crane had not been sanctified in law by even a civil ceremony. Reynolds, having put himself out on a limb, was now obliged to retreat; and Plant appears to have had no inkling of the way the wind was blowing.

With two further perfunctory notes the test issue of *Last Words* was closed. Judge Crane wrote on November 14 that he had received a letter from A. T. Plant, the English executor, who said that Mrs. Crane "has already been paid for the work she expended on the book" (*Last Words*). And in a brief note, dated November 19, he acknowledged receipt of the check for the balance left in Reynolds' hands, $122.27.

APPENDIX THREE

Controversy: Sources of Misinformation

WHATEVER ELSE may be said of Cora Taylor, in her grave or riding out in her victoria, for sixty years she has never ceased to be a figure of conspicuous interest. At her death in 1910, gossip and the lurid backwash of a murder trial in which the murderer, Hammond P. McNeil, won acquittal by libeling Cora, who was then his wife, had already converted her name into a byword and a subject for indecent jokes. The Sheriff of Duval County, a gentleman with a fondness for horseplay, is reported to have called up personally some five or six of Jacksonville's leading citizens next day to announce that each had been left $5,000 in Cora's will—on condition that they act as pall bearers at the funeral. At these tidings, the beneficiaries are said to have hastily left town.

The high flavor of such choice tidbits, and his loathing of Stephen Crane's "horrid books" (*The St. Johns*, p. 283), may have induced Branch Cabell to end his book on the river, subtitled "A Paradise of Diversities," with a mishmash of invention and misrepresentation under the title of "Cora Comes Back." Although Cabell's collaborator, A. J. Hanna, opposed inclusion in the St. John's River book of this colorful, if untrue, elaboration, the chapter stayed in and became, regrettably, almost the only available account of Cora Taylor and her relationship with Crane, the book it adorns having circulated widely among colleges and universities. (*The St. Johns: A Paradise of Diversities*, American River Series [New York: Farrar & Rinehart, 1943]). But the sheriff's witticism points up the fact that Mr. Cabell was by no means the only offender in this respect. Very many others have thought it no sin to slander the memory of a dead woman, who suffered greatly in her fall in society and reaped a harvest of self-sown follies.

For particulars as to Cora's romance with Crane and the two places she operated in the city, before and after the period of their association, Mr. Hanna approached a Jacksonville attorney, R. P. Daniel. Mr. Daniel, in the belief that one George M. Powell had at a time unspecified been Cora's attorney, referred Mr. Hanna to Mr. Powell for details which the latter transmitted in an unpublished letter addressed to Mr. Daniel. For copies in my possession of this letter written to Daniel; of Hanna's rough narrative, which was redrafted by Mr. Cabell to become "Cora Comes Back"; and of an unpublished letter from Carl Bohnenberger to the editor of the *American Mercury*, May 28, 1934, in which Bohnenberger takes issue with another correspondent (Richmond Barrett), I am indebted to John S. Mayfield, of Bethesda, Maryland. A typescript of Bohnenberger's unfinished sketch, "Cora Crane," came to me several years ago from my good friend, Alfred Hanna.

Until his death some ten years ago, George Powell was known to Jacksonville as a talented scapegrace whose considerable legal and social endowments were unfortunately dissipated in an over-avid pursuit of "wine, women, and song." According to his own statement in the letter addressed to R. P. Daniel, he first came to Jacksonville in 1881, as a boy of eight, and soon afterwards moved south with his family to Deland. This would make him born in 1873. It is possible, though not certain, that he had passed his bar examination and been admitted to law practice in Jacksonville at the age of twenty-three—the year of Cora Taylor's meeting with Stephen Crane. But there is no discernible evidence anywhere to sustain George Powell's claim to having been Cora Taylor's legal representative at any time. Known facts, and circumstantial evidence, are all to the contrary:

1. First and foremost, no record exists of any defense action ever handled by Mr. Powell for a defendant listed under the names of Taylor, Crane, Stewart, or McNeil. A check of dockets from 1901 to 1913 in the Clerk's office of the Circuit Court for Duval County turned up four proceedings involving Cora, records of which one of the Deputy Clerks, Miss Abbie Barrs, furnished me. This list,

with explanatory notes supplied me by my relative and family attorney Philip S. May, also of Jacksonville, here follows:

> W. B. Camp vs. Cora Taylor
> No. 758-L. Box 16.
> D. U. Fletcher, Attorney for W. B. Camp.
> H. E. Bowden, Attorney for Cora Taylor.
> Suit filed 2/19/1903 and Dismissed in
> Open Court 5/4/1903.

Says Mr. May, "W. B. Camp was an architect. Suit was pending at about the time of construction of 'The Court' and probably grew out of a controversy about the architect's fee."

> Marion Dickman vs. Cora Crane
> No. 1037-L. Box 44.
> Attorney for Marion Dickman, P. H. Smith.
> Attorney for Cora Crane, D. C. Campbell.
> Suit filed 5/26/1904.
> Praecipe for Dismissal 11/30/1904 and Entry
> same date.
> As action of Assumpsit—Damages $1,000.00
> Declaration not in file.

"An action of assumpsit was a suit for money owing to the plaintiff by the defendant growing out of some contractual relation. Pleas were filed on behalf of Cora by Campbell. She signed the affidavit as to the truth of the pleas which denied the original indebtedness and pleaded payment. The praecipe for dismissal shows that a settlement of the suit was made."

> Charles C. Butler vs. Cora E. Crane
> No. 968-E. Box 45.
> Attorney for the plaintiff, Harwich
> and Farris.
> Attorney for defendant, D. C. Campbell.
> Mortgage Foreclosure—"$8,800.00—Lot 1
> Block 3, Div. "B" LaVilla, etc.
> Dismissed Sept. 26. 1904—Upon Written
> Stipulation and Agreement.

> J. S. Jones vs. Cora McNeil and H. P. McNeil
> No. 1953-L. Box 442.

Attorney for Plaintiff, H. C. Andrews.
Attorney for Defendant, D. C. Campbell.
Cause of action: Plaintiff attacked and bitten
by dog belonging to Cora McNeil. Damages sought $1,000.00. No judgment shown.
Suit filed 11/2/1908—Progress Docket
shows "5-13-1914 Ordered Stricken."

Halstead E. Bowden, Cora's attorney in the first suit, shortly afterwards moved to another city, and D. C. Campbell, who in 1903 was not yet practising law in Jacksonville, began handling her affairs. As indicated in Chapter 8, it is elsewhere on record that Campbell continued as Cora's legal representative to the end of her life. This is in flat contradiction to Powell's statement, which appears to be a fabrication in part from court records with himself substituted in the role of Cora's legal advisor: *"After the Court was finished, as formerly, most of my professional service had to do with protecting her against too violent attempts on the part of creditors to sell the place, which I succeeded in doing with the aid of sundry 'touches' made by her on either very drunk or very affluent friends."* (Italics mine.)

While the Court was under construction Cora's friends in the city, those who were sufficiently well-heeled and also well-disposed, may have come to her assistance with money for her daily needs. That much is probably true. But for the rest, her notes in two Jacksonville banks, attested to by the diary of 1907; interest payments on these bank loans; and D. C. Campbell's outsmarting of the designs of Charles C. Butler, who had loaned her money to build the Court, to oust her from its ownership and take over the business—these give the lie to "sundry touches," which like the rest of his claim seem to have existed chiefly in Mr. Powell's imagination.

2. If George Powell was actually Cora's legal advisor at the time of her meeting with Crane, it is surprising, to say the least, to find nowhere in his narrative any mention of business arrangements connected with her departure from Jacksonville—which is dismissed in a single sentence: "Shortly after this Cora went away, and I heard, joined Crane and went to Greece. . . ." This casual note has a hollow ring, for how could he, in charge of her affairs, not have known what disposition she made of her business—and the

lease on the Hotel de Dream? Why have kept back this *pièce de résistance*, while so evidently eager to tell all?

3. His picture of Cora's later financial plight is equally vague, a hodgepodge of contradictions. For on the one hand we find: "It was shortly after the great fire of May 3, 1901, and houses being scarce, she bought a place from one Edith Powers known as the New York House, on the south side of Ward Street about a block west of where she afterwards built 'The Court.'" But the very next sentence points to "*extreme financial stringency*. One of the girls who returned to America with Cora told me that they arrived on the pier in New York flat broke." The next paragraph however introduces "a nifty little victoria" with "a well setup darkey" in "pongee livery"; and then, "Not content with the New York place and the Victoria, she decided to build a larger place. . . ." All of which, we are invited to assume, was accomplished by means of "sundry touches."

The location of the New York House, as far as we know, is correct. But no Edith Powers is listed in the City Directory; nor does Cora's name appear until 1904, the year after the Court began operation. If Edith Powers was an operator whose name did not appear—as many did not—and if she were also a friend, she may have sheltered Cora in return for the services of hostess until the Court was open for business. The possibility is still remote, as the diary makes no mention of anyone by that name. "One of the girls who returned to America with Cora" perhaps refers to Hattie Mason, whom Cora hustled off on the trip to England in 1907, to prevent her appearance at the trial as a witness against McNeil. But Mr. Powell jumbles facts and chronology here, making it appear that he is discussing one particular sequence of events while pointing to another. As to "the scarcity of houses," it is simply inconceivable that a member of the Jacksonville bar could have been in ignorance of the fact that "the line" had not burned in the great fire! But the crucial evidence which discredits Mr. Powell's story is the fact that *Cora Taylor's alleged purchase of the New York House is not covered by the records pertaining to her property holdings and real estate transactions*. These have already been dealt with in Chapters 1 and 8, and my indebtedness to the Title & Trust Company of Florida for making the complete information available is recorded elsewhere.

Cora's "aloofness," even more pronounced during the Court era than in the old days of the Hotel de Dream, must have piqued more than one gentleman who failed to receive one of the sought after invitations to week-end beach parties at "Palmetto Lodge"—Cora's cottage at Pablo Beach. Whether pique in this case is the explanation of George Powell's peculiar claim to having been her attorney and confidant, or an inverted form of vanity, I leave to the psychologists. Whatever the reasons, a great cloud of witnesses sprang up all of a sudden after Cora Taylor's death—like the blackbirds out of the pie—claiming intimacy with her on one footing or another. Needless to say, the motives of these people were extraordinarily mixed. But the weirdest of all pretenders in this crazy crew was a young man from Massachusetts, who announced himself Cora's illegitimate son! Philip May, who was visited by the young man, became convinced that he was an impostor.

There is surely nothing incriminating in Mr. Powell's occasional lapses of memory, wherein he confuses—years later—the *Commodore* with the *Dauntless*, sister ships in the filibustering fleet carrying arms to Cuba; and makes Victor DeL. Mudge, the divorce lawyer, the husband of Ethel Dreme (whose name he misspells as "Dream," a slip pounced on and exploited by Cabell). Quite another case is the pejorative reference to Cora's "accumulated matrimonial experiences," which gratuitously throws in "Jones" after the unsubstantiated "Taylor," again plucked, perhaps, from court records (J. S. Jones vs. Cora McNeil and H. P. McNeil). Or just Everyman Jones? Cabell elaborates (p. 279): "It seems that after checking out on two or three no-account husbands—Cora was always a little bit vague as to just how many of them—why, she got to living in sin and all sorts of other luxuries on the yacht of a rich bachelor; and they had been drinking their way around a considerable part of the known world."

Taken as a whole, the Powell letter is a jumble of contradictions bearing little relation to the facts on record, which the writer might easily have had at his disposal had he cared to make use of them. This is the first conclusion to be drawn from it. The second is similar, viz., that Mr. Powell is writing not what he knows, but for the most part what he has picked up here and there *after the fact*. The most glaring example of this is in reference to the Conrad letters. Powell knew, of course, that Carl Bohnenberger—Assistant Librarian of the Jacksonville Free Public Library—edited and published Joseph Conrad's letters to Stephen and Cora Crane in the *Bookman* (May-June, 1929), but he had not read them. He very likely did read Thomas Beer's biography of Crane, absorbed from it a sympathetic impression of Cora's rising at midnight to serve food and drink to the visitors swarming on Brede Place, and from the same source also learned of the critic James Huneker's friendship with Crane in New York. So putting two and two together to make five, he has Conrad "describing" in the correspondence the incursions at Brede Place; likewise Huneker, in his autobiography *Steeplejack*. Huneker, of course, was never near Brede Place; and in *Steeplejack* he writes Crane off with only passing mention. (James G. Huneker, *Steeplejack* [New York: Scribner's, 1920], II, 128.)

One other similar instance of transfers after the fact must be mentioned, because it turns up again in Cabell—blown up. Mr. Powell evidently had read Beer's article in the *American Mercury*, "Mrs. Stephen Crane," and noted well a quoted bit from a letter of Richard Harding Davis to Mrs. Charles Sidmore—June 11, 1913: "The common story is that she was the mistress of a Jacksonville politician when Crane met her." Davis is rather notorious for his easy recollection of things after the fact (see Scott C. Osborn to Lillian Gilkes, pp. 75-6n.); since he was not on the scene at the time of which he writes one must conclude that he was repeating local gossip. Skirting the risk of libel, Powell cagily transforms the politician into a gambler "well setup, well dressed," adding, "whose name because of relatives living we will not state." Cabell changes him back into politician, while repeating the mention of living relatives (*The St. Johns*, p. 280). Now it so happens that Powell's description fits none of the politicians who were on the scene in the era of the Hotel de Dream. It fits, with a fair degree of accuracy, one who in the year 1913 entered the Florida Legislature and was one of the most progressive politicians Jacksonville ever produced, in recognition of which fact a grateful citizenry later named a bridge after him. Aside from the fact that Cora Taylor was already three years dead in 1913, the linking of this man's name with hers is simply mischievous nonsense.

In addition to having collaborated on publication of the Conrad letters, Bohnenberger and Norman M. Hill were joint owners of the collection now at Columbia University, originally known as the Bohnenberger-Hill Collection. Mystery surrounds the earlier history of the Crane papers—including the library from Brede Place, which George Powell says was offered to him by Cora and refused. The generally accepted theory is that Bohnenberger and Henry W. Walters, an employe of the Jacksonville Gas Company who became acquainted with Cora in the course of his reading the gas meters at the Court, purchased the collection which had been stored in a trunk for the sum of five hundred dollars. Circumstances point to the conclusion that sometime previously, perhaps during the four days between Cora Taylor's death and the filing of her will for probate, the trunk may have been stolen from the Court by someone aware of the future value of its contents, as the papers were not found among her personal effects. These, together with all other property, including real estate, were left to a Jacksonville businessman, Ernest C. Budd (see Chapter, 8, and Appendix Four).

Bohnenberger, who was killed in an automobile accident in September, 1935, left an unfinished sketch, "Cora Crane," which, though signed with his name, shows evidence of having been written by someone else. Aside from such inexcusable slips in writing "Imogene Clark," for "Imogene Carter"; "Jimmy" Higgins for Billy Higgins, the oiler in the *Open Boat;* "Eben Holden" for Eben Alexander, American Minister to Greece (*Eben Holden* was the title of a novel by Irving Bacheller [Boston: Lothrop, 1900], it is difficult to put together the attitude of hostile aspersion in this piece with Bohnenberger's rather sentimental championship of Cora in the *American Mercury* (May 28, 1934).

But by no ingenuity known to man could the entire collection, including books, have been got into a single trunk! Its very bulk, before cataloguing, must also have presented an obstacle to intelligent use. The explorer plunging in would have need of patience, leisure, a sustaining and disciplined curiosity divested of all bias, if in the process of assembling scattered bits and pieces of the Crane story any sense were to be made of new data unearthed. The preliminary rough cataloguing was probably done by Bohnenberger, no small task in itself. But he unfortunately did not have the necessary leisure for a thoroughgoing examination of the collection's contents, and the temptation to write was too strong. So he romanticized and invented—if the incomplete sketch is, indeed, of his authorship.

Since inaccuracies and distortions in the Bohnenberger manuscript are legion, any attempt to trace them all is but a tedious laboring of the point. I shall deal with four typical examples, three of which are repeated and enlarged upon in Cabell:

1. While presenting Cora as a vampire who transformed Crane into "a doomed and chained man," the author of this dubious narrative appears anxious to soften the judgment slightly by minimizing her "past." To this end, in flagrant violation of facts and dates, he brings Cora and Stephen together for the first time at a dance at the Hotel St. James in "rainy April"—1896. The dance, he says, and the lovers' meeting coincided with Cora's arrival in Jacksonville on the millionaire's yacht the very same evening! He also says that Crane remained in Jacksonville "only seven months" [actually, it was four and a half months], which would put the *Commodore* sinking sometime in October or November instead of January 1, 1897. It is difficult for anyone who knew Bohnenberger, who was thoroughly familiar with the biographical data assembled and set forth in Beer's book, and who when I knew him had the makings of an able scholar, to believe that he could have been guilty of any such careless or willful garbling of the facts on record.

2. The author of the Bohnenberger manuscript, whoever he was, of course had access to the papers now in the Columbia University Crane Collection. A quick glance at Cora's correspondence with the English artist Clement Flower (see Chapter Seven) must have shown him that, before she left England, Flower had painted Crane's portrait. Enough; the portrait, thereafter, hung in the Court! But none of the witnesses I interviewed in Jacksonville who had been inside the Court, including Mr. Henry W. Walters, had ever laid eyes on this portrait, or heard of it; nor has any trace of it yet come to light on this side of the Atlantic. The only sensible conclusion to be drawn from the Flower correspondence, it seems to me, is that since Cora was unable to pay for the portrait—as she confessed to Flower—it was retained by the artist himself. The portrait reappears nevertheless, with romantic embellishments, in Powell's narrative and in "Cora Comes Back."

3. In his unpublished letter to the *American Mercury* Bohnen-

berger claims to have been one of the last persons to walk through the "desolate hallways" of the Court before the red-brick building was pulled down in 1928. In this letter and in the manuscript sketch, its location is given as the corner of Madison and Houston Streets; and Cabell repeats. Powell mentions only Ward Street, which later had its name changed to Houston when a crusading city administration decided to close up the red-light district. The Court is listed in the City Directory at 120 Davis Street and 900 Ward Street, the place actually faced on two streets. But since the main entrance was on Davis Street, this number was the one generally used and is the address given in Cora's diary (1907). Madison Street, which was officially included in the red-light district during Cora's tenure of the Court, parallels Davis Street one block to the east; Bohnenberger's mention of it as the site of the Court is therefore incorrect.

4. In the Bohnenberger manuscript the Court is described as "rather a colossus of a place," which "undoubtedly was to resemble something—either in the woman's life or out of a book of architecture . . . supported on each side by turret-like bulges of brick which gave the place a castle-front, a tinge of romance. . . . The arches were a miniature reflection of vaster ones in medieval castles." And in his letter to the *American Mercury* Bohnenberger is even more explicit: "The architecture was, in a thin-skeleton fashion, reminiscent of Brede Castle. . . . It was an extensive mansion, sumptuous for its day, two stories in height, of bitter red brick, with battlements, a ball room, lovely garden, wide and long veranda . . . and a chapel room, what subtle mockery, spacious diningroom, and other charming attributes."

The metamorphosis of the fourteenth century manor house into a "castle" is perhaps typical of the way in which legend and myth of the grandiose operated in the lives of Cora Taylor and Stephen Crane, changing all that they touched into something larger than reality. No less preposterous is the fabled resemblance between the Court and Brede House; or the myth of an imposing "mahogany" staircase transplanted from Brede Place (where the woodwork was oak). If Bohnenberger was the planter of this giant beanstalk which went on growing after his own death, we find its green tendrils—turrets, battlements, and staircase—blossoming forth again in Powell's narrative and in "Cora Comes Back."

As is readily seen from the photograph reproduced on page 333, the Court was no more a "colossus" than its alleged prototype in Sussex, but a rather sedate-looking edifice about the size of a small apartment building. The two octagonal bay windows at each of the front corners—only one of which is visible in the photograph—are, I suppose, what is meant by "battlements." Brede Manor (see photograph p. 145) has a single tower whose sole resemblance to this pair is its octagonal shape. The "lovely garden" is as shown in the photo. Various snapshots of Cora's "girls," in the Columbia Collection, taken in the backyard of the Court—the "patio" referred to in the Bohnenberger manuscript?—show a second story back veranda such as was common in suburban apartment dwellings of that day and this. But no "rare plant" specimens are detectable with a microscope—unless one chooses to consider in that category the floral backdrops of photographer's studios frequented by the girls to have their likenesses "struck," caressing ostriches and stuffed alligators. I have heard nothing of any "wall" erected there; but an entry in Cora's diary—April 1, 1907—records the purchase of sixty fence posts, thirty-nine of which were for the Court. The photograph of the Court shows fence posts in use along the Davis Street frontage, a privet hedge answering the purpose on the Ward Street side.

The chapel room may be dismissed as pure myth, with nothing more substantial behind it than a crucifix in Cora's bedroom. I have heard—from one source only, Mr. Henry W. Walters—that her Roman Catholic leanings grew stronger toward the end of her life as the shadows closed in. Possibly so; but if true, the crucifix is to date the single piece of evidence.

By all the rules, a historian has the obligation to investigate his sources—though Mr. Cabell may have preferred to let his readers think he was writing fiction. Mr. Cabell cannot be held accountable for ignorance of the facts contained in the papers now at Columbia, and not then available. Other than the Powell letter and the Bohnenberger manuscript, however, the only source on record he appears to have drawn upon was Hammond P. Mc-Neil's bill of complaint in the divorce case. The circumstances, in this instance, hardly tend to improve the plaintiff's record for veracity.

The McNeil murder case was fully reported in both the *Florida Times-Union* and the *Jacksonville Evening Metropolis*, whose files

Mr. Cabell evidently did not consult. He preferred instead—writing fiction—to put the murder in Cora's bedroom, with no other witnesses present. Actually, the murder was committed upon a public road (see Chapter 8) with four other witnesses present, all of whom testified at the preliminary hearing before Justice Greenberg on August 13 (1907) and—except Hattie Mason—later at the trial.

APPENDIX FOUR

The Final Disposition of Cora Taylor's Personal Property and Real Estate

ACCORDING TO the statement of Cora's executor Ernest C. Budd, who under the will was named sole heir to all of her property, real and personal, she left debts amounting to $14,176.18; "and certain personal property inventoried and appraised" at $7,631.11. No valuation was placed on the real estate, which, for reasons presently to be made clear, was sold at auction on the Courthouse steps at a sheriff's sale on April 3, 1911.

Needless to say, no detailed study of Cora's debts checked against assets is possible without all of the bills, receipts, promissory notes, sworn statements of account, etc., which no longer exist. It must suffice here to present the picture somewhat cursorily, in rough outline, stressing only the highlights.

In this connection, it should be noted that originals of the inventory, the list of debts, and of Ernest Budd's Petition to the County Judge's Court (to sell real estate) from which the following interpretation is developed, are among the documents which in recent years have disappeared from the public files in Jacksonville. Copies of these records, however, were obtained previously by Ames W. Williams, and were included in a collection of Crane material later acquired from him by the Syracuse University Library, to whom grateful acknowledgment is herein made.

Included under debts are Cora's mortgage notes on the beach property, $750; 915 Ward Street, $1,200; and C. C. Butler's mortgage on the Court, which had been reduced from $8,800 to $6,300 since assignment was made to the Atlantic National Bank, presumably on or before Butler's death.

Other items in the red column are funeral expenses, $805; unpaid City taxes for 1909; City, State and County Taxes, 1910; insurance on the Court and 915 Ward Street; and two promissory notes in amounts respectively of $250 and $120.71. The authenticity of these various obligations can hardly be in dispute.

But the mists begin to gather when we come to such things as unpaid doctor bills (for the girls), grocery, liquor, and laundry bills, etc., and large sums owing to two meat markets for what would seem to have been supplies for a whole year. Evidently, they were living high off the hog at the Court that year! Presumably, it was the responsibility of Cora's housekeeper, to whom she must have given a limited power of attorney authorizing maintenance purchases, to pay operating expenses out of earnings. These bills are, with a single exception, of Jacksonville origin, none bearing the names of Pablo Beach merchants; and no one, not even Campbell, who might have been expected to keep a watchful eye on the purse strings, seems to have watched the budget. We are familiar with Cora's extravagance at Brede Place, but it never included anything comparable to a bill from the Atlanta Silk Garment Company for $926.50!

Out of the mists that final year there emerges the cloudy image of a woman sick and dying, cruelly fleeced by those she entrusted with the management of her affairs.

There is no point in reproducing here the complete inventory of personal property, but in addition to clothing and jewelry valued at $1000 certain items are of special interest in relation to the total indebtedness. The following are listed among Court properties:

12 doz. pieces flat solid silver		$150.00
1 Silver plate		5.00
1 Gold knife and fork		5.00
Pearl handled cutlery & salt cellars silver		5.00
1 Sewing machine		25.00
Room #20,	Kimball piano & stool	250.00
Ball Room,	Peerless Auto Piano	450.00
	Davenport	35.00

Diningroom, Table & chairs 75.00
　　　　　Buffet 25.00
　　　　　Serving table 10.00
　　　　　Kitchen utensils and stove 100.00
Room #16,　100 books 100.00
Stable [915 Ward Street], 1 Set Harness 20.00
　　　　　1 Black Horse 150.00
　　　　　1 Victoria 175.00
　　　　　1 Rockaway 175.00
　　　　　1 Saddle & Bridle 5.00

Other furnishings at 915 Ward Street, including 76 books and 74 Victor Gramaphone records, totaled $156.

Palmetto Lodge:
　　　　　1 Station Wagon 75.00
　　　　　1 Set Harness 15.00
　　　　　1 Bay Horse 100.00
　　　　　2 Hogs .... 2.50 each
　　　　　2 Heifers about year old .... 6.00 each
　　　　　1 Calf 5.00
　　　　　1 Bull 50.00
　　　　　35 Chickens 17.50
　　　　　40 Pigeons 10.00
　　　　　1 Cow 50.00

Ernest Budd's sworn statement (in petition to sell real estate) declares that "owing to the character of the property and the use that had been made thereof, your orator was compelled to sell the same [personal property] at a sacrifice and your orator sold the same for the·sum of One Thousand Dollars ($1000.00), that being the best price that he could procure therefor." (The livestock was evidently tainted, like the rest of the furniture!)

While a few derived some entertainment from Ernest Budd's legacy, for the most part it created a furor of moral indignation. But Cora Taylor's estate was too rich a plum, in the eyes of certain individuals, to be allowed to fall into the lap of an alcoholic wastrel; a corporation known as the Capital Investment Company was organized in Duval County to prevent such a miscarriage of justice. The president of this perfumed combination was one George W. Russell, a figure familiar in ward politics and in "line" operations after C. C. Butler's death; its vice-president, and very likely the master mind backstage, was none other than Butler's archfoe, David C. Campbell—Cora's attorney.

But Ernest Budd, too, had debts. The bank called in his notes and got judgment, forcing the sale at auction of Cora Taylor's real estate, as above noted; or in the language of the newspaper notice —*Florida Evening Metropolis*, April 3, 1911: "Pursuant to execution issued out of the Circuit Court, for Duval County, on March 1, 1911 in favor of the Barnett National Bank of Jacksonville against Ernest C. Budd for $676.00 and cost, and by virtue of another execution from the same Court, same day, same parties for $784.00 and cost, both of which executions were delivered to the Sheriff March 3, 1911, the Sheriff levied on the land above described on April 3, 1911." The Sheriff's Deed of same date, to the Capital Investment Company, covers "all right, title and interest which Ernest C. Budd, executor and sole heir to the Estate of Cora E. Crane, had on March 3, 1911 or thereafter" in the Court property, 915 Ward Street, and Palmetto Lodge.

The Capital Investment Company presently gave a Warranty Deed to George W. Russell covering the Court property, which had been obtained on a bid of $5,000 in the sale, the mortgage encumbering it assumed by Russell in the conveyance. Then on October 1, 1911 the building was leased to one S. Friend for "a furnished boarding-house," for five years, the lessee paying $24,-400. Contract provided for payments to start at a monthly rental of $250, with an annual increase of $50 per month for the duration.

The total sum realized from the Sheriff's sale was $6,500. Palmetto Lodge brought $1,200. But 915 Ward Street went for a mere $300—one-tenth of the figure Cora had refused in 1907, less than a year after she acquired it, for half of the lot! The other half, the corner lot, changed hands a number of times, was finally sold to Jeffries Meat Market, which has erected on the site a large two-story brick building for use as a warehouse. The price paid in 1941 was $82,000.

By now, certain questions to which I have no answers must have become obvious: (1) Why did the Court permit all of the property to be sold, when the sum total of Ernest Budd's indebtedness in the suit with the bank, exclusive of costs, was under $1,500?

(2) Was there, or was there not, an order of confirmation from the Court authorizing the Sheriff to proceed against the entire corpus? If such an order was ever issued, it is nowhere to be found among existing records on file or available from private sources. (3) Why did not the other Estate creditors come forward, at this time, to assert their claims? Some light on these questions, however incomplete, may possibly be gleaned from the following:

A single piece of Cora's real estate remained in Ernest Budd's hands after the Sheriff and the Capital Investment Company got through, an ocean-front lot adjoining Palmetto Lodge, which she had acquired in December of 1909, presumably paying cash. It was probably upon the basis of this claim that a Petition to Sell Real Estate, filed on April 2, 1912—one year *after* the Sheriff's sale—was initiated. In the Petition Budd is apparently contesting the Sheriff's sale, and it seems altogether probable that he had by this time gotten together with the Estate creditors to undertake this action. The Petition asks that Ernest Budd "be directed to take possession" of Cora's real estate; "and that an order may be made . . . directing and authorizing the sale of said real estate, or so much thereof as may be necessary to pay the debts and obligations of the said Cora E. Crane, deceased"; that a Commissioner be appointed by the Court to superintend a public sale of the property for that purpose, "and that all persons in possession of said real estate or any part thereof surrender possession of the same to your petitioner as Executor of the last will and testament of Cora E. Crane. . . ."

We do not know what action, if any, was taken by the Court thereafter. But George W. Russell seems to have been left undisturbed in his lease of the Court property to S. Friend. Three years later—July 10, 1913—the property was sold to F. P. Lord for $30,000: $1,000 cash down, and $1,000 every sixty days thereafter until full amount was paid, with interest at eight per cent. The agreement recites lease to S. Friend, rents to be paid to Lord according to terms of the lease. Then on May 14, 1914, Lord gave a Quit Claim deed to Russell, who seems to have taken back the property the following year when Lord apparently defaulted.

It is entirely possible, of course, that the Court did order the real estate, or some portion of it, surrendered to Ernest Budd; and that Budd then got together in a deal with the Capital Investment Company and the creditors, which may have included settlement of claims to the creditors, in addition to payment of other personal debts outstanding of Budd's which did not figure in the earlier action brought by the bank.

But by 1916 George W. Russell had come into bad odor with the local authorities, and his departure from the city in haste and secrecy was necessary to avert unpleasant consequences. Also, the reform movement to close up the red-light district was making such headway that the victory of Van Swearingen over J.E.T. Bowden in the city election the following year seemed assured. So on March 16, 1916, George deeded the Court property over to his brother James W. Russell, in a transaction which recites an earlier unrecorded contract to one Daisy E. Mobley (July 15, 1915). He had already, the year before, unloaded 915 Ward Street in a sale for which the price received is not recorded, and in like manner disposed of the Pablo Beach property in 1912.

The election victory of Van Swearingen in 1917 was followed by an immediate and widespread scattering of "line" operators and madams, at which time Daisy E. Mobley—who apparently had taken over S. Friend's old lease on the Court—likewise skedaddled. She and James W. Russell both executed quit claim deeds on the same day—May 31, 1917—to the Atlanta, Birmingham and Atlantic Railway Company, who some while later sold the property to the Atlantic Coast Line Railroad. From 1917, the building itself stood unoccupied, a forlorn shell, the hang-out of thieves and vagrants, until its final demolition in 1928. The site now is a parking lot used by the railroad employees.

But sadder even than this ending were the last years of the Court's active life, when it was re-opened in 1911 as the "Whitehouse Hotel." Gone then were the carefully tended grass plots, the umbrella tree and privet hedge, with every visible trace of the personality of its original owner and creator. The octagonal bay window had been supplanted by a door giving access to the street, and another door cut through on the Ward Street side, thus providing two additional exits for quick getaways in the event of a police raid. These doorways, and the Davis Street main entrance, were hideously daubed with white paint; the stone trim too was painted white. The place was, indeed, nakedly transformed into that which it had never been in Cora Taylor's lifetime—a bawdy house.

Better to become a parking lot!

NOTES ON SOURCES

THE MAIN source of material pertaining to Cora—the things she said or thought, the way she felt about life and certain specific incidents, her impressions and observations on the world she moved in—is of course her notebooks and diaries in the Columbia University Stephen Crane Collection. All source material not otherwise identified is from this collection and is quoted or paraphrased by permission of the Columbia University Libraries. This material includes short quotations such as "Virtue never yet atoned for wrinkles, . . . " (p. 21), her remarks about "good" people (pp. 50-51), etc., as well as the long quoted passages setting forth her views on the night hours (p. 26), on the double standard (p. 47), etc. For a detailed explanation of the uses made in the text of Cora Crane's notebooks and diaries, see Appendix One.

Besides the diaries and notebooks, Cora wrote a great many letters to such friends as the H. G. Wellses, the Joseph Conrads, Mrs. Moreton Frewen; to agents and publishers in both England and the United States; and to relatives, lawyers, and other personal or business acquaintances: William Crane, David Belasco, Hamlin Garland, the United States Secretary of War, etc. These letters, scattered over England and America, are in collections and in private hands, and are generally identified in the notes of the chapter in which they appear.

Also in the separate chapter notes will be found two other primary sources of material concerning Cora, namely, her own writings, published and unpublished, most of which are in holograph manuscript in the Columbia University Crane Collection; and the personal recollections of people who had known her. A particularly valuable source of the latter kind, on which I have drawn heavily, is Thomas Beer's article, "Mrs. Stephen Crane," *American Mercury*, XXXI (March, 1934), pp. 289-295: a collection of letters from friends of Stephen and Cora, written in answer to queries by Mr. Beer or collected by him, and quoted here by the kind permission of Miss Alice Beer.

For background material concerning events in the life of Stephen Crane, and for a number of short quotes from his letters, I am indebted to Thomas Beer's biography, *Stephen Crane: A Study in American Letters* (New York: Knopf, 1927). For certain information not found in Beer I have drawn upon John Berryman's *Stephen Crane*, American Men of Letters Series (William Sloane Associates, 1950). To Daniel G. Hoffman, *The Poetry of Stephen Crane* (New York: Columbia University Press, 1957), I am heavily indebted for material and quotations touching on events, and especially influences, in the lives of both Stephen and Cora. For many quotations from Crane's stories, newspaper articles, and letters, I am indebted to R. W. Stallman, *Stephen Crane: An Omnibus* (New York: Knopf, 1952). References to these four important sources are cited in the notes below, under the headings of Beer, Berryman, Hoffman, and *Omnibus*.

All of the letters written by Stephen Crane, with the exception of five to Moreton Frewen and Mrs. Frewen quoted in Chapter 5, and many of Cora's letters written during their stay in England and after Stephen's death, as well as a large number of letters written to them, have been recently published in *Stephen Crane: Letters*, ed. R. W. Stallman and Lillian Gilkes (New York University Press, 1960). The ones published there for the first time are cited by "*Letters*" and a page number, and are reprinted here by permission of New York University Press.

CHAPTER 1: . . . *the Tall Swift Shadow of a Ship at Night*

THE DESCRIPTION of Cora as a "Tannhäuser Venus," is from a letter by Richmond Barrett in "Correspondence," *American Mercury*, XXXII (June, 1934), xx-xxi. Also from this letter, which contains Barrett's reminiscences of Stephen and Cora in Jacksonville, where he and his family wintered every year, are the remarks on the "class A rating" of the Hotel de Dream, the details on Crane's signing of the little Barrett girl's autograph book, and the incident in which Crane, riding in Cora's victoria, was snubbed by Mrs. Barrett. The remarks about Cora by Richard Harding Davis are from a letter he wrote June 11, 1913, to Mrs. Charles Sidmore, whom Cora knew at Brede as the young girl Vere, published in Thomas Beer's article, "Mrs. Stephen Crane," p. 291 (see also Appendix Three). For the comparison between Cora and the Decadents, see Hoffman, pp. 225-228. The prose-poem sketch, "What Hell Might Be," by Cora Crane, was published in *Smart Set*, November, 1901, p. 41.

The records of Cora Taylor's transactions in connection with the Hotel de Dream are in the possession of the Title and Trust Company of Florida, whose home office is at Jacksonville. These and other public records were saved from the great fire of May 3, 1901, when a citizen of Jacksonville risked his life to drag them out of the burning City Hall and ferried them across the St. John's River in a rowboat. The description of the Hotel de Dream, the quote, "a semi-circular sign . . . ," and other quotes from McCready, are from one of a series of long letters, some eighty manuscript pages, from Ernest W. McCready to Benjamin J. R. Stolper and now in the Columbia University Crane Collection. McCready at the time of which he writes was on the staff of the New York *Herald*. This correspondence is one of two eyewitness accounts to have come down from any source relating to events at the Hotel de Dream; the one other is Ralph D. Paine's expurgated account in *Roads of Adventure* (Boston: Houghton Mifflin, 1922). The McCready letters are dated January 12, 22, and 31, 1934; a portion of the January 22 letter, in which the above material appears, has been published in *Letters*, pp. 339-340. Spelling of the name Hotel de Dream is confused and controversial. Later belittlers of Cora Taylor have seized upon it as an exercise in phonetics and semantics, making her the butt of ridicule. I have adhered to the spelling in the McCready manuscript as probably the one used by Cora herself, reflecting her nonconformist sense of humor colored by romanticism. The comparison drawn between the Hotel de Dream and the sporting houses of the New Orleans Vieux Carré was suggested by the picture given in *Hear Me Talkin To Ya: The Story of Jazz by the Men Who Made It,* ed. Nat Shapiro and Nat Hentoff (New York: Rinehart, 1955).

The facts concerning the Howorth family are from Vital Statistics records in Philadelphia, New York, and Boston, and from property records looked up for me by Mrs. Hazel P. Brook of the New England Historic Genealogical Society. A copy of the pamphlet work by George Howorth is in the Columbia University Crane Collection. The Boston City Directory, 1867, lists Cora's uncle, "George Howorth, Jr. Capt., 1084 Washington Street"—a boarding-house. But the war record of this officer has not come to light in the National Archives. That of William L. Howorth is from Hammersley's *General Register of the U. S. Navy and Marine Corps.* The details of the Holder family history are from a letter written to Cora by her Aunt Mary Holder, letter No. 133 in the Columbia University Crane Collection. For the story of Christopher Holder, I am indebted to Mrs. Hazel P. Brook, Boston genealogist. Cora's remark that her grandfather had left her money "but no guardian" is from Edith Richie Jones, "Stephen Crane at Brede," *Atlantic Monthly,* 194 (July, 1954), 60.

The background on New York in the eighties is mainly from Lloyd Morris, *Incredible New York* (New York: Random House, 1951); but much other unquoted material has also been read and assimilated. The quote about women in the foyer is from p. 261. The article on "Homes for Good Girls" is from the New York *Press,* August 27, 1897. Mrs. Pell's article, quoted from, appeared in the *American Woman's Home Journal* of May 2, 1897.

The details concerning Florida, its development, and its wealthy promoters, at the time of Cora's arrival in Jacksonville, are from Kathryn Trimmer Abbey, *Florida: Land of Change* (Chapel Hill: University of North Carolina Press, 1941), pp. 351-354. A major source for Jacksonville background, in this and Chapter 8, is T. Frederick Davis, *History of Jacksonville* (Florida Historical Society, 1925).

The note concerning Miriam Follin's first marriage is from the biography of her by Madeleine B. Stern, *Purple Passage: The Life of Mrs. Frank Leslie* (Norman, Okla.: University of Oklahoma Press, 1953), pp. 16-17. H. G. Wells' views on women's rights are from *Experiment in Autobiography* (New York: Macmillan, 1934), p. 406. The line quoted from *Hedda Gabler* is from *Six Plays by Henrik Ibsen,* tr. and ed. Eva LeGallienne (Modern Library, 1957), p. 380.

For background material on Stephen Crane, at the time of his meeting with Cora Taylor in Jacksonville, I have relied heavily on Thomas Beer's biography, *Stephen Crane.* The quotation on Crane's urge to make his body "a testing ground for all sensations of living" is from Beer, p. 195. Also from Beer: Crane's remarks on "feminine mules," p. 142; on marriage "a base trick on women," p. 106; on streetwalkers, pp. 148 and 206; on Hell, p. 50; on going to Greece, p. 147; on learning French, p. 53, and on the origin of the pseudonym, "Johnston Smith," for Crane's authorship of *Maggie,* p. 90. Berryman's discussion of brothels being a part of Crane's rebellion is on p. 139 of his book; and Stephen Crane's letter to Edmund Crane is from p. 167. The suggestion that Crane wrote "November 4" for "November 14" on the flyleaf of *George's Mother* is from *Omnibus*, p. 654 f; and Crane's letters to Willis Brooks Hawkins are from pp. 465-476 and 656-658. (Other references to *Omnibus*, in connection with the *Commodore* sinking, are below.) The quoted material from Hoffman on Stephen and Cora's need for each other and on Crane's transference of guilt to the woman appears on pp. 113 and 138 of *The Poetry of Stephen Crane*.

All of the material, quoted or paraphrased, from Crane's letters to Nellie Crouse is from *Stephen Crane's Love Letters to Nellie Crouse*, ed. Edwin H. Cady and Lester G. Wells (Syracuse University Press, 1954). The letters quoted in this chapter will be found on pp. 40-51, *passim*. For the details of Crane's love affair with Lily Brandon Munroe, I am indebted to Mr. and Mrs. Frederick B. Smillie, the son and daughter-in-law of Mrs. Munroe (later Smillie); and to Ames W. Williams, who kept notes from an interview he had several years ago with Lily Brandon Munroe Smillie, then in her eighties and still a beautiful woman.

The quoted and paraphrased material concerning Stephen's appearance, the boyish lock of hair, etc., is from Helen R. Crane, "My Uncle Stephen Crane," *American Mercury* (January, 1934), 24-29. The author of this article is the daughter of an older brother, Wilbur Crane. The long quoted passage describing Crane meeting a girl of the streets is from Robert H. Davis, Introduction to Vol. II, *The Work of Stephen Crane*, ed. Wilson Follett (New York: Knopf, 1925-1927), pp. xvii-xix. Later references to the Knopf edition will refer to it as *Work*.

The scoring sheet for the card game is the back of a holograph manuscript, page 98, of an early draft of *The Red Badge of Courage* in the Houghton Library at Harvard University. It was first described by R. W. Stallman, " 'The Red Badge of Courage': A Collation of Two Pages of Manuscript Expunged From Chapter XII," *Papers of the Bibliographical Society of America*, 49 (Third Quarter, 1955), 273-277.

The quoted and paraphrased material from Corwin Knapp Linson is from two sources: the reference to Cora as a girl who had suffered from "unfortunate circumstances" is from a letter from Linson to Thomas Beer, April 30, 1923, which was found among Beer's papers and made available through the kindness of Miss Alice Beer. It was first published in *Letters*, pp. 326-328. The source of the rest of Linson's remarks is a bound manuscript of his memoirs in the possession of the Syracuse University Library, *Stephen Crane: A Personal Record*, p. 154. The manuscript, edited by Edwin H. Cady, has been published under the title *My Stephen Crane* (Syracuse University Press, 1958), this passage appearing on pp. 101-102.

Crane wrote two love notes "To C. E. S." The first, undated and signed "Stephen Crane," was written during Crane's stay in Jacksonville, the complete text of which was first published in Hoffman, p. 121:

To C. E. S.

Love comes like the tall swift shadow of a ship at night. There is for a moment, the music of the water's turmoil, a bell, perhaps, a man's shout, a row of gleaming yellow lights. Then the slow sinking of this mystic shape. Then silence and a bitter silence—the silence of the sea at night.

Stephen Crane

The second note to Cora, also written at Jacksonville, contains his remarks on brevity as an element of pleasure, the complete text printed here on p. 51. It was first published in Melvin H. Schoberlin's Introduction to *Sullivan County Sketches* (Syracuse University Press, 1949), p. 11.

The copy of the first Appleton edition of *Maggie* (New York, 1896), in which Crane wrote the inscription "To Lyda," has pasted in it by Cora a page from the *Metropolitan Magazine* containing an article by David Belasco on "The Genius of Stephen Crane," in which Belasco speaks of acquiring rights from Mrs. Crane to dramatize Crane's works. There is no indication of how Cora happened to have possession of this copy, which is now in the Columbia University Crane Collection. The first edition copy of *George's Mother*, which Crane inscribed "To an unnamed sweetheart," is in the George Matthew Adams Crane Collection at Dartmouth College. According to Herbert Faulkner West's catalogue description, it was evidently presented by Cora or Stephen to Edward Garnett, whose bookplate it carries. These inscriptions were both published in *Letters*, pp. 139 and 132 respectively.

Crane's remarks on saving a girl who is not a prostitute from being arrested as one are from his article, "Adventures of a Novelist," New York *Journal*, September 26, 1896; an unpaged clipping of the article is in the Columbia University Crane Collection. See also Hoffman, pp. 101 ff. Of the two passages of Crane's poetry printed here, the first is from Poem No. X, the second from "Intrigue," both published in *Work*, VI (*The Black Riders*), pp. 42 and 143 respectively.

The quoted descriptions of the *Commodore* and its fateful voyage are from "Stephen Crane's Own Story," published in the New York *Press*, January 7, 1897, reprinted in *Omnibus*, pp. 465-476; the headlines of the *Commodore's* sinking are from the *Florida Times-Union*, January 3 and 5, 1897, also reprinted in *Omnibus*, pp. 448 and 459. The quote from the "local historian" is from T. Frederick Davis, *History of Jacksonville*, p. 205. For a lively personal account of some of the filibustering exploits of the *Dauntless* and the *Three Friends*, see Ralph D. Paine, *Roads of Adventure* (Boston: Houghton Mifflin, 1922), pp. 144-171. For a challenging though somewhat prejudiced account of the *Commodore* sinking, belittling Crane as a hero and "The Open Boat" as a work of art, see Cyrus L. Day, "Stephen Crane and the Ten-Foot Dinghy," *Boston University Studies in English*, III, 4, 193-213.

The telegrams of Cyrus R. Bisbee, ex-Senator Wilkinson Call, and J. M. Barrs, concerning the use of the *Three Friends* as a mercy ship, are on file in the National Archives, along with those of the Cubans, Paul Rojo and Ricardo Delgado. For knowledge of their existence I am indebted to Mr. Day's article above. All of the other notes and telegrams quoted or cited in connection with the *Commodore* sinking are in the Columbia University Crane Collection. For the sake of persons now living the name of the writer is withheld in the one instance on p. 58.

CHAPTER 2: *Grecian Lark: War and Romance*

THE ACCOUNT of the railroad journey via the Orient Express to the Black Sea, the description of the Bavarian town of Landshut, of Oberammergau, and of other places Cora and Stephen passed through are from Cora's looseleaf diary. Her views on the women of Flanders are from an unpublished article entitled "Dress of the Women of Flanders," intended for the series of syndicated newsletters issued from London, holograph manuscript of which is in the Columbia University Crane Collection. Her story, "The Red Chimneys," was sold to a Chicago syndicate in the autumn of 1900. It probably appeared sometime during the next year, but in what papers or periodicals is not known.

Stephen's article on the Royal Prussian Railway incident was published in the New York *Press*, August 15, 1897, one of ten papers to which the series of ten articles was syndicated. It is incorrectly listed as unpublished in *Stephen Crane: An Exhibition* (New York: Columbia University Libraries, 1956), p. 55. The holograph manuscript is in the Columbia University Crane Collection.

Crane's dispatch, "On Board French Steamer Guardiana," is from "Stephen Crane's Pen Picture of the Powers' Fleet Off Crete," Louisville *Courier-Journal*, Sunday, May 9, 1897. This hitherto unknown dispatch is the discovery of E. R. Hagemann (University of California, Los Angeles), and is included in the collection of Crane's sketches and war dispatches which Mr. Hagemann is preparing with R. W. Stallman for publication by New York University Press. I am indebted to Messrs. Hagemann and Stallman for making the text of the article available for examination in advance of their publication. Crane's story, "The Dogs of War," was first published in the New York *Journal*, May 30, 1897.

The account of the nonexistent fire first appeared in the New York *Press*, Sunday, November 25, 1894, with the title "Fire!" and subtitle "When Everyone Is Panic Stricken." In 1954 Ames W. Williams had the story reprinted in a handsomely bound edition limited to one hundred copies as a Christmas greeting to friends who shared his interest in the work of Stephen Crane. Among those to receive gift copies was an elderly gentleman who happened to have seen Crane's fire piece at the time of its original publication, himself a veteran newspaperman, distinguished in many other fields. This gentleman then wrote to Mr. Williams, revealing with humor and oblique irony the professional secret—which until then he had closely guarded—of Crane's journalistic hoax. The incident is amusingly reported by John S. Mayfield in "Stephen Crane's Curious Conflagration," *The American Book Collector*, VII, 4 (December, 1956), 6-8.

Crane's poetry quoted in this chapter is from *Work*, VI (*The Black Riders*), pp. 72 (Poem No. XL), 142 ("Intrigue"), and 35 (Poem No. III)—the order in which they appear in this chapter.

The letter from Sidney S. Pawling to Stephen Crane, dated December 4, 1896, is quoted from *A Stephen Crane Collection,* by Herbert Faulkner West (Dartmouth College Library, Hanover, New Hampshire, 1948), p. 19. The letter Crane wrote from Basel ("I now know that I am an imbecile of rank. . . .") is from Beer, p. 154. Sylvester Scovel's letter to his wife is from Berryman, p. 183. Originals of the Scovel letters (Scovel to his wife, Athens, May 19, 1897; Stephen Crane to Scovel, Oxted, Surrey, August 1; and Cora Crane to Scovel, Oxted, October 17) are in the possession of Mrs. Frances Scovel Saportas, of St. Louis—or were, in 1950, when Mr. Berryman's book appeared.

The letter of Richard Harding Davis, beginning "Stephen Crane came with me . . . ," is quoted from Scott C. Osborn, "Stephen Crane and Cora Taylor: Some Corrections," *American Literature,* XXVI, 3 (November, 1954), 417. The other Davis letters quoted in this chapter are from Scott C. Osborn, "The 'Rivalry-Chivalry' of Richard Harding Davis and Stephen Crane," *American Literature,* XXXVIII, 1 (March, 1956), 53-54. Originals of the letters are in the possession of Mrs. Hope Harding Davis Kehrig.

Most of the material concerning Harold Frederic is from a critical biography of Frederic by Hoyt C. Franchere and Thomas O'Donnell, now in preparation. See also an unpublished dissertation by Paul Haines, New York University, 1944. The visiting American who wrote of Frederic's home was Lynn Boyd Porter, American novelist and free lance journalist who wrote under the pseudonym "Albert Ross." His letter to Cora, dated January 21, 1899, is in the Columbia University Crane Collection.

The quoted material on Greek demands, by an Associated Press correspondent, p. 83, is from the New York *Press,* April 12, 1897. All other background data relating to the Greco-Turkish war, quoted or paraphrased, unless otherwise indicated are from files of this newspaper. John Bass's story, "How Novelist Crane Behaves on the Battlefield," appeared in the New York *Journal,* Sunday, May 23, 1897. The birdseye of events leading up to the outbreak of war, the "Concert of Power," etc., is also taken from the *Journal* (April, 1897).

For biographical material on Ouida, see Monica Stirling, *The Fine and the Wicked: The Life and Times of Ouida* (New York: Coward-McCann, 1958). Crane's article on her novel, *Under Two Flags,* was published in the *Book Buyer,* January, 1897, and was reprinted in Hoffman, *The Red Badge of Courage and Other Stories,* pp. 185-186. Crane's article is pointed to in Max Beerbohm's essay on Ouida, which appeared two years later (Max Beerbohm, *Works and More,* 1899).

Robert Louis Stevenson's remark on the average woman's lot is from "Talk and Talkers," in *Selected Writings,* ed. with an Introduction by Saxe Commins (New York: Random House, 1947), p. 858.

CHAPTER 3: *Ravensbrook, Oxted: Friendships and Indians*

FOR THE STORY of Velestino's misbehavior in the Paris hotel, I am indebted to Mr. and Mrs. Nicholas Pease. The opinion that Crane took the house at Oxted in order to be near Edward Garnett is from David Garnett, *The Golden Echo* (London: Chatto & Windus, 1954), p. 62. The impressions furnished by Mr. Edmund Gosse, the young girl Vere (later Mrs. Charles Sidmore), Sanford Bennett, C. Thomas Janeway, and other witnesses both friendly and unfriendly to Cora Crane, are quoted or paraphrased from Beer's article, "Mrs. Stephen Crane," pp. 289-295. (A drawing of the living room at Brede Place by Kate Howarth is in the scrapbook recently found there by Mr. Roger M. Frewen.)

The letter from Cora to Moreton Frewen, dated June 10, 1898, is in the possession of Mr. Roger M. Frewen and is used by his kind permission; it was first published in *Letters*, pp. 181-182. Her letter to Sylvester Scovel, October 17, 1897 (see Chapter 2, Notes), and her letter to Sanford Bennett, November 29, 1897, are from Berryman, pp. 189-190 and 203. Her remark to a friend about her having no sense about money is also from Berryman, p. 203.

Cora's notes on women's fashions are from a newsletter date-lined October 1, published October 10, 1897, New York *Press*, p. 16. The holograph manuscript is in the Columbia University Crane Collection. Her letter on society beauties is from the issue of August 29.

Crane's letter to James G. Huneker about the English believing "anything wild or impossible you tell them," and his note to Sanford Bennett, before he sailed for Cuba, are from Beer, pp. 167-168 and 177, and his note of December 3, to an unknown recipient, referring to his staying in a hotel to write, from p. 166. His letter to Sylvester Scovel, October 17, 1897, is from Berryman, p. 189. His letter to Paul R. Reynolds concerning the authorship of the London newsletters is from Berryman, p. 182. (Berryman's citation of this letter was, of course, without knowledge of the existence of the London newsletters or the collaboration from which they came.) Crane's letter to Paul Revere Reynolds is reproduced whole in *Omnibus*, pp. 668-670. From *Omnibus*, pp. 632-633, comes Crane's letter to Willis Brooks Hawkins ("I am no longer a black sheep but a star"); his long letter to William H. Crane, October 29, 1897, is from pp. 661-665; his letter of November 11, 1897, to Joseph Conrad, pp. 665-666; to Paul R. Reynolds, saying he was "buckling down" (February 7, 1898), p. 677; the early letter (May 29, 1892) to Acton Davies, p. 591 and note; to Reynolds (to sell "The Monster") and Davies (to collect old debts), pp. 671-672.

Crane's remark about Stevenson not having "passed away far enough," and the details, quoted and paraphrased, of his argument with Frederic over "The Monster" and "The Nigger of the Narcissus" are from Beer, pp. 160 and 167-168. Crane's remarks on Hueffer are quoted from Ford Madox (Hueffer) Ford, "Stephen Crane," in *Portraits from Life* (Boston, New York: Houghton Mifflin, 1937), p. 35; and Hueffer's opinion of Crane's reception in England is from p. 28. Crane's observations on Ireland are from *Work*, XI (*Midnight Sketches*, "Irish Notes"), 169-171 *passim*. His remarks on the reaction of the British public to Ogden Goelet's yacht are quoted from a newsletter in the New York *Press*, August 22, 1897.

The letters of Joseph Conrad to Stephen and Cora Crane were edited and published by Carl Bohnenberger and Norman M. Hill in the *Bookman*, May-

June, 1929. Originals of the Conrad letters, including four unpublished letters to Cora, one of which is from Conrad and three from Mrs. Conrad, are now in the Columbia University Crane Collection. All quotations in this and later chapters, unless otherwise noted, are from this source. Conrad's description of Crane is from Joseph Conrad, *A Personal Record* (Garden City: Doubleday, Page & Co., 1923), p. 103. His statement that he was "the blind agent of fate" the day Crane left for Cuba is from his Introduction to Beer, p. 33.

The letters of Harold and Kate Frederic to the Cranes, quoted or paraphrased in this and later chapters, are in the Columbia University Crane Collection and they are used here by special arrangement. Frederic's long letter to Cora, February 8, 1898, was first published in *Letters*, p. 174.

The letter from Charles Woodruff Woolley, Sr., to Cora Crane was written December 19, 1899.

The letter from George Mabon, Amy Leslie's attorney, to Willis B. Hawkins is from the Dartmouth Library, and is reprinted here by its kind permission.

CHAPTER 4: *Ravensbrook: Heartache, Waiting, the Prodigal's Return*

THE LETTER from Cora Crane to Mrs. Moreton Frewen, June 4, 1898, and her letter to Mr. Frewen, June 16, are from a group of five unpublished letters of Cora Crane, four of which are to Moreton Frewen, and the originals of which are in England, presumably in private hands. The Bancroft Library of the University of California owns a positive microfilm copy of the set, from which prints were obtained. These Cora Crane letters are part of a collection of some 41 reels of correspondence pertaining to Moreton Frewen, and the use here made of them is by permission of the Bancroft Library, which does not control copyright. The originals of Cora's letter to Moreton Frewen of June 10 (cited in Chapter 3) and the one written about December 22, 1898, are in the possession of Mr. Roger M. Frewen and used here by his kind permission. They are not among the group on microfilm at the Bancroft Library.

The June 16 note from Cora to an unknown recipient, concerning Crane's whereabouts, is in the Clifton Waller Barrett Collection and was first published in *Letters*, p. 182. The inquiry of the Secretary of War to Major General J. F. Wade is in the National Archives, as is Cora's letter to the Secretary, which was published in the *Colophon*, April, 1940. Cora's letter of September 25, 1898, to Paul R. Reynolds, and her subsequent communications to him, are from the Clifton Waller Barrett Collection, Alderman Library, University of Virginia. The September 25 letter was published in *Letters*, pp. 186-187. A portion of it originally appeared, undated, in *Paul Revere Reynolds*, a biographical sketch by Frederick Lewis Allen, privately published, 1944, and was reprinted in *Omnibus*, p. 684. The original holograph letters from Cora Crane to Edward Garnett, of late December, 1898, and January 10 and 19 (Chapter 5), 1899, are in the Yale University Library, and were first published in *Letters*, pp. 203-206.

The letter from Henry James concerning the Frederic children and others in later chapters, unless otherwise noted, are from a group of some sixteen unpublished letters and notes from James in the Columbia University Crane Collection. All are addressed to Cora Crane but one, a note to "Mr. and Mrs. Crane" scribbled on a visiting card. The letter from Robert Barr to Cora Crane, September, 1898, and others in later chapters are all from the Columbia University Crane Collection unless otherwise noted. Also from Columbia is the letter from W. J. Fisher to Cora Crane, which is dated May 25, 1899. All other correspondence bearing on this episode of the Frederic children is of late 1898 and 1899.

The letter from Stephen Crane to Mrs. Bolton Chaffee is from Beer, p. 196; his letter to Mrs. William Sonntag is from "Mrs. Stephen Crane," p. 163; to Ripley Hitchcock, which Stallman dates March 15, 1896, from "Stephen Crane's Letters to Ripley Hitchcock," ed. R. W. Stallman, *Bulletin of the New York Public Library*, LX, 7 (July, 1956), 329 ff. His letter to an unknown recipient, about staying in England, is from *Omnibus*, p. 685 n. The letter from Crane to Reynolds is from *Omnibus*, pp. 682-683, where it was reprinted from *Paul Revere Reynolds*.

The information concerning Crane's appeal for aid for Mrs. Frederic is from a letter from J. Nicol Dunn, editor of the London *Morning Post*, to Stephen Crane, February 14, 1900.

William Crane's letter to Beer, and the letter from Henry Sonntag to Beer, telling of the incident between Crane, the Sonntags, and the New York policeman, are from "Mrs. Stephen Crane," pp. 291-292. The letter from William H. Crane to Paul R. Reynolds, November 10, 1898, is in the Barrett Collection and reproduced here by kind permission of Mr. Barrett and the Alderman Library of the University of Virginia. The letter from David S. Meldrum to William Blackwood, p. 155, is from *Joseph Conrad: Letters to William Blackwood and David S. Meldrum*, ed. William Blackburn (Duke University Press, 1958), pp. 31 ff.

The passage from an early draft of *The Red Badge of Courage* is from a holograph manuscript page, number 102, in the Houghton Library, Harvard University. The complete text, with other variants, was first published in R. W. Stallman's definitive edition of *The Red Badge* recently issued in the New American Library Series (Signet Books), where the line beginning "no sympathy for the rabbit and the weed" and ending with "his own capacity for pity" has been omitted through a printer's error. The marking at the top, "A page of the original MS of Red Badge," is incorrectly attributed by Mr. Stallman to Stephen Crane. The handwriting in this inscription is that of Cora Crane.

Cora's story, "Cowardice," is in holograph manuscript in the Columbia University Crane Collection. It appeared in the *Nottinghamshire Guardian*, October 4, 1902, one of the papers served by the Northern Newspaper Syndicate to which the story was originally sold. I am indebted to Mr. Roger M. Frewen for loan of newspaper text, and to Mr. W. N. Rees, editor of the *Nottinghamshire Guardian*, for microfilm.

Frederic's remark about Henry James, "an effeminate old donkey," is from

Beer, pp. 151-152; Crane's feelings about Congressmen and Senators, from pp. 199-200; and the quote from James Huneker, from p. 207. Berryman's remark on a typical Crane character ("pretentious and scared") is from p. 280 of his book. The article, "Cuban Gossip," is from the September 10, 1898, issue of the *Florida Times-Union and Citizen*, from the collection of Florida newspaper files in the P. K. Yonge Memorial Library, University of Florida. The information from Jessie Conrad is from (Mrs. Joseph Conrad,) "Recollections of Stephen Crane ," *Bookman*, LXIII (April, 1926), 134-135.

Details pertaining to Moreton Frewen, the episode of the Kipling manuscript, etc., are from Anita Leslie, *The Remarkable Mr. Jerome* (New York: Holt, 1954). Information on the architectural history of Brede Place, Sir Goddard Oxenbridge, and the ghost legend is from an article by Viscountess Wolseley in the *Sussex County Magazine*, III (October, 1929), 671 ff. The story of Sir Goddard's will is from a series of articles by David McLean, Nos. 4 and 5, "Brede Place, Sussex and America," *Sussex County Magazine* (July-August, 1931), 540 ff. I am indebted to R. W. Stallman for loan of these now scarce issues, the gift of Mr. Roger M. Frewen. Details of smuggling operations are from Edmund Austen, *Brede: The Story of a Sussex Parish* (Rye, Sussex: Adams and Sons, 1947), pp. 126-130.

CHAPTER 5: *Brede Place: Ghosts at a Christmas Party*

THE LETTERS from Cora Crane to Mrs. Edward Pease are in the possession of Commander Melvin H. Schoberlin, USN, to whom I am indebted for permission to quote from them here. The one of February 12, 1899, was first published in *Letters*, pp. 210-211, where it is wrongly dated February 13; the other letter is unpublished. The letter from Cora Crane to Mrs. H. G. Wells, dated July 28, 1899, is one of a group of seven letters from Cora Crane in the H. G. Wells Collection at the University of Illinois, two of which are to Mrs. Wells and five to H. G. Wells. Permission to quote from them is by special arrangement for which I am indebted to Professor Gordon N. Ray and the Library of the University of Illinois. The letter from Cora Crane to Mrs. Moreton Frewen, dated January 16, 1900, is used by the kind permission of Roger M. Frewen, who has the original. The post cards Stephen and Cora sent from Paris to the Brede dogs, referred to in Edith Richie Jones' article, "Stephen Crane at Brede," are in the Columbia University Crane Collection.

Stephen Crane's letters to Sanford Bennett are from Beer, pp. 210 and 221-222. His angry note to someone who had upset Cora is from Berryman, p. 248, and his letter to George Wyndham, from pp. 244-245. His letters to Moreton Frewen and Mrs. Frewen are from a group of five unpublished letters of Stephen Crane, four of which are to Moreton Frewen, recently unearthed at Brede Place and now in the possession of Roger M. Frewen, by whose kind permission they are quoted here. The letter from Stephen Crane to James B. Pinker, and others from Stephen and Cora in later chapters, are from a group of 22 letters from Stephen Crane and 33 from Cora to Pinker, now in the George Arents Crane Collection at Syracuse University (typescript copies only—the originals are in the possession of Commander Melvin H. Schoberlin). Crane's letter to John Northern Hilliard is from *Omnibus*, pp. 679-680, where it is incorrectly ascribed to Joseph O'Connor. His letter to Mark Barr, September 29, 1899, is in the possession of Mr. Philip M. Barr and used by his kind permission. First published in *Letters*, p. 232. His letter to H. B. Marriott-Watson is in the Berg Collection at the New York Public Library and is quoted by permission of the Trustees of the Library. A type-script copy of Crane's contract with Methuen is among the papers in the Columbia University Crane Collection.

The letter from Henry James, thanking Cora for photographs of the garden party, is from Daniel G. Hoffman, "An Unwritten Life of Stephen Crane," in *Columbia Library Columns*, II, 2 (February, 1953), 15. The letter from Edmund Crane, others quoted from William Howe Crane and his daughter Helen, to Stephen and Cora, and many others from members of the Crane family, are in the Columbia University Crane Collection; another large group of Crane family letters is in the Newark Public Library. Robert Barr's letter to Cora, cited in Chapter 4, refutes those who have him scared by the Brede ghost (see Berryman, p. 249, and *Joseph Conrad and His Circle*, p. 73); the doggerel verses are in the possession of Mr. Roger M. Frewen.

Crane's remarks beginning "People tell me . . ." and his outburst to Mark Barr are from Beer, pp. 218-219 and 232. The story of the Wellses' use of corn leaves for salad is from Berryman, pp. 249-250. The guest who remembered Cora's resourcefulness in setting up house at Brede is Edith Richie Jones, and this and other recollections by her are all from her article, "Stephen Crane at Brede." The memoirs of Karl Edwin Harriman appeared in *The Critic*, July, 1900. The description of dinner at Brede Place is from Jessie Conrad, *Joseph Conrad and His Circle* (New York: Dutton, 1935), p. 73. Mrs. Conrad's description of Cora's bedroom and her remarks on Crane's guitar-play-ing are from her article, "Recollections of Stephen Crane." (For an enter-taining account of some of Mrs. Conrad's exaggerations, which should be checked against her own story in *Joseph Conrad and His Circle*, see David Garnett, *The Golden Echo*, p. 63.)

The passage from Lady Churchill is from *The Reminiscences of Lady Randolph Churchill* (New York: Century, 1908), p. 60. A copy of the Con-stitution and By-laws of the Society of American Women in London is in the British Museum.

The material quoted from the *Southeastern Advertiser* and the *Manchester Guardian* is from newspaper clippings in Cora Crane's scrapbook found at Brede Place and kindly made available by Mr. Roger M. Frewen. For a copy of the Christmas dinner menu I am also indebted to Mr. Frewen. The account of the main performance of *The Ghost*, including the quotation, "in spite of the prevailing epidemic . . . ," is from a review in the *Sussex Express, Surrey Standard, & Kent Mail*, Friday, January 5, 1900, quoted in John D. Gordan, "The Ghost at Brede Place," *Bulletin of the New York Public Library*, De-cember, 1953. A manuscript page from page one of *The Ghost*, in the hand-writing of Stephen Crane and bearing at the top a note in Cora's hand: "Ste-phen Crane's MS." is in the possession of Mr. Frewen. The catalogue, *Stephen*

Crane: An Exhibition, arranged and described by Joan H. Baum, with a Foreword by Professor Lewis Leary (New York: Columbia University Libraries, 1956), lists two pages of typescript and three of manuscript "in an unknown hand" held in the collection now at Columbia. The "unknown hand" is certainly Cora's. The Berg Collection at the New York Public Library also has "seven typescript pages . . . including what seems to be the whole of Act I plus the first page of Act II" (see John D. Gordan, "The Ghost at Brede Place").

H. G. Wells' account of the Christmas house party is from *Experiment in Autobiography*, p. 523. The quotations from A. E. W. Mason are from a letter to Vincent Starrett, October 4, 1945, now in the possession of R. W. Stallman, and published in *Letters*, pp. 342-345.

CHAPTER 6: *Brede Place: The Ghost Goes Home*

CORA CRANE's letter of June 3, 1900, to Moreton Frewen, and her second note of the same date, are in the Bancroft Library, University of California, and used by permission of the Bancroft Library. The original of the letter from Cora Crane to Corwin Knapp Linson, written September 28, 1900, is in the George Arents Crane Collection at Syracuse University. Stephen Crane's letter to Sanford Bennett, asking him to watch after Conrad, is in Berryman, p. 259.

Kate Frederic's letter to Cora, asking if Stephen meant her to write as well as research some of the *Battle* articles, is in the Columbia University Crane Collection. The letter from Robert Barr to a friend is from Beer, p. 237.

Crane's remark to Willis Clarke, "I'm just a dry twig . . . ," and his observation, "Men have never much deserved Christ and Buddha . . . ," are from Beer, pp. 233 and 225. His words to Robert Barr about death are from a letter Barr wrote to Karl Edwin Harriman, June 8, 1900, published in *Omnibus*, pp. 694 ff., where it appears under the heading, "To An Unknown Recipient."

The original of the announcement in Helen Crane's handwriting that friends of Stephen Crane could pay their last respects is in the Berg Collection at the New York Public Library. Cora's remark to Stephen's nieces about ghosts and tombstones is told in a letter from Edith F. Crane to Lillian Gilkes, September 30, 1959.

The quotation from Hueffer (Ford Madox Ford) is from *Portraits from Life*, pp. 32-33. For photocopy of the poster and the clipping from the *Southeastern Advertiser* I am indebted to Roger M. Frewen. Sanford Bennett's description of Cora pacing the hall is from Beer's "Mrs. Stephen Crane," p. 295. The report from Jessie Conrad that Cora went without meals at Dover is from *Joseph Conrad and His Circle*, p. 74.

A copy of the *Memorandum of Agreement* between Cora and Frederick L. Bowen is among the papers at Columbia University. For the interpretation of Crane's will I am indebted to Arthur A. Donigian of Hackensack, New Jersey.

CHAPTER 7: *London: Stone of Stumbling; A Decision Taken*

THE LETTER from Cora Crane to Corwin Knapp Linson, October 18, 1900, is in the George Arents Collection at Syracuse University, and was published in *Letters*, pp. 319-320. The two letters from Cora to Hamlin Garland, August 8 and September 17, 1900, are in the American Literature Collection of the Library of the University of Southern California, and were published in *Letters*, pp. 308-309 and 316-317. (Garland's article in the *Saturday Evening Post* appeared in the issue of July 28, 1900.)

The letters from Cora Crane to James B. Pinker, August 2, 3, 24, and 25, 1900, and the undated one, p. 301, are in the George Matthew Adams Collection at Dartmouth. The original of her letter of August 15, 1900, is in the possession of Commander Melvin H. Schoberlin, to whom I am indebted for permission to quote. Cora's letter of April 26, 1901, to Paul R. Reynolds is in the Clifton Waller Barrett Collection at the University of Virginia.

Most of the originals of the letters from Cora Crane to G. H. Perris are in the Yale University Library: August 28, September 9 and 11, October 13 and 23, November 11 and 23, and December 23, 1900, and April 24 and 27, and December 2, 1901. Another letter of August 28, 1900, telling about the run-in with her landlady, is in the George Arents Collection at Syracuse University, and was first published in the *Crouse* letters, p. 82. Cora's letter to Perris objecting to a "15%" agent's fee, dated September 13, 1900, is one of four letters from Cora to Perris in the possession of L. V. Scagell, London. Her remarks to Perris on "José and the Saints" and "The Lavender Trousers" are from a letter dated October 26, 1900, the original of which is in the possession of Commander Melvin H. Schoberlin, who kindly made it available.

I am also indebted to Mr. Schoberlin for Cora's letter to Louis Senger, October 22, 1900, which is in his possession. Her letter to Agnes Crane, December 16, 1900, is in the possession of Miss Edith F. Crane, who kindly furnished typescript. The note referring to Belasco, "allowing him to show play to managers . . . ," is in Cora's handwriting on the envelope of a letter from David Belasco about *The O'Ruddy*, postmarked Aix-les-Bains, August 10, in the Columbia University Crane Collection.

Holograph manuscripts of Cora's stories, "Arundel Castle," "The 17th Regiment of Light Dragoons," "The Lavender Trousers," "Elbridge Carter's Dream," "The Red Chimneys," "Cowardice," and "An Old World Courtship," are in the Columbia University Crane Collection. Holograph manuscript of "The Squire's Madness," begun by Stephen Crane and finished by Cora, and of the unpublished article, "The Greco-Turkish Question," begun by Cora and finished by Stephen, are also in the Columbia Collection. Cora completed Crane's unfinished story, "The Man from Duluth," and probably also "The Surrender of Forty Fort," but these manuscripts are untraced. Three manuscript pages of "The Battle of Forty Fort," likewise finished by Cora, are in the Barrett Collection at the University of Virginia.

The quoted material on James' character, Mrs. Headway, is from the story, "The Siege of London," in *The Great Short Stories of Henry James*, ed. Philip Rahv (New York: Dial Press, 1944), p. 309. Karl Edwin Harriman's article advertising *The O'Ruddy* and mentioning Cora's literary excursions appeared in *The Critic*, XXXVII, 3 (March, 1901), 14-16.

The incident of Cora's meeting with the young man whose sister had died is from a letter by George Hyslop in Beer's "Mrs. Stephen Crane," p. 293. The meeting at the restaurant between Cora and Vere is described in a letter from Vere (Mrs. Charles Sidmore), also in "Mrs. Stephen Crane," p. 295. The information on Cora's small art collection is from a letter from P. G. Huardel to Cora Crane, April 19, 1901. The details on Poultney Bigelow are from his *Seventy Summers*, an autobiography in two volumes (New York: Longmans, Green, 1925).

My authority for the statement that Crane had read *The Light That Failed* before writing *Maggie* is James B. Colvert, "The Origins of Stephen Crane's Literary Creed," University of Texas *Studies in English*, XXXIV (1955), 182. See also R. W. Stallman, "The Scholar's Net: Literary Sources," *College English*, XVII, 1 (October, 1955).

Reynolds' letters to Cora about *The Red Badge* and *The O'Ruddy* are in the Columbia University Crane Collection. See also his correspondence with Alice Kauser, New York dramatists' agent, in the Clifton Waller Barrett Collection at the Alderman Library, University of Virginia. The letters from Alfred T. Plant to James B. Pinker, October 10 and December 19, 1900, are from the Clifton Waller Barrett Collection. The letter from William H. Crane to Paul R. Reynolds, November 6, 1901, is one of a large group of letters in the Barrett Collection, several of which are from William Crane to Reynolds, dealing with the wrangle over *Last Words*. In this group also are Cora's letters to Reynolds about *Last Words*, and two others from Joseph H. Coates of the publishing house.

The information that William Crane bought up his brothers' shares of stock, etc., is from Helen R. Crane, "My Uncle Stephen Crane," *American Mercury*, p. 26. The details of his handling of Stephen's estate are from William H. Crane's "Accounting of Proceedings in the Administration of the Estate of Stephen Crane, Deceased," on file in public records. The report of the accident involving Stephen's horse, "Peanuts," is from a letter from Edith F. Crane to Edith R. Greenburg, editor, Indiana University Press, September 30, 1959, and published here with the kind permission of Miss Crane.

CHAPTER 8: *The Court*

FOR RECORDS pertaining to Cora Taylor's purchase of the Court property I am indebted to the Title & Trust Company of Florida, and its president, Mr. Alton B. Wetherington. For interpretation of Cora's second mortgage to C. C. Butler, and other items pertaining to her real estate, I am indebted to Mr. George E. Drady of the Title & Trust Company. Subject matter bearing on the various lawsuits in which Cora Taylor was involved is taken from records in the Circuit Court for Duval County at Jacksonville; interpretation is based on notes supplied me by Philip S. May, Jacksonville attorney. The episode of the threatened suit, and Cora's reply, comes from the daughter of the contractor who furnished building materials.

For facts pertaining to the burials assumed by Cora, including that of Harry Parker, I am indebted to Mr. S. A. Kyle, mortician, who told me that Cora more than once "turned matters over" to someone else representing her—as in the case of Jeannette Raymond. There may have been still other instances in which her name is not shown on the records.

The story of Carry Nation's trip "down the line" appeared in the *Florida Times-Union*, February 14, 1908. The "august political body" which went "down the line" in 1911 was apparently the Democratic State Committee; the episode is described in an article by Albert Williamson, owner and publisher of *The Floridian*. The election-eve parade of the girls in red tights was reported by Helen Hunt (Mrs. Byron West), for the *Florida Evening Metropolis*, and appeared in a June (1915) issue of the paper. (Election day was June 15, 1915.)

The information revealed on the witness stand concerning McNeil and his relations with Cora is from Testimony and Proceedings in the Preliminary Trial of Hammond P. McNeil in Justice Court, Eighth Justice District, Duval County, August 13, 1907—before Justice A. Greenberg. A copy of this testimony, some eighty pages, which must have been obtained for Cora by her attorney (Campbell), is in the Columbia University Crane Collection; it appears to be the only one in existence, the original having disappeared from the files of the local court. The account of the murder in this chapter is reconstructed in toto from the Testimony at the Preliminary Trial, and lines in quotation marks are as they appear in the record.

The tongue-lashing given Hammond P. McNeil is from the *Florida Evening Metropolis*, June 7, 1907, p. 1. From the same paper, December 4, 1907, p. 1, is the reporter's comment on the arguments of the defense, after McNeil's acquittal. The account of the death of McNeil is from the *Florida Evening Metropolis*, May 14, 1913; McNeil died intestate on May 14, leaving an estate with an appraiser's valuation of $20,000, but, having over-extended himself with debt in excess of assets, the estate was insolvent.

The letter from Cora Crane to Alfred T. Plant, Jacksonville, July 9, 1905, is in the Columbia University Crane Collection.

All of the letters written to Cora in this chapter are in the Columbia University Crane Collection: R. J. Horner & Co., Furniture Makers, Upholsterers and Importers, West 23rd Street, New York, September 25, 1906, to Mrs. Stephen Crane, P.O. Box 480, Jacksonville; Mrs. Moreton Frewen, Inver Lodge, Galway, September 27, 1904, to Cora Crane; Hoyt De Friese to Cora McNeil, undated; Henry James, November 26, 1907, to Cora McNeil; Jessie Conrad, Someries, October 22, 1907, to Cora McNeil; Clara Frewen, December 2, 1907, to Cora McNeil; Florence Forbes-Bentley, Bay Tree Cottage,

Beckley, East Sussex, December 7, 1908, to Cora McNeil; Joseph Conrad to Cora McNeil; and Kate Frederic, July 1, 1909, to Cora [McNeil].

Cora's birth date on her headstone is incorrect, whether because Ernest Budd—who was a good deal younger than Cora—did not know her age or because she had misrepresented it to him. She was born in 1865.

The date of her death also appears incorrectly on the Death Certificate as September 5, an error repeated in obituaries in the *Florida Evening Metropolis* and *Florida Times-Union* of September 6, 1910. The correct date, September 4, is given in Ernest C. Budd's Petition to the County Judge's Court (Probate), for Duval County, to sell real estate—copy of which is in the George Arents Crane Collection at Syracuse University. Both newspaper articles contain numerous inaccuracies. The one in the *Florida Evening Metropolis* was probably written by Cora's old friend, W. R. Carter, the editor and owner of the paper, who from motives of friendship was no doubt anxious to gloss over the scandalous aspect and overemphasize her literary achievements. Copies of the *Times-Union* article are in the Crane Collections at Columbia and Syracuse Universities.

A short time before her death, Cora had bought the Evergreen Cemetery lot in which she was buried.